Meeting the Innovation Challenge:

Leadership for Transformation and Growth

Meeting the Innovation Challenge:
Leadership for Transformation and Growth

SCOTT G. ISAKSEN

Creative Problem Solving Group
Buffalo, USA

JOE TIDD

SPRU – University of Sussex
Brighton, UK

John Wiley & Sons, Ltd

Other Wiley Editorial Offices

John Wiley & Sons Inc., 111 River Street, Hoboken, NJ 07030, USA

Jossey-Bass, 989 Market Street, San Francisco, CA 94103-1741, USA

Wiley-VCH Verlag GmbH, Boschstr. 12, D-69469 Weinheim, Germany

John Wiley & Sons Australia Ltd, 42 McDougall Street, Milton, Queensland 4064, Australia

John Wiley & Sons (Asia) Pte Ltd, 2 Clementi Loop #02-01, Jin Xing Distripark, Singapore 129809

John Wiley & Sons Canada Ltd, 22 Worcester Road, Etobicoke, Ontario, Canada M9W 1L1

Wiley also publishes its books in a variety of electronic formats. Some content that appears in print may
not be available in electronic books.

Library of Congress Cataloging-in-Publication Data

Isaksen, Scott G.
     Meeting the innovation challenge : leadership for transformation and growth /
Scott G. Isaksen, Joe Tidd.
         p. cm.
     Includes bibliographical references and index.
     ISBN 0-470-01499-7 (pbk. : alk. paper)
  1. Leadership.   2. Organizational change.   3. Creative ability.   I. Tidd, Joseph, 1960–
II. Title.
     HD57.7.I83 2006
     658.4′092–dc22   2006001051

British Library Cataloguing in Publication Data

A catalogue record for this book is available from the British Library

ISBN-10: 0-470-01499-7 (pbk)
ISBN-13: 978-0470-01499-8 (pbk)

Typeset in 10/15pt Sabon by SNP Best-set Typesetter Ltd, Hong Kong
Printed and bound in Great Britain by Antony Rowe Ltd, Chippenham, Wiltshire
This book is printed on acid-free paper responsibly manufactured from sustainable forestry
in which at least two trees are planted for each one used for paper production.

CONTENTS

Part 3 Transformation Methods

PREFACE

There is an urgent need for new and improved thinking about leadership, creativity and innovation. Older leadership models, tried and true practices, and previous innovation strategies do not adequately address today's challenges. Academics, consultants and popular writers have drawn leadership and management apart. Similarly, research and practice of innovation has emphasized strategic and organizational factors, whereas research and practice on creativity have focused on individual and group factors. However, successful organizational transformation and managing change demand *both* leadership *and* management as well as creativity *and* innovation. The purpose of this book is to integrate and expand research and practice of leadership and management, and innovation and creativity.

The idea for this book began in 2001 when we met to receive our respective awards for our previous work at the Conference of the European Association of Creativity and Innovation in the Netherlands. Members voted *Managing Innovation: Integrating Technological, Market and Organizational Change* (Tidd, Bessant and Pavitt, 2001) as the 'best book on innovation', and *Creative Approaches to Problem Solving* (Isaksen, Dorval and Treffinger, 2000) the 'best book on creativity'. We believed then, and believe now, that there is considerable scope to integrate the research and practice of the fields of creativity and innovation to support organizational transformation and growth.

Why is a new book on this topic needed at this time?

Broadened response to change

Managers are facing broadening demands on their time and attention to a dynamic and uncertain environment. No organization is insulated from the requirements of being able to broaden their responsiveness to change. Organizations in both the private and public sectors face an increasingly ambiguous environment. Under these conditions, managers must learn how to become more flexible and agile in order to respond successfully.

More inclusive leadership

Organizations have traditionally conceived of leadership as a heroic attribute, appointing the few 'real' leaders to high-level senior positions in order to get them through the hard times. Many observers within organizations are becoming cynical about this approach and are beginning to think about the need to recognize and utilize a wider range of leadership practices. Leadership needs to be conceived of as something that happens across functions and levels. New concepts and frameworks are needed in order to embrace this more inclusive approach to leadership.

Exploiting a broader range of creative talents

Organizations have typically viewed creativity as belonging to a gifted few (usually placed within the design, research and development or marketing functions). As a result, the development and implementation of innovation strategy has been limited. There is increasing recognition of the need to move beyond this narrow view of who has creative talent to how a broader range of talents might be applied. The contributions of innovation and creativity need to be understood as a source of competitive advantage. Organizations need to find ways to recognize and apply the full spectrum of creative talent represented in the entire employee population.

Integrating innovation, leadership and creativity

The best-selling *Innovator's Dilemma* by Christensen argues that disruptive innovation should be managed differently from routine innovation, and that the two demand different resources and organization. Conversely, in the popular *Winning Through Innovation*, Tushman argues that organizations must become 'ambidextrous', balancing both demands. Our book helps to integrate these different perspectives.

The questions and discussion must move beyond, 'What is the difference between leadership and management?' to 'How do we use a full spectrum of creative leadership skills to improve our responses to the needs for change?'

How does *Meeting the Innovation Challenge* meet the need?

Balanced integration

There are thousands of books on creativity, innovation, change and leadership, offering a diversity of models, ideas and perspectives. Very few books attempt to integrate these key concepts. What is needed is a productive synthesis of what we know about leadership and creativity – a balanced integration. This book seeks to link leadership and management, and innovation and creativity within the context of change.

Our particular emphasis will be on resolving the unnecessary and unproductive distinction that is made between leadership and management. When it comes to transformation and growth, organizations need both sets of skills.

A systems approach

Meeting the Innovation Challenge is about taking a systems approach. This means deliberately focusing on method, people, context and need. As such, this book offers a specific system that links the two dimensions of people and situation with two additional dimensions of process and content (methods and outcomes). Most other books deliberately try to focus on only one or two of these ingredients.

Practical suggestions and helpful resources

Many of the existing books offer perspectives and insights; few offer practical suggestions and resources. *Meeting the Innovation Challenge* will provide practical models, frameworks and resources to help those who live and work within organizations, with a particular emphasis on senior management.

How does this book go beyond other publications to provide a new contribution?

A *new framework for creative leadership*

Meeting the Innovation Challenge is organized around a model of creative leadership that builds on past work, but adds some recent perspectives from the fields of change management, personality psychology, innovation management and social psychology. As a result, the model seeks to integrate what is known, and to resolve a few of the inherent paradoxes and tensions in previous literature.

The multidimensional views of leadership raise the issue of context as an important factor, beyond concern of task and people. Recent social psychological research has introduced concern for change as a third factor for leadership behavior, in addition to concern for task and people. This recent insight forms the basis for our model of creative leadership. We deliberately include three main dimensions: concern for task, concern for people and concern for change.

In addition, we take another insight from the work of personality psychology and place it on this third change dimension. For example, there is a great deal of writing about the fundamental difference between leadership and management. This literature abounds and has generally promoted the argument that leaders have vision and think creatively, while managers are merely drones and just focus on doing things better. This distinction has led to a general devaluation of management. Emerging work in the field of creativity on styles of creativity and management initiative informs us that it is useful to keep preference distinct from capacity. Creativity is present both when doing things differently and doing things better. This means that leadership and management may be two constructs on a continuum, rather than two opposing views.

Leadership and climate

One of the most important roles that leaders play within organizational settings is to create the climate. Climate creation has a great influence on organizational performance. This book provides specific information on the dimensions of the climate for creativity and change, and some suggestions for leaders for creating appropriate climates.

Change methods and context

This book also goes beyond other publications by deliberately including information and guidance regarding many different change methods. Most other books keep their focus on one method and all the suggestions and recommendations deal with only that method. *Meeting the Innovation Challenge* applies the systematic approach and identifies how different methods of managing change are appropriate in different contexts.

Who should read this book?

The book is written for practicing managers, and for postgraduate study and post-experience training in change or innovation management, leadership and creativity. It will be most relevant to managers within private or public organizations, particularly those who face managing change projects. These leaders of change will generally work across functional boundaries but will include:

- research and development managers;
- new product development managers;
- project and program managers;
- divisional heads (who coordinate numerous other functions);
- senior managers who are launching strategic change initiatives;
- change consultants.

Such individuals will benefit by increasing the awareness and importance of their role, considering more elements of the larger system, and working toward sharing a common systemic framework when working together on challenges. In short, any change agent who needs to assist in implementing initiatives to improve or modify organizations stands to benefit from this book. We have attempted to balance the need for academic rigor, drawing upon a wide range of our own and others' research and experience, and practical models and guidance, trying to avoid the all-too common simplistic 'cook book' approach.

What's in this book?

In this book we will outline the need for taking a systemic approach to change and transformation. The first chapter will outline the four key elements in this system. Then we include parts on each of the elements. Part 1, focusing on the outcomes of transformation, includes a chapter on building the Janusian organization that outlines a spectrum of change. The next chapter in Part 1 attempts to integrate what we know about creativity and innovation as important partners in producing transformation. Chapter 4 on developing blockbusters includes what we have learned about breakthrough products and services and how these are created.

Part 2, on the role people play in transformation, also includes three chapters. Chapter 5 summarizes and integrates what we have learned about both leadership and management and outlines a new model for creative leadership. The next chapter describes the role of ownership and how the social roles of client and sponsor are key to creating transformation. Chapter 7 outlines how teamwork can be applied to produce extraordinary results.

Part 3, on transformation methods, includes a chapter on how to manage various change methods. Chapter 9 summarizes information on 20 different change methods. The final chapter in Part 3 illustrates how one particular change method, creative problem-solving, can be applied to new product and service development.

The context for transformation is the focus for the fourth and final part of the book. Here we deal first with the difference between culture and climate and provide a model for organizational change. Chapter 12 digs a little deeper into the concept of climate and outlines the dimensions of the Situational Outlook Questionnaire. The final chapter illustrates how using this measure can change the climate and offers suggestions for those who lead and manage organizations.

This book represents the first major effort to work across two large and important domains. We have learned a great deal in the process, but certainly know that this effort is more of a journey than a destination. We both look forward to continuing the journey and the future learning that implies.

Scott Isaksen, Buffalo, New York, USA
Joe Tidd, Brighton, Sussex, UK
January 2006

ABOUT THE AUTHORS

Scott Isaksen

Dr Isaksen is the President and Chief Executive Officer of the Creative Problem Solving Group Inc. and the Senior Fellow of its Creativity Research Unit. A former professor and director of the Center for Studies in Creativity he has published 160 books, articles and chapters including: *Creative Problem Solving: The Basic Course* (Bearly Ltd, 1985), *Frontiers of Creativity Research: Beyond the Basics* (Bearly Ltd, 1987), *Understanding and Recognizing Creativity: The Emergence of a Discipline* (Ablex, 1993), *Nurturing and Developing Creativity: The Emergence of a Discipline* (Ablex, 1993), *Creative Approaches to Problem Solving* (Kendall/Hunt, 1994, 2000) and *Facilitative Leadership* (Kendall/Hunt, 2000). Scott has conducted more than 1200 programs and courses by working with over 200 organizations and groups in more than 27 states or provinces and 20 different countries. Scott serves as a visiting faculty member to various universities and as a consulting editor for the *Journal of Creative Behavior*.

Scott is a regular faculty member for Ogilvy and Mather's Senior Leadership Program, Oxford's International Leadership Program, PwC's Leadership Conferences, and has provided numerous workshops for a variety of organizations. He continues to conduct research on creativity, creative problem-solving, styles of problem-solving and the climate for creativity – and works with graduate students and professionals around the world to do so.

Joe Tidd

Dr Tidd is a physicist with subsequent degrees in technology policy and business administration. He is Deputy Director and Professor of Technology and Innovation Management at SPRU (Science and Technology Policy Research), University of Sussex, and visiting Professor at University College London, Copenhagen Business School and the Rotterdam School of Management. He was previously Head of the Management of Innovation Specialization and Director of the Executive MBA Programme at Imperial College.

Dr Tidd has worked as policy adviser to the Confederation of British Industry (CBI), responsible for industrial innovation and advanced technologies. There he developed and launched the annual CBI *Innovation Trends Survey*, and presented expert evidence to three Select Committee Enquiries held by the House of Commons and House of Lords. Prior to working for the CBI, Dr Tidd was a researcher for the five-year, $5 million International Motor Vehicle Program organized by the Massachusetts Institute of Technology (MIT) in the US. He has worked on research and consultancy projects on technology and innovation management for consultants Arthur D. Little, CAP Gemini and McKinsey, and technology-based firms such as ASML, Applied Materials, BT, Marconi, National Power, NKT and Nortel Networks. He is the winner of the Price Waterhouse Urwick Medal for contribution to management teaching and research, and the Epton Prize from the R&D Society.

He has written six books and more than 70 papers on the management of technology and innovation, the most recent being *From Knowledge Management to Strategic Competence* (Imperial College Press, 2nd edn, 2006); *Managing Innovation: Integrating Technological, Market and Organizational Change* (John Wiley & Sons, Ltd, 3rd edn, 2005); and *Service Innovation: Organizational Responses to Technological Opportunities and Market Imperatives* (Imperial College Press, 2003). He is also Managing Editor of the *International Journal of Innovation Management*.

ACKNOWLEDGMENTS

From Scott

Our work in the field of creativity, like so many fields, allows us to state that we are standing on the shoulders of giants. Alex F. Osborn founded the tribe to which I belong. He was a founding partner of Batten, Barton, Durstine and Osborn, a Madison-Avenue advertising firm. Based on his challenge of getting 'creatives' and 'suits' to work together on client campaigns, he developed the first deliberate description of creative problem-solving outlined in his book *Applied Imagination*. Most people will recognize the term 'brainstorming', but fewer realize that it was Alex who developed it. I never met Alex, but his work provided the foundation for my learning about creativity.

The efforts of Sidney Parnes and Ruth Noller to validate a deliberate educational program to teach creativity at Buffalo State College provided the crucible for my early learning. Sid was Ruth's mentor, and Ruth has been my mentor since 1970. Her unconditional acceptance and encouragement have been a source of inspiration for me, and many others. She and I started work on some parts of this book and she influenced much of the thinking and learning about all four main concepts.

I met Don Treffinger after joining the faculty at the Center for Studies in Creativity and we have enjoyed a friendship and colleagueship for more than 25 years. Together with some students and other academic colleagues, we took some bold steps to build on the foundation with which we were entrusted. As a result, we made some important advances in creative problem-solving, started the Cognitive Styles Research Project and the Creative Climate Research Project. This work started at the university, but soon outgrew the academic environment and now continues through the Center for Creative Learning and the Creative Problem Solving Group (CPSB). The colleagues and associates of both organizations have continued to challenge our thinking and help us learn great things. Particular thanks go to Brian Stead-Dorval, Ken Lauer, Barbara Babij, Alex Britz, Keith Kaminski, John Gaulin, Luc DeSchryver, Andy Wilkins, Ed Selby and Glenn Wilson.

Four other organizations have provided rich insights and valuable contributions to my learning. After joining the faculty at the university I was able to work with the Center for Creative Leadership and learned that organizations were seriously interested in creativity. Thanks to Stan Gryskiewicz, Anne Faber, Ken and Mim Clark, David Campbell, and many others in Greensboro, North Carolina. Another organization was the Creative Education Foundation and its annual Creative Problem Solving Institute (CPSI). This event provided the opportunity to be influenced by J.P. Guilford, Don MacKinnon, E. Paul Torrance, Moe Stein and Charlie Clark. CPSI also provided experiences that directly influenced this book through partnership with Ruth Noller. We worked together on early versions of the Leadership Development Program and other events that shaped our learning.

The European Association for Creativity and Innovation and the many people who attend its biannual conference have provided a rich and varied set of opportunities to learn from people from many different cultures. Particular thanks go to Pros Vanasmoel, Han Van der Meer, Jan Buis and many others. It was through one special event during one of these conferences that Joe and I met. The fourth organization that must be acknowledged is the Creativity Research Unit at CPSB. Particular thanks go to Göran Ekvall, Geir Kaufmann and Michael Kirton for their direct influence on my learning. Thanks also to Harry Grace and Michael Johnson for their spiritual guidance and friendship.

Working with so many great people in a variety of client organizations has allowed me to test and develop much of my thinking and learning. Particular thanks go to Alf Tonneson, Simon McMurtrie and so many others at International Masters Publishers; Rita Houlihan and Ros Passman, and others from IBM; Don Taylor and others at Exxon-Mobil; Wayne Lewis, Trevor Davis, Frank Milton and others at PricewaterhouseCoopers; Mary Boulanger and Nancy Hann from Armstrong; Susan Ede and many others from Procter & Gamble; and so many others!

Finally, I must acknowledge those who helped in the writing of this book. Bill Shephard provided general support and encouragement and major assistance on the chapter on alternative change methods. Jesse Bergeron has assisted with editorial and graphic support. And most of all I must thank my family, Marves, Kristin, Erik and Kristen, who have tolerated the loss of their husband and father on weekends, evenings and even during vacations! The mistakes and omissions are mine!

From Joe

I would like to thank all my colleagues and students at SPRU (Science and Technology Policy Research), University of Sussex, and CENTRIM (the Centre for Research in Innovation Management), University of Brighton. For the past three years we have occupied a new, purpose-built facility – the Freeman Centre. This complex constitutes the largest academic center in the world devoted to research, training and development in the area of science, technology and innovation policy and management. The community of scholars includes 60 faculty, 80 PhD students and 70 postgraduate students. The environment and learning experience at the Freeman Centre is unique, and embodies three principles consistent with the central message of this book: interaction, collaboration and creativity.

SPRU's work is independent, multidisciplinary and international in scope. It is concerned with the scientific and technological challenges that confront decision-makers in government, industry and international agencies, and with the public debates that surround these challenges. We have engaged in world-class research and teaching on issues relating to scientific discovery and technological change since 1966, and celebrate SPRU's 40th anniversary in 2006. Our primary aim is to deepen understanding of the place of science, technology and innovation in the global economy for the benefit of government, business and society. See www.sussex.ac.uk/spru for details of our current work.

Our research, consultancy and development work has also influenced this book. This includes recent projects for the UK ESRC (Economic and Social Research Council) on the evolution of business knowledge, and international collaborative projects such as MINE (Managing Innovation in the New Economy), and has involved many innovative companies, including Applied Materials, Arup, ASML, Atkins, Jacobs, Mott MacDonald, Ricardo, Stork Protech, Vernalis and WRc plc.

I would also like to thank the team at John Wiley & Sons, Ltd, for their continuing support for our work on creativity, innovation and entrepreneurship. See www.managing-innovation.com for examples of recent developments.

Chapter 1

TAKING A SYSTEMIC APPROACH TO CHANGE

change initiatives such as delayering, outsourcing and networking will not succeed if done piecemeal. To reap the benefits of organizational innovation, firms must think and act holistically and make changes on several fronts in careful alignment[1]

Introduction

Transformation for innovation and growth is at the forefront of the agenda for many who work within organizations. In his work on disruptive innovation, Clayton Christensen identifies the many challenges organizations now face, and why so many fail to respond to these.[2] Today, everyone seems to be involved in planning or implementing some sort of change program or innovation initiative. At the same time, organizations must competently manage existing operations and businesses, what Michael Tushman calls the 'ambidextrous organization'.[3] In his ground-breaking study *Good to Great: Why Some Companies Make the Leap . . . and Others Don't*, Jim Collins describes a recipe for success that places leadership at the center.[4] Our research and experience inform us that those who initiate change need to have a good understanding of the nature of organizations, as well as the dynamics of innovation and change. This means that we must have a workable model for how organizations function that includes the key levers or factors for change. Rather than simply trying to pull a single lever, in this chapter we outline the need for a more systemic approach.

Most change programs aren't worth the effort

Researchers at Harvard have confirmed what many of us already knew. They examined the change efforts of Fortune 100 companies between 1980 and 1995 and found that virtually all had implemented at least one change program with an average investment of $1 billion per organization. The results were disappointing. Only 30% produced an improvement in bottom-line results that exceeded the company's cost of capital. Only 50% led to an improvement in market share price.[5] Similarly, most major programs of business process re-engineering (BPR) have failed to deliver the promised improvements in productivity or quality, for example two-thirds of 600 BPR cases studied experienced marginal or zero benefit, and many have simply been used as an excuse for rationalization and downsizing, e.g. typically 20% reduction in staff is experienced.[6] Most recently, many large private and public organizations have invested in some form of enterprise resource planning (ERP) as a catalyst for change, but 'such systems force change on an organization structure, working practices, policies and procedures that can hinder innovation'.[7]

Many managers, researchers, academics and consultants have speculated about why most change efforts are not very successful.[8] A common shortcoming is for a senior management team to design and announce a major change effort without the involvement and participation of others in the organization. They decide to train all members of their organization to enable implementation. Their single-minded reliance on training usually results in ineffective implementation and a condemnation of training. Another common pitfall is to limit participation in the leading of the change effort, only to find out later that participation should have been broadened and more inclusive from the start. Leaders of change efforts often fail to consider the entire situation. Some organizations seem to announce a new major change effort every few months and then wonder why people appear overwhelmed or resistant.

We know of other change initiatives that focused on creating a special place within the larger organization to foster innovation and transformation. These 'innovation centers' or corporate ventures have also had a mixed degree of success. Typically half fail, mainly due to problems of integration with the rest of the organization, internal territorial infringements, and differences between the culture and style of managers in the parent firm and venture.[9] Change efforts that fail can create major barriers to any future change endeavors. Change initiatives that fall short result in huge wastes of time, money and attention, and this has a big effect on the general vitality of the organization. Once an organization has gone through a change approach that does not work, the credibility of leadership is reduced within the organization. This affects not only the change effort, but the day-to-day operations as well. Exhibit 1.1 gives some examples where change has been introduced without a broader perspective.

Exhibit 1.1   Fashion statements versus behavioral change in organizations

It takes time, effort and money to try new things, it disrupts and disturbs the day-to-day working of the firm, it can upset organizational arrangements and requires effort in acquiring and using new skills. Not surprisingly most organizations are reluctant learners – and one strategy that they adopt is to try to short cut the process by borrowing ideas from other organizations.

While there is enormous potential in learning from others, simply copying what seems to work for another organization will not necessarily bring any benefits and may end up costing a great deal and distracting the organization from finding its own ways of dealing with a particular problem. The temptation to copy gives rise to the phenomenon of particular approaches becoming fashionable – something which every organization thinks it needs in order to deal with its particular problems.

Over the past 20 years we have seen many apparent panaceas for the problems of becoming competitive. Organizations are constantly seeking for new answers to old problems, and the scale of investment in the new fashions of management thinking have often been considerable. The *original* evidence for the value of these tools and techniques was strong, with case studies and other reports testifying to their proven value within the context of origin. But there is also extensive evidence to suggest that these changes do not always work, and in many cases that they lead to considerable dissatisfaction and disillusionment.

Examples include:

- quality circles, total quality management/ISO9000/Six Sigma;
- benchmarking best practice;
- business process re-engineering (BPR);
- 'Japanese', lean or agile manufacturing;
- knowledge management;
- enterprise resource planning (ERP).

What is going on here demonstrates well the principles behind behavioral change in organizations. It is not that the original ideas were flawed or that the initial evidence was wrong. Rather, it was that other organizations assumed that they could simply be copied, without the need to adapt them, to customize them, to modify and change them to suit their circumstances. In other words, there was no learning, and no progress toward making them become routines, part of the underlying culture within the organization.

Source: Adapted from Tidd, J., Bessant, J. and Pavitt, K. (2005) *Managing Innovation*. Chichester: John Wiley & Sons, Ltd.

We know of no single change method that is guaranteed to work for all situations: 'The most common mistake managers make is to use only one approach or a limited set of them regardless of the situation.'[10] We would treat any single quota or formula to guide the degree of participation for a change effort as naive. Simply guessing or ignoring the situational outlook for change can doom any initiative to fail. Too narrow a focus or being unclear about the desired outcome will also endanger the success of any change effort. We believe that you can increase the likelihood of successful change initiatives by taking a systemic approach.

We have had experience in attempting to help numerous organizations address the need for change and transformation by delivering programs designed to help participants use specific change methods. Our research into the impact of these programs tells us that other factors, like the environment or management support, were key to successful implementation. When we only focused on the method and associated tools, the impact was generally low.

We assert that a systemic approach is more productive than many of the existing ways organizations currently manage their change efforts. Rather than a single-minded focus on the results, leadership needs to consider a variety of critical factors in order to effectively implement change. For change agents, this means going beyond a single and preferred method. This kind of approach has also been referred to as integrated, comprehensive or inclusive.[11] As an additional resource, we have included a list of the top 10 barriers to effective change at the end of this chapter.

Why do organizations need to guide change?

There are three basic reasons why organizations need to be able to effectively respond to change. These include: the escalating pace and volume of change, dealing with greater complexity and more intense competition.

Increasing pace and volume

The pace of change within and external to organizations is increasing.[12] Organizations face continuous changes in senior leadership. Time is being compressed in the marketplace. Companies must get new and improved products and services to the market faster than ever before. Organizations face an increased volume of change in comparison with earlier times. With trade liberalization and the opening of markets have come a massive upsurge in overall activity and the number of players in the game. It is estimated, for example, that the entire volume of world trade that took place during 1950 is now transacted in a single day! Competition has intensified and much of it is being driven by innovation in products, services and processes.

Growing complexity

The second reason for the importance of organizational change is the increasing complexity with which organizations must deal.[13] Complexity is fed by major levels of growth within companies, mergers, acquisitions, outsourcing, offshoring and the scarcity of qualified people for key jobs. The impact of government policies and regulation is also on the rise due to a growing role within the workplace, e.g. for people with disabilities, retirement and health benefits, etc. Legislation can add additional force to changing the rules of the game – for example, the continuing effects of clean air and related environmental pollution legislation have had enormous and cumulative effects on industries involved in chemicals, materials processing, mining and transportation, both in terms of products and processes. Current directives such as those of the European Union around waste and recycling mean that manufacturers are increasingly having to take into account the long-term use and disposal of their products as well as their manufacture and sales – and this is forcing innovation in products, processes and administrative models, such as whole-life costing. The expanding growth rate of knowledge, information and data is also feeding complexity.

Intensifying competition and globalization

Finally, increasing competition within all markets, and on a global level, means that the costs of not changing can be too high for organizational survival.[14] Organizations face severe declines in profits and perceived decreases in value in the marketplace should they be unable to anticipate and respond to competitors' actions. There is also the ever-present need to improve customer satisfaction and existing products and services while developing new avenues for future growth. The production of knowledge has become far more global, particularly in the newly industrializing countries. For example, the number of engineering degrees awarded in 1998 in the USA was 62 000, in Europe 159 000, but in Asia around 280 000.

These issues face all types of organization. Private businesses, large global corporations, not-for-profits, educational or academic institutions and governmental agencies all face the challenges of change and increasing turbulence. This problem – of managing both the discontinuous and the steady state – emerges frequently and can be triggered not only by radical technology or significant market change. It can come from reframing a business model – such as has happened with the 're-invention' of the airline industry around low-cost models, or the music industry based on downloading. Table 1.1 gives some examples of such triggers for discontinuity. Common to these is the need to recognize that under discontinuous conditions we need different approaches to organizing and managing change.

In such turbulent and rapidly changing times, in order to survive and prosper organizations must be prepared to renew their products and processes on a continuing basis. A study by Shell suggested that the average corporate survival rate for large companies was only about half as long as that of a human being, and of the 500 companies originally making up the Standard and Poor 500 list in 1857, only 74 remained on the list through to 1997.[15] One indicator of the possibility of doing this comes from the experiences of organizations that have survived for an extended period of time. While most organizations have comparatively modest life-spans, there are some that have survived at least one and sometimes multiple centuries. Looking at the experience of these '100 club' members – firms like 3M, Corning, Procter & Gamble, Reuters, Siemens, Philips and Rolls-Royce – we can see that much of their longevity is down to having developed a capacity to innovate on a continuing basis. They have learned – often the hard way – how to manage the process (both in its 'do better' and 'do different' variants) so that they can sustain performance.

The distinction between commercial and not-for-profit organizations is irrelevant when considering the need for change. While private sector firms may compete for the attentions of their markets through offering new things or new ways of delivering them, public sector and nonprofit organizations use innovation to help them compete against the challenges of delivering healthcare, education, law and order, etc. They are similarly preoccupied with process innovation (the challenge of using often scarce resources more effectively or becoming faster and more flexible in their response to a diverse environment) and with product innovation – using combinations of new and existing knowledge to deliver new or improved 'product concepts' – such as decentralized healthcare or community policing.[16]

Table 1.1 Sources of discontinuity

Triggers/sources of discontinuity	Explanation	Problems posed	Examples (of good and bad experiences)
New market emerges	Most markets evolve through a process of growth, segmentation, etc. But at certain times completely new markets emerge that can not be analyzed or predicted in advance or explored through using conventional market research/analytical techniques	Established players don't see it because they are focused on their existing markets May discount it as being too small or not representing their preferred target market – fringe/cranks dismissal Originators of new product may not see potential in new markets and may ignore them, e.g. text messaging	Disk drives, excavators, mini-mills Mobile phone/SMS where market that actually emerged was not the one expected or predicted by originators
New technology emerges	Step change takes place in product or process technology – may result from convergence and maturing of several streams (e.g. industrial automation, mobile phones) or as a result of a	Don't see it because beyond the periphery of technology search environment Not an extension of current areas but completely new field or approach	Ice harvesting to cold storage Valves to solid-state electronics Photos to digital images

Table 1.1 *Continued*

Triggers/sources of discontinuity	Explanation	Problems posed	Examples (of good and bad experiences)
	single breakthrough (e.g. LED as white light source)	Tipping point may not be a single breakthrough but convergence and maturing of established technological streams, whose combined effect is underestimated Not invented here effect – new technology represents a different basis for delivering value, e.g. telephone vs telegraphy	
New political rules emerge	Political conditions that shape the economic and social rules may shift dramatically – for example, the collapse of communism meant an alternative model	Old mindset about how business is done, rules of the game, etc. are challenged and established firms fail to understand or learn	Centrally planned to market economy, e.g. former Soviet Union Apartheid to post-apartheid South Africa – inward and insular to externally linked

	– capitalist, competition – as opposed to central planning – and many ex-state firms couldn't adapt their ways of thinking	new rules	Free trade/globalization results in dismantling protective tariff and other barriers and new competition basis emerges
Running out of road	Firms in mature industries may need to escape the constraints of diminishing space for product and process innovation and the increasing competition of industry structures by either exit or by radical reorientation of their business	Current system is built around a particular trajectory and embedded in a steady-state set of innovation routines that militate against widespread search or risk taking experiments	Medproducts Kodak Encyclopaedia Britannica Preussag Mannesmann
Sea change in market sentiment or behavior	Public opinion or behavior shifts slowly and then tips over into a new model – for example, the music industry is in the midst of a (technology-enabled) revolution in delivery systems from buying records, tapes and CDs to direct download of tracks in MP3 and related formats.	Don't pick up on it or persist in alternative explanations – cognitive dissonance – until it may be too late	Apple, Napster, Dell, Microsoft vs traditional music industry

Table 1.1 Continued

Triggers/sources of discontinuity	Explanation	Problems posed	Examples (of good and bad experiences)
Deregulation/shifts in regulatory regime	Political and market pressures lead to shifts in the regulatory framework and enable the emergence of a new set of rules, e.g. liberalization, privatization or deregulation	New rules of the game but old mindsets persist and existing player unable to move fast enough or see new opportunities opened up	Old monopoly positions in fields like telecommunications and energy were dismantled and new players/combinations of enterprises emerged. In particular, energy and bandwidth become increasingly viewed as commodities. Innovations include skills in trading and distribution – a factor behind the considerable success of Enron in the late 1990s as it emerged from a small gas pipeline business to becoming a major energy trade – unquantifiable chances may need to be taken

Fractures along 'fault lines'	Long-standing issues of concern to a minority accumulate momentum (sometimes through the action of pressure groups) and suddenly the system switches/tips over – for example, social attitudes to smoking or health concerns about obesity levels and fast-foods	Rules of the game suddenly shift and then new pattern gathers rapid momentum wrong-footing existing players working with old assumptions. Other players who have been working in the background developing parallel alternatives may suddenly come into the limelight as new conditions favor them	McDonald's and obesity Tobacco companies and smoking bans Oil/energy and others and global warming Opportunity for new energy sources like wind-power
Unthinkable events	Unimagined and therefore not prepared for events, which – sometimes literally – change the world and set up new rules of the game	New rules may disempower existing players or render competencies unnecessary	9/11

Table 1.1   Continued

Triggers/sources of discontinuity	Explanation	Problems posed	Examples (of good and bad experiences)
Business model innovation	Established business models are challenged by a reframing, usually by a new entrant who redefines/reframes the problem and the consequent 'rules of the game'	New entrants see opportunity to deliver product/service via new business model and rewrite rules – existing players have at best to be fast followers	Amazon.com Charles Schwab Southwest and other low-cost airlines
Shifts in 'techno-economic paradigm' – systemic changes that impact whole sectors or even whole societies	Change takes place at system level, involving technology and market shifts. This involves the convergence of a number of trends that result in a 'paradigm shift' where the old order is replaced	Hard to see where new paradigm begins until rules become established. Existing players tend to reinforce their commitment to old model, reinforced by 'sailing ship' effects	Industrial Revolution Mass production

| Architectural innovation | Changes at the level of the system architecture rewrite the rules of the game for those involved at component level | Established players develop particular ways of seeing and framing their interactions – for example who they talk to in acquiring and using knowledge to drive innovation – according to this set of views. Architectural shifts may involve reframing but at the component level it is difficult to pick up the need for doing so – and thus new entrants better able to work with new architecture can emerge | Photo-lithography in chip manufacture |

Source: Adapted from Tidd, J., Bessant, J. and Pavitt, K. (2005) *Managing Innovation*. Chichester: John Wiley & Sons, Ltd.

The example of downsizing

Despite the need for a comprehensive spectrum of change efforts, many of the initiatives that organizations currently undertake are merely aimed at cost cutting, 'headcount reduction,' and 'right-sizing'. Some efforts are taken to improve the existing business, like quality management or cycle-time reduction. Still fewer initiatives are being taken to develop fundamentally new ways of working or new business opportunities.

Recent evidence regarding the results of downsizing points to the need for better navigation of change efforts. Although the expected benefits from downsizing include lower overheads, decreased bureaucracy, faster decision-making, smoother communication, increased productivity and generally making an organization more efficient than its competitors, the actual results are disappointing. They include:

- More than 50% of the 1468 firms that restructured reported that productivity remained stagnant or deteriorated after downsizing.[17]
- 74% of the senior executives surveyed within the 1468 firms indicated that they had experienced problems with trust, morale and productivity.[18]
- Of 1005 downsized firms surveyed by the *Wall Street Journal*, only 46% had actually cut expenses, 32% had increased profits, 22% had increased productivity, and 22% had reduced bureaucracy.[19]
- 58% of the 1005 companies reported that employee morale was severely affected with some companies indicating a severe impact on the survivors.[20]
- Many organizations report an initial upsurge in productivity immediately after downsizing, but then become depressed and lethargic.[21]
- Stock prices of firms that downsized during the 1980s lagged behind the industry average in the 1990s.[22]
- Most firms do not succeed in their original effort and end up downsizing again, a year later on average.[23]
- Depression was a regular occurrence among most people involved in downsizing.[24]

As you can see from these results, downsizing as a way of dealing with the need for change does not offer the expected benefits. In summarizing their exploratory study on downsizing, Kets de Vries and Balsz called for the creation of a mindset that concentrates unwaveringly on finding new learning opportunities that lead to innovative practices in the workplace.[25] They outlined the need to reframe downsizing toward corporate transformation; the process of continuously aligning the organization with its environment and the shaping of an organizational climate in which the enduring encouragement of new challenges stands as central.

Downsizing also offers a key lesson for those who seek to guide change. Those who chose this approach to improving effectiveness probably did not make a mindful choice. For a while, it seemed as though every organization was going through some downsizing effort. It became a major line of service for some consultancies, who regularly offered senior management a prepackaged 5%, 10% or 20% solution. Our point is that the change effort became a trend and this encouraged decision-makers within organizations to go along with a poor choice. The alternative is to make a more mindful choice after considering some important key factors.

This is what we mean by making a more systemic approach to guiding change. It means considering the centrality of people issues in successfully implementing change, while also thinking about the situation, climate or culture. It also means considering a number of possible approaches to accomplishing the desired outcomes. Even the effects of downsizing can be dealt with productively.[26] But the main message is that anyone who sees the need for change must look beyond a single, well-defined or prepackaged solution. It pays to look at the larger picture.

A survey of high performers

Research conducted by PricewaterhouseCoopers (PwC) examined the gaps between the most innovative companies and the lowest performers from among the *Times* Top 1000 organizations in the United Kingdom.[27] They found that a number of key factors separated the top 20% of those organizations earning the highest percentage of turnover from new products and services (introduced within the last five years) from those earning the lowest. The study identified three basic capabilities that characterized the more successful organizations. They were: having a deliberate process for idea management, building a creative climate and following an inclusive approach to leadership (Figure 1.1).

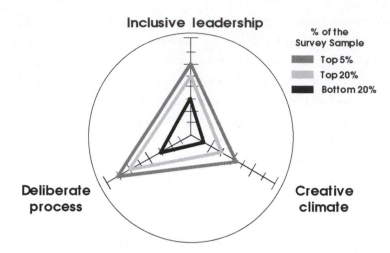

Figure 1.1 The three capabilities
Source: Adapted from: Davis, T. (2000) *Innovation and Growth: A Global Perspective*. London: PricewaterhouseCoopers.

Deliberate process

High performers are very deliberate about their processes for generating, storing and retrieving ideas. Ideas are viewed as options to solve problems and the high performers are most interested in problems that come from the marketplace. They view creative problem-solving as being one of the best ways of engaging in discovering new ideas for things that will be useful for their business. The highest performers invest in understanding the underlying needs of clients and customers and deliberately attempt to deal with the 'messy stuff'. The lowest performers in the PwC survey thought that high-quality new ideas came mainly from senior management. The highest performers see everybody as having potentially valuable ideas.

Creative climate

The high performers go about getting more high-quality ideas by paying attention to everyday behavior and language. They create the right climate or environment for ideas and alternatives to thrive and grow, and encourage everyone to get involved. The high performers have the capability to establish and maintain productive workplaces.

Inclusive leadership

High performers have a much wider and more inclusive view of leadership. They have the capability to engage everyone in the creative process. They have rewritten the contract between leaders and their constituents such that it is often hard to tell the difference between them. The relationship between leaders and followers creates the productive climate for idea management.

The PwC research clearly shows that high-performing organizations take a systemic approach to sustaining change. When we examine organizations that are highly productive, they create climates for change, deliberately manage ideas and redesign leadership to promote creativity. Those in the top 5% of those surveyed are doing all three of these things better and more often than their less-productive counterparts. They do not focus on only one of these factors. They take deliberate steps to work on multiple fronts.

Our systemic approach

The PwC study illustrates the importance of taking a systemic approach. Organizations are understood as temporary solutions invented by people to accomplish more than is possible alone or as a small group. They are dynamic, living systems. As they get larger and their purposes become broader, organizations function as complex interacting systems.

A system is an organized and connected group of things that are associated in such a way that, according to Aristotle, the whole is greater than the sum of its parts. Taking a systemic approach to change means carefully considering all the interrelated elements of the whole change situation. Real change is messy, involving false starts, recycling between stages, dead ends, jumps out of sequence, etc. A seminal program of case studies-based research looking at widely different innovation types explored the limitations of simple models of the process.[28] It drew attention to the complex ways in which innovations actually evolve over time, and derived some important modifiers to the basic model:

- Shocks trigger innovations – change happens when people or organizations reach a threshold of opportunity or dissatisfaction.
- Ideas proliferate – after starting out in a single direction, the process proliferates into multiple, divergent progressions.

- Setbacks frequently arise, plans are overoptimistic, commitments escalate, mistakes accumulate and vicious cycles can develop.
- Restructuring of the innovating unit often occur through external intervention, personnel changes or other unexpected events.
- Top management plays a key role in sponsoring – but also in criticizing and shaping – innovation.
- Success criteria shift over time, differ between groups and make innovation a political process.
- Innovation involves learning, but many of its outcomes are due to other events that occur as the innovation develops – making learning often 'superstitious' in nature.

This effort could easily become overly complex or even completely unmanageable, so we have outlined four main elements for taking a systemic approach to change. Our current model for guiding change includes four main dimensions: people, need or desired outcomes, context or situational readiness, and the method or approach to managing change (see Figure 1.2). This model has been derived as a result of taking an ecological approach to our research, as well as a descriptive approach to creative problem-solving.[29] From the conceptual point of view, creativity can be approached as a function of person, process, product and context.

When change is viewed from a systemic point of view, a very similar framework is useful. The four main elements of a model for change management include people, context, need and method. When considering change within organizations it is natural to think about the people and the context or place involved in the change. This is related to the person–environment fit issue.[30] An additional dimension includes the

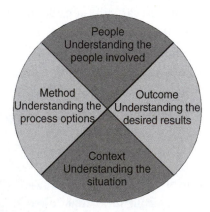

Figure 1.2 A model for guiding change

need and the method that relates well to the content–process issue. Each of the four main elements will be explored in more detail below.

People

Most change (revitalization as well as transformation) requires the involvement and active participation of a large number of people. Managers, leaders and followers will face ambiguity and discomfort during times of change. How the tension created by these messy situations is handled depends on the quality of leadership and the environments they create. The recent critiques of the $4.7 billion reengineering industry focus their explanations of the 70% failure rate on the overemphasis on engineering and ignoring the human dimension.[31] A detailed study of a six-year business process re-engineering (BPR) program concluded that:

> As opposed to the orthodox definition of BPR as a tool for radical change in a short period of time . . . BPR was part of the attempted change programme which affected the company's operations. This change in the processes would not have led to the desired results if it had not been aligned with the strategy of the company and joined to the changes in the management system, the organization, the technology and labour relations system . . . leadership and change management are of great importance.[32]

According to a study conducted by Arthur D. Little, the single biggest stumbling block to change is an absence of adequate leadership and direction, not a fear of failure or lack of reward. The study of 350 senior executives from 14 major sectors of industry reported that:

> Some 64 percent of the respondents said their companies' most daunting barrier to implementing change was a lack of buy-in among managers and employees that change was necessary in the first place. Four out of ten executives further identified turf battles, the absence of a senior management champion, and a lack of adequate implementation skills as major barriers.[33]

Organizational leadership creates the climate within which people operate and interact. This climate will impact how people will behave and whether or not they will use their creativity to identify and resolve challenges and opportunities. Dealing with change within organizations means that questions and answers will come from different places. People still need to run the day-to-day operations while the change processes are going on. There are many implications for a new kind of leadership that will be required to manage creative kinds of change. Questions that need to be asked include:

- What kind of change leadership exists (are there clear sponsors and leaders)?
- How ready are others in the organization to participate in a change program?
- How much diversity exists in the organization (cultural, functional, styles, etc.) and how well is it managed?
- What have people learned that will help or hinder future change?
- How have people managed their creativity resources?

The model for creative leadership (described in more detail in Chapter 5) illustrates that contemporary views of leadership must go well beyond the two classic dimensions of paying attention to people and tasks. A full spectrum of change must also be included that allows for focusing on management competencies when there are relatively stable conditions. As the need for a more extraordinary level of performance increases, then different leadership practices and strategies are required. Finally, when you need to operate at the edge of chaos, more attention is focused on establishing and maintaining intensely productive relationships with people and establishing higher performing work systems.

PricewaterhouseCoopers (PwC) researchers were able to identify 10 fundamental characteristics that differentiate the highest from the lowest performers among those organizations surveyed. A major insight from the study was that people surveyed within most of the successful organizations considered trust to be the most significant characteristic. Specifically, they reported a higher degree of management trust; in each other and in them by others.[34]

The trust factor describes an important aspect of the quality of relationships among people in organizations that are successful at introducing change. Kouzes and Posner reported the existence of a wide-spread credibility gap within organizations. They stated:

> Credibility is mostly about consistency between words and deeds. People listen to the words and look at the deeds. Then they measure the congruence. A judgment as 'credible' is handed down when two are consonant.[35]

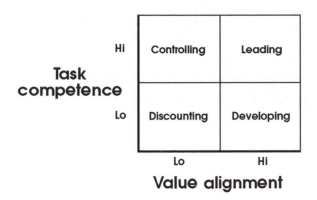

Figure 1.3   Trust includes competence and values

Their study also indicated that although more than 80% of office workers believed that it was important that management be honest, upright, and ethical, less than 40% of the workers believed that it was true for them. They point to the trust factor in overcoming cynicism and distrust and in closing the credibility gap.

Trust is commonly understood as a single thing, usually having to do with the level of assured reliance on someone's character or degree of truth. Rather than being a single dimensional factor, trust is being seen more frequently by researchers as multidimensional.[36] These multidimensional views approach trust as the willingness to be vulnerable to another based on belief of competence and values; particularly those of honesty, concern and alignment of words and actions.

As you can see from Figure 1.3, trust can be illustrated both as a belief in the competence of the individual to perform various tasks and the degree to which an individual is in agreement with a certain set of values. When seen in this way, trust can be understood in terms of the interaction of values and competence. When we have low belief in someone's competence and their values are very different, this diversity is not seen as important or valuable in the organization. The result is that that people who are characterized this way may be discounted. When someone is seen as very competent but holding a different value set, you are likely to see controlling behavior and use of power to keep the individual aligned. When values are clearly aligned, the response may be to develop the competencies that are needed for accomplishing the task. When you know that the person is competent and holds a similar value set, you will want to get out of their way and let them lead.

The key issue when it comes to change leadership is the kind of ownership and sponsorship that exists to enable people to make the change happen (see Chapter 6 on owning up to change). People within organizations who are being asked to change must be able to trust their leaders. As Kouzes and Posner indicated:

> To take people to places they have never been before, leaders and constituents must be on the same path. And to get people to join the voyage of discovery voluntarily requires that the aims and aspirations of leaders and constituents are harmonious.[37]

Context

The people often make the place. Managing change means understanding the situational readiness for the transformation, and the forces operating for and against the initiative. This key area relates very strongly to the finding from the PwC study identified as creating the climate.

Organizations develop particular ways of behaving that become 'the way we do things around here' as a result of repetition and reinforcement. These patterns reflect an underlying set of shared beliefs about the world and how to deal with it, and form part of the organization's culture. They emerge as a result of repeated experiments and experience around what appears to work well – in other words, they are learned. Over time the pattern becomes more of an automatic response to particular situations, and the behavior becomes what can be termed as 'routine'.

This does not mean that it is necessarily repetitive, only that its execution does not require detailed conscious thought. The analogy can be made with driving a car; it is possible to drive along a stretch of motorway while simultaneously talking to someone else, eating or drinking, listening to and concentrating on something on the radio or planning what to say at the forthcoming meeting. But driving is not a passive behavior; it requires continuous assessment and adaptation of responses in the light of other traffic behavior, road conditions, weather and a host of different and unplanned factors. We can say that driving represents a behavioral routine in that it has been learned to the point of being largely automatic.

In the same way, an organizational routine might exist around how projects are managed or new products researched. For our purposes, the important thing to note is that routines are what makes one organization different from another in how they carry out the same basic activity. We could almost say that they represent the particular 'personality' of the firm. Each enterprise learns its own particular 'way we do things around here' in answer to the same generic questions – how it manages quality, how it manages people, etc. It follows that some routines are better than others in coping with the uncertainties of the outside world, in both the short and the long term. And it is possible to learn from others' experience in this way; the important point is to remember that routines are organization-specific and must be learned. Simply copying what someone else does is unlikely to help, any more than watching someone drive and then attempting to copy them will make a novice into an experienced driver. There may be helpful clues that can be used to improve the novice's routines, but there is no substitute for the long and experience-based process of learning.

There is an important negative side of routines. They represent, as we have seen, embedded behaviors that have become reinforced to the point of being almost second nature – 'the way we do things around here'. Therein lies their strength, but also their weakness. Because they represent ingrained patterns of thinking about the world, they are resilient – but they can also become barriers to thinking in different ways; thus, when the 'way we do things round here' becomes inappropriate, but when the organization is too committed to the old ways to change. So it becomes important, from the standpoint of managing change, not only to build routines but also to recognize when and how to destroy them and allow new ones to emerge.

We now have improved ways of diagnosing organizational health. In much the same way that medicine has moved away from treating obvious symptoms, we can now examine the vital signs that tell us how ready the organization is to innovate and lead change. We use these assessments to examine the strengths, weaknesses and needs within an organization. One assessment we use is the Situational Outlook Questionnaire (SOQ) that is described in more detail in Chapter 12. It measures nine dimensions that have been found to be important for a climate for creativity and change (see Figure 1.4).

- Challenge and involvement
- Playfulness and humor
- Freedom
- Conflict
- Trust and openness
- Idea support
- Idea time
- Debate
- Risk-taking

Figure 1.4 Situational Outlook Questionnaire (SOQ) dimensions
Source: Adapted from Göran Ekvall, Swedish Council for Management and Work Life Issues

In addition to these measures, a few of the major questions to consider include:

- How has the organization handled change in the past (history)?
- What are the current changes the organization faces (map the landscape)?
- What kinds of resources are available to help implement the change effort?
- How is power used in making decisions and taking action?
- To what extent do people have a clear idea about the vision and values of the organization?

The model for organizational change (described in more detail in Chapter 11) illustrates a few of the key attributes that impact the overall performance of individuals, groups and the organization. When we examine the context, these are the characteristics on which we check. From our experience, there are usually very different levels of readiness in every workplace. Mental models are important because they help us frame the issues that need managing – but therein also lies the risk. If our mental models are limited then our approach to managing is also likely to be limited. Examples of such 'partial thinking' here include seeing change as a single isolated change rather than as part of a wider system. Table 1.2 provides an overview of the difficulties that can arise if we take a partial view of innovation.[38]

The SOQ contains a number of open-ended questions that help to obtain information on many of the factors in the model for organizational change. If the leaders within the organization desire radical innovation and change, then we must know that the capabilities are within the organization to develop and sustain this kind of change. Whatever the kind of change, it will be helpful to think about the context from the point of view of the individual, the team or group as well as the entire organization.

Outcomes

The actual change itself is a major factor that influences how the change program should work. The sponsors and leadership community must be very clear and specific about the desired future vision as well as the core values to be held constant. The image of the desired outcome must answer the question of core purpose for the change. The reason and concurrent emotion for the change helps people see what needs to be done and when it needs to be accomplished. At a basic level, the structures and behaviors needed to help enable incremental improvements to be incorporated into the

Table 1.2 Problems of partial views of change

If change is only seen as . . .	. . . the result can be
The province of specialists	Lack of involvement of others, and a lack of key knowledge and experience input from other perspectives
Understanding and meeting customer needs	Lack of technical progression, leading to inability to gain competitive edge
Advances along the technology frontier	Producing products or services that the market does not want or designing processes that do not meet the needs of the user and whose implementation is resisted
The province only of large firms	Weak, small firms with too high a dependence on large customers. Disruptive innovation as apparently insignificant small players seize new technical or market opportunities
Only about 'breakthrough' changes	Neglect of the potential of incremental innovation. Also an inability to secure and reinforce the gains from radical change because the incremental performance ratchet is not working well
Only about strategically targeted projects	May miss out on lucky 'accidents' that open up new possibilities
Only associated with key individuals	Failure to utilize the creativity of the remainder of employees, and to secure their inputs and perspectives to improve innovation
Only internally generated	The 'not invented here' effect, where good ideas from outside are resisted or rejected
Only externally generated	Innovation becomes simply a matter of filling a shopping list of needs from outside and there is little internal learning or development of technological competence
Only concerning single firms	Excludes the possibility of various forms of inter-organizational networking to create new products, streamline shared processes, etc.

Source: Adapted from Tidd, J., Bessant, J. and Pavitt, K. (2005) *Managing Innovation*. Chichester: John Wiley & Sons, Ltd.

day-to-day standard operating procedures of the organization are different to more radical projects that will require more specialized. At the limit, the organization may need to review the whole bundle of routines that it uses for managing innovation when it confronts discontinuous conditions and the 'rules of the game' change.

The conventional distinction between incremental and radical innovation can be misleading; there is a need to differentiate between the nature of technology inputs and market and organizational impact. Major advances or breakthroughs along the *technological* frontier can disrupt the rules of the game,[39] but they are not the only mechanism. The influential work of Clayton Christensen drew attention to cases where the *market* was the effective trigger point.[40] His distinctive observation was that with each generation almost all of the previously successful players in what was a multimillion dollar market failed to make the transition effectively and were often squeezed out of the market or into bankruptcy. The problem is not a failure to cope with a breakthrough in the technological frontier, but the emergence of new *markets* with very different needs and expectations. In essence, the existing players were too good at working with their mainstream users and failed to see the longer-term potential in the newly emerging market. Their systems for picking up signals about user needs and feeding these into the product development process were all geared around existing markets and industry norms.

In order to focus on the right questions for people and situational issues, we must know as much as possible about the desired outcome. People must know and understand if they are dealing with an incremental improvement or a total transformation. Those guiding change are responsible to explain the scope and scale of the desired change. We must answer questions like:

- What is the kind and degree of novelty required within the future image?
- What will not change (the core ideology)?
- When must the outcome be accomplished (long or short term)?
- What is the relationship between this new desired outcome and the current organizational strategy?
- Will new structures, systems, policies and procedures be required to sustain the desired outcome or just improvements in existing ones?

The core issues within the area of need include determining the degree of clarity of the image of the outcome or result and determining the kind of novelty desired. People will need to be able to develop a personal image of the desired outcome and take initiative to get there.

Method

The method or approach to change depends upon the people and the situation, as well as the desired outcome. Knowing what outcome you desire, along with understanding the people and place issues, does not tell you how to manage the change. When we know enough about these issues, we can then plan the most appropriate approach. We can then answer important questions such as:

- How mindful does our approach need to be (do we need to instill mental disciplines during this unique opportunity to learn or do we just want to take a transparent approach)?
- How fast does our approach need to be (do we need to build in some fast-track activities or do we want the entire effort coordinated and fully planned)?
- How broad does the leadership community need to be?
- What's the plan for engaging others within the organization?
- Can we use some common process approach or do we need to develop one?

Much recent work recognizes the limits of linear models and tries to build more complexity and interaction into the frameworks. Increasingly, there is recognition of some of the difficulties around what is often termed the 'fuzzy front end' where uncertainty is highest, but there is still convergence around a basic process structure as a way of focusing our attention. The balance needs to be struck between simplifications and representations that help thinking – but just as the map is not the same as the territory it represents so they need to be seen as frameworks for thinking not as descriptions of the way the process actually operates.

Our approach to managing change relies on searching to understand as much as possible about the entire system surrounding the change. Then we design and implement an appropriate approach. We often rely on the flexible application of creative problem-solving (CPS) as well as other models and tools. Our application of CPS is formed by learning about the sponsors, clients and others involved in leading the change, plus an understanding of the context and the image of the preferred future. Chapter 9 provides numerous examples of change methods, beyond CPS, that can be helpful in guiding any change effort.

Beware those who offer the 'magic bullet'! Methods provide tools and helpful means for people to engage in change. They are not replacements for being mindful about the purpose or the philosophy surrounding the tools. All methods have their costs and benefits, and they differ in terms of their ability to fit various circumstances. Different methods and tools will be appropriate in different contexts,[41] and in many cases tools alone are simply insufficient or may even be dysfunctional.[42] That's the whole reason for taking a systemic approach. Without such a systematic approach, managers may.

> navigate between two deadly extremes: on the one hand, ill-conceived and arbitrary decisions made without systematic study and reflection – *extinction by instinct*, and on the other hand, a retreat into abstraction and conservatism that relies obsessively on numbers, analyses and reports – *paralysis by analysis*.[43]

Conclusions

There is no question that organizations, and the people within them, will need to find ways to cope with and embrace increasing demands for change. Rather than the 'method of the month' approach currently being taken, we will need to find better and more effective ways to unleash the creative talents of people within the organization. Taking a more systemic approach to this fundamental task is likely to improve the success rate most organizations experience when enacting change.

Our experiences with a variety of organizations support this view. A division of a global information systems company with which we worked faced major challenges in the marketplace. A patent on a large systems IT product was about to expire and the competition had a much-improved and lower-priced product ready to enter the market. The division faced major layoffs and the possibility of shutting down. We took a systemic approach and one of the interventions was a workshop for the senior management team of the division. Results included:

- common recognition of the challenges and the opportunities facing the organization;
- acceptance of their role in taking initiatives outside the normal ways of working;
- rejection of the 'inevitable' layoffs and shut down;
- using the cross-functional diversity within the division to consider a variety of new and potentially useful ways of using the talents and unique resources available to them;
- a plan to develop and implement up to five new business units designed to take advantage of their unique strengths and experiences to meet needs within the marketplace.

The acid test is that three years later the division had fully implemented the plan for four of the five business units. They had saved 85%–90% of the positions and were even more viable than before the transition. They are seen as a major profit center for the global organization and are now looking to hire more people and take on new markets. Similar stories can be told within the healthcare industry, educational programs and even churches.

Our approach to managing change is different from many others in that it is based on more than 55 years of extensive research and development in the fields of creativity and innovation, and has been shaped by working with a variety of private and public sector organizations in different countries.[44] Although we have focused our energy on a particular change method, we hope that others can benefit from the more general insights for guiding change efforts. We have had the pleasure of working with numerous senior executives, presidents, executive directors, chief executive officers and boards over the past 15 years. Most of our work has been about creative change. We have searched the academic literature for the latest research and evidence, and have interpreted this using our own experience. We can offer the following top 10 reasons why change efforts are often unsuccessful.

Top 10 barriers to effective change: a recipe for failure

1. Do not establish or communicate a great enough sense of urgency

If change efforts are to be believed and accepted, they must be shared in the context of clearly compelling reasons for doing things differently. The reasons for the change must be clearly communicated (at least six different ways and many times) and must be referred to when the change initiative is being adjusted or evaluated.

2. Keep the leadership for the change small in number and concentrated at the top of the organizational chart

All successful change efforts require the active involvement and participation of a leadership community. Initiators of change must create an inclusive guiding coalition that includes some from outside the traditional hierarchy. This can be through informal means or the creation of task forces or strategic project teams.

3. Initiate change without a blueprint

Trying to guide a major change effort without a complete strategic architecture is like flying blind. Before launching a major change effort, people need to know what will not change (core ideology = core values and purpose) as well as what will change (vision and mission). The blueprint must be balanced or people will become confused and frustrated and spend precious energy dealing with the noise surrounding the change effort. The blueprint must also be believable (even with some imagination) in order to avoid the massive amounts of resistance and cynicism that will naturally surround change.

4. Keep the strategic architecture a secret and avoid communicating successes

If you have a blueprint, then it must be shared broadly and consistently throughout the organization. If the many actions and behaviors associated with change do not make sense to the people within the organization, they will invent their own interpretation of the events to make meaning from it all.

5. Ignore or pretend that resistance does not exist

Those who guide change will need to confront and remove the big obstacles in order to maintain the credibility of the change effort. People may not agree with the reasons for change, the direction or nature of the solution, or the costs of the implications for implementation. Emotions and fear may breed a lack of trust in those leading the initiative. Part of the change initiative must include methods and approaches of dealing with resistance (in ways that are consonant with the core values).

6. Believe that short-term wins are not important

The momentum for the change effort can be sustained by explicitly planning for and creating short-term wins. These actions provide evidence that the longer-term journey is worth the effort. It also helps to break the larger journey down to some smaller, and more attainable, milestones.

7. Declare victory at the earliest signs of progress

It is too easy to interpret early signs of progress as completion. Those guiding change must remain steadfast and accept the long-term nature of complex and creative change. While it is important to celebrate successes, don't confuse arriving at a milestone with obtaining the destination.

8. Focus mainly on the existing leaders of today

In order to sustain the long-term implementation of systemic change, the next generation of leaders within the organization must be prepared for their role.

9. Use only one method or approach

Creative change will require the skillful learning and use of a variety of methods.

10. Behave as though all people are highly resilient and always ready for more change

People have different levels of readiness for change and the anxiety it creates. It takes energy to cope with doing things better and differently. It takes a skillful eye to determine how heavy a load people are already carrying.

References

1. Pettigrew, A. (1999) Organizing to improve company performance: a report from the Warwick Business School. *Hottopics*, 1: 1–5.

2. Christensen, C. & Raynor, M. (2003) *The Innovator's Solution: Creating and Sustaining Successful Growth*. Boston, MA: Harvard Business School Press.

3. Tushman, M.L. (2002) *Winning Through Innovation*. Boston, MA: Harvard Business School Press. Tushman, M.L. & O'Reilly, C.A. (1997) *Winning Through Innovation: A Practical Guide to Leading Organizational Change and Renewal*. Boston, MA: Harvard Business School Press.

4. Collins, J. (2001) *Good to Great: Why Some Companies Make the Leap . . . and Others Don't*. New York: Harper Business.

5. Nohria, N. (1996) From the M-form to the N-form: taking stock of changes in the large industrial corporation. *Harvard Business School Working Paper 96-054*.

6. CSC Index (1994) *The State of Re-Engineering*. London: CSC Index.

7. Trott, P. & Hoecht, A. (2004) Enterprise Resource Planning (ERP) and its impact on the innovative capability of the firm, *International Journal of Innovation Management*, 8(4): 380–398.

8. Argyris, C. (1993) *Knowledge for Action: A Guide to Overcoming Barriers to Organizational Change*. San Francisco: Jossey-Bass. Kotter, J.P. (1995) Leading change: why transformation efforts fail. *Harvard Business Review*, 73: 59–67.

9. Buckland, W., Hatche, A. & Bikinshaw, J. (2003) *Inventuring*. McGraw-Hill. Chesborough, H. (2003) *Open Innovation: The New Imperative for Creating and Profiting from Technology*. Boston: Harvard Business School Press.

10. Kotter, J.P. (1999) *John P. Kotter on What Leaders Really Do*. Boston, MA: Harvard Business School Press.

11. Nadler, D.A. (1998) *Champions of Change: How CEOs and Their Companies are Mastering the Skills of Radical Change*. San Francisco: Jossey-Bass. Taffinder, P. (1998) *Big Change: A Route-Map for Corporate Transformation*. New York: John Wiley & Sons, Inc. Goyder, M., Hartley, N. & Goldenberg, P. (1995) *Tomorrow's Company: The Role of Business in a Changing World*. London: The Royal Society for the Encouragement of the Arts, Manufacturing and Commerce.

12. Conner, D.R. (1995) *Managing at the Speed of Change: How Resilient Managers Succeed and Prosper Where Others Fail*. New York: Villard Books. Conner, D.R. (1998) *Leading at the Edge of Chaos: How to Create the Nimble Organization*. New York: John Wiley & Sons, Inc.

13. Stacey, R.D. (1996) *Complexity and Creativity in Organizations*. San Francisco: Berrett-Koehler Publishers.

14. Robinson, A.G. & Stern, S. (1997) *Corporate Creativity*. San Francisco: Berrett-Koehler Publishers.

15. Foster, R. & Kaplan, S. (2001) *Creative Destruction*. Boston, MA: Harvard University Press.

16. Tidd, J. & Hull, F. (2003) *Service Innovation: Organizational Responses to Technological Opportunities and Market Imperatives*. London: Imperial College Press.

17. Henkoff, R. (1994) Getting beyond downsizing. *Fortune*, 129: 30–34.

18. *Ibid.*

19. Bennett, A. (1991) Management: downsizing does not necessarily bring an upswing in corporate profitability. *Wall Street Journal*, 6 June, p. B–1.

20. *Ibid.*

21. Applebaum, S.H., Simpson, R. & Shapiro, B.T. (1987) The tough test of downsizing. *Organizational Dynamics*, 16: 68–79.

22. Baumohl, B. (1993) When downsizing becomes dumbsizing. *Time*, 15 March, p. 55.

23. Pearlstein, S. (1994) Corporate cutbacks yet to pay off. *Washington Post*, 4 January, p. B–6.

24. Kets de Vries, M.V.R. & Balazs, K. (1997) The downside of downsizing. *Human Relations*, 50: 11–51.

25. *Ibid.*

26. Noer, D.M. (1997) *Breaking Free: A Prescription for Personal and Organizational Change*. San Francisco: Jossey-Bass.

27. Davis, T. (2000) *Innovation Survey and Growth: A Global Perspective*. London: PricewaterhouseCoopers.

28. Van de Ven, A.H., Angle, H.L. & Poole, M.S. (2000) *Research on the Management of Innovation*. Oxford: Oxford University Press.

29. Isaksen, S.G., Dorval, K.B. & Treffinger, D.J. (2000) *Creative Approaches to Problem Solving* (revd edn). Dubuque, IA: Kendall/Hunt Publishing. Isaksen, S.G., Dorval, K.B. & Treffinger, D.J. (1994) *Creative Approaches to Problem Solving*. Dubuque, IA: Kendall/Hunt Publishing. Isaksen, S.G., Puccio, G.J. & Treffinger, D.J. (1993) An ecological approach to creativity research: profiling for creative problem solving. *Journal of Creative Behavior*, 23(3): 149–170.

30. Puccio, G.J., Talbot, R.J. & Joniak, A.J. (1993) Person-environment fit: using commensurate scales to predict student stress. *British Journal of Educational Psychology*, 63: 457–468.

31. Conner, D.R. (1998) *Leading at the Edge of Chaos: How to Create the Nimble Organization*. New York: John Wiley & Sons, Inc.

32. Albizu, E., Olazaran, M. & Simon, K. (2004) BPR and change management, *International Journal of Innovation Management*, 8(4): 355–380.

33. Loos, K. (1993) *Managing Organizational Change: How Leading Organizations are Meeting the Challenge*. Cambridge, MA: Arthur D. Little, Inc.

34. Davis, T. (2000) *Innovation*. London: PricewaterhouseCoopers.

35. Kouzes, J.M. & Posner, B.Z. (1993) *Credibility: How Leaders Gain and Lose it, Why People Demand it*, p. 47. San Francisco: Jossey-Bass.

36. Rousseau, D.M., Sitkin, S.B., Burt, R.B. & Camerer, C. (1998) Not so different after all: a cross-discipline view of trust. *Academy of Management Review*, 23: 393–404. Kramer, R.M. & Tyler, T.R. (eds) (1996) *Trust in Organizations: Frontiers of Theory and Research*. Thousand Oaks, CA: SAGE. Mishra, A.K. (1996) Organizational responses to crises: the

centrality of trust. In *Trust in Organizations: Frontiers of Theory and Research* (eds R.M. Kramer & T.R. Tyler) pp. 261–287. Thousand Oaks, CA: Sage. Reynolds, L. (1997) *The Trust Effect: Creating High Trust High Performance Organization*. London: Nicholas Brealey Publishing.

37. Kouzes, J.M. & Posner, B.Z. (1993) *Credibility: How Leaders Gain and Lose it, Why People Demand it*, p. 47. San Francisco: Jossey-Bass.

38. Tidd, J., Bessant, J. & Pavitt, K. (2005) *Managing Innovation: Integrating Technological, Market and Organizational Change* (3rd edn). Chichester: John Wiley & Sons, Ltd.

39. Utterback, J. & Acee, H.J. (2005) Disruptive technologies: an expanded view, *International Journal of Innovation Management*, 9(1): 1–18.

40. Christenson, C. (1997) *The Innovator's Dilemma*. Boston, MA: Harvard Business School Press.

41. Tidd, J. & Bodley, K. (2002) The affect of project novelty on the new product development process. *R&D Management*, 32(2): 127–138.

42. Benders, J. & Vermeulen, P. (2002) Too many tools? On problem-solving in new product development projects. *International Journal of Innovation Management*, 6(2): 163–186.

43. Darnton, G. & Darnton, M. (1997) *Business Process Analysis*. International Thomson Press.

44. Isaksen, S.G., Dorval, K.B. & Treffinger, D.J. (2000) *Creative Approaches to Problem Solving* (revd edn). Dubuque. IA: Kendall/Hunt Publishing.

Part 1

THE OUTCOMES OF TRANSFORMATION

Chapter 2

BUILDING THE JANUSIAN ORGANIZATION

again and again we see the dichotomy of the creative process . . . whereas some of these conditions require suspension of control, and openness to the almost automatic effusions of the primary sources, others require the greatest discipline, acuteness, control, checking, and discussion. And all of them must occur in a general atmosphere of devotion, dedication and commitment[1]

Those who lead within organizations are facing unprecedented challenges and opportunities. The very survival of these organizations depends on the ability of those who lead and follow to develop creative responses to the many different tensions and opportunities facing the individuals, teams and the organization itself.

This book is about meeting the innovation challenge. We have argued that taking a systemic approach to change and transformation is more productive than focusing on only one element of the system. The purpose of this chapter is to lay out the need for this kind of leadership and to point out how it relates to facilitation, mentoring and servant leadership. We will explain the title of this chapter first, point out the main challenges facing the Janusian organization and then highlight how each of the chapters of this book help to meet the challenges.

Who is Janus?

Janus is one of the most well-known Roman gods and he presides over beginnings.[2] We preserve this today by having our first month named for him (January). He was the god of coming in and going out as well as beginnings and endings. It is believed that he was connected to water, as there are five shrines to Janus built in Rome and they are all placed near crossings over the river or other waterways.

Janus had an important role to play during times of war. Based on a legend, when the Forum was under siege by the Sabines, Janus caused jets of boiling water to gush forth and keep them at bay.[3] The doors of the shrine to Janus near the Argiletum entrance to the Forum were left open in times of war and left closed in times of peace. Augustus, for example, closed these doors with great ceremony to mark the end of the civil wars that brought him to power.

Janus is depicted on many Roman coins with two faces and had four faces on coins produced during the second century BC. Some depictions have shown Janus with six faces. The reason the most common depiction of Janus had two faces was because he was the god of beginnings and endings so he could look in both opposing directions at the same time.

What is Janusian thinking?

The reason Janus was chosen as the inspiration behind Janusian thinking is that he had to look in two opposing directions at the same time. As the god of doorways he looked outside and inside at the same time. Rothenberg[4] used this attribute to coin the phrase 'Janusian thinking'. He described the Janusian process as:

> actively conceiving multiple opposites or antitheses simultaneously . . . During the course of the creative process, opposite or antithetical ideas, concepts, or propositions are consciously conceptualized as simultaneously coexisting. Although seemingly illogical and self-contradictory, these formulations are constructed in clearly logical and rational states of mind to produce creative effects. They occur as early conceptions in the development of scientific theories and artworks and at critical junctures at middle and later stages of the creative process, these simultaneous antitheses or simultaneous opposites usually undergo transformation and modification and are seldom directly discernable in final creative products.[5]

Rothenberg[6] provided evidence that this kind of process exists in both the arts and sciences, and in most creative endeavors. He has collected historical and anecdotal evidence, as well as a large amount of data from his psychiatric practice, to support his theory.[7]

Active and simultaneous consideration of opposites appears to be a key aspect of creating new and useful responses across a variety of fields. We find support for this idea from a number of key creativity researchers and writers, particularly those who are interested in the creative process. At the core, Janusian thinking is an attempt to describe an aspect of the creative process, a process that is in motion and is dynamic.

Gordon[8] reported that his inquiry into the creative process yielded the synectics approach. He described this approach as based on the Greek meaning for synectics, the joining together of different and apparently irrelevant elements. Gordon's synectics method was based on similar evidence to Rothenberg's, as well as a few studies conducted with artists and professionals. The research and method supports the general idea of Janusian thinking.

Koestler studied the act of creation from the point of view of literature, science and the arts. He described the essence of the creative process as:

> the perceiving of a situation or idea . . . in two self-consistent but habitually incompatible frames of reference . . . I have coined the term bisociation in order to make a distinction between the routine skills of thinking on a single plane, as it were, and the creative act, which . . . always operates on more than one plane.[9]

Koestler used the term 'bisociation' in a way similar to Gordon's use of synectics and Rothenberg's use of Janusian thinking.

Arieti[10] suggested that the creative individual blends the worlds of mind and matter; and the rational and irrational. He explained the creative process as one in which the individual integrates archaic, obsolete or seemingly irrelevant notions with normal logical processes in what seems to be a magical synthesis. The result is the emergence of the new, unexpected, and desirable notion.

The ability to understand and develop meaningful new connections from resolving structural opposition seems to be at the core of the creative process. Many of the current approaches to creative problem-solving have some features that express this creative tension. We have called this the dynamic balance between generating many, varied and unusual alternatives and focusing on these to screen, select and support those options.[11]

What is a Janusian organization?

If we take the key ingredient of Janusian thinking to be the simultaneous consideration and resolution of opposing views or perspectives, it shouldn't be too hard to

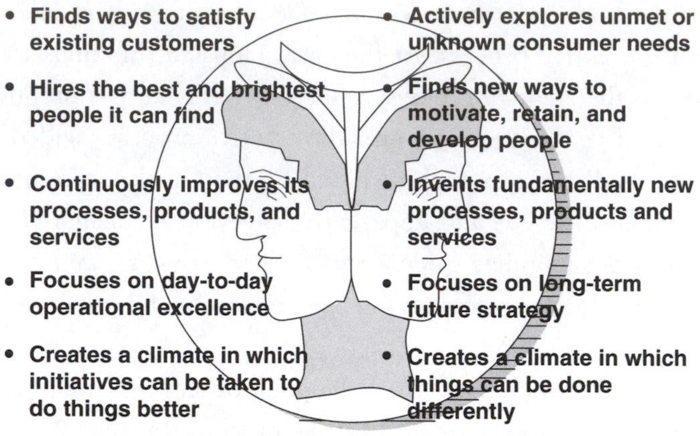

- Finds ways to satisfy existing customers
- Hires the best and brightest people it can find
- Continuously improves its processes, products, and services
- Focuses on day-to-day operational excellence
- Creates a climate in which initiatives can be taken to do things better

- Actively explores unmet or unknown consumer needs
- Finds new ways to motivate, retain, and develop people
- Invents fundamentally new processes, products and services
- Focuses on long-term future strategy
- Creates a climate in which things can be done differently

Figure 2.1 The Janusian organization

consider the organizational implications of this tension. Organizations must be able to stimulate and manage a full spectrum of change initiatives.[12] We have developed Figure 2.1 to illustrate a few of the key features of the Janusian organization.

Crisis and renewal

Hurst[13] outlined the need for organizations to be able to manage the full cycle of crisis and renewal. He described the rhythms of renewal as a cycle that includes birth, growth, maturation and death, and illustrates this cycle occurring in numerous organizations including 3M and Nike. One of the key ingredients of his cycle is the concept of creative destruction. For example, our normal reaction to forest fires is to think of them as destructive. They are necessary, however, for the white pole pines to reproduce and renew the forest. In other words, creative destruction precedes renewal. This makes sense to any one who gardens, as pruning stimulates growth, as long as you don't destroy the source of life altogether.

Focusing on what will and will not change

Collins and Porras[14] studied 18 visionary organizations and found that they were not forced into the 'either-or' mindset. They were guided more frequently by the 'yes-and' view that allowed them to pursue distinctly different options at the same time. Collins and Porras found that these visionary organizations were able to maintain unusually long periods of sustained growth and staying power by working around a clear and consistent core ideology that would rarely change, and a vision of itself that changed frequently. In fact, it was this dualism of continuity and change that seemed to make the truly exceptional companies different from the others. The 18 organizations studied by Collins and Porras outperformed others in the stock market by a factor of 16 to 1.

Incremental and discontinuous change

Tushman and O'Reilly described the tyranny of success that plagues many organizations. They indicated that it is often the strategy, structure and systems that made the organization successful and that also dampen its ability to innovate and change. They stated that:

> The managerial challenge is clear but daunting. Long-term organizational success requires streams of innovation – systematically different kinds of innovation over time. These innovation streams run counter to forces for organizational inertia. Given these contrasting forces for change and stability, managers need to create ambidextrous organizations – organizations that celebrate stability and incremental change as well as experimentation and discontinuous change simultaneously.[15]

These ambidextrous organizations manage these streams of innovation by encouraging different kinds of systems and structures for the diversity of change within the streams. The organizations must learn to play two games at once. They must be able to evolve productively through periods of incremental adaptation and ride the rough waves of discontinuity.

Increasing support for 'yes-and' approaches

More and more writers, researchers and thinkers are pointing out that it takes a Janusian-like organization in order to succeed. Sjostrand[16] actually refers to the Janus factor as he supported the need for managers to be able to respond to both the rational and irrational. Gryskiewicz[17] points out the need for organizations to be able to respond to, and even embrace, positive turbulence. De Geus[18] pointed out that the living company is one that resolves the dilemma between tolerance and control by aggressively pursuing both goals. While freedom and tolerance are necessary for learning, control is needed to maintain cohesion. Over and over again, we are discovering the importance of a Janusian stance in order to ensure long-term survival of organizations.

Why do Janusian organizations need to lead for change and transformation?

The changing landscape upon which organizations must travel necessitates the move to a more systemic approach and the need to embrace a Janusian stance. Those who pilot organizations can no longer behave as if they are in stable and calm waters. In order to hold and integrate the broader spectrum of challenges and the inherent tension created by this dynamic, those who manage organizations will need to master the dynamics of change. Rather than relying on a narrow set of change strategies, leaders at all levels of the organization will need a broad set of tools and methods from which to choose.

Taking a systems approach means moving beyond the singular focus on, and search for, the great leader. Of course, we can learn important lessons from studying the lives of leadership icons. A systems view of leadership requires that we see leaders as intimately interconnected to the world. It requires that we seek to understand the patterns and interrelationships that influence leaders' behavior and the reactions and behaviors of those that are led. As we learn more about the entire context we can develop those skills and insights into specific strategies for helping new and existing leaders face the challenges of creative change.

The need to lead creative change is supported by many who have critiqued organizational change initiatives.[19] These critiques have sought to examine and differentiate a variety of change strategies. These initiatives range from those strategies that focus on knowledge and management, to those that aim to improve motivation or increase skills. What the critiques tell us is:

- *Knowledge is not enough*. Knowing *about* is different from knowing *how*. Many change strategies assume that people are rational and that all they need to do, in order to change, is to be informed. Information exchange can be a useful strategy but must be coupled with some other approach to ensure implementation and acceptance. Leading creative change is about what and how; content and process. It places creative leadership in the context of change in a way that integrates knowing and applying.

- *Focus on collaboration.* Many change strategies imply some sort of consultant-like interaction where the solution or answer is given to the target population. Leading creative change is more about a close and inclusive working relationship described as co-creation. The quality of leadership greatly affects the ability of a group, division or organization to make productive use of the diverse array of talents.
- *Look at the larger picture.* There is no guarantee that a wise person who attains power will act wisely. We need to consider the forces and roles surrounding the individual. In the best case, we would be able to understand these factors in a way that made them amenable to intervention. Leading creative change approaches this need from the point of view of a set of interacting elements that form a complex whole, the organization functioning in its context. It is this systems view that represents a departure from many previous resources for those who guide change.

Leading creative change is not just an individual affair. It deliberately focuses on all the relevant players, the situation or context, as well as the method and desired outcomes. Many approaches to managing change focus mainly on the outcome, under the belief that given the high quality of the result, change will happen automatically to allow for its acceptance. Keeping an eye on the larger picture increases the likelihood of reducing errors in judgment.

Link insight with action

Strategies for change are often focused on the use of power held by a few to convince or coerce. Other strategies suggest the complete reverse, that everyone is a leader of change. These strategies often include resources that are full of insights but leave something to be desired when it comes to guiding action and implementation. In other words, many resources take a stand and provide a point of view, but leave figuring out the practical implications to the reader. Leading creative change outlines the full spectrum of change strategies and then provides models and frameworks for action.

Rather than making choices within dichotomies, or two mutually exclusive or contradictory elements, we need to think more about spectra, continua and systems. One key aspect of tension is change itself.

Spectrum of change

The future of civilization as we know it depends on our ability to respond effectively to change. Individuals, groups and organizations as well as communities, governments and international organizations are all learning how to deal with increasing demands to change, cope with complexity and handle competition. Although leaders know this, change is often conceived as turmoil and turbulence.

Change can be defined as both a verb (to make or become different) or as a noun (the process or result of making or becoming different). As a verb it means to cause to pass from one state to another; to vary in form or essence, or to alter or make different. As a noun it means any variation or alteration in form, state, quality or essence; or a passing from one state to another. Other words people often use that share similar meaning include: alteration, improvement, modification, variation, substitution, conversions, transformation or metamorphosis.

Leading creative change has to do with transforming yourself, groups with which you work, and organizations within society. This is an exceptional challenge and can only be done by those who have a deep commitment. Even with high levels of commitment, people will be limited by how much transition and change they can productively assimilate. Creative change includes change that is both novel and useful. As a result, there is real tension involved in leading creative change.

Change has been a hot topic from very early in human history. One of the earliest debates about change took place between Heraclites and Parmenides during the fifth century BC.[20] The reigning philosopher of the time, Parmenides, believed that change was impossible, that all things are one and never change. This was very likely a comforting position because it implied that life was stable and certainly predictable. Heraclites was on the other side of the debate. Heraclites believed that you could never walk into the same river twice, as they are ever flowing, everything always changes. In retrospect, Heraclites was right. Change is a constant. It's not like we have a choice about change today. It's all around us.

One of the challenges about change is that people often mean different things when they use this word. Some use change to describe a minor alteration or modification of something, a 'tweak', adjustment or fine tuning of something. Others use the word

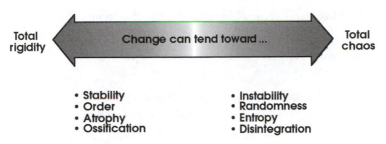

Figure 2.2   A spectrum of change
Source: Adapted from Stacey, R. (1993) Strategy as order emerging from chaos. *Long Range Planning*, *26*: 10–17; and Kirton, M.J. (1995, April) KAI Certification Conference, Buffalo, NY.

'change' to describe the making of a radical difference or transformation. We believe that it is more helpful to see change and transformation occurring on a spectrum.

Change and transformation occur on a continuous spectrum ranging from total and continuous change on the one end, and moving toward no change on the other. This spectrum provides the theoretical spread of possible change. Much like the theoretical spread of temperature, human beings can tolerate and function only within a rather narrow range. The spectrum of change entails the full range of change from evolution to revolution (Figure 2.2).

In the spirit of Janusian thinking, it is more helpful to consider change including a full range of outcomes, processes, people and environments. Rather than taking an either-or approach to change – either we change or we don't change – we propose taking a Janusian approach. We need to include the full spectrum of outcomes, from minor improvements to radical departures, into consideration when thinking about change and transformation. Organizations we lead and manage need to have the widest tolerable range of process strategies at their disposal. Since people will differ regarding their preferences for various kinds of change, we need to include the broadest possible range of people along the full spectrum of change preferences. We also need to be able to establish working environments that tolerate and embrace different outcomes, people and processes.

Kirton stated that it was not so much a matter of people resisting change; it was that they resist particular kinds of change. They may also resist change if people who prefer different kinds of change are promoting it. Those who prefer continuous change prefer very little structure in their lives. The change they prefer tends toward chaos, instability, randomness, disintegration and entropy. Others tend to prefer more structure in their lives and generally prefer change that tends toward order, stability, structure, ossification and atrophy. Thus, Kirton's[21] notion of styles of creativity, problem-solving and decision-making seems to apply to the area of change as well.

The spectrum of change relates to the idea that people have differing capacities for absorbing change. Thus, people can have different capacities for assimilation as well as different preferences for the kinds of change they wish to absorb. This insight has some powerful implications for leaders who are trying to manage change. Different approaches and strategies may be needed to work with people who have these diverse preferences.

The change spectrum also applies to different kinds of outcomes and desired results. Beyond personal preferences, some situations demand different kinds of change.[22] Some changes are incremental, adaptive or developmental. These changes end up being close to the current objective, usually have clearly defined measures of success and often relate to a strategy of optimization (minor improvement, spin, tweaking). Other contingencies associated with incremental change include: limited resources; a relatively stable environment; a need for craftsmanship and attention to detail; and a desire for short-term benefits.

Other situations call for a more discontinuous, radical or exploratory kind of change. These changes come from a vision of a great future opportunity, a fundamental technological breakthrough, or some other major paradigm shift. The source for this kind of change may also come from the fact that incremental change simply isn't working – you seem to be 'hitting the wall'. Exploratory or radical changes are associated with the requirements for an entirely new design, needing to change the game or facing an urgent crisis. This kind of change is appropriate when seeking long-term benefits and it is possible to commit flexible resources.

Given this entire spectrum of change, it is not surprising that there would be a variety of approaches to change management. Once again, when we examine the variety of change-management approaches, it becomes clear that we need to take a Janusian stance.

Spectrum of change-management strategies

Michael Beer and Nitin Nohria[23] organized a conference at Harvard to bring together the best and most experienced scholars and practitioners in organizational change to develop a common framework. Their hope was that this framework would

---

Exhibit 2.1

The US financial services group Capital One saw major growth over the period 1999–2002, equivalent to 430%, and built a large customer base of around 44 million people. Its growth rate (30% in turnover 2000–2001) makes it one of the most admired and innovative companies in its sector. But,

> innovation at Capital One cannot be traced to a single department or set of activities. It's not a unique R&D function, there is no internal think-tank. Innovation is not localized but systemic. It's the lifeblood of this organization and drives its remarkable growth . . . It comes through people who are passionate enough to pursue an idea they believe in, even if doing so means extending well beyond their primary responsibilities.

Chevron Texaco is another example of a high-growth company that incorporates – in this case in its formal mission statement – a commitment to high involvement innovation. It views its 53 000 employees worldwide as 'fertile and largely untapped resources for new business ideas'. Texaco believed that nearly everyone in the company had ideas about different products the company could offer or ways it could run its business. It felt it had thousands of oil and gas experts inside its walls and wanted them to focus on creating and sharing innovative ideas.

---

place diverse theories and practices in perspective and help practitioners confront choices among change strategies and types of consultants.

They invited a speaker to take a point of view regarding a particular change strategy and then another speaker to present the opposing point of view. Then a third paper examined the pros and cons of each. The net result was that there was a good case to be made for both points of view. For example, one of the issues was that change needed to be directed and led from the very top of the organization. The opposing view was that change often required broad participation and involvement throughout the organization. The bottom line was that there is a certain amount of truth in both points of view. What seemed to matter are the specific circumstances and the kind of change being sought.

Those who lead and manage organizations must be able to deploy a range of change-management strategies that are designed to fit the specific circumstances of the actual change, the organization itself, and the larger context of the market. This means that

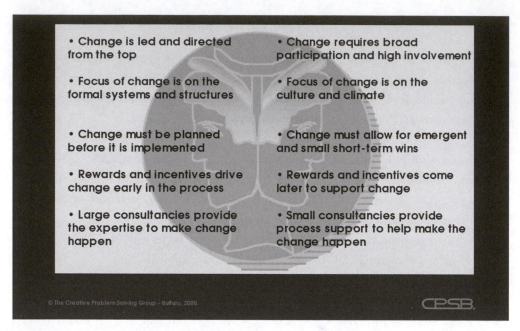

Figure 2.3   Approaches to change
Source: Adapted from Beer, M. and Nohria, N. (eds) (2000) *Breaking the Code of Change*. Boston: Harvard Business School Press.

organizations must have the capacity to lead change from top-down and bottom-up perspectives and have both a planned change strategy and one that allows for emergent influences. This is clearly another example of the need to build a Janusian organization.

Conclusion

Bennis[24] described the post-bureaucratic organization's demand for a new type of leader. This new type of leader is one who can inspire and empower; who is a maestro, not a master; a coach, not a commander. He supports this claim by pointing out that tomorrow's organizations will be networks, clusters, cross-functional teams, temporary systems and everything but pyramids. These new leaders will need to establish a climate supportive of using both problem-solving and problem-finding in order to resolve the creative tension the organization faces. Bennis stated that:

In the post-bureaucratic world, the laurel will go to the leader who encourages healthy dissent and values those followers courageous enough to say no. It will go to the leader who exults in cultural differences and knows that diversity is the best hope for long-term survival. These new leaders will not have the loudest voice, but the most attentive ear. Instead of pyramids, these post-bureaucratic organizations will be structures built of energy and ideas, led by people who find their joy in the task at hand, not in leaving monuments behind.[25]

Leading creative change is an approach to understanding leadership that integrates what we know from studying leadership and provides a fresh new perspective on the entire spectrum of strategies that leaders need to be able to employ.

Leading creative change is designed to help those who face the Janusian challenge. For, as Kets de Vries and Florent-Treacy have found, the most successful leaders have played two roles at the same time. The successful leaders envision, empower and energize their constituents as they perform their charismatic role. Leaders must also play an architectural role involving the improvement of organizational design and stimulating or rewarding appropriate follower behavior. In short, leaders must have a variety of skills and abilities in order to effectively handle the Janusian tension.

Kets de Vries and Florent-Treacy indicated that:

> Truly great leaders recognize that leadership is an art whose aim is to create an environment that stimulates and exhilarates, fostering excitement that leads employees to become completely absorbed in their tasks and achieve peak performance.[26]

We will dig deeper into the kind of leadership and management that is required to build this Janusian organization in Chapter 5 on leading and managing for transformation.

References

1. Arieti, S. (1976) *Creativity: The Magic Synthesis*. New York: Basic Books, p. 379.
2. Morford, M.P.O. & Lenardon, R.J. (1995) *Classical Mythology* (5th edn). White Plains, NY: Longman.

3. Rothenberg, A. (1971) The process of Janusian thinking in creativity. *Archives of General Psychiatry*, 24: 195–205.

4. Rothenberg, A. (1999) Janusian process. In *Encyclopedia of Creativity – Volume 2* (eds M. Runco & S.R. Pritzker), pp. 103–108. New York: Academic Press.

5. Rothenberg, A. (1979) *The Emerging Goddess: The Creative Process in Art, Science and Other Fields*. Chicago: University of Chicago Press.

6. Rothenberg, A. (1996) The Janusian process in scientific creativity. *Creativity Research Journal*, 9: 207–231.

7. Rothenberg, A. (1998) *The Creative Process in Psychotherapy*. New York: Norton.

8. Gordon, W.J.J. (1961) *Synectics: The Development of Creative Capacity*. New York: Harper & Row.

9. Koestler, A. (1964) *The Act of Creation*, pp. 35–36. New York: Macmillan.

10. Arieti, S. (1976) *Creativity: The Magic Synthesis*. New York: Basic Books, p. 379.

11. Isaksen, S.G., Dorval, K.B. & Treffinger, D.J. (1997) *Toolbox for Creative Problem Solving: Basic Tools and Resources*. Buffalo, NY: Creative Problem Solving Group – Buffalo.

12. Kirton, M.J. (1961) *Management Initiative*. London: The Acton Society Trust – Unwin Brothers.

13. Hurst, D.K. (1995) *Crisis and Renewal: Meeting the Challenge of Organizational Change*. Boston: Harvard Business School Press.

14. Collins, J.C. & Porras, J.I. (1997) *Built to Last: Successful Habits of Visionary Companies*. New York: HarperBusiness.

15. Tushman, M.L. & O'Reilly, C.A. (1997) *Winning Through Innovation: A Practical Guide To Leading Organizational Change and Renewal*, p. 14. Boston: Harvard Business School Press.

16. Sjostrand, S.E. (1997) *The Two Faces of Management: The Janus Factor*. London: Thompson Business.

17. Gryskiewicz, S.S. (1999) *Positive Turbulence: Developing Climates for Creativity, Innovation, and Renewal*. San Francisco: Jossey-Bass.

18. De Geus, A. (1997) *The Living Company: Habits for Survival in a Turbulent Business Environment*. Boston: Harvard Business School Press.

19. Chin, R. & Benne, K.D. (1976) General strategies for effecting changes in human systems. In *The Planning of Change*, 3rd edn (eds W.G. Bennis, K.D. Benne, R. Chin & K.E. Corey), pp. 22–45. New York: Holt, Rinehart & Winston.

20. De Brabandere, L. (2005) *The Forgotten Half of Change: Achieving Greater Creativity Through Changes in Perception*. Chicago: Dearborn.

21. Kirton, M.J. (1994) *Adaptors and Innovators: Styles of Creativity and Problem Solving*. London: Routledge.

22. Tushman, M.L. & O'Reilly, C.A. (1997) *Winning Through Innovation: A Practical Guide To Leading Organizational Change and Renewal*, p. 14. Boston: Harvard Business School Press.

23. Beer, M. & Nohria, N. (eds) (2000) *Breaking the Code of Change.* Boston: Harvard Business School Press.

24. Bennis, W. (1993) *Beyond Bureaucracy: Essays on the Development and Evolution of Human Organizations.* San Francisco: Jossey-Bass.

25. *Ibid.*

26. Kets de Vries, M.F.R. & Florent-Treacy, E. (1999) *The New Global Leaders: Richard Branson, Percy Barnevik and David Simon*, p. xxv. San Francisco: Jossey-Bass.

Chapter 3

CREATIVITY AND INNOVATION FOR TRANSFORMATION

constant revolutionizing of production, uninterrupted disturbance of all social conditions, everlasting uncertainty . . . all old-established national industries have been destroyed or are daily being destroyed. They are dislodged by new industries . . . whose products are consumed not only at home, but in every quarter of the globe. In place of old wants satisfied by the production of the country, we find new wants . . . the intellectual creativity of individual nations become common property[1]

The quote demonstrates that uncertainty is not new, and reminds us of a major imperative for promoting creativity and innovation for organization renewal and transformation – the fact that we are doing so against a constantly shifting backdrop, creating conditions that may rewrite the rules of the game.

However, managing change is too often seen as an end in itself, perhaps following merger or acquisition, rebranding, or as a symbolic gesture of new senior management. In other cases there may be some specific end goal, but too often this is simply to reduce costs in some way. In contrast, we shall argue that transformation should aim for the renewal of an organization, to promote growth through greater creativity and innovation.

We believe that 'doing different' is very different to the more common aim of simply 'doing cheaper or better'. Specifically, we shall argue that we need to change both *the way we think* – individual cognition – and *the way we work* – organizational routines – to achieve transformation. In this chapter we identify how creativity and innovation can be combined to help create new processes, new products and new businesses.

Neither creativity nor innovation alone is sufficient. Initiatives on creativity tend to focus mainly on individuals and groups, and their ability to think differently and generate novel ideas, but without a clear commercial outcome. Innovation, on the other hand, has been concerned primarily with the organizational processes and tools necessary to translate ideas into new processes, products, services or businesses. Clearly, organizational transformation requires us to integrate the two fields, and demands changes both in individual behavior and organizational processes. We show how we can create the ability to identify new opportunities, and to exploit these in more effective ways.

New challenges, old responses

When faced with problems of performance, or even a more fundamental crisis, organizations typically react by implementing incremental improvements or changes. However, such responses are often insufficient, or worse, inappropriate. Existing strategies, however successful in the past, are often a poor guide to how best to respond to future demands, what has been called the 'Icarus Paradox'.[2] Recent research on strategic transformation shows that successful organizations achieve 'non-traumatic' transformation through a combination of: proactiveness, experimentation, a willingness to challenge existing business models, top management commitment and multi-level involvement.[3] This is a far cry from traditional approaches to strategic planning and managing change.

The most durable organizations have had to change dramatically to survive changes in their environments. Nokia, founded in the early 19th century, originally had Wellington boots and toilet paper among its product range, but is now one of the largest and most successful in the world in the telecommunications business. Nokia began life as a lumber company, making the equipment and supplies needed to cut down forests in Finland. It moved through into paper and from there into the 'paperless office' world of IT – and from there into mobile telephones. Another mobile phone player – Vodafone Airtouch – grew to its huge size by merging with a firm called Mannesman, which since its birth in the 1870s, has been more commonly associated with the invention and production of steel tubes! Tui is the company that now owns Thomson the travel group in the UK, and is the largest European travel and tourism services company. Its origins, however, lie in the mines of old Prussia where it was established as a public sector state lead mining and smelting company!

In a process as uncertain and complex as this, luck plays a part. There are cases where success comes by accident – and sometimes the benefits arising from one lucky break are enough to cover several subsequent failures. But real success lies in being able to repeat the trick – to manage the process consistently so that success, while never guaranteed, is more likely. And this depends on understanding and managing the process such that little gets left to chance. Research suggests that consistent success is based on the ability to learn and repeat these behaviors; it's similar to the golfer

Gary Player's comment that 'The more I practice, the luckier I get . . .' IBM has transformed itself many times, from its original focus on computer hardware for mainframes, to the creation of the PC industry, provision of software and applications, exploitation of intellectual property, and most recently, consulting services.

Serendipity is an important trigger for innovation, but only if the conditions exist to help it emerge.[4] However, transformation does not happen by accident, but from an environment in which people have the freedom to explore alternative directions and some resources to support this. It is also a problem of 'mindset' – organizations have particular ways of framing the world and their activities within it and may dismiss ideas that do not easily fit that frame. For example, Xerox developed many technologies in its laboratories in Palo Alto that did not easily fit their image of themselves as 'the document company'. These included Ethernet (later successfully commercialized by 3Com and others) and PostScript language (taken forward by Adobe Systems). Chesborough[5] reports that 11 of 35 rejected projects from Xerox's labs were later commercialized with the resulting businesses having a market capitalization of twice that of Xerox itself.

So what do we have to manage? We suggest that there is a core process concerned with renewing what the organization offers, its products and/or services, and the ways in which it generates and delivers these. Whether the organization is concerned with bricks, bread, banking or baby care, the underlying challenge is still the same. This is as much a challenge for nonprofit organizations – in police work, in healthcare, in education the competition is still there, and the role of innovation still one of getting a better edge to dealing with problems of crime, illness or illiteracy. How to use creativity and innovation to survive and grow?

From 'doing better' to 'doing different'

Transformation is essentially about learning and change, and is often disruptive, risky and costly. So, it is not surprising that individuals and organizations develop many different cognitive, behavioral and structural ways of reinforcing the status quo. It requires energy to overcome this inertia, and the determination to change the order of things. We see this in the case of individual inventors who champion their ideas against the odds, in entrepreneurs who build businesses through risk-taking behavior and in organizations that manage to challenge the accepted rules of the game.

Before we go too much further it will be worth defining our terms. What do we mean by 'transformation'? Essentially there are two dimensions: the type of change and degree of change (Figure 3.1). Types of change include:

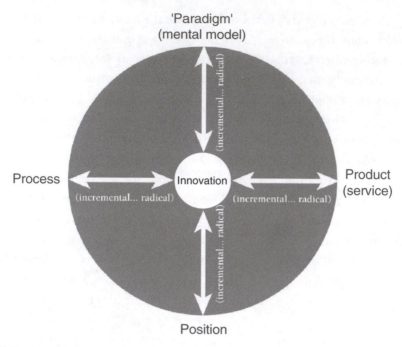

Figure 3.1 Innovation space

Source: Tidd, J., Bessant, J. & Pavitt, K. (2005) *Managing Innovation*. Chichester: John Wiley & Sons, Ltd.

- 'product or service' – changes in the things (products/services) that an organization offers;
- 'process' – changes in the ways in which they are created and delivered;
- 'position' – changes in the context in which the products/services are introduced;
- 'paradigm' – changes in the underlying mental models that frame what the organization does.

Process and product innovation are necessary, but not sufficient for organizational transformation. Incremental process improvements can have a profound cumulative effect on the cost and quality of products and services, and incremental product differentiation can sometimes be highly profitable. However, such innovations, and even more radical process and product innovations, can often occur without significant changes in strategy or organizational structure. In contrast, significant changes in position may demand more fundamental changes in how an organization relates to its customers and suppliers. Radical changes in paradigm demand organizational transformation.

Recent examples of 'paradigm' innovation – changes in mental models – include the shift to low-cost airlines, the provision of online insurance and other financial services, and the repositioning of drinks like coffee and fruit juice as premium 'designer' products. Although in its later days Enron became infamous for financial malpractice, it originally came to prominence as a small gas pipeline contractor that realized the potential in paradigm innovation in the utilities business. In a climate of deregulation, and with global interconnection through grid distribution systems, energy and other utilities like telecommunications bandwidth increasingly became commodities that could be traded much as sugar or cocoa futures.

The second dimension to change is the degree of novelty involved. Clearly, updating the styling on our car is not the same as coming up with a completely new concept car that has an electric engine and is made of new composite materials as opposed to steel and glass. There are degrees of novelty in these, running from minor, incremental improvements right through to radical changes that transform the way we think about and use them. Sometimes these changes are common to a particular sector or activity, but sometimes they are so radical and far-reaching that they change the basis of society – for example the role played by steam power in the Industrial Revolution or the ubiquitous changes resulting from today's communications and computing technologies.

As far as managing the process is concerned, these differences are important. The ways in which we approach incremental, day-to-day change will differ from those used occasionally to handle a radical step change in product, process or business. But we should also remember that in the case of paradigm changes it is the *perceived* degree of novelty that matters; novelty is very much in the eye of the beholder. For example, in a giant, technologically advanced organization like Shell or IBM advanced networked information systems are commonplace, but for a small car dealership this might still represent a major challenge.

Radical changes in organizational paradigms require a new set of approaches to managing and organizing creativity and innovation – for example, how the firm searches for weak signals about potential discontinuities, how it makes strategic choices in the face of high uncertainty, how it resources projects that lie far outside the mainstream of its innovation operations, etc. Established and well-proven routines for 'steady-state' conditions may break down here – for example, an effective 'stage gate' system would find it difficult to deal with high-risk project proposals that lie at the fringes of the firm's envelope of experience. Developing new behaviors more appropriate to these conditions – and then embedding them into routines – requires a different kind of learning.

Table 3.1 indicates some of the ways in which enterprises can obtain strategic advantage through innovation.

Table 3.1 Strategic advantages through innovation

Mechanism	Strategic advantage	Examples
Novelty in product or service offering	Offering something no one else can	Introducing the first . . . Walkman, fountain pen, camera, dishwasher, telephone bank, online retailer, etc. . . . to the world
Novelty in process	Offering it in ways others cannot match – faster, lower cost, more customized, etc.	Pilkington's float glass process, Bessemer's steel process, Internet banking, online bookselling, etc.
Add/extend range of competitive factors	Move basis of competition – e.g. from price of product to price and quality, or price, quality, choice, etc.	Japanese car manufacturing, which systematically moved the competitive agenda from price to quality, to flexibility and choice, to shorter times between launch of new models, and so on – each time not trading these off against each other but offering them all
Timing	First-mover advantage – being first can be worth significant market share in new product fields	Amazon.com, Yahoo – others can follow, but the advantage 'sticks' to the early movers

Reconfiguring the parts of the process	Rethinking the way in which bits of the system work together – e.g. building more effective networks, outsourcing and coordination of a virtual company, etc.	Zara, Benetton in clothing, Dell in computers, Toyota in its supply chain management
Transferring across different application contexts	Recombining established elements for different markets	Polycarbonate wheels transferred from application market like rolling luggage into children's toys – lightweight micro-scooters
Rewriting the rules, new business models	Innovation is all about finding new ways to do things and to obtain strategic advantage – so there will be room for new ways of gaining and retaining advantage	Napster. This firm began by writing software that would enable music fans to swap their favourite pieces via the Internet – the Napster program essentially connected person-to-person (P2P) by providing a fast link. Its potential to change the architecture and mode of operation of the Internet was much greater, and although Napster suffered from legal issues followers developed a huge industry based on downloading and file sharing

Source: Adapted from Tidd, J., Bessant, J. & Pavitt, K. (20005) *Managing Innovation*. Chichester: John Wiley & Sons, Ltd.

When things happen that lie outside the 'normal' frame and result in changes to the 'rules of the game', doing more of the same 'good practice' routines may not be enough, and may even be inappropriate to dealing with the new challenges. Instead, we need a different set of routines – not to use instead of but as well as those we have developed for 'steady-state' conditions. It is likely to be harder to identify and learn these, in part because we don't get so much practice – it is hard to make a routine out of something that only happens occasionally. But we can observe some of the basic elements of the complementary routines that are associated with successful transformation. These tend to be associated with highly flexible creative and innovative behaviors (Table 3.2).

Searching and scanning

One of the greatest challenges facing organizations today is the effective management of people and projects to innovate, in the broadest sense, and that the motivation to innovate, and the kinds of innovation pursued, depends on perceptions of environmental opportunities and risks.[6] We know that the best leaders in such cases have substantial technical expertise, but also need creative cognitive capacity and the ability to support innovative people and projects.

Searching or scanning the external environment consists of identifying, filtering and evaluating potential opportunities from outside the organization, including related and emerging markets and technologies, competitors, regulations and other changes in the environment. For example, a study of corporate entrepreneurship in 169 companies concluded that 'opportunity recognition, which is a precursor to entrepreneurial behavior, [is] often associated with a flash of genius, but in reality is probably more often the end result of a laborious process of environmental scanning'.[7]

A major challenge to identify potential sources of discontinuous innovation is to pick up relevant trigger signals, which may be from unfamiliar sources, or only very weak and emerging. Most of the time, organizations have an effective filter that channels search activities into spaces where they are likely to be fruitful in helping the organization with its agenda based on 'doing what we do but better'. Under these conditions the search routines described above work well and the space within which it is carried out – the 'selection environment' – is clearly defined.

But in the case of discontinuous innovation these signals may lie in unexpected places, often far from the areas covered by the 'normal' radar screen of the organization. Worryingly, the source of disruption often comes from outside that industry. So

Table 3.2 Different management archetypes

Phase in process	Type 1 – Steady state – 'doing better' archetype	Type 2 – Discontinuous – 'doing different' archetype
1. Searching and scanning – individual cognition and interpretive schema – how managers see and make sense of the world	There is an established set of 'rules of the game' by which other competitors also play Particular pathways in terms of search and selection environments and technological trajectories exist and define the 'innovation space' Strategic direction is highly path-dependent	No clear 'rules of the game' – these emerge over time but cannot be predicted in advance Need high tolerance for ambiguity – seeing multiple parallel possible trajectories 'Innovation space' defined by open and fuzzy selection environment Probe and learn experiments needed to build information about emerging patterns and allow dominant design to emerge Highly path-independent
2. Strategic decision-making and problem solving	Makes use of decision-making processes that allocate resources on the basis of risk management linked to the above 'rules of the game'. (Does the proposal fit the business strategic directions? Does it build on existing competence base?). Controlled risks are taken	High levels of risk-taking since no clear trajectories – emphasis on fast and lightweight decisions rather than heavy commitment in initial stages. Multiple parallel bets, fast failure and learning as dominant themes. High tolerance of failure but risk is managed by limited commitment

Table 3.2 Continued

Phase in process	Type 1 – Steady state – 'doing better' archetype	Type 2 – Discontinuous – 'doing different' archetype
	within the bounds of the 'innovation space'. Political coalitions are significant influences maintaining the current trajectory	Influence flows to those prepared to 'stick their neck out' – entrepreneurial behavior
3. Implementing new organizational operating routines	Operates with a set of routines and structures/procedures that embed them, which are linked to these 'risk rules' – for example, stage gate monitoring and review for project management	Operating routines are open-ended, based around managing emergence
		Project implementation is about "fuzzy front end', light-touch strategic review and parallel experimentation. Probe and learn, fast failure and learn rather than managed risk
	Search behavior is along defined trajectories and uses tools and techniques for R&D, market research, etc., which assume a known space to be explored – search and selection environment	Search behavior is about peripheral vision, picking up early warning through weak signals of emerging trends
	Network building to support innovation – e.g. user involvement, supplier partnership, etc. – is on basis of developing close and strong ties	Linkages are with heterogeneous population and emphasis less on established relationships than on weak ties

Source: Adapted from Tidd, J., Bessant, J. & Pavitt, K. (2005) *Managing Innovation*. Chichester: John Wiley & Sons, Ltd.

even those large incumbent firms that take time and resources to carry out research to try and stay abreast of developments in their field may find that they are wrong-footed by the entry of something that has been developed in a different field. The massive changes in insurance and financial services that have characterized the shift to online and telephone provision were largely developed by IT professionals, often working outside the original industry. In extreme cases, we find what is often termed the 'not invented here' (NIH) effect, where a firm finds out about a technology but decides against following it up because it does not fit with their perception of the industry or the likely rate and direction of its technological development. Famous examples of this include Kodak's rejection of the Polaroid process or Western Union's dismissal of Bell's telephone invention. In a famous memo dated 1876 the Board commented: 'This "telephone" has too many shortcomings to be seriously considered as a means of communication. The device is inherently of no value to us.'

Challenging the way that the organization sees things – the corporate mindset – can sometimes be accomplished by bringing in external perspectives. IBM's recovery was due in no small measure to the role played by Lou Gerstner who succeeded at least in part *because* he was a newcomer to the computer industry, and was able to ask the awkward questions that insiders were oblivious to. In similar fashion when Wellington, a Canadian insurance company, embarked on a radical transformation of its business in 1990, the entire management team was brought in from other sectors.

The problem is compounded by the fact that sometimes the very routines that help an organization working under steady state conditions to pick up early on key signals may actively conflict with those designed to help it pick up signals about discontinuities. For example, we have seen that it is good innovation management practice to listen to customers and to respond to their feedback. The problem with this is that customers are often stuck in the same mindset as the firm selling to them: they can see ways of improving on the features of existing products, but they cannot imagine an entirely different solution to their needs. One of the significant themes in Christensen's[8] research on disruptive innovation was that existing 'value networks' – systems of suppliers and customers – effectively conspire with each other so that when a new proposition is put to them involving a different bundle of innovation characteristics they reject it because it doesn't match what they were expecting as a development trajectory.

It's a little like the old joke about the drunk who loses his keys somewhere in the distant darkness but who is searching for them under the nearest lamppost because there is more light there. Familiar search routines are very effective but inevitably will reveal only what the organization expects to find in such familiar territory. The challenge under discontinuous conditions is to develop greater peripheral vision.[9]

Developing peripheral vision involves actively searching in unexpected places – for example, by seeking out fringe users and pre-early adopters in the population who have a higher tolerance for failure. These groups are often prepared to explore new areas and will accept that learning is a function of experimentation – an example might be the early beta test users of new software. Indeed, the good practice precepts around long-term close links with suppliers may be challenged; instead of seeking strategic alliances organizations may need to exploit weaker ties and go for 'strategic dalliances'.[10]

For example, working with lead users is critical to the development and adoption of innovative processes and products. As the title suggests, lead users demand new requirements ahead of the general market of other users, but are also positioned in the market to significantly benefit from the meeting of those requirements.[11] Where potential users have high levels of sophistication – for example, in business-to-business markets such as scientific instruments, capital equipment and IT systems – lead users can help to co-develop innovations, and are therefore often early adopters of such innovations. The initial research by Von Hippel suggests that lead users adopt an average of seven years before typical users, but the precise lead time will depend on a number of factors, including the technology life cycle. A recent study identified a number of characteristics of lead users:[12]

- *Recognize requirements early* – are ahead of the market in identifying and planning for new requirements.
- *Expect high level of benefits* – due to their market position and complementary assets.
- *Develop their own innovations and applications* – have sufficient sophistication to identify and capabilities to contribute to development of the innovation.
- *Perceived to be pioneering and innovative* – by themselves and their peer group.

This has two important implications. First, those seeking to develop innovative products and services should identify potential lead users with such characteristics to contribute to the co-development and early adoption of the innovation. Second, that lead users, as early adopters, can provide insights to forecasting the diffusion of innovations. For example, a study of 55 development projects in telecommunications computer infrastructure found that the importance of customer inputs increased with technological newness, and moreover, the relationship shifted from customer surveys and focus groups to co-development because 'conventional marketing techniques proved to be of limited utility, were often ignored, and in hindsight were sometimes strikingly inaccurate'.[13] Clayton Christensen and Michael Raynor make a similar point in their book *The Innovator's Solution,* and argue that conventional segmentation of markets by product attributes or user types cannot identify potentially disruptive innovations (Exhibit 3.1).

Exhibit 3.1   Identifying potentially disruptive innovations

In their book *The Innovator's Solution: Creating and Sustaining Successful Growth* (Harvard Business School Press, 2003), Clayton Christensen and Michael Raynor argue that segmentation of markets by product attributes or type of customer will fail to identify potentially disruptive innovations. Building on the seminal marketing work of Theodore Levitt, they recommend *circumstance*-based segmentation, which focuses on the 'job to be done' by an innovation, rather than product attributes or type of users. This perspective is likely to result in very different new products and services than traditional ways of segmenting markets. One of the insights this approach provides is the idea of innovations from *non-consumption.* So instead of comparing product attributes with competing products, identify target customers who are trying to get a job done, but due to circumstances – wealth, skill, location, etc. – do not have access to existing solutions. These potential customers are more likely to compare the disruptive innovation with the alternative of having nothing at all, rather than existing offerings. This can lead to the creation of whole new markets, for example, the low-cost airlines in the USA and UK, such as Southwest and Ryanair or Intuit's QuickBooks.

The problem is of course not simply about mechanisms for picking up the signals – under these conditions it is also very much about how the organization reacts to them. In some ways, organizations behave in a fashion similar to individuals who exhibit what psychologists call 'cognitive dissonance' – that is, they interpret signals coming in as reinforcing what they want to believe. Even if the evidence is strongly in other directions they have the capacity to deceive themselves – in part because they have so much investment (financial, physical and emotional) in preserving the existing model. Numerous examples exist where such cognitive blinkers stopped otherwise 'smart' organizations from reacting to external challenges as their core competencies became core rigidities.[14] Polaroid's problems with the entry into digital imaging is a good case in point. In many ways the IBM story is typical – a giant organization that received plenty of early warning about the emerging challenge from decentralized network computing but failed to react fast enough and nearly lost the business as a result. In similar fashion, Microsoft were latecomers to the Internet party and it was only the result of a major focused reorientation – a turn of the tanker at high speed steered by Bill Gates himself – that they were able to capitalize on the opportunities posed.

That said, organizations can put in place more open-ended search routines and these include picking up and amplifying weak signals, using multiple and alternative perspectives, using technology antennae to pick up early warning signals, working with fringe users and deploying future search routines of an open-ended variety (e.g. multiple alternative scenarios).[15] For example, Nokia created an 'insight and foresight' group whose role was to look for changes in the marketplace three to five years out.

There is also scope for using signal generation and processing capacity *within* the organization itself – for example, by exploring more at the periphery of the firm – using subsidiaries, joint ventures or distributors as sources of innovation. An example here is Smirnoff Ice – a highly successful European brand for Diageo that originated in Australia as a local product, Stolichnaya Lemon Russki, before it was picked up by the corporate marketing department as a product with global potential.[16]

The lack of such capability can explain many failures, even among large and well-established organizations. For example:

- The failure to recognize or capitalize on new ideas that conflict with an established knowledge set – the 'not invented here' problem.
- The problem of being too close to existing customers and meeting their needs too well – and not being able to move into new technological fields early enough.
- The problem of adopting new methods or technology – following managerial or technological fashions – without an underlying strategic rationale.

As we have seen, successful organizations in the steady state work closely with customers and suppliers, they make use of sophisticated resource allocation mechanisms to select a strategically relevant portfolio of projects, they use advanced project and risk management approaches in developing new products and processes, and so on. These routines are the products of well-developed adaptive learning processes, which give the firm a strong position in managing innovation under steady state conditions – but they also act as a set of barriers to picking up signals about, and effectively responding to, innovation threats and opportunities associated with discontinuous shifts. Christensen's[17] work on 'the innovator's dilemma' highlights this problem of a virtuous circle that operates in a successful firm and its surrounding value network, and describes in detail the ways in which their markets become disrupted by new entrants.

While some research suggests existing incumbents do badly, we need to be careful here. Not all existing players do badly – many of them are able to build on the new trajectory and deploy/leverage their accumulated knowledge, networks, skills and financial assets to enhance their competence through building on the new opportunity. Equally, while it is true that new entrants – often small entrepreneurial firms – play a strong role in this early phase, we should not forget that we see only the successful players. We need to remember that there is a strong ecological pressure on new entrants, which means that only the fittest or luckiest survive.

It is more helpful to suggest that there is something about the way searching and scanning occur under these conditions that poses problems. Good practice of the 'do better' kind can actively militate against success. How do enterprises pick up signals about changes if they take place in areas where they don't normally do research? How do they understand the needs of a market that doesn't exist, yet will shape the eventual package that becomes the dominant design? This requires much more than simply more or better tools for searching, or increased 'networking'. It demands a fundamental change in the way we perceive and interpret our environment; in short, changes in the way we think.

Changing the way we think involves three basic elements:

1. It is *cognitive*, but is inferred from behavior. It occurs internally, in the mind or cognitive system, and must be inferred indirectly.
2. It is a *process* that involves some manipulation of or set of operations on knowledge in the cognitive system.
3. It is *directed* and results in behavior that 'solves' a problem or is directed toward a solution.[18]

Cognitive science is a contemporary field that tries to answer questions about the nature of knowledge, its development and deployment.[19] It is an interdisciplinary field that includes psychology, philosophy, linguistics, anthropology, artificial intelligence and the neurosciences. Problem-solving has always been a central concept within cognitive science but, more recently, creativity has become an important construct within this field.[20] Given the complexity of these fields, great care is necessary in order to develop useful and valuable applications and implications of them for future research and practice.

Creativity in searching and scanning

The cognitive sciences have provided many insights into many aspects of creativity, the most relevant being an understanding and nurturing of the creative process. This focus includes consideration of mental operations, heuristics and problem-solving strategies (among other items). This does not mean that characteristics of the creative person are irrelevant, as individual differences in mental representations and functioning are acknowledged and studied. In fact, as you can see from Figure 3.2, the best way to understand creativity is through a systemic approach.

In fact, those who study creativity often refer to four overlapping themes.[21] Briefly, research on *person* has led to the identification of many personality characteristics, cognitive abilities, and behavioral or biographical events associated with individual creativity. However, aspects of emotion, context and culture are generally de-emphasized within the mainstream of cognitive science.[22] Work in the area of *process* has delineated various stages and strategies within the creative process. Studies of creative *products* have revealed important variables that distinguish more creative from less creative products as perceived by different people for different purposes. Finally, investigators have identified *environmental* factors that facilitate or inhibit creative performance (press, climate, culture and context). Despite some confusion and contradictions implied by much of the research, there does appear to be some agreement on a few of the basic themes or strands. For example, most researchers have pointed out

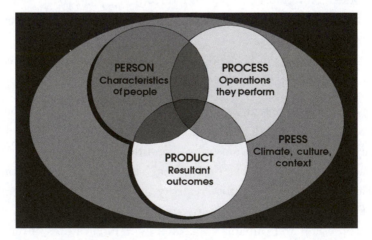

Figure 3.2   Systemic approaches to creativity

the need to differentiate the kind of creativity associated with radical novelty and major significant breakthroughs from the more common notions of personal creativity.[23]

We will use the following definition of creativity:

> Creativity is the making and communicating of meaningful new connections to help us think of many possibilities; to help us think and experience in varied ways and using different points of view; to help us think of new and unusual possibilities; and to guide us in generating and selecting alternatives. These new connections and possibilities must result in something of value for the individual, group, organization, or society.[24]

In relation to search and scanning, one emerging development within the field of creativity that has relevance is the distinction between level and style of creativity.[25] Creativity research has historically focused on defining, assessing and developing the level of creativity ability. This relatively new focus on style focuses more on preferred mode or manner of applying creativity. This distinction between the style of problem-solving and level or capacity is important, and studies confirm that creative cognitive style and capacity are different.[26]

Once we understand our own style preferences, we can approach the task of challenging the way that we think and respond more constructively, rather than viewing the task merely as attaining proficiency with an externally imposed, fixed set of tools or techniques. If we can better assess our own strengths and needs more effectively it becomes easier to understand and accept the principle that there is more than one 'right way'.

Pure cognitive approaches tend to ignore or underplay the social and cultural environment, whereas as the socio-cognitive perspective also takes into account mental processes and actions of individuals, but in addition considers the influence of culture and routines. Studying either individual cognition or social interactions separately is pointless. A socio-cognitive approach focuses on knowledge acquisition, sense making, intelligence, dissemination, implementation and improvisation, connected by organizational culture.[27]

Social cognition is concerned with how people interpret and construct their social environment. This approach emphasizes the role of culture, communication and groups in organizations. The different levels of the organization must be integrated, and through the interaction of individual cognition and social processes a collective cognitive representation is created. Unlike the crude managerial models of cognition that focus on the interaction of cognitive processes, based on computer models of information processing, a social cognition approach focuses on organizing, change and innovation. It focuses not only on the information processing and response to external stimuli, but also the social context in which people do their thinking, judgment and sense making. Key aspects include:

1. Information acquisition and dissemination, including the capture of information from a wide range of sources, requiring attention and perception.
2. Intelligence, the ability and capability to interpret, process and manipulate information.
3. Sense making, giving meaning to information.
4. Unlearning, the process of reducing or eliminating pre-existing routines or behaviors, including discarding information.
5. Implementation and improvisation, autonomous behavior, experimentation, reflection and action. Using information to solve problems, for example, during new product development or process improvement.

Individual cognition and creativity is anything but unidimensional, and can best be described and understood by using an interactionist or ecological approach.[28] We are concerned with the interaction of several variables within a specific context, very much like the ecologist who explores the interactions among living and nonliving components within an ecosystem. One of the goals is to understand better and build more effectively upon the multifaceted nature of creativity, through an interactionist, rather than only reductionist, approach. Our goal is to understand the natural interactions among the sources that lead to creative productivity. Unlike the blind men in the well-known parable, we seek to study the whole elephant, not just its parts. Our approach builds upon the ecological and interactionist views, and we adopt a concept of profiling. Profiling refers to the development of a multidimensional framework to help understand, predict and facilitate creativity. This approach takes into account a constellation of cognitive and personality characteristics; dimensions of the situation, such as climate and culture; elements of the task; process behaviors; and product or outcome qualities. Two important premises clearly emerge and must be addressed.

First, creative productivity does not come about (or fail to come about) only as a result of what is present (or absent) within the individual; it is influenced by time, other people, places, settings, domain-specific knowledge and strategies that people can use individually or in groups. Therefore, no one is, in an absolute sense, always more or less creative. We must ask, creative at what, when, how, where, why and with whom. We shouldn't 'look for' creativity as something fixed and static; it waxes and wanes dependent on a combination of multiple factors. Thus, the goal of profiling is *not* to ask, 'How creative is this person?' It is not just to aggregate several independent data sources in order to obtain an overall index or categorization of the person. Rather, it is to help identify, for a particular task or goal, in a certain setting and under particular circumstances, the person's creative strengths or talents, the best ways to put them to use, and plans to enable us to incorporate those talents into a meaningful and effective instructional or training experience.

Second, creativity is not just something that happens to people; it is actively and deliberately employed, monitored and managed. Creativity can be enhanced and nurtured. Research has demonstrated that specific process tools and strategies can be used to increase creative-thinking skills. Process dimensions may be defined in many ways, but an individual's profile reflects a particular set of process skills. The exact nature of the targets or goals of the profiling effort must always be clearly specified. For example, we would expect that there is an interaction between individuals' style of creativity, the nature of the products they produce and their perception of the psychological climate of their workplace on problem-finding behavior.

Strategic decision-making and problem-solving

Senior management play an important role in shaping an organization's response to changes in the environment, in particular where there are potential discontinuities that demand the ability to reframe existing mental models. Despite an increasing interest in managerial cognition, there has been relatively little effort to link top management mental models with strategic choice in the face of dynamic and potentially discontinuous environments.

Sometimes strong leadership is critical to carrying the company forward into new territory. When Intel was facing strong competition from Far Eastern producers in the memory chip market, Groves and Noyce reported on the need to 'think the unthinkable', i.e. get out of memory production (the business on which Intel had grown up) and to contemplate moving into other product niches. They trace their subsequent success to the point where they found themselves 'entering the void' and creating a new vision for the business.

Broadly speaking, these problems have been approached from three perspectives:

1. the cognitive, which emphasizes the role of individuals, typically leadership;
2. the social, which stresses the contribution of teams and groups; and
3. organizational, which focuses on the structures, climate and processes.

One critical issue arising from these different perspectives is the relative effort needed between cognitive and social interventions, and the interaction between the cognitive and social. Some of the factors having a moderating effect on leadership and creativity are the type of the job and task, the nature of the followers, work group processes, and organizational structure and climate.[29]

The evidence to support a socio-cognitive approach is growing. A study of major pharmaceutical firms' responses to the emerging potential and threat of biotechnology found that senior managerial cognition had a separate and measurable effect on strategic responses.[30] They found that managerial sense making, including the recognition and interpretation of information from the technological and market environments, was a significant explanatory factor in the different strategic responses of the firms studied. A study of major oil companies found that managerial and organizational cognition was one of the reasons why companies come to different conclusions and strategies when presented with essentially the same environment and information.[31] The interpretative frame of managers was based on prior experience and beliefs, and influenced the perceptions and understanding of technological dynamics and expectations of market opportunities. Therefore, there were very different approaches to the application of technological innovation, and the balance between strategies based on improving efficiency versus growth.

Restricted cognition can have a similar effect at group and functional levels. Studies of research and development have found that measures of cognitive ability are associated with project performance. In particular, differences in reflection, reasoning, interpretation and sense making influence the quality of problem formulation, evaluation and solution, and therefore, ultimately the performance of research and development. A common weakness is the oversimplification of problems characterized by complexity or uncertainty, and the simplification of problem framing and evaluation of alternatives.[32] This includes adopting a single, prior hypothesis, selective use of information that supports this, devaluing alternatives, and illusion of control and predictability. Similarly, marketing managers in the same organization have been found to have very similar cognitive maps, and share assumptions concerning the relative importance of different factors contributing to new product success, such as the degree of customer orientation versus competitor orientation, and the implications of relationship between these factors, such as the degree of interfunctional coordination.[33] So the evidence indicates the importance of cognitive processes at the senior management, functional, group and individual levels of an organization. More generally, problems of limited cognition include:[34]

- *reasoning by analogy* – which oversimplifies complex problems;
- *adopting a single, prior hypothesis bias* – even where information and trails suggest that this is wrong;
- *limited problem set* – the repeated use of a narrow problem-solving strategy;
- *single outcome calculation* – which focuses on a simple single goal and a course of action to achieve it, and denying value trade-offs;
- *illusion of control and predictability* – based on an overconfidence in the chosen strategy, a partial understanding of the problem and limited appreciation of the uncertainty of the environment;
- *devaluation of alternatives* – emphasizing negative aspects of alternatives.

Changing mind set and refocusing organizational energies requires the articulation of a new vision, and there are many cases where this kind of leadership is credited with starting or turning round organizations. Examples include Jack Welch of GE, Steve Jobs (Pixar/Apple), Andy Groves (Intel) and Richard Branson (Virgin). While we must be careful of vacuous expressions of 'mission' and 'vision', it is also clear that in cases like these there has been a clear sense of, and commitment to, shared organizational purpose arising from such leadership.

In other cases the need for change is perceived, but the strength or saliency of the threat is underestimated. IBM experienced difficulties in the early 1990s in responding to the emerging 'client-server' and network shift in computing away from mainframes, and this is a good example of a firm that believed it had seen and assessed the threat but which nearly drove the company out of business. Similarly, General Motors found it difficult to appreciate and interpret the information about Japanese competition, preferring to believe that their access in US markets was due to unfair trade policies rather than recognizing the fundamental need for process innovation that the 'lean manufacturing' approach pioneered in Japan was bringing to the car industry. Christensen, in his studies of disruptive innovation in the computer hard drive industry, and Tripsas and Gravetti, in their analysis of the problems that senior management at Polaroid experienced in making the transition to digital imaging, provide powerful evidence to show the difficulties established firms have in interpreting the signals associated with a new and potentially disruptive innovations (Exhibit 3.2).

Even when senior management do identify a potential threat, they can misinterpret, underestimate or simply ignore it. The influential work of Clayton Christensen drew attention to cases where the *market* was the effective trigger point. He studied a number of industries in depth and particularly focused on the hard-disk drive sector

Exhibit 3.2   Leadership and transformation at Polaroid and Kodak

Polaroid was a pioneer in the development of instant photography. It developed the first instant camera in 1948, the first instant colour camera in 1963, and introduced sonar automatic focusing in 1978. In addition to its competencies in silver halide chemistry, it had technological competencies in optics and electronics, and mass manufacturing, marketing and distribution expertise. The company was technology-driven from its foundation in 1937, and the founder Edwin Land had 500 personal patents. When Kodak entered the instant photography market in 1976, Polaroid sued the company for patent infringement and was awarded $924.5 million in damages. Polaroid consistently and successfully pursued a strategy of introducing new cameras, but made almost all its profits from the sale of the film (the so-called razor/blade marketing strategy also used by Gillette), and between 1948 and 1978 the average annual sales growth was 23%, and profit growth 17% per year.

Polaroid established an electronic imaging group as early as 1981, as it recognized the potential of the technology. However, digital technology was perceived as a potential technological shift rather than as a market or business disruption. By 1986 the group had an annual research budget of $10 million, and by 1989, 42% of the R&D budget was devoted to digital imaging technologies. By 1990, 28% of the firm's patents related to digital technologies. Polaroid was therefore well-positioned at that time to develop a digital camera business. However, it failed to translate prototypes into a commercial digital camera until 1996, by which time there were 40 other companies in the market, including many strong Japanese camera and electronics firms. Part of the problem was adapting the product development and marketing channels to the new product needs. However, other more fundamental problems related to long-held cognitions: a continued commitment to the razor/blade business model and pursuit of image quality. Profits from the new market for digital cameras were derived from the cameras rather than the consumables (film). Ironically, Polaroid had rejected the development of ink-jet printers, which rely on consumables for profits, because of the relatively low quality of their (early) outputs. Polaroid had a long tradition of improving its print quality to compete with conventional 35 mm film.

Faced with developments in digital imaging technology, Kodak redefined its business as 'pictures, not technology', stressing that the market competencies were still relevant to the digital photographic markets, but it lacked the relevant technological competencies. The board hired George Fisher from Motorola to be the new CEO. Fisher pursued a two-tier strategy for new business development. For the medical imaging business, Kodak acquired a number of specialist digital technology firms, including Imation Corporation, which had developed a hybrid dry laser imaging technology. It combined these new competencies with its existing market knowledge, as it accounted for around 30% of the global medical imaging market at that time.

For the consumer imaging market, Kodak established a new digital and applied imaging division, but this suffered from the parent company's organizational routines, which had evolved to monitor relatively stable mass markets and slow moving technology, and were therefore inappropriate for digital imaging at that time. As a result of organizational problems, the division was made organizationally independent in 1997, and in 1998 formed a joint venture with Intel to develop the 'Picture CD' project. Similarly, initial attempts to develop digital cameras in the existing consumer imaging division resulted in cameras that failed to meet the technological and market demands. These developments were also later moved to the new digital and applied imaging division, which had routines more suited to the needs of emerging technologies and markets. A series of successful products followed, and by 2004 Kodak had 20% of the global market share in digital cameras.

Sources: Derived from Tripsas, M. & Gavetti, G. (2000) Capabilities, cognition, and inertia: evidence from digital imaging. *Strategic Management Journal*, 21: 1147–1161; and Macher, J.T. & Richman, B.D. (2004) Organizational responses to discontinuous innovation. *International Journal of Innovation Management*, 8(1): 87–114.

because it represented an industry where a number of generations of dominant design could be found within a relatively short history. His distinctive observation was that with each generation almost all of the previously successful players in what was a multimillion dollar market failed to make the transition effectively and were often squeezed out of the market or into bankruptcy. In 1976 there were 17 major firms in the industry; by 1995 of these only IBM remained a player. During that period 129 firms had entered the industry – but 109 exited. Yet these were not noninnovative firms – quite the reverse. They were textbook examples of good practice, ploughing a high percentage of sales back into R&D, working closely with lead users to understand their needs and develop product innovations alongside them, delivering a steady stream of continuous product and process innovations and systematically exploring the full extent of the innovation space defined by their market. So what explains why such apparently smart firms fail?

The answer was not their failure to cope with a breakthrough in the technological frontier – indeed, all of the technologies that were involved in the new dominant designs for each generation were well-established, and many of them had originated in the laboratories of the existing (and later disrupted) incumbents. What was changing was the emergence of new *markets* with very different needs and expectations. Generally, these involved players who were looking for something simpler and cheaper to meet a very different set of needs – essentially outside or at the fringes of the mainstream.

For example, the pioneers of the personal computer (Apple, Atari, Commodore, etc.) in the mid-1970s were trying to make a machine for the home and hobby market – but for a fraction of the price and with much less functionality than the existing mainstream minicomputer market where high-capacity, fast access disk drives were required. Messrs Jobs, Wozniak and colleagues would be quite satisfied with something much less impressive technically but available to fit their tight budget of the kind of hobbyists to whom their product was initially addressed. The trouble was that they were not taken seriously as an alternative market prospect by the established suppliers. The early days of the PC industry were characterized by enthusiasm among a group of nerds and geeks running small and highly speculative ventures. These hardly represented a serious alternative market to the multi billion dollar business of supplying the makers of mainstream mini computers. As Steve Jobs described their attempts to engage interest,

> So we went to Atari and said, 'Hey, we've got this amazing thing, even built with some of your parts, and what do you think about funding us? Or we'll give it to you. We just want to do it. Pay our salary, we'll come work for you.' And they said, 'No.' So then we went to Hewlett-Packard, and they said, 'Hey, we don't need you. You haven't got through college yet.'

In essence, existing successful players are too good at working with their mainstream users and fail to see the longer-term potential in newly emerging markets. Their systems for picking up signals about user needs and feeding these into the product development process are all geared around existing products and user needs. And their success in meeting these needs helped their businesses to grow through keeping up with that industry. We shouldn't be surprised at this – new markets do not emerge in their full scale or with clearly identifiable needs but start out as messy, uncertain and risky places with small size and dubious growth prospects.

Although techniques to support more creative strategic decision-making and problem-solving can be can be taught and learned, they are best suited for the solution of real-life problems. We are not referring here to the elegant strategy models and sophisticated but abstract tools taught by business schools and touted by consultants. We are concerned with how to identify and implement more creative and innovative solutions.

This requires a problem to be considered 'real', and to be owned by someone. A problem becomes 'real' only when it involves an emotional or affective commitment as well as an intellectual or cognitive one; it must have a personal frame of reference. Second, it must not have an already existing solution. Third, merely naming something a 'real' problem does not necessarily make it so for a particular individual or group. Finally, the purpose of a 'real' problem is to contribute something new or bring about some sort of change.[35]

Ownership of the problem is also critical.[36] Ownership for a challenge means that the problem-solver has some degree of influence, authority and decision-making responsibility for implementing the solutions. It also means that the problem-owner is motivated and willing to submit the challenge to systematic problem-solving efforts and is interested in following through on the results. Finally, in order for someone to have ownership in a challenge, there must be a deliberate and explicit search for something new. In short, in order for ownership to exist, there must be influence, interest and imagination (see Chapter 6 on owning up to change).

Leadership can influence perceptions of the environment in two ways: first, the need for change, and second, the appropriate type of response, that is the generation, testing and implementation of ideas. The critical condition for translation of the situational assessment into innovative behaviors is that a manager judges a need for change, and that the organization is susceptible to change.[37] Clearly, a feedback loop exists from the second to the first assessment. With greater perceived situational control (authority to act, resources, time, etc.) a manager will increase their sensitivity and aspiration for innovation, and conversely if they perceive their control to be lower, their sensitivity in the primary appraisal will be reduced.

Much of the above discussion on corporate mind set creates difficulties downstream in terms of decision-making. If the proposed new project doesn't fit the existing ways of seeing then it has a very poor chance of entering, never mind surviving in the strategic portfolio. The challenge is not simply one of dealing with a risk-averse approach that favors doing well-understood things as opposed to totally new ones. It is also about the difficulties of predicting where and how novel ideas might move forward. As Christensen points out, one of the common problems in the many cases of disruptive innovation that he looked at was that at the outset the new prospects did not offer much apparent market potential. They tended to represent innovation opportunities that were technically risky and that had limited market potential – it was only later, as they grew to multimillion or even billion dollar businesses that the scale of missed opportunity became apparent. Most well-managed resource allocation systems would tend to favor less radical bets that offered better returns in the short term.

Given the complexities involved, the outcomes of investments in innovation are uncertain, so that the forecasts (of costs, prices, sales volume, etc.) that underlie project and program evaluations can be unreliable. According to Joseph Bower, management finds it easier, when appraising investment proposals, to make more accurate forecasts of reductions in production cost than of expansion in sales, while their ability to forecast the financial consequences of new product introductions is very limited indeed. This last conclusion is confirmed by the study by Edwin Mansfield and his colleagues of project selection in large US firms. By comparing project forecasts with outcomes, he showed that managers find it difficult to pick technological and commercial winners.

Dealing with uncertainty is reflected in how successful managers allocate resources to such projects.[38] In particular, they:

- encourage *experimentation* and *incrementalism* – step-by-step modification of objectives and resources, in the light of new evidence;
- use *simple rules* models for allocating resources, so that the implications of changes can be easily understood, and recognise that *different types* of project should be evaluated by *different criteria*;
- use *sensitivity analysis* to explore if the outcome of the project is 'robust' (unchanging) to a range of different assumptions (e.g. 'What if the project costs twice as much, and takes twice as long, as the present estimates?');
- seek the reduction of *key uncertainties* (technical and – if possible – market) before any irreversible commitment to full-scale – and costly – commercialization;
- make explicit from the outset criteria for *stopping* the project or program.

In other words, the successful allocation of resources to innovation depends less on robustness of decision-making techniques than on the organizational processes in which they are embedded. According to Mitchell and Hamilton, there are three (overlapping) categories of projects that large firms must finance.

Business investment

This is the development, production and marketing of existing and better products, processes and services. In such projects, the appropriate question is: 'What are the potential costs and benefits in continuing with the project?' It involves relatively large-scale expenditures, evaluated with conventional financial tools. However, the best performing firms also use strategic methods.[39]

Strategic positioning

These activities are in between knowledge-building and business investment, and an important – and often neglected – link between them. They involve feasibility demonstration, in order to reduce uncertainties and to build in-house competence. For this type of project, the appropriate question is: 'Is the program likely to create *an option* for a profitable investment at a later date?' Comparisons are sometimes made with financial 'stock options', where (for a relatively small sum) a firm can purchase the *option* to buy a stock at a specified price, before a specified date – in anticipation of increase in its value in future. Market analysis should be broad (e.g. where could genetic engineering create new markets for vegetables in a food company?). A variety of evaluation methods may be used, but they will be more judgmental than rigorously quantitative.

Knowledge-building

This is the early stage and relatively inexpensive research for nurturing and maintaining expertise in fields that could lead to future opportunities or threats. It is often treated as a necessary overhead expense, and sometimes viewed with suspicion (and even incomprehension) by senior management obsessed with short-term financial returns and exploiting existing markets, rather than creating new ones. With knowledge-building programs, the central question for the company is: 'What are the potential costs and risks of *not* mastering or entering the field?' Formal market research has almost no value in such cases.

Creativity in strategic decision-making and problem-solving

A number of models of the creative process can be helpful to those who need to engage in strategic decision-making and problem-solving. One proven and practical process for challenging the way we perceive things includes four main components.[40]

The first component is planning your approach and includes two stages. These stages require you to think about your thinking and problem-solving. The first, called 'appraising tasks', is characterized by surveying the desired outcome or required task, learning about the people involved and assessing the environment surrounding the task. The second, called 'designing process', allows the problem-solver to apply what was learned during appraising tasks to develop a customized approach to using the three process components. These include:

1. understanding the problem;
2. generating ideas;
3. planning for action.

Understanding the problem

Understanding the problem includes a systematic effort to define, construct or formulate a problem. Although many researchers have focused on problem-finding as a process separate from problem-solving, such a distinction may be arbitrary especially within the context of a flexible or descriptive approach. It is not necessarily the 'first' step, nor is it necessarily undertaken by all people. Rather than prescribing an essential problem-finding process, understanding the problem involves active construction by the individual or group through analyzing the task at hand (including outcomes, people, context and methodological options) to determine whether and when deliberate problem structuring efforts are needed. This stage includes the three stages of constructing opportunities, exploring data and framing problems.

An opportunity is a broad statement of a goal or direction that can be constructed as broad, brief and beneficial. The opportunity generally describes the basic area of need or challenge on which the problem-solver's efforts will be focused, remaining broad enough to allow many perspectives to emerge as one (or a group) looks more closely at the situation. Exploring data includes the generating and answering of questions to bring out key data (information, impressions, observations, feelings, etc.) to help the problem-solver(s) focus more clearly on the most challenging aspects and concerns of the situation. Framing problems includes the seeking of a specified or targeted question (problem statement) on which to focus subsequent effort. Effectively worded problem statements invite an open or wide-ranging search for many, varied and novel options. They are stated concisely and are free from specific limiting criteria.

This component has been widely applied to assist in strategic decision-making and problem-solving. Management teams have considered many, varied and unique opportunities and focused on those that offer the best future organizational results. These teams have explored a variety of data to better understand their market, competition and internal strengths and weaknesses. They have also applied their creativity to framing a variety of specific problem statements that have shaped projects and initiatives for change.

Generating ideas

Generating ideas includes the generating of options in answer to an open-ended or invitational statement of the problem. This component has only one stage that contains both a generating and focusing phase. During the generating phase of this stage, the person or group produces many options (fluent thinking), a variety of possible options (flexible thinking), novel or unusual options (original thinking) or a number of detailed or refined options (elaborative thinking). The focusing phase of generating ideas provides an opportunity for examining, reviewing, clustering and selecting promising options. Although this stage includes a focusing phase, its primary emphasis is generative.

Generating ideas has also been widely applied to assist those who engage in strategic decision-making and problem-solving. Brainstorming is the widely known tool to assist groups in generating ideas, but it can be applied whenever a group needs to consider many, varied and unusual alternatives.[41]

Planning for action

Planning for action is appropriate when a person or group recognizes a number of interesting or promising options that may not necessarily be useful, valuable or valid without extended effort and productive thinking. The need may be to make or develop effective choices, or prepare for successful implementation and social acceptance. The two stages included in the component are called 'developing solutions' and 'building acceptance'.

When developing solutions, promising options may be analyzed, refined or developed. If there are many options, the emphasis may be compressing or condensing them so that they are more manageable. If there are only a few promising options, the challenge may be to strengthen each as much as possible. There may be a need to rank or prioritize a number of possible options. Specific criteria may be generated and selected upon which to evaluate and develop promising options or select from a larger pool of available alternatives. Although there may be some generating in this stage, the emphasis is primarily on focusing.

Building acceptance involves searching several potential sources of assistance and resistance for possible solutions. The aim is to help prepare an option or alternative for improved acceptance and value. This stage helps the problem-solver identify ways to make the best possible use of assisters and avoid or overcome possible sources of resistance. From considering these factors, a plan of action is developed and evaluated for implementation.

Both developing solutions and building acceptance are critical areas for those who must engage in strategic decision-making and problem-solving. If an organization is to make use of original ways to compete in the market, they must have the capability to invest effort and energy in screening, selecting and supporting and strengthening new concepts and solutions. Once the new concepts and ideas are developed, the next logical focus of attention is to prepare them for the marketplace and acceptance from key stakeholders.

Changing organizational routines

The idea of organizational 'routines' plays a central role in theories of innovation. The concept has intuitive appeal, resonating with mundane experience of repeated patterns in organizational life, and it holds promise of connections between theory and practice – notably, management practice. Routines are seen as regular and predictable behavioral patterns of the firm. Routines are seen as essentially *collective* constructions for the coordination of organizational knowledge in developing, maintaining and extending competencies and capabilities within the innovative firm. Research on the sociology of organizations has begun to explore the dual nature of routines:[42] as practical constructions within organizations they serve contingently as sites of both reproduction/stability and creation/change.

Despite proliferating interpretations, Becker[43] points to some consensus around effects of routines in terms of:

1. enabling coordination;
2. providing a degree of stability in behavior;
3. enabling tasks to be executed in the subconscious and hence economizing on limited cognitive resources; and
4. binding knowledge, including tacit knowledge.

Most of the time the routines work well as a basis for organizing and managing 'what we do but better'. This is often the bulk of an organization's activity and paying attention to these factors demonstrably helps create the conditions for success. But there are occasions when discontinuous conditions emerge and where existing routines do not always help deal with the new challenge. Indeed, on occasions doing more of the old routines may be positively the wrong thing to do.

We have become used to seeing routines as a source of strength within the organization, but the downside is that the mind set that is highly competent in doing certain things can also block the organization from changing its mind. Thus, ideas that challenge the status quo face an uphill struggle to gain acceptance; innovation requires considerable energy and enthusiasm to overcome barriers of this kind. One of the concerns in successful innovative organizations is finding ways to ensure that individuals with good ideas are able to progress them without having to leave the organization to do so.

We should also recognize the problem of *unlearning*. Not only is learning to learn a matter of acquiring and reinforcing new patterns of behavior – it is often about forgetting old ones. Letting go in this way is by no means easy, and there is a strong tendency to return to the status quo or equilibrium position – which helps account for the otherwise surprising number of existing players in an industry who find themselves upstaged by new entrants taking advantage of new technologies, emerging markets or new business models. Managing transformation requires the capacity to cannibalize and look for ways in which other players will try and bring about 'creative destruction' of the rules of the game. Jack Welch, former CEO of General Electric, is famous for having sent out a memo to his senior managers asking them to tell him how they were planning to destroy their businesses! The intention was not, of course, to execute these plans but rather to use the challenge as a way of focusing on the need to be prepared to let go and rethink – to unlearn.

Change can be conceptualized along two dimensions:

1. the context of the change initiative in the organization; and
2. the relations of the change project to the institutional environment.[44]

The relationship of the organization to its environment is a two-way process in which the organization influences its environment, but the environment will also influence the organization. This leads to two very different potential processes of change: eruptive, which is characterized by anarchic self-development and entrepreneurship; or isomorphic, which is imposed through formal systems and processes. A rhetoric of participation and self-actualization can help mobilize, motivate and induce creativity, but presents the danger of opportunistic, symbolic 'change rhetoric', which simply results in a placebo effect rather than any real lasting change. However, to achieve real change, informal strategies and rhetoric have ultimately to be validated within the formal power structure, which is the central role of implementation. Therefore, successful organizational change depends on how the gap between the informal and formal systems is handled. Informal systems focus on practice, professional understanding and problem-solving, whereas formal systems focus on function. Real change demands both informal involvement and formal legitimacy, and combines institutional explanations of isomorphic change, with the need for eruptive and entrepreneurial processes.

Drawing on her own extensive experience and the research on managing change, Smale[45] argues that organizations too often follow simplistic step change programs promoted by management gurus and consultants, rather than basing their action on evidence of how successful change programs work. She identifies a number of common beliefs:

- *Cascade* – the idea that change trickles down or cascades down through an organization from senior management through staff and middle managers, down to the lowest levels.
- *Anthropomorphic* – the belief that 'new methods develop', 'ideas spreading' throughout social networks or communities.
- *Evolution or natural selection* – that an organization will naturally 'select' the superior practices, technologies and so on, based on economic or other logic.
- *Pilot projects or the Trojan horse* – many gurus and consultants advocate a series of pilot programs prior to more widespread change management.

- *Change requires major restructuring* – managers focus on changing the structure of the organization.
- *Best practice or evidence-based practice* – once 'best practice' is established this can be disseminated.

She advocates breaking down objectives into specific component cases of change; for example, new work practices or introduction of new technology. This is helpful because it makes the process more manageable, but also because it helps to identify what needs to be changed and what does not, and differences in the discrete changes or innovation. She develops a three-phase change process:

1. *Identify the specific changes or innovations needed* as different types of innovation will demand different approaches and support, 'what needs to change, and what should stay the same', for example:
   - What are the characteristics of the innovation, and what do we know about implementing this type of innovation?
   - What are the complementary changes or systemic requirements?
   - How radical or incremental is it perceived to be in this context?
   - Are there examples of similar innovations elsewhere that we can draw upon or use as support?
2. *Mapping the significant people* to identify who needs to do what to whom, 'who sees what as a problem', for example:
   - Who is initiating change, and who is it 'being done to'?
   - Who has to do what differently?
   - Who experiences what losses and what gains?
   - How are significant people responding to change?
   - Who are the change agents, and who is supporting them?
3. *Understand the context of change* to exploit compatible forces and minimize conflicts, for example:
   - How does the innovation effect the relationship between significant people?
   - How compatible is the innovation with other changes or current practices?
   - What is the culture of the organization and is it supportive?
   - How does it effect the relationship of the organization with other organizations e.g. suppliers, customers, regulators?

The first phase is often omitted from the 'standardized' implementation programs advocated by management gurus and by consultants. The nature of the project or innovation will fundamentally influence how is should be implemented and the likelihood of success.

Creativity in changing organizational routines

When we consider how research and practice in creativity can contribute to changing organizational routines, we think it best to return to the overall interactionist and ecological approach. There are numerous contingencies that those who lead and manage organizations can consider and use. We propose the following five dimensions to help understand, predict and facilitate creativity; we will briefly review each of the five dimensions.

Personal orientation contingencies

Personal orientation includes what is traditionally thought of as characteristic of the creative person as well as the creative abilities associated with creativity. These include personality traits traditionally associated with creativity, such as openness to experience, tolerance of ambiguity, resistance to premature closure, curiosity and risk-taking, among others. They also include such creative thinking abilities as fluency, flexibility, originality and elaboration. Expertise, competence and knowledge base also contribute to creative efforts.

We believe that people can be selected and developed on the basis of many of these characteristics. Building awareness and competence in managing a diversity of problem-solving styles can also assist in changing organizational routines (see Chapter 7 on teamwork for transformation).

Situational outlook contingencies

Situational outlook involves many elements surrounding the context. These include an individual's perception of the organizational climate and culture, the predominant leadership styles and behaviors, and the nature and function of the reward systems and structures. People's perceptions and conceptions of their work and the overall strategic orientation (e.g. growth or decline of industry or market) are also important aspects of the situation. The ways in which people understand and react to their situation also lead to variations in assessing or selecting tasks. The amount of reward and leadership support for creativity, the values and norms regarding outcomes, or the impact of perceived external constraints on individuals' motivation can also be influenced by the contingencies within situational outlook.

Taking deliberate steps to assess and develop an appropriate organizational climate creates the opportunity for initiative to be taken. There are numerous resources and approaches to explicitly create the context for changing organizational routines (see Chapters 11, 12 and 13 for more information).

Task contingencies

Our ecological view departs significantly from past interactionist descriptions of creativity by including a task dimension. Task appraisal arises from the interaction between personal orientation and situational outlook. A preliminary analysis of the task provides an understanding of the nature of the intended outcomes and the factors influencing success, such as the extent to which the task is ambiguous, complex or novel, and the degree to which an individual owns or can influence the problem or opportunity. The actual content or domain of the challenge can be either well-defined and clearly structured or fuzzy, ill-defined and ambiguous. A task like writing a research report in the history of the American presidency may offer the typical high-school student quite a challenge, but it is fairly well-defined and clearly structured. This would be identified as more of a problem-solving task. The problem of determining key characteristics for successful global leadership is much more fuzzy, rather ill-defined and somewhat ambiguous. This challenge requires much more definition and investment in thinking that would be characterized as original or novel. What is meant by successful? What is global leadership? How might we actually determine those key characteristics?

Scoping tasks that allow for deliberate creative thinking and encouraging others within all levels of the organization to do the same increases the probability that new and useful ideas and suggestions will result. Setting clear priorities on these tasks also increases the likelihood that these ideas will be implemented. See Chapter 8 on managing change methods for more information on how these contingencies can be applied.

Creative process contingencies

This dimension focuses on the methodology, process or strategies needed. This describes the nature of the pathway toward the solution. On the one hand, a method can be well-known, a clear and standard approach is available, and the pathway is determined and simple. On the other side of the dimension are problems for which there is no known or determined method or for which the approach is extremely complex. Effective practitioners have long since passed the view of the process as a fixed sequence of prescribed steps and activities. To be effective, it is necessary to make deliberate decisions about the components, stages and techniques that will be appropriate and valuable, given the purpose and intended outcomes of the process. Potential interaction effects can be investigated among the three major components: understanding the problem, generating ideas and planning for action.

By deliberately introducing new change methods, those who lead and manage organizational routines can introduce new ways of working. There are a variety of change methods from which to choose (see Chapter 9 on alternative change methods).

Desired outcomes

The outcome dimension refers to the results of process. Outcome contingencies differ from task contingencies in that the latter relate more to the initial or desired results. Outcome contingencies deal with the actual or real results of the process. These may be tangible (e.g. concreteness) or intangible (e.g. satisfaction). The nature of the results can be considered from the point of view of the product or outcome itself, or by how well it is diffused and accepted by others. Outcomes can also be assessed for their level of novelty, usefulness and other criteria. Some tasks require outcomes that are readily available or already exist. The challenge for the problem-solver is to discover them. Other tasks require the invention or active construction of the outcome. Here, the needed outcome is not currently or readily available. The desire for certain outcome qualities, such as novelty, usefulness or completeness, may be influenced by elements found in personal orientation.

Organizational routines can be changed by emphasizing and focusing on new sorts of outcomes. Strategic decisions can be taken to ensure that the appropriate levels of novelty and usefulness are pursued along with the desired market positioning of the outcomes.

Conclusion

The challenge seems to be to develop ways of managing under the highly uncertain, rapidly evolving and changing conditions that result from a dislocation or discontinuity. The kinds of organizational behavior needed here will include things like agility, flexibility, the ability to learn fast, the lack of preconceptions about the ways in which things might evolve, etc. – and these are often associated with new, small firms. There are ways in which large and established players can also exhibit this kind of behavior but it does often conflict with their normal ways of thinking and working.

As we will see throughout the book, a key challenge in managing transformation for creativity and innovation is the ability to create ways of dealing with both sets of challenges 'doing better' and 'doing different', and if possible to do so in 'ambidextrous' fashion, maintaining close links between the two rather than spinning off completely separate ventures.

References

1. Marx, K. & Engels, F. (1848) *The Manifesto of the Communist Party*.
2. Miller, D. (1990) *The Icarus Paradox: How Exceptional Companies Bring about Their Own Downfall*. New York: HarperCollins.
3. Johnson, G. (2005) *Successful Strategic Transformers*. British Academy of Management Conference, Oxford, 13–15 September.
4. Austin, J.H. (1977) *Chase, Chance, and Creativity: The Lucky Art of Novelty*. New York: Columbia University Press.
5. Chesborough, H. (2003) *Open Innovation: The New Imperative for Creating and Profiting from Technology*. Boston: Harvard Business School Press.
6. Mumford, M.D. (2003) Editorial: special issue on leading for innovation, *Leadership Quarterly*, 14(4–5): 1–4.
7. Barringer, B.R. & Bluedorn, A.C. (1999) The relationship between corporate entrepreneurship and strategic management. *Strategic Management Journal*, 20: 421–444.
8. Christensen, C. (1997) *The Innovator's Dilemma*. Boston: Harvard Business School Press.
9. Winter, S. (2004) Specialized perception, selection and strategic surprise: learning from the moths and the bees. *Long Range Planning*, 37: 163–169.

10. Philips, W., Lamming, R., Bessant, J. & Noke, H. (2004) Promiscuous Relationships: Discontinuous Innovation and the Role of Supply Networks. In *IPSERA Conference*. Naples, Italy.

11. Von Hippel, E. (1986) Lead users: a source of novel product concepts, *Management Science*, 32(7): 791–805. Von Hippel, E. (1988) *The Sources of Innovation*. Oxford: Oxford University Press.

12. Morrison, P.D., Roberts, J.H. & Midgley, D.F. (2004) The nature of lead users and measurement of leading edge status, *Research Policy*, 33: 351–362.

13. Callahan, J. & Lasry, E. (2004) The importance of customer input in the development of very new products, *R&D Management*, 34(2): 107–117.

14. Leonard, D. (1992) *Wellsprings of Knowledge*. Boston: Harvard Business School Press.

15. Christensen, C.M., Anthony, S.D. & Roth, E.A. (2005) *Seeing What's Next: Using the Theories of Innovation to Predict Industry Change*. Boston: Harvard Business School Press.

16. Bessant, J. & Francis, D. (2004) Developing parallel routines for product innovation. In *11th PDMA Product Development Conference*. Dublin, Ireland: EIASM, Brussels.

17. Christensen, C. (1997) *The Innovator's Dilemma*. Boston: Harvard Business School Press.

18. Mayer, R.E. (1983) *Thinking, Problem Solving, Cognition*. New York: W.H. Freeman and Co.

19. Gardner, H. (1985) *The Mind's New Science: A History of the Cognitive Revolution*. New York: Basic Books.

20. Boden, M.A. (1991) *The Creative Mind: Myths and Mechanisms*. New York: Basic Books.

21. Isaksen, S.G., Puccio, G.J. & Treffinger, D.J. (1993) An ecological approach to creativity research: profiling for creative problem solving. *Journal of Creative Behavior*, 27(3): 149–170.

22. Gardner, H. (1985) *The Mind's New Science: A History of the Cognitive Revolution*. New York: Basic Books.

23. Maslow, A.H. (1976) Creativity in self-actualizing people. In *The Creativity Question* (eds A. Rothenberg & C.R. Hausman), pp. 86–92. Durham, NC: Duke University Press. Stein, M.I. (1987) Creativity at the crossroads: a 1985 perspective. In *Frontiers of Creativity Research: Beyond the Basics* (ed S.G. Isaksen), pp. 417–427. Buffalo, NY: Bearly Ltd.

24. Isaksen, S.G. & Treffinger, D.J. (1985) *Creative Problem Solving: The Basic Course*. Buffalo, NY: Bearly Ltd.

25. Kirton, M.J. (1976) Adaptors and innovators: A description and measure. *Journal of Applied Psychology*, 61: 622–629. Kirton, M.J. (1989) A theory of cognitive style. In *Adaptors and Innovators: Styles of Creativity and Problem Solving* (ed M.J. Kirton), pp. 1–36. London: Routledge.

26. Tefft, M.E. (1990) *A Factor Analysis of the TTCT, MBTI and KAI: The Creative Level-Style Issue Re-Examined*. Unpublished master's thesis, State University College at Buffalo, Buffalo, NY. Isaksen, S.G. (2004) The progress and potential of the creativity level-style

distinction: Implications for research and practice. In *Creativity and Problem Solving in the Context of Business Management* (eds W. Haukedal & B. Kuvaas), pp. 40–71. Bergen, Norway: Fagbokforlaget.

27. Akgun, A.E., Lynn, G.S. & Byrne, J.C. (2003) Organizational learning: a socio-cognitive framework. *Human Relations*, 56(7): 839–868.

28. Isaksen, S.G., Puccio, G.J. & Treffinger, D.J. (1993) An ecological approach to creativity research: profiling for creative problem solving. *Journal of Creative Behavior*, 27(3): 149–170.

29. Mumford, M.D. & Licuanan, B. (2004) Leading for innovation: conclusions, issues and directions. *Leadership Quarterly*, 15(1): 163–171.

30. Kaplan, S., Murray, F. & Henderson, R. (2003) Discontinuities and senior management: assessing the role of recognition in pharmaceutical firm response to biotechnology. *Industrial and Corporate Change*, 12(4): 203–233.

31. Acha, V. (2004) Technology frames: the art of perspective and interpretation in strategy. *SPRU Electronic Working Paper Series*, 109.

32. Tenkasi, R.V. (2000) The dynamics of cognitive oversimplification processes in R&D environments: an empirical assessment of some consequences. *International Journal of Technology Management*, 20(5/6/7/8): 782–798.

33. Tyler, B.B. and Gnyawali, D.R. (2002) Mapping managers' market orientations regarding new product success. *Journal of Product Innovation Management*, 19(4): 259–276.

34. Walsh, J.P. (1995) Managerial and organizational cognition: notes from a field trip. *Organization Science*, 6(1): 1–41.

35. Renzulli, J.S. (1982) What makes a problem real: stalking the illusive meaning of qualitative differences in gifted education. *Gifted Child Quarterly*, 26: 147–156.

36. Isaksen, S.G. & Treffinger, D.J. (1985) *Creative Problem Solving: The Basic Course*. Buffalo, NY: Bearly Ltd.

37. Krause, D.E (2004) Influence-based leadership as a determinant of the inclination to innovate and of innovation-related behaviors. *Leadership Quarterly*, 15(1): 79–102.

38. Dvir, D. & Lechler, T. (2004) Plans are nothing, changing plans is everything: the impact of changes on project success. *Research Policy*, 33: 1–15.

39. Cooper, R., Edgett, S. & Kleinschmidt, E. (2001) Portfolio management for new product development: results of an industry practices study, *R&D Management*, 31(4): 361–380. Tidd, J. and Bodley, K. (2002) The affect of project novelty on the new product development process. *R&D Management*, 32(2): 127–138.

40. Isaksen, S.G. & Treffinger, D.J. (2004) Celebrating 50 years of reflective practice: versions of creative problem solving. *Journal of Creative Behavior*, 38: 75–101. Isaksen, S.G., Dorval, K.B. & Treffinger, D.J. (2000) *Creative Approaches to Problem Solving: A Framework for Change*. Dubuque, IA: Kendall/Hunt. Treffinger, D.J., Isaksen, S.G. & Stead-Dorval, K.B. (2005) *Creative Problem Solving: An Introduction* (4th edn). Austin, TX: Prufrock Press.

41. Isaksen, S.G. & Gaulin, J.P. (2005) A reexamination of brainstorming research: implications for research and practice. *Gifted Child Quarterly*, 49: 315–329.

42. Feldman, M.S. & Pentland, B.T. (2003) Reconceptualizing organizational routines as a source of flexibility and change. *Administrative Science Quarterly*, 48(1): 94–118.

43. Becker, M.C. (2005) Organizational routines: a review of the literature. *Industrial and Corporate Change*, 13(4): 643–677.

44. Finstad, N. (1998) The rhetoric of organizational change. *Human Relations*, 51(6): 717–739.

45. Smale, G. (1998) *Managing Change through Innovation*. London: The Stationery Office.

Chapter 4

CREATING BLOCKBUSTERS

commercial breakthroughs do not happen in a single explosive moment but proceed through a series of events – of smaller breakthroughs in concept, in technologies, in emotion, in organization, in the marketplace. There are no general rules for what happens. But it is clear that, as a breakthrough concept forms into something consumers eventually will buy, there are both moments when traditional management can be terribly destructive and moments when responsive people in traditional management roles can save the concept from destroying itself[1]

No discussion of transformation and growth would be complete without including the topic of blockbuster products and services. This kind of product has a dramatic effect on the organization that produces it, as well as the marketplace. This chapter will describe blockbuster products and provide some insight into how they are developed.

When we think about innovation, the main emphasis is about taking an idea or invention through development to commercialization or use in the marketplace. A great deal of work has been done over the past few decades to define and share best practices for new product development,[2] but one of the proponents of these practices has issued a warning that the balance of products in most organization's portfolios is off. Cooper[3] has indicated that most organizations seem preoccupied with minor modifications, tweaks and line extensions, rather than with what he calls 'true' innovation – new to the world.

One reason for the shortfall of new to the world innovation is the lack of clear best practices for the front end of new product development (see Chapter 10 on applying CPS as a change method). Peter Koen and his colleagues are doing some promising work in this area, and clear best practices for the 'fuzzy' front end are just beginning to emerge.[4] Others are joining this effort. Based on working at the Palo Alto Research Center, Mark and Barbara Stefik[5] have assembled stories and strategies on breakthroughs. They point out that radical breakthroughs can launch new industries or transform existing ones.

What are blockbusters?

When we hear the word 'blockbuster', we often think of current movies that are box-office hits. Some recent examples are *Titanic*, *Harry Potter*, *Star Wars*, etc. We call a movie a blockbuster when it brings in surprising levels of earning at the box office. People seem to swarm and create long lines to get to see one. It's not only about the movie but all the other products and services that stem from the characters and plot. Clothing, toys and a variety of other items emerge rather quickly around a blockbuster movie. Collectors and fans become a market for all sorts of memorabilia and the after market can last for generations. These movies can change the way we look at the world and enter our vocabulary with a deep sense of meaning. But blockbuster products can come from many different industries.

Blockbuster products are those that seem to overcome all barriers within the market. These sorts of products and services grab a hold of many segments within the market and produce surprising results. They can change the way we work and live. When we have asked groups of executives and managers to describe blockbusters, they have provided many different descriptions and examples. Blockbusters imply:

- Big impact for the organization and the market – Microsoft launched Windows and now controls 80%–85% of the entire PC software industry.
- Luck – during the 1960s Spence Silver discovered glue that would not dry, melt or stick to anything, yielding the ubiquitous Post-it note.
- Obvious in retrospect – in 1899 Johan Vaaler simply bent just a thin piece of steel wire into a double oval shape and invented the paper clip.
- Consumers really want it, even if they didn't ask for it – in 1973 Dr Martin Cooper invented the first cell phone at Motorola Dynatac. In 2002, 425 million units were sold.
- Kicks in, takes off soon after launch, rolls out quickly – since 1993 Puma was becoming a trendy brand. Madonna went on stage wearing Sparcos in Summer 2001, and by 2003 Puma saw a 40% increase in turnover.
- Broad scope and spread, appeals to a wide market – McDonald's founded a restaurant on fast and efficient preparation of hamburgers in 1948. Sold to Ray Kroc in 1953, the chain included 30 000 stores in 119 countries in 2004.

- Unknown and unmet needs are met – in 1970 Ray Damadian invented magnetic resonance imaging (MRI) that now provides a widely used noninvasive method for medical diagnosis.
- Starts a new trend – the first digital camera for the consumer market, introduced in 1994, used a computer and was connected to the computer via a serial cable. In 2006 about 71 million units will be sold.
- Timely, catches a wave of interest and desire – despite the admonition of the president of Digital Equipment that 'there is no reason anyone would want a computer at home', Apple launched the personal computer, Apple II, in 1975 with an easy modem interface and color graphic capability.
- Eureka, having an inspirational quality – Virgin Blue, Southwest and Jet Blue launch discount services having clearly different, exciting and profitable service with high levels of customer loyalty and satisfaction.
- Represents a disruptive change or a response to one – the World Wide Web was initiated by Tim Berners-Lee in 1991. Usage is currently at about 758 million and had a growth rate of 111% from 2000 to 2004.

Characteristics of creative products

Susan Besemer is one researcher who has been studying characteristics of creative products for more than 20 years. Her search for an answer to 'What makes a product creative?' has produced a model and an assessment.[6] The model is based on the identification of criteria for creativity in products and outcomes of all kinds. This includes art, inventions, consumer products, household goods, written works, etc. The characteristics in her model fall within three main categories: novelty, resolution and style. We would, indeed, expect a blockbuster product to be new, meet a need and be presented in an aesthetically pleasing way. Let's look a little deeper into these three areas.

Novelty

Blockbuster products must have some degree of originality. They must be new, unusual or unique in some way. Remember that you can consider novelty along a spectrum – like the spectrum of change described in Chapter 2. Is the product breaking fundamental new ground as something radical and exploratory, or is it a new development or incremental improvement on something else? Motorola's introduction of the cell phone was something that bore little resemblance to anything else in the market and introduced a practical application of new technology. It broke new ground and quickly became pervasive and ever-present across markets and segments. On the other hand, when Polycom created the SoundStation, there were other, more clunky and inefficient conference phones in the market. The novelty of the SoundStation was its technical ability to allow the group to have a normal conversation with the absent participant (without yelling, leaning in toward the device or missing key bits of the conversation).

Resolution

Any product must be able to work and function as it's supposed to in order for consumers to want it. Even the most novel product or service must conform to a few basic rules. It must solve a problem or close the gap between a desired future and the current reality. In a way, all creative products must be somewhat logical, useful or valuable. Blockbuster products fill a need that is known or generally unknown.

Corning's development and commercialization of fiber optics is a good example of resolution. Early fiber optic cables suffered tremendous loss of efficiency in carrying light. Through persistent and substantial investment in technical research and development, Corning was eventually able to reduce the loss of efficiency dramatically. Meanwhile, the standard in the marketplace was the use of copper wire for telecommunications. Clearly, fiber optics was a highly novel technology. It was not until Corning had made a few major sales and demonstrated in an understandable way that fiber optics could carry 65 000 times more information than conventional copper wire that it became a blockbuster.

Style

How a product or service presents itself to the user is part of its presentation style. How well a product presents itself as a whole – its look and feel – is important. Creative products are well-crafted as a result of sustained efforts to polish, finish and continuously improve the outcome. They are also elegant in that they are simple to use or understand and refined. Apple's iPod is a good illustration of style. The thin, fashionable and user-friendly iPod combines the ability to download music from iTunes, playing digital music, manage music libraries on computers or the iPod, PDA functions, and games with ease of use and the distinctive 'earbud'-type earphones. There are currently four generations of this product available to the market, each offering improvements like longer battery life, providing a single product that works with Macs and Windows. Apple's iPod has dominated the US digital music player sales with over 92% of the market for hard drive players and more than 65% of the market for all types of players. As of January of 2005, over 10 million units had been sold. As we write this book, the iPod nano is making quite a splash in the market.

A blockbuster outcome must possess at least some of all three of these dimensions and more likely a high level of one or two. In addition to these characteristics, blockbusters generally have both broad and deep appeal in the market, likely because they address a need, desire or aspiration that is profoundly held by many.

Blockbusters are the dream for all sorts of organizations. They can be tangible products or intangible outcomes. Businesses may strive to produce blockbuster consumer products, movies, books, etc. Nonprofit organizations may seek to create blockbuster fundraising or stewardship campaigns, advertising and marketing efforts, and new processes and procedures that change their industries.

Given the ubiquitous interest in breakthrough blockbuster outcomes, it is surprising that little is known about how they are developed. The following sections of this chapter will outline what we currently know about how they are developed, as well as illustrate the entire system outlined in Chapter 1.

How are blockbusters developed?

When we have asked managers to describe how blockbusters were developed, the answers included assertions that the process was mysterious or completely intuitive, and many highlighted the importance of luck, accidental discoveries, serendipity, etc. Of course, there are examples of blockbusters that have depended on lucky happenstance, like the discovery of penicillin. There are other examples of products that hit the mark primarily due to changes in the marketplace, like DuPont's entering the market with an excellent grade of gunpowder just as the war of 1812 was starting. But these circumstances are really outside of anyone's control. There are no levers to pull to order a lucky discovery, or predict completely new trends and developments in the marketplace (although you can certainly endeavor to be aware of them). The idea that 'luck favors the prepared mind' is the only guidance that we can offer here.

We have discovered a vast literature on innovation, creativity and change, and this is summarized in this book, but very little information on the development of block-buster products and services has emerged. One notable exception includes the work of two professors from the Stevens Institute of Technology. Gary Lynn and Richard Reilly conducted a 10-year study of more than 700 teams and the inside stories of nearly 50 of the most successful products ever launched. They referred to these as 'true blockbusters'. They compared and contrasted those organizations and teams that developed and commercialized blockbuster products with their unsuccessful counter-parts. They were able to identify five key practices that explained how new product development teams created great new products (see Table 4.1).

All five practices operate as a system; blockbuster teams must excel in all five practices all the way through the new product development (NPD) process. All the pieces of the puzzle need to come together.

> We evaluated all the teams in our database on a ten-point scale. Based on our statistical analysis of more than 700 teams, we found that if your teams perform all five practices poorly (scoring only ones), their chances of launching a blockbuster is less than 1 percent. If, however, your team scored ten on all five practices, your chances of succeeding are 98 percent and of developing a blockbuster increase to over 70 percent. But not a single one of our blockbuster teams achieved that level of excellence for every practice. This means that even if your team doesn't score tens across the board, you can still achieve blockbuster success.[7]

From their studies, five major practices emerged. The size of the organization did not seem to matter; neither did the type of product. If you were to compare your team's performance with teams in their database that scored fives across the board, your chances of achieving a blockbuster would be less than 5%. If you were able to move all the practices from five to eight, your chances would improve to more than 40%. These practices are described for you in more detail below.

Commitment of senior management

Those teams that developed blockbusters had the full support and cooperation from senior management. These senior managers functioned as sponsors for the project (for

Table 4.1 The five keys to developing blockbuster products

Incremental products (Improvements on what is currently available)	Radically new products (Use untested technology and create a new market category)
Senior management is integrally involved with every aspect of the NPD process and gives the team the needed authority to proceed	Senior management support is more focused on providing adequate (but not excessive) funding and giving the team the needed autonomy and authority, not day-to-day involvement
There is a clear and stable vision to guide the NPD efforts and create the key requirements of any project, and these 'project pillars' are specified before the efforts begin	The initial vision is cloudy and the vision emerges over time – it takes longer to develop clear, compelling and stable project parameters
Rapid and iterative prototyping is done to learn about what works with customers	Since the lead time is longer and the market continually changes, it takes extensive experimenting and following a 'probe and learn' approach
A variety of formal and informal information exchange approaches are utilized within and across teams	Cross-team learning is less important and the information exchange is much more focused on within-team members
Agreed goals and objectives are the focus on coherent and cohesive teamwork	All team members share a common understanding of the project's overall goal, but the specific objectives emerge and shift as the project continues. The team follows these shifts and works to clarify the objectives together

more information about this role see Chapter 6 on owning up to change). They took on an active and intimate role by either involving themselves intimately on the project, or at least providing the backing for the team. Senior managers would often provide more of a 'hit and run' kind of involvement for those teams that did not produce blockbusters. We have also researched the development of blockbuster products within a very specific industry. One of our clients was a global continuity products publishing and marketing company with a presence in more that 28 countries. They had some great historical success in developing and commercializing a number of blockbuster products, but had not produced one in a while.

We were commissioned to conduct a study focusing on obtaining a deeper understanding of how these blockbusters were developed to enable and encourage the development of new ones. Senior management identified historical products that were blockbusters by their own industry standards. We confirmed the financial performance of these products and then set out to interview those who were directly involved in their development. We had amazingly open access to the products, people, and sales and marketing data, and the interviews provided many additional insights about the development of blockbusters.

Our study allowed us to interview the key people who had primary responsibility for developing blockbuster continuity products. These products worked across many markets, generated considerable revenue (the nine different products generated over €4 billion) and were purchased for sustained periods of time (a key success factor for the continuity business). Our study supports the five practices, or method, discovered by Lynn and Reilly, so we will include some examples from both sources.

For example, from our interview with one of the key product developers we learned just how senior management support sometimes serves to keep the development team on track. One team was focusing on an entirely new format for a product. Instead of the traditional card format, the team was using CDs. The founding CEO was very excited about the new format and was also supportive of the team. He did, however, influence the team to consider adjusting the traditional format so that it would fit with the new one (much to the initial chagrin of the team). Because of the CEO's influence and the respect the team had for him, they tested his suggestion and were amazed with the spectacular results. Without the CEO's intimate involvement in the project, the product would never become a blockbuster. He had the business strategy in mind, as well as the excitement for the new format. It was up to him to be familiar enough with what the team was actually trying to accomplish and help drive the process through a critical stage.

Clear and stable vision

Another key practice that Lynn and Reilly discovered was the importance of having a clear and stable vision to guide the product development team. They refer to this as having specific and enduring parameters, something they call 'project pillars', to guide the team. These pillars are the key requirements or 'must haves' for the new product.

Rafferty and Griffin[8] found that two factors had a greater influence on creativity and innovation than overall 'transformational leadership': articulating a vision and inspirational communication. They define a vision as 'the expression of an idealized picture of the future based around organizational values', and inspirational communication as 'the expression of positive and encouraging messages about the organization, and statements that build motivation and confidence'. They found that the expression of a vision has a negative effect on followers' confidence, unless accompanied with inspirational communication. Mission awareness is a strong predictor of the success of R&D projects, the degree to which depends on the stage of the project. For example, in the planning and conceptual stage, mission awareness explained two-thirds of the subsequent project success.[9] Leadership clarity is associated with clear team objectives, high levels of participation, commitment to excellence, and support for innovation.[10] Leadership clarity, partly mediated by good team processes, is a good predictor of team innovation.

When Polycom was developing the SoundStation the founder was clear about what was needed. He formulated three main pillars for the new teleconferencing product. It had to have superb audio quality that would allow for a normal conversation. It had to be easy to use so it could not include lots of complex buttons or chords. The new product also had to be aesthetically pleasing and fit the context of an executive boardroom. Even though the team was facing numerous challenges and a tight deadline, there was to be no wavering.

The main source for developing these clear and stable project pillars is based on an intimate knowledge of the customer. In our research, the CEO of the publishing company (who was personally responsible for numerous blockbusters) had asserted 'The only chance to be successful in product development is if you have the ability of moving yourself into the customer's mind. If you cannot engage in that sort of fantasy, you can't develop products.' Another senior manager who was also responsible for a number of blockbusters told his story about when he was developing a new health-related product. He had been looking at what the company had done previously, and the efforts of competitors, while forming the product concept. Then he related the following:

It was more by accident because I had tonsillitis and I went into the public encyclopedia and looked and it was so full of scientific pictures, X-ray pictures and so on. It didn't help me a lot and the language was quite difficult for me to understand. So I thought, what do you do when you have a disease or an illness like that? What do you want to know yourself? I mean of course you don't want to see X-ray pictures, you want to stand in front of the mirror and look at your mouth and see some symptoms of tonsillitis. And then what else do you want to know, the symptoms, fever, headache, etc? You want to have an easy explanation what it is. You want to know how you get it, how it's treated, what can I do myself. When should I see a doctor and what will he or she do? What will happen with the disease? Will I die from it? How long will it take? It's very basic. It's like that for everyone. Is it dangerous? How can I avoid having it in future and some other important information, and so on?

This empathic and personal understanding of what the customer needs in a health product was directly responsible for the development of another blockbuster for the company.

Another example of how important it is for you to have a clear and stable vision for your product comes from IBM. The IBM PC had clear and unwavering purposes: beat Apple and do it within a year. The team never allowed the overall schedule or purpose to change. In fact, a majority of the charts used to obtain approval for the project were also used to get the go ahead for launch. The IBM PC was highly successful. IBM sold 35 000 by the end of the year it was launched (five times the estimate), and replaced Apple as the front-runner in the personal computer market. A completely different story is told about the IBM PCjr. Work started on this product shortly after the success of the PC. The major difference was that there was never a clear vision for the project. Senior management kept wavering about the focus being the home as well as the business market, making many changes to the requirements along the way. The IBM PCjr was not a blockbuster or even a basic success.

Improvisation

Teams that produced blockbuster products were completing the traditional stages of NPD; they were taking a different approach to their process. Rather than going through the gates step-by-step, waiting for a final decision to be made about going forward, they simply continued to sell the concept and obtain insight from consumers. There are two key aspects to this practice. Blockbuster teams focused on getting an early prototype out quickly to learn how customers would respond. Once they learned how customers responded, they then continued to take new prototypes out for more continuous feedback. This fast, iterative process was critical to their success.

Although you may think that these blockbuster teams were undisciplined, they nearly always had to meet a hard and fast deadline. They were also more likely to monitor their progress and costs than the less successful teams.

One company, Datex-Ohmeda (now part of GE) provides an excellent example of the value of fast prototyping. They are in the business of designing, building and selling anesthesia and healthcare equipment. They were aware that the practitioner using their equipment had a challenge working all the controls, keeping the mask on the patient, squeezing the bag, and keeping their eye on the patient. At first, they were going to invest a great deal in reengineering the controls. After the product development manager went out and applied some tools to obtain consumer insight, it became clear that the existing project was not going to meet the challenge. The team went through a deliberate process of examining all the different problems the practitioners were facing and eventually landed on a new product that would combine controls and squeezing the bag, allowing simplification and improved focus on the patient.

The new product concept had some hurdles. How would it fit into their existing equipment lines? Some felt that it was a little too revolutionary. Initial survey results were not very promising. The breakthrough came when the product manager took the first working prototype to a medical conference and put the device into the hands of the practitioners. Of these, 100% said that they wanted to buy it right then and there. This gave the team and the company the confidence to continue with the development and produce further iterations of the product, until it was doable and able to be produced. The cost of the new product was less than the initial project to reengineer the controls.

Related evidence for improvisation comes from our own research into blockbusters. The need for continuous attention and care was a common theme across all nine products we studied. Published products underwent continuous improvement, even after they were launched. Some were updated and reintroduced into other markets.

The iterative part of the process allows for more approximate thinking. It allows for more exploration and discovery along the way. One of the subjects in our study who was responsible for a major blockbuster product said it best. He said:

Nobody is that brilliant that they can see the end product from the beginning. They may have a vision of what the end product may look like or what the experience of using it will be (or must be) like. It's more like having a dialogue with the product – in trying to get the end results you may ditch what you've done and try something else. You may just have to accept that you may come up with something you never thought you would produce and you might be better off for it.

Information exchange

Effective communication and information exchange was another key practice identified by Lynn and Reilly. Many blockbuster outcomes require the use of cross-functional teams. Exchanging information openly and clearly on a cross-functional team can be challenging to say the least. Not only do specific functions have their own specialized language, they also often have conflicting interests. Lynn and Reilly report that those teams that were successful in developing blockbusters used both transactive and mechanistic memory and knowledge sharing. The transactive type of memory and information is based on interpersonal transactions with other team members. Team members can call on each other through a variety of informal and personal ways like casual conversation, phone calls and meetings. Mechanistic memory and knowledge exchange happens through some sort of system for recording, storing, retrieving and reviewing information. Team members can access this information as it is needed. Both types of information exchange can be enabled for virtual team working, but all teams need some face-to-face time.

Lynn and Reilly share the story of the development of the Apple II e computer and contrast this successful story with the development of the Lisa. Wozniak and Jobs used something called 'the war room' during the development of the Apple II e computer. The war room was a conference room in which they could assemble all the bits of information they needed. Anyone could find out about who was doing what and the status of the development at any time. Inputs from all functions were recorded on handwritten notes and displayed for all to see. People involved in the development could stand around interacting with each other and the information. The Apple II e was introduced in 1983 and became an instant blockbuster product.

The war room was contrasted with the way information was exchanged during the development of the Lisa. After basking in the success of the Apple II e, Jobs and Wozniak hired others and invested in more appropriate offices. The war room was transformed into a more corporate center with typed notes replacing the handwritten Post-its, an informal place to hang out replaced by a more formal and stiff environment. People on the project did not feel comfortable exchanging information this way. The lack of effective information exchange, among other factors, allowed the project to go way outside its cost allowance (and target consumer price) and the Lisa was almost an immediate flop.

Effective communication is such an obvious requirement for information exchange but it is often overlooked. In our research, we had one case in which a product development team was floundering until someone joined the team with excellent facilitation skills. She clarified the roles and structured the exchange of information in such a way that new insights became immediately apparent. The person responsible for the product pointed to that intervention as key to developing his blockbuster product.

Collaboration under pressure

Our own research and that of Lynn and Reilly confirms the importance of effective teamwork for the development of blockbusters. These teams are generally cross-functional in nature, and must often deal with occasional outsiders to bring in a new perspective or expertise. Collaboration in the face of conflicting functions and other sources of internal and external pressure requires a number of facilitating factors (including those mentioned above).

- *Strong senior management participation.* During the development of blockbusters, it is important to have the direct involvement of sponsors and senior managers. This ensures that the project pillars are consistently explained and reinforced and that appropriate support, resources and focus are maintained.
- *Unified goal and deadlines.* The teams responsible for developing blockbusters worked with clear deadlines and common interest and commitment to achieve them. They were able to move beyond the clash that often accompanies cross-functional working and maintain the momentum to lever their complementary skills.
- *Clear roles and responsibilities.* Those teams that produced blockbuster products were composed of members who knew why they were on the team. They also had clear demands and requirements for contributing to the development of the successful outcomes.
- *Balance the voice of the customer with the shared concept of the outcome.* The teams we studied were able to unify the insights they gained from the consumer with the desired outcome. This constant balance allowed them to adjust and fine-tune their understanding of both the market need and the product concept.

One of the product developers offered a key insight for effective teamwork. She said:

> There is always a little anxiety in any product development process and I think this is where the team plays an important role. Ours was a small team, so if a component was too expensive we could work it out right away. Things did not tend to slip because of competing priorities. Everybody was engaged. Because we only had a few products in our category – maybe three or four – we did not have 13 babies to take care of, we only had four. If there was a labeling issue for the package or if there was a component in the promo package that did not look right or something was too expensive we could immediately deal with it and make the product economically feasible and still meet the needs we knew about. We had a very tight team.

What about more radical products?

Most of the five practices outlined above could fit very well for improvements within a known market category. Did we learn about any differences for a blockbuster that uses untested technology or creates a new market category?

Lynn and Reilly indicated that the more radical products included the same five keys, but with a twist (see Table 4.1). Senior management support is still important, but given the extraordinarily long lead time for many radical blockbusters, they do not have as much active, direct day-to-day involvement. Lynn and Reilly describe senior management involvement as 'arm's length support'. Chortatsiani[11] found the same change in the role of senior management in novel innovations in financial services. She found that the differences in the success of the more novel projects was not the result of differences in the *amount* of involvement of the leaders, but rather the *type* of involvement. Looser control, or delegation of the work to teams, in such cases, leads to more effective new product development.

Since it may take longer for the outcome pillars to become clear, radical development may need to tolerate a more ambiguous image from the start. If you are trying to accomplish something brand new, you cannot use traditional market research tools.[12] As a result, the insights needed from the market may take longer to assist in developing the clear vision of the outcome. For example, a recent empirical study identified a key role for so-called 'lead users' in more radical innovations.[13] These users are unlikely to be existing customers, but are ahead of the market in identifying and planning for new requirements, and have sufficient sophistication to identify and capabilities to contribute to development of the innovation. Similarly, a study of 55 development projects in telecommunications computer infrastructure found that the importance of customer inputs increased with technological newness, and moreover, the relationship shifted from customer surveys and focus groups to codevelopment because: 'conventional marketing techniques proved to be of limited utility, were often ignored, and in hindsight were sometimes strikingly inaccurate'.[14]

Although prototyping is still important for radical outcomes, the probe and learn approach will take longer. Taking radically new outcomes to the market for feedback is difficult, at best, as the consumers have no reference point to use as a basis to evaluate the product or service. As a result, much of the early testing may go on within the development team.

For example, IDEO, the global design and development consultancy, finds conventional market research methods insufficient and sometimes misleading for new products and services, and instead favors the use of direct observation and prototyping. Behind its rather typical Californian wackiness lies a tried and tested process for successful design and development:[15]

- Understand the market, client and technology.
- Observe users and potential users in real life situations.
- Visualize new concepts and the customers who might use them, using prototyping, models and simulations.
- Evaluate and refine the prototypes in a series of quick iterations.
- Implement the new concept for commercialization.

The first critical step is achieved through close *observation* of potential users in context. As Tom Kelly of IDEO argues:

> We're not big fans of focus groups. We don't much care for traditional market research either. We go to the source. Not the 'experts' inside a (client) company, but the actual people who use the product or something similar to what we're hoping to create . . . we believe you have to go beyond putting yourself in your customers' shoes. Indeed we believe it's not even enough to *ask* people what they think about a product or idea . . . customers may lack the vocabulary or the palate to explain what's wrong, and especially what's *missing*.

The next step is to develop prototypes to help evaluate and refine the ideas captured from users:

An iterative approach to problems is one of the foundations of our culture of prototyping . . . you can prototype just about anything – a new product or service, or a special promotion. What counts is moving the ball forward, achieving some part of your goal.

Teamwork is still valuable, but the way the team must work will be different. The teams must operate a little tighter with more information exchange occurring within the team rather than across teams. The focus of the teamwork may also be on learning more about the market and the consumer than on sharing cross-functional expertise. The information exchange requires even more openness and tolerance of ambiguity along the way.

Who develops blockbusters?

In addition to finding out how blockbusters were developed, our study discovered that it took a special kind of person to be involved in the process. Most of the research has centered on members of new product development teams and program managers.

From the description above of the method for developing blockbusters, you can see that the process is a challenging one requiring some unique characteristics on the part of those who play key roles along the way. We have found a number of specific characteristics of those we interviewed.

Persistence to overcome resistance

Many in our study found their journey difficult at times. They indicated that when you work on something that is new, numerous sources of resistance emerge. One blockbuster product developer described the difficulty. He said:

When your job is to develop fundamentally new products you are ordered to do nothing else during your working day but break new ground and then all of a sudden you are told that what you are working on will never work. Why? Because it's new ground. That was a bit frustrating, but anyway we at least got through it.

He, along with others in our study, indicated that it takes a person with a certain amount of resilience and persistence to overcome the many sources of resistance. During some of the times when the resistance is at its peak, the commitment and belief in the outcome can be source of inspiration. One of our subjects described it this way:

> I was one of the people who refused to let the product die. In fact, I wasn't the only one – there were others on our team who felt the same way. We felt like the sword of Damocles was hanging over us. I wasn't even an employee of the company but I know how I felt. It was very clear to me that there were periods of optimism followed by absolute periods of crisis that had to be resolved in one way or another. There was one night we had to send and receive a thousand faxes to get through one challenge. You get through it by being sort of self-interestedly determined, like we must do this – we have no choice.

Toleration of ambiguity and lack of control

The development of blockbusters requires that the people involved can deal effectively with a lack of clarity, particularly when dealing with radical blockbusters. Sometimes, the consumer needs cannot be identified in traditional ways and take some time to understand. At other times, the actual product concept can take a while to emerge. One participant in our study described it this way:

> Our company has never been sort of painfully risk-averse, but there are many here who are ultimately obsessed with control. I think it's the toleration of a lack of control that has helped us succeed in developing blockbusters. Everyone finds lack of control scary, but what I would argue is that if you find that scary, then go work somewhere else. Lack of control is absolutely what developing blockbusters is all about.

Intrinsic motivation for the task

Those who have developed blockbusters described an internal and personal passion and enjoyment in pursuing the outcome. This is very close to what Teresa Amabile refers to as intrinsic motivation. It is the kind of motivation that is derived for its own sake, not for the purpose of seeking external reward, recognition, fame, profit or glory. Part of the motivation for the developers we studied was an intense personal curiosity about other people – their interests, their motivations and aspirations. Another part of the motivation was in the actual product they were pursuing. One of our subjects described it this way:

> I think one of the main differences about the team that developed this blockbuster was that everyone was so enthusiastic about the product. They just loved the product and they were glad and proud to be working on it. Even the illustrators who came in only occasionally to our team gatherings would hang around and come and visit because they loved the product too. Most of the illustrators we work with seem to be lonely people, but they would hang around with us because the subject was close to their heart, one they could really enjoy.

A *creative personality*

When you start looking at the kind of characteristics we found in those who were involved in developing blockbusters, there is a striking similarity to the creative personality. For example, Rossman[16] studied inventors and those who pursued patents for their insights. Table 4.2 shows the answers of 710 inventors to the question, 'What motivates or incentives cause you to invent?'

You will notice that the top two responses are consistent with Amabile's[17] notion of intrinsic motivation. The motivation for inventors and those who develop blockbuster products appear to be somewhat similar. They share a high degree of personal energy and passion for what they do. This energy helps them sustain the development process.

A great deal has been written about the creative personality and individual characteristics associated with creative behavior.[18]. MacKinnon studied the personality of creative architects and offered the following summary of his findings:

> What most generally characterizes the creative individual as he has revealed himself in the Berkeley studies, it is his high level of effective intelligence, his openness to experience, his freedom from crippling restraints and impoverishing inhibitions, his esthetic sensitivity, his cognitive flexibility, his independence in thought and action, his unquestioning commitment to creative

Table 4.2 Why do inventors invent?	
What motives or incentives cause you to invent? The following are answers given by 710 inventors to the question, 'What motives or incentives cause you to invent?'	
Love of inventing	193
Desire to improve	183
Financial gain	167
Necessity or need	118
Desire to achieve	73
Part of work	59
Prestige	27
Altruistic reasons	22
Laziness	6
No answers	33

endeavor, and his unceasing striving for solutions to the ever more difficult problems that he constantly sets for himself.[19]

Of course, other people play key roles in the development of blockbuster outcomes. We have already underscored the importance of senior leadership and sponsorship that supports the process. These sponsors champion the effort, demonstrate a belief in the product and can make tough decisions and 'hard calls'. They also provide cover for the developers (who need this protection at times) and keep the momentum going.

In a way, those involved in the development of blockbusters find themselves in the middle. They must have leaders and sponsors within the organization and at the same time they are passionate about the insights from consumers and the market. The development of blockbusters requires consumer intimacy so that the outcomes can appeal to aspirational needs – but not too distant needs, or the outcome does not make any sense to the consumer. The products and outcomes are derived from rich insight based on broad and deep consumer needs and this insight serves to guide the work all along the way.

When it comes to developing blockbusters, the people involved are key to successful development. There is some emerging evidence that finding ways to match certain personalities and preferences to various parts of the new product development process can yield important benefits. One study found that certain types of personalities and styles involved in the early stages of new product development outearned other types by a factor of 95 times when measuring corporate profits.[20] The key was to help people understand their natural preferences and then find ways for them to find their best location and role within the process. A similar approach was undertaken by another organization and was found to increase their effective use of intellectual property, pilot plant efficiency, the number of new launches, and decrease their speed to launch.[21]

Do blockbusters require a special environment?

Our research into blockbusters also pointed out the need for the kind of environment that would allow creative people to flourish. The developers we interviewed told us that a relaxed and informal atmosphere helped them achieve challenging and intrinsically motivating goals. They used descriptors like energy, enthusiasm, freedom and feeling connected to describe the right working environment. They also confirmed that they needed some time to explore and play with ideas, but not too much time. The importance of safety in working relationships, trust and a no-blame climate also came up. One participant indicated that:

> We needed to be able to experiment. We would do some tests but it was important to have a no-blame culture in the team so that if people want to try new things out and try different suppliers and so on, we had a chance in a safe context.

One of our participants took some degree of pride in describing his organizational climate. He made it clear that formal, executive types and those who enjoy bureaucracy did not belong in the development of blockbusters. He was head of one of the external partner agencies. He said:

> Well, we're not a corporation. We are a creative company. Unless we create, we've got nothing. Creativity is inherently a risk, if that's what you want to call it. I don't want to call it that because I believe it isn't a risk. Our hit rate at the time of the development of this blockbuster was a good bet. Typically, if you talk with our main competitor, their hit rate is one in three or four. If you talk to others in our industry, their hit rate is one in ten. For us, it was seven in ten. Why, I don't know. Maybe we were more talented or we did

few products giving us more time and attention for each, but I think we were probably less executive about our work and much more creative . . . blokes in offices might see things as good ideas, but actually what we've been talking about is not about executives. It's not an executive that's directly involved in creating blockbusters. It's the same in the film and music business. You don't get great groups with briefcases and ties and offices and nine o'clock in the morning stuff. Film directors don't do that, art directors don't do that, no one out there who produced anything we want does it.

The quality and access to the external environment was also important for the development of blockbusters. Since ideas for blockbusters can come from a variety of internal and external sources, it was helpful to use the business concept and strategy as a springboard to guide the search while remaining open to new formats, features, content and approaches. Another point our participants made rather emphatically was the centrality of staying close to consumers. Many of those we interviewed pointed out how important is was for them to keep the voice of the customer close to their development work. The environment had to allow for some surprises along the way and a great deal of freedom to pursue insights from within and outside the team.

A recent review of the research on innovative climates confirmed that a number of factors contribute to project success: inspirational communication, intellectual stimulation, a high quality leader–member exchange (LMX) and boundary-spanning activities.[22] The boundary-spanning and championing roles are critical inside and outside the organization. The value of this role depends on the kinds of exposure and interactions that take place. In social network theory, the strength of the relationship between two people, or the 'tie' between them, is a function of the amount of interaction, emotional intensity and reciprocity. Social network theory and research predicts that weak ties are better than strong ties for creativity. This is because weak ties are more likely to connect two very different networks, and other links between the two networks are much less likely, whereas stronger ties are likely to indicate less diversity, more social pressure to conform and greater redundancy in the individual relationships between members of the two groups. In contrast, weak ties tend to connect people with diverse perspectives and knowledge.

Typically, much of the basis of innovation lies at a system level involving networks of internal and external suppliers and partners configuring knowledge and other resources to create a radically new offering. Discontinuous innovation is often problematic because it may involve building and working with a significantly different set of partners than those the firm is accustomed to working with. Whereas 'strong ties' – close and consistent relationships with regular partners in a network – may be important in enabling a steady stream of continuous improvement innovations, evidence suggests that where firms are seeking to do something different they need to exploit much weaker ties across a very different population in order to gain access to new ideas and different sources of knowledge and expertise.[23] Therefore, a peripheral position in the network combined with boundary-spanning ties with many connections outside of the network is more likely to result in greater creativity and more radical innovation as it provides exposure to a wider range of people and information than a more central position.[24]

We will deal further with the environment, culture and climate for creativity, innovation and transformation in Chapters 11, 12 and 13.

Implications and conclusion

If you want to develop blockbuster products and services, you will need to attend to all four elements of the change system. You must be clear about the desired outcome, at least in terms of what needs to be done to meet consumers' needs and kind of creativity you desire as a result. Lynn and Reilly called the specific elements in the desired outcome 'project pillars'. You will need to establish and manage a deliberate process that promotes cross-functional teamwork, and integrate the practices outlined above. The right people must be on the team and they need to be supported by appropriate leadership and sponsorship. The working environment must support the people and the process. The climate within the team is critical, but a broader organizational climate conducive to creativity and change is optimal.

Once again, only paying attention to one element of the system will decrease the likelihood of success. Only focusing on the outcome and ignoring the people, context and method will not encourage the development of blockbuster services or products. There are no guarantees that following the suggestions in this chapter will produce a blockbuster, but if these elements are not managed well, your chances of success will be much lower.

Much of the research summarized in this chapter has dealt with companies that produce concrete products for the market. We would assert that the insights gleaned from this research would be applicable to any kind of organization seeking to produce outcomes that can change the way they work and how they contribute to the marketplace. For example, in our study of 108 service firms in the UK and USA, we found that a strategy of rapid, reiterative redevelopment (RRR) was associated with higher levels of new service development success and higher service quality.[25] This approach to new service development combines many of the benefits of the polar extremes of radical and incremental innovation, but with lower costs and risks. This strategy is less disruptive to internal functional relationships than infrequent radical service innovations, and encourages knowledge transfer and reuse.

For example, in 1995 the American Express Travel Service Group implemented a strategy of RRR. In the previous decade, the group had introduced only two new service products. In 1995, a vice-president of product development was created, cross-functional teams were established, a formal development process adopted, and computer tools, including prototyping and simulation, were deployed. Since then, the group has developed and launched more than 80 new service offerings, and has become the market leader.

References

1. Ranganath Nayak, P. & Ketteringham, J.M. (1986) *Breakthroughs! How the Vision and Drive of Innovators in Sixteen Companies Created Commercial Breakthroughs that Swept the World.* New York: Rawson Associates, pp. 345–346.
2. Belliveau, P., Griffin, A. & Somermeyer, S. (2002) *The PDMA Toolbook for New Product Development.* New York: John Wiley & Sons, Inc.
3. Cooper, R.G. (2005) Your NPD portfolio may be harmful to your business's health. *PDMA Visions*, 29: 22–26.
4. Koen, P.A., Ajamian, G.M., Boyce, S. *et al.* (2002) Fuzzy front end: effective methods, tools and techniques. In *The PDMA Toolbook* (eds P. Belliveau, A. Griffin & S. Somermeyer), pp. 5–35.
5. Stefik, M. & Stefik, B. (2004) *Stories and Strategies of Radical Innovation Breakthrough.* Cambridge, MA: MIT Press.
6. Besemer, S.P. (1998) Creative product analysis matrix: testing the model structure and a comparison among products. *Creativity Research Journal*, 11: 333–346. Besemer, S.P. (2000) Creative product analysis to foster innovation. *Design Management Journal*, Fall, pp. 59–64.
7. Lynn, G.S. & Reilly, R.R. (2002) *Blockbusters: The Five Keys to Developing Great New Products.* New York: HarperBusiness, p. 207.
8. Rafferty, A.E. & Griffin, M.A. (2004) Dimensions of transformational leadership: conceptual and empirical extensions, *Leadership Quarterly*, 15(3): 329–354.
9. Pinto, J. & Slevin, D. (1989) Critical success factors in R&D projects, *Research-Technology Management*, 32: 12–18.
10. West, M.A., Borrill, C.S., Dawson, J.F. *et al.* (2003) Leadership clarity and team innovation in health care, *Leadership Quarterly*, 14(4–5): 393–410.

11. Chortatsiani, E. (2003) Product development in financial services: picking the right leader for success. In *Service Innovation: Organizational Responses to Technological Opportunities and Market Imperatives* (eds J. Tidd & F. Hull). London: Imperial College Press.

12. Tidd, J. & Bodley, K. (2002) The affect of project novelty on the new product development process. *R&D Management*, 32(2): 127–138.

13. Morrison, P.D., Roberts, J.H. & Midgley, D.F. (2004) The nature of lead users and measurement of leading edge status. *Research Policy*, 33: 351–362.

14. Callahan, J. & Lasry, E. (2004) The importance of customer input in the development of very new products. *R&D Management*, 34(2): 107–117.

15. Kelly, T. (2002) *The Art of Innovation: Lessons in Creativity from IDEO*. New York: HarperCollinsBusiness.

16. Rossman, J. (1931) *The Psychology of the Inventor: A Study of the Patentee*. Washington, DC: The Inventors Publishing Company.

17. Amabile, T.M. (1996) *Creativity in Context: Update to the Social Psychology of Creativity*. Boulder, CO: Westview Press.

18. Arieti, S. (1976) *Creativity: The Magic Synthesis*. New York: Basic Books. Barron, F. & Harrington, D.M. (1981) Creativity, intelligence and personality. *Annual Review of Psychology*, 32: 439–476. Maslow, A.H. (1959) Creativity in self-actualizing people. In *Creativity and its Cultivation* (ed H.H. Anderson), pp. 83–95. New York: Harper. Selby, E.C., Shaw, E.J. & Houtz, J.C. (2005) The creative personality. *Gifted Child Quarterly*, 49: 300–314. Ward, T.B., Smith, S.M. & Vaid, J. (1997) *Creative Thought: An Investigation of Conceptual Structures and Processes*. Washington, DC: American Psychological Association.

19. MacKinnon, D.W. (1978) *In Search of Human Effectiveness: Identifying and Developing Creativity*. Buffalo, NY: Creative Education Foundation, p. 186.

20. Stevens, G. & Burley, J. (2003) Piloting the rocket of radical innovation – selecting the right people for the right roles dramatically improves the effectiveness of business development. *Research Technology Management*, March–April, pp. 16–25.

21. Stevens, G., Burley, J. & Swogger, K. (2003) Dow Chemical achieves major transformation of PO&E R&D group: personality oriented approach improves NPD results. *PDMA Visions*, 27: 6–10.

22. Elkins, T. & Keller, R.T. (2003) Leadership in research and development organizations: a literature review and conceptual framework, *Leadership Quarterly*, 14(4–5): 587–606.

23. Philips, W., Lamming, R., Bessant, J. & Noke, H. (2004) *Promiscuous Relationships: Discontinuous Innovation and the Role of Supply Networks*. In *IPSERA Conference*. Naples, Italy.

24. Perry-Smith, J.E. & Shalley, C.E. (2003) The social side of creativity: a static and dynamic social network perspective. *Academy of Management Review*, 2891: 89–106.

25. Tidd, J. & Hull, F.M. (eds) (2003) *Service Innovation: Organizational Responses to Technological Opportunities and Market Imperatives*. London: Imperial College Press.

Part 2

THE PART PEOPLE PLAY

Chapter 5

LEADING AND MANAGING FOR TRANSFORMATION

the fundamental purpose of management is to keep the current system functioning. The fundamental purpose of leadership is to produce useful change, especially non-incremental change[1]

Introduction

Leading and managing others is one of the most important aspects when it comes to guiding and engaging people in systemic change. Certain types and styles of leadership and influence have a clear impact on creativity, innovation and transformation.[2]

The purpose of this chapter is to provide you with a summary of the major historical approaches to understanding leadership as well as the emerging and contemporary approaches to this topic. This provides you with a foundation for exploring the major issues and challenges facing those who lead and manage for transformation, innovation and creativity.

We offer a model for creative leadership that links leadership and management in the context of change and transformation. Change and transformation imply doing something in a new way. Creativity is all about newness that is useful and involves an awareness of people, method, desired outcome or result, as well as place or context. Innovation is the conversion of new and useful ideas and concepts into something of commercial or social value. Leadership and management are critical influence factors on all of these acts and behaviors.

Historical approaches to leadership

Leadership is a sophisticated concept and its study is an ancient art. There are numerous discussions from the classical era from thinkers like Plato, Caesar and Plutarch.

The Chinese classics, Egyptians and Greeks also provided insight into the question of defining leadership. The *Oxford English Dictionary* notes the appearance of the word 'leader' in the English language as early as 1300, but notes that the word 'leadership' did not appear until the first half of the 19th century. We believe that this reflects our early interest in the person, as opposed to a later interest in the behavior associated with leadership.

The contribution that leaders make to the performance of their organizations can be significant. Upper echelons theory argues that decisions and choices by top management have an influence on the performance of an organization (positive or negative!), through their assessment of the environment, strategic decision-making and support for innovation. The results of different studies vary, but the reviews of research on leadership and performance suggest that leadership directly influences around 15% of the differences found in performance of businesses, and contributes around an additional 35% through the choice of business strategy.[3] So directly and indirectly, leadership can account for half of the variance in performance observed across organizations.

The mechanism through which leaders can influence performance include strategic decision-making, often made under conditions of ambiguity and complexity, with limited information. At higher levels of management the problems to be solved are more likely to be ill-defined, demanding leaders to conceptualize more. While demographic indicators such as age, tenure and education are not good predictors of top management performance, psychological indicators have a better record of predicting performance.

There are as many different definitions of leadership as there are people who have attempted to study the concept, leading one prominent writer to indicate that leadership is one of the most observed and least understood phenomena on earth.[4]

Despite the many differences in defining leadership, it is possible to identify at least three main approaches to understanding the concept. We prefer to call these approaches one-, two- and multidimensional. These refer to a rather simplistic but potentially useful description or summary of the major historical approaches to studying leadership.

One-dimensional approaches

One-dimensional approaches to studying leadership have focused on identifying the specific traits and characteristics of leaders. The precursor to this approach was the 'great man' theory of leadership that was based on the idea that heroes and great leaders were endowed with unique qualities that captured the imagination of the masses. The efforts of researchers following this tradition have been aimed at uncovering the basic determinants of effective leadership by examining the internal qualities that must be present in the individual.

This historical one-dimensional approach is reminiscent of the search for the Holy Grail. The research of Stodgill and others[5] clearly indicated that it was next to impossible to devise a single and short list of predictors of highly effective leaders. Instead, researchers were able to identify a long list of characteristics that might have something to do with being effective in certain situations.[6] These lists usually included characteristics like 'leaders are':

- Bright, alert and intelligent;
- Those who seek responsibility and take charge;
- Skillful in their task domain;
- Administratively and socially competent;
- Energetic, active and resilient;
- Good communicators.

Although these lists may describe some characteristics of some leaders in certain situations, measures of these traits yield highly inconsistent relationships with being a good leader.[7] In short, there is no short and universal list of enduring traits that all good leaders must possess.

Two-dimensional approaches

Researchers who took a two-dimensional approach changed their locus of attention from stable traits within the individual toward the actual behavior of leaders. Their aim was to discover the pattern of leadership behavior that leads to effective group performance. Questionnaires were developed by researchers to have respondents describe their leaders by the frequency with which they displayed specified behaviors.[8] These ratings were analyzed and fell into four main factors.[9] The two factors that accounted for the bulk of leader behavior were called *consideration* and *initiation of structure*. These factors were supported by the Ohio State[10] and Michigan[11] studies.

Consideration included behavior items concerned with friendliness, openness of communication with subordinates, recognition of contributions, leader supportiveness, and other items related to establishing and maintaining good relationships with subordinates. Consideration, as a leadership factor, has to do with paying attention to people and human relations.

Initiating structure included behaviors concerned with directing subordinates, clarifying roles, planning and other task-oriented behaviors related to the efficient use of resources and attaining the task goals. The initiating structure factor focuses on a leader's concern for getting the work done.

These two basic dimensions have been referred to in a variety of ways, as: employee-centered versus production-centered, concern for people versus concern for production, supportive versus directive behavior, and group maintenance versus task-related activities. This two-dimensional approach is represented by the managerial grid promoted by Blake and Mouton (Figure 5.1).[12]

Whatever these two basic dimensions of leadership behavior are called, one of the major challenges with this approach is the perception that it is necessary to be high on both scales. Indeed, this perception was supported by research.[13] The drawback is that you may be led to believe that there might be one best style for all situations. This case is still being argued in the leadership literature and can be observed in many practical situations.

Studies in different contexts identify not only the technical expertise of leadership influencing group performance but also broader cognitive ability, such as creative problem-solving and information-processing skills. For example, studies of groups facing novel, ill-defined problems confirm that both expertise and cognitive processing skills are key components of creative leadership, and are both associated with effective performance of creative groups.[14] Moreover, this combination of expertise and cognitive capacity is critical for the evaluation of others' ideas. A study of scientists found that they most valued their leaders' inputs at the early stages of a new project, when they were formulating their ideas and defining the problems, and later, at the stage where they needed feedback and insights to the implications of their work. Therefore, a key role of creative leadership in such environments is to provide feedback and evaluation, rather than to simply generate ideas.[15] This evaluative role is critical, but is typically seen as not being conducive to creativity and innovation, where the conventional advice is to suspend judgment to foster idea generation. Also, it suggests that the conventional linear view that evaluation follows idea generation may be wrong. Evaluation by creative leadership may precede idea generation and conceptual combination.

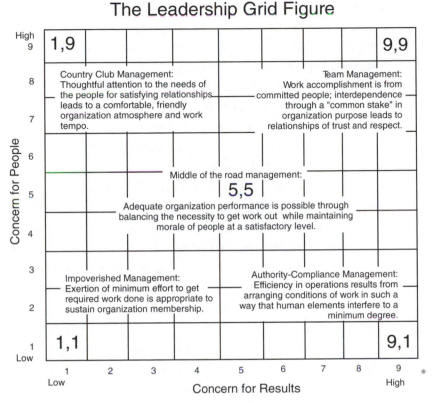

Figure 5.1 Blake and Mouton's managerial grid
Source: Blake, R.R. & Mouton, J.S. (1985) *The Managerial Grid III: The Key to Leadership Excellence*. Houston, TX: Gulf Publications. Reproduced by permission.

Multidimensional approaches

The center of attention for the multidimensional or contingency approach to studying leaders was viewing leadership through an increasingly complex set of considerations. There have been a variety of multidimensional approaches including: situational leadership, Fiedler's contingency model, Vroom and Yetton's contingency model and the path-goal theory.

The starting point of the *situational approaches* was that different contexts required different leadership functions to be performed. Leaders were seen as needing to fulfill different functions in situations with different tasks. The situational approaches emphasized the leader's qualities and behaviors that were appropriate to a group in a specific situation. One popular situational leadership approach emphasized the readiness or developmental level of followers as a key factor in determining the appropriate style to be applied.[16]

For example, Ehrhart and Klein[17] found that the orientation of followers influences their preference for different leadership types, and those with intrinsic work values such as responsibility, challenge and initiative prefer to work under a charismatic leader, whereas workers who take a more instrumental approach to work as a means of extrinsic reward, do not. However, followers' values and achievement orientation are only moderately related to a preference for charismatic leadership over relationship- or task-orientated leadership. This suggests that follower characteristics are much more than simply dependent variables influenced by leadership, or even moderators, but rather a reciprocal relationship (similar to the leader–member exchange approach). In this way, the selection and decision of whether or not to follow a leader becomes more active, based on the extent to which the leader is perceived to represent the interests and values of followers.

The quality and nature of the leader–member exchange (LMX) has been found to influence the creativity of subordinates.[18] A study of 238 knowledge workers from 26 project teams in high-technology firms identified a number of positive aspects of LMX, including monitoring, clarifying and consulting, but also found that the frequency of negative LMX were as high as the positive, around a third of respondents reporting these.[19] Therefore, LMX can either enhance or undermine subordinates' sense of competence and self-determination. However, analysis of exchanges perceived to be negative and positive revealed that it was typically *how* something was done rather than *what* was done, which suggests that task and relationship behaviors in leadership support and LMX are intimately intertwined, and that negative behaviors can have a disproportionate negative influence.

One of the challenges with the situational approach was that it centered on task differences and followers' level of readiness to engage in these tasks to the exclusion of many other important variables in the context. Those involved in the situational approach gave little attention to the processes of leader–follower relations over time.[20] The approach paved the way for more complex approaches to understanding leadership. Examples of these more complex approaches include the Bass transactional/transformational typology, Fiedler's contingency model, Vroom and Yetton's model for leadership styles and decision-making, and the path-goal theory.

Within the *Bass transactional/transformational typology* a distinction made is between a task orientation and a people orientation, and transformation versus transactional leadership.[21] This suggests that leadership styles can be positioned on some scale of leader proactiveness, ranging from avoidance or laissez-faire at the bottom of the range, through transactional somewhere in the middle, to transformational at the top. Others identify a focus on personal values and standards, so-called 'ideological' leadership, and a focus on social needs and requirements for change, or 'charismatic' leadership.[22] Most argue that innovation and creativity are associated with transformation leadership qualities.[23]

Leadership style is said to be either *transactional* or *transformational*. A transactional style is a 'mutual influence between leaders and followers' working on the basis of 'a reciprocal exchange relationship of costs and benefits'.[24] Decision-making takes place in a stable and certain framework where bureaucratic authority, formal rules, regulation, procedures and legitimate power are all visible and regularly exercised. The basis for guiding work is exchange, such as work done for money, security or other rewards but also effort, responsibility, honesty and fairness. Transformational leadership, on the other hand, is based not on physical rewards but on motivation. It works through a process in which leaders and followers raise one another to higher levels of morality and motivation. Transformational leaders often initiate and implement changes in the structure and strategy of the business and to people, challenging and changing the core beliefs, culture, structure and strategy, outcomes, careers, products and markets of the company and sometimes an organization from one design archetype to another (organizational transformations). Transformational leadership formulates, defines and restates overall values, vision and mission, strategic directions and organizational forms; it empowers and mobilizes commitment to new directions, energizes people in action.

Bass[25] considered charisma (later renamed 'influence'), intellectual stimulation, inspired motivation and individual consideration to be significant components of the construct of transformational leadership and, while there is limited empirical support for the effectiveness of the transformational leadership style in total, there is significant support for some of its sub-dimensions under certain conditions. For example, charismatic leadership, which includes a sense of mission, articulating a future-oriented, inspirational vision based on powerful imagery, values and beliefs, might be expected to be highly predictive of organizational performance under conditions of perceived environmental uncertainty. Research indicates that charismatic leadership does influence performance, but equally under all environmental conditions, with no interaction with uncertainty.[26] Innovation champions provide enthusiastic support for new ideas and relate the innovation to a variety of positive organizational outcomes by using their informal networks to promote the innovation throughout the organization.[27] However, they do not need to get directly involved in developing ideas.

However, intellectual stimulation by leaders has a stronger effect on organizational performance under conditions of perceived uncertainty. Intellectual stimulation is the most underdeveloped component of transformational leadership, and includes behaviors that increase others' awareness of and interest in problems, and develops their propensity and ability to tackle problems in new ways. It is also associated with commitment to an organization.[28] Stratified system theory (SST) focuses on the cognitive aspects of leadership, and argues that conceptual capacity is associated with superior performance in strategic decision-making where there is a need to integrate complex information and think abstractly in order to assess the environment. It also is likely to demand a combination of these problem-solving capabilities and social skills, as leaders will depend upon others to identify and implement solutions.[29] This suggests that under conditions of environmental uncertainty, the contribution of transformational leadership is not simply, or even primarily, to inspire or build confidence, but rather to solve problems and make appropriate strategic decisions.

Rafferty and Griffin[30] propose other sub-dimensions to the concept of transformational leadership that may have a greater influence on creativity and innovation, including articulating a vision and inspirational communication. They define a vision as 'the expression of an idealized picture of the future based around organizational values', and inspirational communication as 'the expression of positive and encouraging messages about the organization, and statements that build motivation and confidence'. They found that the expression of a vision has a negative effect on followers' confidence, unless accompanied with inspirational communication. Independent of vision, inspirational communication was associated with RBSE (role breadth self-efficacy), commitment and interpersonal helping behaviors. Mission awareness, associated with transformational leadership, has been found to predict the success of R&D projects, the degree to which depends on the stage of the project. For example, in the planning and conceptual stage, mission awareness explained 67% of the subsequent project success.[31] Leadership clarity is associated with clear team objectives, high levels of participation, commitment to excellence and support for innovation.[32] Leadership clarity, partly mediated by good team processes, is a good predictor of team innovation. The effects are significant, with good team processes predicting up to 37% of the variance in team innovation, and clarity of leadership 17%. Conversely, a lack of clarity about or over leadership is negatively associated with team innovation. This suggests that the tendency to focus on the style of leadership may be premature, and that the initial focus should be on maximizing leadership clarity and minimizing leadership conflict, which appears to be critical in all cases. The specific style of leadership, however, is more contingent upon the team context and nature of task.

Chortatsiani[33] examined the effects of different leadership styles on the success of routine and more novel innovation in financial services. She found that a transformational approach was a significant factor in determining the success of the more novel service innovations, much more so than a transactional style. One interpretation is simply that transformational leaders are better at selecting the projects that have a greater chance of success, or that they are better at negotiating which projects they will assume responsibility for. More likely, however, is that the more novel innovation projects require skills not possessed by transactional leaders. For example, the study showed that the differences in the success of the more novel projects was not the result of differences in the *amount* of involvement of the transformational or transactional leaders, but rather the *type* of involvement. Conversely, for the more routine development projects, transformational leaders were found to delegate more of their responsibilities than transactional leaders. This may be because the transformational leaders find the tasks involved in the more routine development projects lack interest, or that they believe they can add little by getting directly involved. Looser control, or delegation of the work to teams, in such cases, leads to accelerated product development. Transactional leaders can be more effective when they have to work and operate in a more stable organizational environment or when they have to deal with low-risk activities rather than with major innovations that entail high risks.

The creative leader needs to do much more than simply provide a passive, supportive role, to encourage creative followers. Perceptual measures of leaders' performance suggest that in a research environment the perception of a leader's technical skill is the single best predictor of research group performance, with correlation in the 0.40–0.53 range.[34] Keller[35] found that the type of project moderates the relationships between leadership style and project success, and found that transformational leadership was a stronger predictor in research projects than in development projects. This strongly suggests that certain qualities of transformational leadership may be most appropriate under conditions of high complexity, uncertainty or novelty. Indeed, studies comparing the effects of leadership styles in research and administrative environments have found that transformational leadership has a greater impact on performance in a research environment than in an administrative one, although the effect is positive in both cases; whereas, a transactional style has a positive effect in the administrative context, but a negative effect in the research context.[36]

Experimental work indicates that transformational leadership can enhance motivation and empowerment of direct followers, and increase their level of development, but not necessarily their internalization of values or active engagement.[37] In addition, transformational leadership also has a positive effect on the performance of indirect followers. The processes that influence direct and indirect followers are different, and over time result in different outcomes. In general, the initial developmental level of followers predicts the ratings of transformational leadership, but for direct followers these decline over time, and increase over time for indirect followers.[38] This suggests that transformational leadership is not an inherent trait, but can change over time by direct leader–follower relations.

Fiedler's contingency model was based on the idea that the performance of a group or an organization depends on the degree to which the leader's personality matched the requirements of the leadership situation.[39] Certain types of individuals are primarily motivated to seek close interpersonal relations, while others are primarily motivated by the esteem that comes from accomplishing a task. The degree to which the situation provides the leader with control and influence is determined by three dimensions: leader–member relations, task structure and position power.

Vroom and Yetton[40] offered another contingency model that was concerned with factors affecting decision-making and organizational leadership. The point was to specify particular styles of decision-making called forth by various situational factors. They offered three main leadership styles including: autocratic, consultative and group-oriented. These three styles can yield different levels of effectiveness based on the three criteria of quality of solution, time required to arrive at it and acceptance of it by subordinates. The model also considered situational factors including: the importance of decision quality; the degree to which the needed information is available to the leader and to followers; the degree to which the problem is structured; and how much subordinate acceptance is probable and critical to implementing the solution. A revised version of the model expanded the number and kind of problem attributes to be considered in making choices about leadership behavior.[41]

The *path-goal theory* was originally proposed by Evans[42] and later extended by House.[43] According to this theory, the leader's function is to define a path along which the followers expend effort to achieve a group goal. Followers can be guided to do things that they believe will produce satisfying outcomes. The leader's motivational function is to increase the number and kinds of personal payoffs to followers for attaining goals. The leader makes the paths to these payoffs easier to travel by clearly pointing them out, reducing the barriers, and increasing opportunities for the satisfaction of the followers. The path-goal theory encompasses four categories of leader behavior[44] including: supportive, directive, participative and achievement-oriented leadership. The other contingencies include the personal characteristics of the followers (such as degree of authoritarianism, internal or external control, etc.) and the environmental and task demands the subordinates face (such as the degree of structure or amount of challenge inherent in the goal).

The three major approaches (one-, two- and multidimensional) to understanding leadership have provided the major foundation for continuing research and development. There are, however, a number of more recent developments within the field that offer much promise for those within organizations who are facing the innovation and transformation challenge.

Contemporary approaches to leadership

Current researchers, writers and consultants are building on the rich historical work and making new contributions to our understanding of leadership. Some important thinkers are returning to the major lessons of the past and examining them for relevance and completeness. They are also renewing their concern for applying their new insights to the practices and behaviors within ever changing organizations. These more contemporary approaches to leadership include a focus on strategies and practices, as well as the discovery of a new dimension for leadership behavior.

Bennis and Nanus – leadership strategies

In offering a new theory of leadership, Bennis and Nanus[45] suggested that we examine the leadership context that includes commitment, complexity and credibility. They also suggested that one of the main problems with the historical view of leadership was that it ignored the importance of power. Power is the basic energy needed to initiate and sustain action or the capacity to translate intention into reality and then sustain it. They saw leadership as the wise use of power.

As a result of interviewing 90 successful leaders (CEOs, corporate presidents or board chairmen, and 30 from the public sector) who were working to achieve mastery over the present confusion their organizations were facing, Bennis and Nanus[46] identified four main themes. These four themes were distinct areas of competency or human-handling skills that all 90 leaders embodied. These strategies included managing attention through vision, meaning through communication, trust through positioning, and the creative deployment of self.

Bennis and Nanus described effective leaders as capable of deploying their ideas and themselves in a way that created more exposure and risk than others. This is transformative leadership[47] and is described as leaders who can shape and elevate the motives and goals of followers. According to Bennis and Nanus:

> Transformative leadership achieves significant change that reflects the community of interests of both leaders and followers; indeed, it frees up and pools the collective energies in pursuit of a common goal.

Kouzes and Posner – leadership practices

Kouzes and Posner[48] were concerned about how leaders get extraordinary things done within organizations. Their work is about the practices leaders use to turn challenging opportunities into remarkable successes. After conducting a large-scale research program that included analyzing thousands of surveys, case studies and interviews surrounding experiences that led a group to achieve some extraordinary accomplishment, they found some interesting similarities across much of their data. The stories that these leaders told revealed a consistent pattern of behavior.

More than 70% of the behaviors identified from their research were described by five practices. Each of the five leadership practices consists of two basic strategies. The first practice is that leaders who accomplish extraordinary things challenge the process. This means they search for opportunities and experiment and take risks. The kinds of behaviors associated with these strategies include: seeking challenges, staying up to date, challenging the status quo, looking for ways to innovate, and experimenting and taking risks.

The second practice is inspiring a shared vision by envisioning the future and enlisting the support of others. Effective leaders frequently describe a desired future that we can create together. They share their future dreams and communicate a positive outlook for their future together.

The third practice is enabling others to act, including fostering collaboration and strengthening others. The behaviors related to this practice include involving others in planning, treating others with respect, allowing others to make decisions, developing cooperative relationships and creating an atmosphere of trust.

The fourth practice is modeling the way and it includes setting an example and planning small wins. The kinds of behaviors leaders demonstrate here include: being clear about their own philosophy of leadership, breaking projects into smaller steps, assuring that the values are adhered to, letting others know about beliefs and values, and setting clear goals and milestones.

The final practice is encouraging the heart and it consists of recognizing contributions and celebrating accomplishments. To encourage the heart, leaders celebrate milestones, recognize the contributions of others, give praise for a job well done, give the team appreciation and support, find ways to celebrate and tell others about the group's work.

Kouzes and Posner's work has become increasingly popular and they have broadened the conception of leadership from being about a select few at the top of the organizational hierarchy, to being everyone's business. Further, they have pointed out the centrality of the quality of the relationship between leaders and their constituents as the core context to examine the potential for transformation.

Ekvall's leadership and change

The classic two-dimensional model of leadership has been widely accepted and grew out of research in relatively stable contexts. The 1970s and 1980s have ushered in a new era characterized by changing markets and increased need for organizational transformation. Ekvall and his colleagues have demonstrated, in a series of studies, the appearance of a new dimension for leadership behavior.[49] Their research confirms the existence of the two well-established dimensions, which they call production-centered and employee-centered leadership. The new third dimension deals with change and development and includes a focus on: offering ideas about new and different ways of doing things; pushing for growth; initiating new projects; experimenting with new ways of doing things; and thinking about and planning for the future (Figure 5.2).

This third dimension of leadership behavior is supported by Nanus, who asserts that leaders of today need to be highly skilled in anticipating the future. Further, he stated:

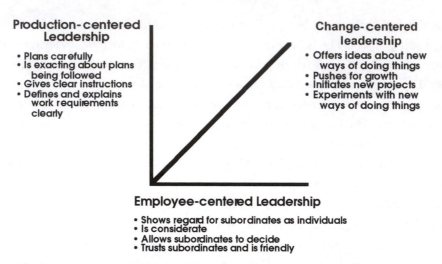

Production-centered Leadership
- Plans carefully
- Is exacting about plans being followed
- Gives clear instructions
- Defines and explains work requirements clearly

Change-centered leadership
- Offers ideas about new ways of doing things
- Pushes for growth
- Initiates new projects
- Experiments with new ways of doing things

Employee-centered Leadership
- Shows regard for subordinates as individuals
- Is considerate
- Allows subordinates to decide
- Trusts subordinates and is friendly

Figure 5.2 Ekvall & Arvonen's change-centered leadership model
Source: Ekvall & Arvonen (1991) and (1994).[49] Reproduced with permission.

Leaders take charge, make things happen, dream dreams and then translate them into reality. Leaders attract the voluntary commitment of followers, energize them, and transform organizations into new entities with greater potential for survival, growth and excellence. Effective leadership empowers an organization to maximize its contribution to the well being of its members and the larger society of which it is a part. If managers are known for their skills in solving problems, then leaders are known for being masters in designing and building institutions; they are the architects of the organization's future.[50]

Similarly, Sternberg and his colleagues[51] suggest a typology of creative leadership that consists of three broad leadership styles: those that accept existing ways of doing things, those that challenge existing ways of doing things, and those that synthesize different ways of doing things. Therefore, typical management models developed to help explain and prescribe leadership in routine or more normative contexts are unlikely to be relevant or effective in more novel and uncertain environments.

These more contemporary approaches to examining leadership provide an emerging view of leadership taking place within increasing complexity, ambiguity and novelty.[52] One of the challenges leaders have in dealing with change under these conditions is unleashing creativity.

Servant leadership

Following the seminal writings of Robert Greenleaf, the concept of the servant as leader seems to gaining some momentum.[53] Having worked as director of management research at AT&T he considered himself a lifelong student of how things get done in large complex organizations. Greenleaf's central idea is that great leaders must first serve others. True creative leadership emerges from those whose primary motivation is a desire to help others.

This approach to leadership is being adopted by a variety of for-profit and nonprofit organizations as a long-term transformational approach to life and work.

Collins' level-five leadership

Jim Collins, and his colleagues, started by studying 18 premier and admired companies that made an imprint on the world, which had multiple generations of chief executives, and had been founded before 1950. Each of these visionary companies was compared with one of its competitors. The results of the six-year study were published in *Built to Last*. One of the key contributions of the study was the finding that companies that were successful in the long term knew what they could and should change and things that needed to remain constant. But the companies in this first study were already great. The question remained, 'How do good companies turn themselves into great companies?'

This question was addressed in the second major research effort and the findings were published in *Good to Great*.[54] Although Collins did not want to set out to study leadership (he had given explicit instructions to downplay the role of top executives), it came up quite clearly as a factor when good companies make a transformation into great companies. The *Good to Great* study included 11 companies that made it through a long set of criteria and numerous comparison companies. In every one of the good-to-great companies they found a leader that created superb results, had unwavering resolve to produce the best long-term outcomes and possessed a compelling modesty, acted with calm determination, and channeled ambition into the organization. This unique combination of personal humility with professional will made up the highest level in a hierarchy of executive capabilities that Collins identified in the research.

The hierarchy starts with highly capable individuals who make productive contributions through their talents, knowledge, skills and good work habits. The next level is contributing team members who add their individual capabilities to the achievement of group goals and work together well with other team members. The next level is the competent manager. At this level, the competent manager organizes people and resources toward the efficient pursuit of organizational objectives. The effective leader is at the fourth level. The effective leader generates commitment to and energy for a clear and compelling vision and stimulates high performance standards. It is the level five leader who builds enduring greatness through a paradoxical blend of humility and will. No matter when the transition took place, how big the organization, whether it was a consumer or industrial company, all the good-to-great companies had a level five leader (and the comparison companies did not).

The literature on leadership and change is booming. There are thousands of books available for those who have an interest in leadership and change. In addition, the published literature in academic journals is also flourishing. Given this expansive interest in the topic, we are observing a number of critical issues. The first major issue is the current status of the relationship between leadership and management.

Leading versus managing

A recent review of the research and literature on the management of innovation and change concluded that:

> much of the folklore and applied literature on the management of innovation has ignored the research by cognitive psychologists and social psychologists . . . as a consequence, one often gets an impression that . . . innovators have superhuman creative heuristics or abilities to 'walk on water'.[55]

Organizations have traditionally conceived of leadership as a heroic attribute, appointing a few 'real' leaders to high-level senior positions in order to get them through difficult times. However, many observers and researchers are becoming cynical about this approach and are beginning to think about the need to recognize and utilize a wider range of leadership practices. Leadership needs to be conceived of as something that happens across functions and levels. New concepts and frameworks are needed in order to embrace this more inclusive approach to leadership.

For example, there is a great deal of writing about the fundamental difference between leadership and management. This literature abounds and has generally promoted the argument that leaders have vision and think creatively ('doing different'), while managers are merely drones and just focus on improving productivity or quality ('doing better'). This distinction has led to a general devaluation of management. Emerging work on styles of creativity and management suggests that it is useful to keep preference distinct from capacity. Creativity is present both when doing things differently and doing things better. This means that leadership and management may be two constructs on a continuum, rather than two opposing characteristics.

There are numerous examples we can use to illustrate this tension. Some literature points out that leaders should inspire risk-taking while managers tend to avoid risk-taking.[56] Others point out that leaders focus on developing strategy that fits the organizational context while managers gently 'tweak' the existing system.[57] The general thrust from much of the literature characterizes leadership as more important than management. Leaders look outward. Managers look inward. Leaders take initiative and confront the established order, managers maintain order and seek control. Some writers assert that leaders set the organizational context while managers merely plan and execute.[58]

Some dispute the image that leaders focus on only the strategic issues and managers handle the tactical implementation of those issues. In outlining the importance of execution as a way to identify and close the gap between what a company's leaders want to achieve and the ability of their organization to achieve it, Larry Bossidy and Ram Charan pointed out the potential damage of thinking about leading and managing as either-or:

> Lots of business leaders like to think that the top dog is exempt from the details of actually running things. It's a pleasant way to view leadership: you stand on the mountaintop, thinking strategically and attempting to inspire your people with visions, while managers do the grunt work. This idea creates a lot of aspirations for leadership, naturally. Who wouldn't want to have all the fun and glory while keeping their hands clean? Conversely, who wants to tell people at a cocktail party, 'My goal is to be a manager,' in an era when the term has become almost pejorative? This way of thinking is a fallacy, one that creates immense damage.[59]

Although there is inherent tension between these two topics, effective transformation and innovation will require a reasonable integration of these interdependent roles. Risk-taking will only be acceptable if people are both inspired and clear expectations are established and reinforced. Strategy must be developed and modified as new challenges and opportunities surface. Both leaders and managers must look inside and

Doing things right	AND	Doing the right things
Management		**Leadership**
• Short-term, day-to-day tactics		• Long-term, strategic horizon
• Cool, aloof, analytic		• Inspiration, passion, caring
• Deal with stability and certainty		• Deal with turbulence, uncertainty
• Direct, administer and control		• Influence, serve and support
• Do things better		• Do things differently
• Transactional		• Transformational

Figure 5.3 Management and leadership

outside. Transformation will require both leaders and managers to take initiative and provide balancing structure. As you can see in Figure 5.3, our experience and research supports an integrative approach rather than an 'either-or' approach.

Our particular emphasis is on resolving the unnecessary and unproductive distinction that is made between leadership and management. When it comes to innovation and transformation, organizations need both sets of skills. We develop a model of innovation leadership that builds on past work, but adds some recent perspectives from the fields of change and innovation management, and personality and social psychology. This multidimensional view of leadership raises the issue of context as an important factor, beyond concern for task and people. This approach suggests the need for a third factor in assessing leadership behavior, in addition to the traditional concerns for task and people. Therefore, we integrate three dimensions of leadership: concern for task, concern for people and concern for change.

Challenges of leading and managing change

A recent A. D. Little study surveyed 350 top executives from 14 different industrial sectors regarding the ways in which their organizations were managing and leveraging change.[60] Nearly half the executives characterized a new strategic direction or new organizational structure as the most significant change affecting their organization. The motives behind much of the change were reducing overheads and cutting costs as well as focusing on customer and employee satisfaction. The survey found that the single biggest stumbling block to change is often an absence of adequate leadership and direction, not a fear of failure or lack of reward. In addition, leadership was found to be the most critical factor in implementing the change.

The good news is that a majority of the executives surveyed were satisfied with the progress toward their company's change endeavors. The not-so-good news was that more than 68% of the respondents confirmed that their organizations had experienced unanticipated problems in the change process. Many of the executives were very clear about how they would improve future change efforts. They said that:

> . . . they would do more: spend more time planning, demand greater top management commitment, communicate goals more clearly and broadly, make sure many more people throughout their organizations buy in, and then move more quickly to implement desired changes.[60]

Managing change methods

There has been an increase in the development and use of change methods as a result of increasing demands to change. Most organizations have utilized methods like business process reengineering, total quality management or continuous improvement. A change method is a proposed way of dealing with a needed transformation. Change methods are ways that individuals, groups and organizations deal regularly with demands for novelty and improved effectiveness. These can be changes in the marketplace, customer needs, technology, regulations, weather or the structure of knowledge. They are ways in which people cope with modifications, major or revolutionary shifts, and incremental improvements. Change methods can be reactive or proactive; implicit or explicit; deliberate or unintentional.

The reason for the increasingly large number of change methods is, in part, due to the existence and need to cope with many different kinds of change. Another reason for the proliferation is that programs, procedures and strategies seem to have a shorter shelf life than before. Those who learn and apply change methods need some way to decide which method to use for what purposes. The methods they choose also need to fit both the people involved and the situation in which the method is applied.[61] We include an entire section of this book on managing change methods, as this is a key aspect of leading and managing for transformation (see Chapter 8 on managing change methods). We also provide sampling of the many change methods available as well as some specific strategies and tactics for managing these methods.

Beyond simple prescriptions

Change often involves something new, may create some ambiguity and usually contains some level of complexity. To varying degrees, change creates a need for people to use their problem-solving ability and creativity. Many change methods offer a prescribed series of activities to meet the needs of any change situation. These prescriptive methods provide a predetermined pathway to deal with a particular kind of change. If you are looking for a step-by-step recipe for dealing with change, then a prescriptive method will suit you.

Coyne and Subramaniam[62] identified the same tendency within the broad area of strategy. They indicated that the secret of devising successful strategies under conditions of high uncertainty lies in ascertaining just how uncertain the environment really is and then tailoring strategy to that degree of uncertainty. They called this 'situational analysis' and were critical of any strategist who would simply apply any strategy method because of having a bias toward or against any particular approach. The idea that leaders and managers must move beyond closed and prescriptive approaches to change is supported by many others.[63]

An example of a prescriptive method includes the earlier approaches to creative problem-solving (CPS). Whatever the need or task, situation or people involved, you started at stage one and 'ran through' the process to the final stage. There are many other methods that call for following a predetermined series of steps. We have devised task appraisal to help us explore the nature of the desired results or outcomes, the nature of the people involved in the task and the situation surrounding the task. After considering these factors and deciding that there is sufficient ownership, knowing the need for novelty and that the task is within the appropriate strategic direction, we qualify the use or modification of our method.[64] When we qualify or design the use of any particular method, we identify it as taking a descriptive versus prescriptive approach.

Descriptive methods provide frameworks that can be flexibly used to meet a variety of needs for change. The cost for this increased flexibility and applicability is that you must now make choices and decisions about how to use the method. Rather than having your pathway predetermined, you are now creating a map that provides a variety of choices for your journey. Our recent work with CPS takes a descriptive

Descriptive	Prescriptive
Flexible framework	Predetermined pathway
Realistic – based on observation and experience	Authoritative – determined by custom or expertise
Open – many choice points	Targeted – approaches and outcomes are specified

Figure 5.4 Two approaches to change

approach in that the stages, components and tools are used after considering the people, the context and the desired outcomes. Then the process is tailored for that specific journey. Only those stages or tools that are needed are used or applied. We provide an example of the application of CPS in Chapter 10 on applying CPS as a change method.

Ownership and change roles

Isaksen and Treffinger[65] defined ownership as having a sufficient degree of interest, influence and imagination for a particular task. Having interest for a task means that you are motivated and committed to work on it and will invest a sufficient level of energy to get it done. Having influence means that you have an appropriate level of authority, responsibility and accountability to make the task yours. Having imagination implies that you are ready, willing and able to develop and hold an image of a new and desired future. There is room for novelty in your task. These characteristics are absolutely essential to initiate and sustain a change initiative. Ownership needs to show up in a variety of ways and on a variety of levels to support the management of change.

Ownership can occur on a variety of levels, including: the individual; a partnership; a team, task force or group; across a number of teams, groups or functions; within an entire organization; across a number of organizations or within a sector or system; or on a global level. If you are to take ownership for change, then you must have an appropriate scope of sponsorship. The sponsor's ownership is characterized by being able to provide the appropriate sanction and validate the initiative or change effort. You must either be the sponsor, or must have direct knowledge regarding the sponsorship for the change you are attempting to manage.

Connor[66] defined sponsorship as an essential role in implementing an organizational change because the sponsor has the legitimizing power and authority necessary to enable and sustain the initiative. For change to be successfully implemented, the sponsor must demonstrate strong commitment by: being dissatisfied with current reality; having an image of what must be changed; believing that there is a real need for the change; understanding the scope and impact of the change (who will or may be affected); understanding and committing the needed resources; and showing consistent and sustained support for the change.

Connor[67] also defined change agents, targets and advocates as other critical roles when an organization is faced with change. The change agent is the individual or group responsible for implementing the change. Targets are those who must actually change. Advocates are those who want or desire to achieve a change but do not have the real power to legitimize it.

All the change roles outlined by Connor must have a degree of ownership for the change, but the sponsor(s) must have acknowledged and confirmed that the change is appropriate, needed and supported. The challenge is to locate the lowest possible level within the organization for the sponsor to both initiate and sustain the change.

One of the dangers of qualifying sponsorship when leading change is that all change may be held up until the chief executive officer finds the time and focuses attention on sponsoring all changes. Connor promoted the notion of cascading sponsorship to find the lowest possible level within the organization to locate the initiating and sustaining sponsors. Katzenbach and his colleagues[68] identify this challenge and called for attention to be focused on those deep within the organization to be real change leaders. The goal is to push ownership and enliven sponsorship throughout the organization, rather than waiting for permission from those at the top.

Leading creative change is not done with the simple writing of a memo or issuing a commandment from the top of the organization. Ownership and change roles must be considered. When it comes to using any particular change method, there must be a client or customer (internal or external) for the outcomes of all sessions, initiatives or interventions. The anticipated results must be legitimized by confirming that the client is either the sponsor, or has the appropriate degree of sponsorship, for authorizing the outcomes from the work. More information on owning up to change is found in Chapter 6.

Research on innovation over the past 40 years has confirmed that contrary to the common caricature of the lone maverick innovator, 'top management commitment' is one of the most common prescriptions associated with successful innovation;[69] the challenge is to translate the concept into reality by finding mechanisms that demonstrate and reinforce the sense of management involvement, commitment, enthusiasm and support. In particular, there needs to be long-term commitment to major projects, as opposed to seeking short-term returns. Since much of innovation is about uncertainty, it follows that returns may not emerge quickly and that there will be a need for 'patient money'. This may not always be easy to provide, especially when demands for shorter-term gains by shareholders have to be reconciled with long-term technology development plans. One way of dealing with this problem is to focus not only on returns on investment but on other considerations, like future market penetration and growth or the strategic benefits that might accrue to having a more flexible or responsive production system.

Part of this pattern is also top management acceptance of risk. Innovation is inherently uncertain and will inevitably involve failures as well as successes. Successful innovation management thus requires that the organization be prepared to take risks and to accept failure as an opportunity for learning and development. This is not to say that unnecessary risks should be taken – rather, as Robert Cooper[70] suggests, the inherent uncertainty in innovation should be reduced where possible through the use of information collection and research.

We should not confuse leadership and commitment with always being the active change agent. In many cases, innovation happens in spite of the senior management within an organization, and success emerges as a result of guerrilla tactics rather than a frontal assault on the problem. Much has been made of the dramatic turnaround in IBM's fortunes under the leadership of Lou Gerstner who took the ailing giant firm from a crisis position to one of leadership in the IT services field and an acknowledged pioneer of e-business. But closer analysis reveals that the entry into e-business was the result of a bottom-up team initiative led by a programmer called Dave Grossman. It was his frustration with the lack of response from his line managers that eventually led to the establishment of a broad coalition of people within the company who were able to bring the idea into practice and establish IBM as a major e-business leader. The message for senior management is as much about leading through creating space and support within the organization as it is about direct involvement.

Innovation is essentially about learning and change and is often disruptive, risky and costly. So, it is not surprising that individuals and organizations develop many different cognitive, behavioral and structural ways of reinforcing the status quo.

Innovation requires energy to overcome this inertia, and the determination to change the order of things. We see this in the case of individual inventors who champion their ideas against the odds, in entrepreneurs who build businesses through risk-taking behavior and in organizations that manage to challenge the accepted rules of the game.

Creative leadership

When we consider innovation, transformation and growth, the kinds of challenges that managers and leaders face require creativity. The tasks tend to be more ambiguous, ill-defined or fuzzy, rather than clearly structured or well-defined. The potential solutions and ways of solving them tend to be complex, unknown or untested rather than known, predetermined or simple. The outcomes and results are new, requiring discovery and invention rather than simply applying something that already exists. This situation demands creativity – the making and communicating of something new and useful.

Your challenge is to consider how you might manage and lead creatively. The implication here is that you will need to link and integrate your expertise and experience in order to provide a more creative kind of problem-solving. This implication has importance for you as the leader or manager, the groups and teams with which you work, and the organization as a whole. In short, we need to connect creativity and leadership.[71]

We see creative leadership as an inclusive process or mutual influence and communication in which the leader functions as a catalyst for navigating change along its full spectrum. This conception of creative leadership includes behaviors related to both leading and managing. It also includes an implicit assertion that part of the challenge is to provide energy for overcoming inertia.

We have already pointed out that there is a great deal of debate and tension between the roles of leader and manager. Leading seems to be focused on the future and on all the strategically important things, while management is seen as merely dealing with day-to-day maintenance functions. We see this situation as nonproductive. These distinctions between leading and managing are interesting and important, but only insofar as they encourage mindfulness. If the distinctions breed the outright discounting of management, then organizations will necessarily see creativity as linked only to leading and not to managing. This would encourage people in organizations to miss out on the many powerful and productive linkages between creativity and management.[72]

Our approach deliberately builds on the recent developments to acknowledge the importance of change when considering leadership.[73] Adding the dimension of change expands the traditional focus on task and people, and provides the opportunity to include the full spectrum of incremental improvement to paradigm breaking as the appropriate scope for leadership.

Linked to learning

Creative leadership involves an intense level of learning for the leader as well as for those being led. Leadership for transformation involves making sense out of ambiguity and ill-structured situations. Those who lead and manage must be able to integrate their experience with what is known, with learning about what is yet to be known. This holds true for the leader and extends to those being led. The people being managed and led need ways to seek meaning in their efforts.[74]

If learning is a key element, then the leader will very likely be involved in stimulating training, teaching and taking on the role of educator. From this perspective, remember that to educate means to draw out that which is within, not to pour or stuff into from the outside. As Gardner[75] has maintained, the key to renewal and growth is the release of human energy and talent. The focus on learning, from the perspective of creative leadership, is on the importance of using experience and reflection.[76] The importance of learning for organizations has been increasingly pointed out. For example, Argyris & Schön indicated that:

> Now in the mid-1990's, it is conventional wisdom that business firms, governments, nongovernmental organizations, schools, health care systems, regions, even whole nations and supranational institutions need to adapt to changing environments, draw lessons from past successes and failures, detect and correct the errors of the past, anticipate and respond to impending threats, conduct experiments, engage in continuous innovation, build and realize images of a desirable future. There is virtual consensus that we are all subject to a 'learning imperative,' and in the academic as well as the practical world, organizational learning has become an idea in good currency.[77]

Includes the whole system

A second connection created by linking creativity and leadership is that of leading systemically or ecologically. This means considering the whole system rather than any one of its constituent parts.[78] This involves searching for the big picture while realizing that you can never really see and comprehend everything that needs to be considered. Thinking and acting systemically has a great deal to do with staying open and looking for possibilities. Seeing creative leadership as an inclusive process means that our concern is not limited to the outcome or the method, but also includes the people who might be involved and the situational factors.

Creative leadership includes understanding people, desired outcomes, methods and context. It's about helping people use the style and level of creativity they have to produce novel and useful results. It also involves creating an environment or atmosphere that supports the productive engagement in creative processes. The role of a creative leader requires a constant conscious consideration of multiple factors aimed at understanding, recognizing and then nurturing the full spectrum of creative talent in people.

Rather than having one best style, approach or answer, the leader must have the capacity for great flexibility in behavior. This flexibility includes being aware of the factors in the situation including the general orientation of the people involved in the task, the nature of the desired outcomes, the context or culture surrounding the task and the method being applied. In short, the creative leader must work together with constituents to invent meaningful and new responses to many, varied and unique situations, demands and challenges. This increased range of behaviors applies to concern for task as well as for people and transforms the traditional role of the leader. More information about systemically guiding change is found in Chapter 1.

Linked to facilitation

In order to lead flexibly and promote individual, team and organizational learning, leaders need to build relationships based on involvement and participation. This aspect of creative leadership focuses on the influence and energy that the leader brings to the group. Leadership is, after all, a group affair. This relationship and group-based role is called 'facilitation'. The responsibilities of the facilitator are rather complex.[79] An effective facilitator must also be an excellent trainer or teacher as well as an ecological leader.

Generally, a facilitator is someone who helps others accomplish their tasks. In this sense, a leader needs to be able to facilitate rather than command. When we deal more specifically with CPS, the facilitator is the person who takes primary responsibility for the process and procedures with which the group will be involved toward the accomplishment of a desired outcome.[80] In this way, the facilitator assumes a special social role in managing change creatively. Within the framework of CPS there are three distinct leadership roles: the facilitator who focuses on process, the client who primarily owns the content and outcomes of the session, and the resource-group members. These group members provide input, suggestions and alternatives to support the client's task. When these social roles work well together, you have a group-oriented situation resembling servant leadership.[81]

Leaders and managers can also influence the cognitive processes that underlie creative problem-solving.[82] Leaders and managers can provide time, tools and training to employees, as well as encourage others to use these resources at appropriate times and on challenging tasks that promote innovation and change.

This facilitative approach to leadership focuses on the quality of relationships between the leader and his or her constituents. It is this leader–follower interaction that is at the heart of creative leadership. Indeed, those who are led have made it very clear what they expect of their leaders. Those who are seen as credible leaders are seen as being honest, truthful and competent.[83] Facilitative leadership is more than simply focusing on the process approach you are taking in order to benefit a client or sponsor. It is a philosophy of leadership based on service to others.

A model for creative leadership

The model for creative leadership we currently use to integrate what we know about leadership, creativity and change contains three basic dimensions: a focus on tasks; a focus on people; and a concern for change. This model builds on the insights provided by Ekvall and Arvonen regarding the new third dimension of leadership behavior.[84] If you take the spectrum of change (described in detail in Chapter 2 on building the Janusian organization) and impose it as the third dimension, you can organize a spectrum of creative leadership that includes management competencies, leadership practices and strategies and leading at the edge of chaos (see Figure 5.5). The situation and needs determine where you are on the change spectrum, and therefore, the most appropriate default position for your behavior. Leaders and managers must be able to use a variety of styles and behaviors that are contextualized to fit the interaction of people and tasks.

We believe that a multilevel perspective is needed, based on the historical and emerging trends and research. As a result, we will explore the individual, group or team, and organizational implications along the full spectrum of change.

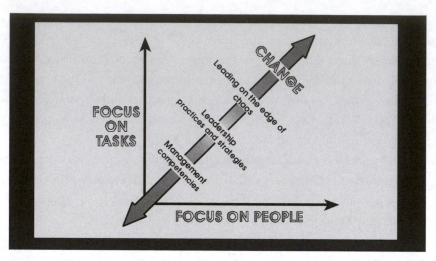

Figure 5.5 A model for creative leadership

Management competencies

Creative leadership within a relatively stable situation, one that is lower on the change spectrum, can be assisted by ensuring that the appropriate competencies are present. Management competencies are causally related to effective or superior performance in a specific job.[85] That is, that organizational effectiveness will be at its highest when managers possess the competencies to perform the tasks demanded within their contexts. Well-established managerial competencies like searching for and processing information, concept formation, conceptual flexibility, managing interaction, oral presentation ability, etc. would seem to be sufficient for making improvements and modifications within a relatively stable environment.

One of the most comprehensive studies about what great managers do was conducted by the Gallup organization and reported by Buckingham and Coffman in their book *First Break all the Rules*.[86] The study included over a million employees from a broad range of companies, industries and countries in order to discover the most important needs demanded by the most productive employees. On the basis of their analysis of the vast amount of data generated through their research, the authors were able to identify 12 key questions that captured the most information and the most important information with key implications for managers. In fact, the opinions about these 12 questions were formed by the employee's interaction with his or her immediate manager. Things like policies, procedures, pay, benefits or the overall company did not matter as much. It was the manager who was the key, not even the strong charismatic corporate leader.

Of the 12 questions, six had the strongest links to the most business outcomes like productivity, profitability, retention and customer satisfaction. The implications for managers were clear. The key management competencies derived from these questions include:

1. Providing people with clear expectations about work.
2. Outfitting people with required materials and equipment to get the job done.
3. Establishing opportunities for people to their very best work.
4. Giving consistent recognition and praise for good work.
5. Caring for people – as individuals.
6. Encouraging personal and professional development.

These managerial competencies are not too far removed from what we've already identified as leadership practices and strategies.

Rather than minimizing or marginalizing management, our approach recognizes that creative change can and does occur here. New policies and procedures are developed and implemented. Improved planning and control procedures are often put in place that more effectively integrate people and tasks. Creative leadership also occurs here, as very dramatic and significantly useful changes can bring new ways of making the current system run more efficiently and effectively. Providing effective management and introducing appropriate change that focuses on improving existing products, services and processes establishes the foundation and resources for making more radical changes.

At an individual level, the manager or leader must be able to provide clear expectation about the work to be done and kind of relationships that will enable the work to be accomplished. At a group or team level, the challenge is to provide a more integrative or facilitative function focusing on obtaining clarity, generating ideas and alternatives and then gaining consensus and agreement on the plan for action. You must have organization-wide systems and procedures to ensure that managers and leaders are open to new insights that are derived both internally and externally.

Leadership practices and strategies

Creative leadership is often related to accomplishing extraordinary results, outcomes that are both new and useful. As outlined above, leadership practices and strategies are patterns of behaviors that help people within teams and organizations to do more than function well within a stable system. These behaviors help people to create and deal with a range of change including making major new improvements for existing lines of work to creating entirely new lines of business.

At an individual level, people who are being led and managed need to see those who exert influence as credible and having an appropriate degree of expertise. In order to have the potential for influence, the quality of the interpersonal relationships is key. A larger than normal amount of energy commitment and trust are foundations to accomplish something extraordinary. This holds true at the group or team level as well. The added challenge for leaders and managers is to focus the attention of the group on obtaining clarity about the required degree of structure without limiting the group too much. At an organizational level, this requires an investment in selecting and developing leaders who can effectively deploy the full range of leadership practices (Figure 5.5).

Leading at the edge of chaos

The very high end of the change spectrum has been likened to white water, turbulent times and the edge of chaos. There is an emerging view among those who write about life in today's organizations that traditional and established views of leadership may not be sufficient for dealing with the future. Our concepts of leadership are being influenced by the new sciences that challenge the 17th century mechanistic view of the world.[87] Stacey's notions of organizations being complex adaptive systems containing both formal and shadow systems helps describe a few of the challenges facing leaders who venture into this level of change. He indicated:

> What both effective systemic thinking and effective leadership can do is to contain much higher levels of anxiety than would otherwise be possible, making it feasible for groups to be creative even when information flows, individual diversity, and connectedness are at very high levels. Systemic thinking and leadership are human strategies that make it more possible for us to survive at the edge of chaos than other species.[88]

Support for this new form of leadership comes from a variety of sources. One of the main implications for this kind of leadership is a high degree of integration of working on the task and working with others. Bennis and Biederman studied six great groups including: Disney Animation, Xerox Palo Alto Research Center, the team responsible for Clinton's election and re-election, Lockheed's skunk works, the experimental Black Mountain College, and the Manhattan Project. As a result of examining these six case studies of extraordinarily effective groups, they assert that the increasing need for collaboration and co-operation is actually beginning to temper the lone individualistic hero image of the great man approach to leadership. They stated that:

> The organizations of the future will increasingly depend on the creativity of their members to survive. And the leaders of those organizations will be those who find ways to both retain their talented and independent-minded staffs and to set them free to do their best, most imaginative work. Conventional wisdom about leadership and teams continues to glorify the leader at the expense of the group. Great groups offer a new model in which the leader is an equal among Titans. In a truly creative collaboration, work is pleasure, and the only rules and procedures are those that advance the common good.[89]

This new notion of leadership is also supported by Block's concept of stewardship. His basic idea is that stewardship is a means of achieving fundamental change in the way we govern our organizations and institutions. He stated that:

> Stewardship is defined in this book as the choice to preside over the orderly distribution of power. This means giving people at the bottom and the boundaries of the organization choice over how to serve a customer, a citizen, a community. It is the willingness to be accountable for the well being of the larger organization by operating in service, rather than in control, of those around us. Stated simply, it is accountability without control or compliance.[90]

Leading within this degree of turmoil creates an extraordinary need for productive, close and intense relationships among people. Farson described organizations as fragile monoliths. He explained their vulnerability as stemming from having a hard time accepting the importance of the relationships among the people within them. Rather than seeing organizations as enduring and sacrosanct structures, they are really nothing more than temporary solutions and relationships among people. Farson indicated that:

> Individuals are very strong, but organizations are not. Part of the reason why we don't recognize the vulnerability of organizations is that we have a hard time believing that the relationships that make them work are real. Even psychologists sometimes think of organizations as simply collections of individuals. But relationships – the bonds between people – are very real, and they have a life of their own. To a great extent they determine the behavior of an organization and the people within it.[91]

These relationships can be very personal and occur as one-on-one interactions, as in mentoring.[92] These relationships can and do happen within the context of groups and across functions and cultures within organizations (see Chapter 7 on teamwork for transformation). They can also be broad as in personal and professional networks outside any formal organizational boundaries. As in any relationship, like friendship and insurance, the time to develop and strengthen it is before you need it. These close personal and professional relationships can be extremely important during chaotic times because they help reduce anxiety and feelings of being alone. The high level of trust and openness also help provide the opportunity for support and honest feedback.

At the high end of the change spectrum, the need is for high levels of performance within the entire system of people, outcome, method and place. We need the full spectrum of leading and managing in order to create organizations that will be versatile and nimble. The model of creative leadership we have presented here illustrates the need for building these capacities and potentials into the very fabric of your organizations. We offer this model as an initial integration of what we have learned on the basis of our experience and research. A great deal more work remains to be done to further develop the model and the many implications that can be derived from it.

Conclusion

Creative leadership involves learning, leading systemically or ecologically, and facilitating. Why are these actions and practices important? The basic reasons fall into three broad categories of response: the demand for novelty and newness; the increasing demands to deal with complexity; and the need to clarify ambiguity. All three of these are the result of increasing demands for dealing and managing change and transformation.

From old to new

Creative leadership is largely about establishing a climate and context that is open to change. This climate provides the opportunity to deal with original, fresh and unfamiliar ways of solving problems and achieving opportunities. With increasing demands for change, more and more novel outcomes need to be invented. Everything changes all the time. There are increasing demands to keep up with the latest developments and information that is recent. How leaders invent outcomes that respond to change is a critical ingredient in why it is important to understand creative leadership. How they promote learning and renewal is critical to the success of their constituents.

From chaos to community

Change implies a large amount of complexity. Managing change often includes the use of cross-functional or cross-cultural teams and individuals. This implies an increasing need to understand and appreciate diverse backgrounds, approaches, preferences and behavior. Creative leadership now means helping constituents deal with the often perplexing challenge of puzzling interpersonal differences and getting dissimilar people to work together. There is a need for a common language for change, especially for creative and cooperative kinds of problem-solving.

From confusion to clarity

The need for change also increases the degree of ambiguity involved in the leader's work. Change is often accompanied by lack of clarity and uncertainty. Creative leadership involves developing a shared vision and promoting goal clarity. In order to deal with the vague and undetermined implications of change, the creative leader needs a flexible framework, a high degree of credibility and an ability to keep the focus on content or process clear. The creative leader is able to work together with constituents to decide what is needed and to hold a common and clear image of the desired future state.

Leading creative change means integrating what we know about leadership and management. It also implies pushing our knowledge to the limits and having the courage to make some discoveries along the way. If we can make progress in doing so, we will be able to help people in organizations go well beyond simply coping with change. Leaders will be able to embrace the future change, complexity and ambiguity with less anxiety for themselves and their constituents. Our hope is that this work will contribute to helping us all productively make the transition into the 21st century and beyond.

References

1. Kotter, J.P. (1999) *John P. Kotter on What Leaders Really Do*. Boston, MA: Harvard Business Review, p. 11.

2. Mumford, M.D., Scott, G.M., Gaddis, B. & Strange, J.M. (2002) Leading creative people: orchestrating expertise and relationships. *Leadership Quarterly*, 13: 705–750.

3. Bowman, E.H. & Helfat, C.E. (2001) Does corporate strategy matter? *Strategic Management Journal*, 22: 1–23.

4. Burns, J.M. (1978) *Leadership*. New York: Harper & Row.

5. Bass, B.M. (1981) *Stogdill's Handbook of Leadership: A Survey of Theory and Research* (Revised and expanded edn). New York: The Free Press. Bass, B.M. (1990) *Bass and Stogdill's Handbook of Leadership* (3rd edn). New York: The Free Press.

6. Clark, K.E. & Clark, M.B. (1990) *Measures of Leadership*. Greensboro, NC: The Center for Creative Leadership. Clark, K.E., Clark, M.B. & Campbell, D.P. (1992) *Impact of Leadership*. Greensboro, NC: The Center for Creative Leadership.

7. Mann, R.D. (1959) A review of the relationships between personality and performance in small groups. *Psychological Bulletin*, 56: 241–270.

8. Hemphill, J.K. & Coons, A.E. (1957) Development of the leader behavior description questionnaire. In *Leader Behavior: Its Description and Measure* (eds R.M. Stogdill & A.E. Coons). Columbus, OH: Ohio State University, Bureau of Business Research.

9. Halpin, A.W. & Winer, B.J. (1957) A factorial study of the leader behavior descriptions. In *Leader Behavior: Its Description and Measure* (eds R.M. Stogdill & A.E. Coons). Columbus, OH: Ohio State University, Bureau of Business Research.

10. Fleishman, E.A. (1953) The description of supervisory behavior. *Journal of Applied Psychology*, 37: 1–6. Fleishman, E.A. (ed.) (1967) *Studies in Personnel and Industrial Psychology*. Homewood, IL: Dorsey Press. Fleishman, E.A. (1973) Twenty years of consideration and structure. In *Current Developments in the Study of Leadership* (eds E.A. Fleishman & J.G. Hunt), pp. 1–37. Carbondale: Southern Illinois University Press.

11. Likert, R. (1961) *New Patterns of Management*. New York: McGraw-Hill. Likert, R. (1967) *The Human Organization*. New York: McGraw-Hill.

12. Blake, R.R. & Mouton, J.S. (1964) *The Managerial Grid*. Houston: Gulf Publications. Blake, R.R. & Mouton, J.S. (1985) *The Managerial Grid III: The Key to Leadership Excellence*. Houston, TX: Gulf Publications.

13. Blake, R.R. & Mouton, J.S. (1982) Comparative analysis of situationalism and 9,9 management by principle. *Organizational Dynamics*, 10: 20–43. Stogdill, R.M. (1974) *Handbook of Leadership*. New York: The Free Press.

14. Connelly, M.S., Gilbert, J.A., Zaccaro, S.J. *et al.* (2000) Exploring the relationship of leader skills and knowledge to leader performance. *Leadership Quarterly*, 11: 65–86. Zaccaro, S.J., Gilbert, J.A., Thor, K.K. & Mumford, M.D. (2000) Assessment of leadership problem-solving capabilities. *Leadership Quarterly*, 11: 37–64.

15. Farris, G.F. (1972) The effect of individual role on performance in creative groups. *R&D Management*, 3: 23–28.

16. Blanchard, K.H. (1985) *SLII: A Situational Approach to Managing People*. Escondido, CA: Blanchard Training and Development. Hersey, P. (1984) *The Situational Leader: The Other 59 Minutes*. Escondido, CA: The Center for Leadership Studies. Hersey, P. & Blanchard, K. (1969) *Management of Organizational Behavior*. Englewood Cliffs, NJ: Prentice-Hall. Hersey, P. & Blanchard, K. (1982) *Management of Organizational Behavior: Utilizing Human Resources* (4th edn). Englewood Cliffs, NJ: Prentice-Hall.

17. Ehrhart, M.G. & K.J. Klein (2001) Predicting followers' preferences for charismatic leadership: the influence of follower values and personality. *Leadership Quarterly*, 12: 153–180.

18. Scott, S.G. & Bruce, R.A. (1994) Determinants of innovative behavior: a path model of individual innovation in the workplace. *Academy of Management Journal*, 37(3): 580–607.

19. Amabile, T.M., Schatzel, E.A., Moneta, G.B. & Kramer, S.J. (2004) Leader behaviors and the work environment for creativity: perceived leader support. *Leadership Quarterly*, 15(1): 5–32.

20. Hollander, E.P. (1978) *Leadership Dynamics: A Practical Guide to Effective Relationships*. New York: The Free Press.

21. Bass, B.M. (1998) *Transformational Leadership: Industrial, Military and Educational Impact*. New Jersey: Lawrence Erlbaum Associates.

22. Strange, J.M. & Mumford, M.D. (2002) The origins of vision: charismatic versus ideological leadership. *Leadership Quarterly*, 13: 301–323.

23. Howell, J.M. & Higgins, C.A. (1990) Champions of technological innovaton. *Administrative Science Quarterly*, 35: 317–341. Keller, R.T. (1992) Transformational leadership and performance of research and development project groups. *Journal of Management*, 18: 489–501.

24. Van de Ven, A.H., Angle, H.L. & Poole, M.S. (2000) *Research on the Management of Innovation*. Oxford: Oxford University Press.

25. Bass, B.M. (1998) *Transformational Leadership: Industrial, Military and Educational Impact*. New Jersey: Lawrence Eribaum Associates.

26. Walderman, D.A., Javidan, M. & Varella, P. (2004) Charismatic leadership at the strategic level: a new application of upper echelons theory. *Leadership Quarterly*, 15(3): 355–380.

27. Howell, J.M. & Boies, K. (2004) Champions of technological innovation: the influence of contextual knowledge, role orientation, idea generation, and idea promotion on champion emergence. *Leadership Quarterly*, 15(1): 123–143.

28. Rafferty, A.E. & Griffin, M.A. (2004) Dimensions of transformational leadership: conceptual and empirical extensions. *Leadership Quarterly*, 15(3): 329–354.

29. Mumford, M.D., Zaccaro, S.J., Harding, F.D. *et al.* (2000) Leadership skills for a changing world: solving complex social problems. *Leadership Quarterly*, 11: 11–35.

30. Rafferty, A.E. & Griffin, M.A. (2004) Dimensions of transformational leadership: conceptual and empirical extensions. *Leadership Quarterly*, 15(3): 329-354.

31. Pinto, J. & Slevin, D. (1989) Critical success factors in R&D projects. *Research-Technology Management*, 32: 12–18. Podsakoff, P.M., Mackenzie, S.B., Paine, J.B. & Bachrach, D.G. (2000) Organizational citizenship behaviors: a critical review of the theoretical and empirical literature and suggestions for future research. *Journal of Management*, 2693: 513–563.

32. West, M.A., Borrill, C.S., Dawson, J.F. *et al.* (2003) Leadership clarity and team innovation in health care. *Leadership Quarterly*, 14(4–5): 393–410.

33. Chortatsiani, E. (2003) Product development in financial services: picking the right leader for success. In *Service Innovation: Organizational Responses to Technological Opportunities and Market Imperatives* (eds J. Tidd & F. Hull). London: Imperial College Press.

34. Andrews, F.M. & Farris, G.F. (1967) Supervisory practices and innovation in scientific teams. *Personnel Psychology*, 20: 497–515. Barnowe, J.T. (1975) Leadership performance outcomes in research organizations. *Organizational Behavior and Human Performance*, 14: 264–280. Elkins, T. & Keller, R.T. (2003) Leadership in research and development organizations: a literature review and conceptual framework. *Leadership Quarterly*, 14: 587–606.

35. Keller, R.T. (1992) Transformational leadership and performance of research and development project groups. *Journal of Management*, 18: 489–501.

36. Berson, Y. & Linton, J.D. (2005) An examination of the relationships between leadership style, quality, and employee satisfaction in R&D versus administrative environments. *R&D Management*, 35(1): 51–60.

37. Dvir, T., Avolio, B.J. & Shamir, B. (2002) Impact of transformational leadership on follower development and performance: a field experiment. *Academy of Management Journal*, 45(4): 735–744.

38. *Ibid.*

39. Fiedler, F.E., Chemers, M.M. & Bons, P.M. (1980) Implications of the contingency model for improving organizational effectiveness. In *Perspectives in Leader Effectiveness* (eds P. Hersey & J. Stinson), pp. 15–29. Ohio University: The Center for Leadership Studies.

40. Vroom, V.H. & Yetton, P.W. (1973) *Leadership and Decision Making*. Pittsburgh, PA: University of Pittsburgh Press.

41. Vroom, V.H. & Jago, A.G. (1988) Managing participation: a critical dimension of leadership. *Journal of Management Development*, 7: 32–42.

42. Evans, M.G. (1970) Extensions of a path-goal theory of motivation. *Organizational Behavior and Human Performance*, 5: 277–298.

43. House, R.J. (1971) A path-goal theory of leader effectiveness. *Administrative Science Quarterly*, 16: 321–339.

44. House, R.J. & Mitchell, T.R. (1974) Path-goal theory of leadership. *Journal of Contemporary Business*, 3: 81–97.

45. Bennis, W.G. & Nanus, B. (1985) *Leaders: The Strategies for Taking Charge: Four Keys to Effective Leadership*. New York: Harper.

46. *Ibid.*

47. Burns, J.M. (1978) *Leadership*. New York: Harper & Row.

48. Kouzes, J.M. & Posner, B.Z. (1995) *The Leadership Challenge: How to Get Extraordinary Things Done in Organizations*. San Francisco: Jossey-Bass. Posner, B.Z. & Kouzes, J.M. (1992) *Psychometric Properties of the Leadership Practices Inventory*. San Diego, CA: Pfieffer & Company.

49. Ekvall, G. (1988) *Förnyelse och friktion*. Stockholm: Natur och Kultur. Ekvall, G., Arvonen, J. & Nystrom, H. (1987) *Organisation och innovation*. Stockholm: Studentlitteratur. Ekvall, G. & Arvonen, J. (1991) Change-centered leadership: an extension of the two-dimensional model. *Scandinavian Journal of Management*, 7: 17–26. Ekvall, G. & Arvonen, J. (1994) Leadership profiles, situation and effectiveness. *Creativity and Innovation Management*, 3: 139–161.

50. Nanus, B. (1992) *Visionary Leadership: Creating a Compelling Sense of Direction for Your Organization*. San Francisco: Jossey-Bass, p. 10.

51. Sternberg, R.J., Kaugman, J.C. & Perez, J.E. (2003) A propulsion model of creative leadership. *Leadership Quarterly*, 14(4–5): 455–473.

52. Kotter, J.P. (1999) *John P. Kotter on What Leaders Really Do*. Boston, MA: Harvard Business Review.

53. Greenleaf, R.K. (1973) *The Servant as Leader*. Peterborough, NH: Center for Applied Studies. Spears, L.C. (ed.) (1995) *Reflections on Leadership: How Robert K. Greenleaf's Theory of Servant-Leadership Influenced Today's Top Management Thinkers*. New York: John Wiley & Sons, Inc. Spears, L.C. (ed.) (1998) *Insights on Leadership: Service, Stewardship, Spirit and Servant Leadership*. New York: John Wiley & Sons, Inc. Spears, L.C. & Lawrence, M. (eds) (2002) *Focus on Leadership: Servant Leadership for the 21st Century*. New York: John Wiley & Sons, Inc.

54. Collins, J. & Porras, J.I. (1994) *Built to Last: Successful Habits of Visionary Companies*. New York: HarperBusiness. Collins, J. (2001) *Good to Great: Why Some Companies Make the Lead and Others Don't*. New York: HarperBusiness.

55. Van de Ven, A.H., Angle, H.L. & Poole, M.S. (2000) *Research on the Management of Innovation*. Oxford: Oxford University Press.

56. Bethel, S.M. (1995) Servant-leadership and corporate risk-taking: when risk-taking makes a difference. In *Reflections on Leadership: How Robert K. Greenleaf's Theory of Servant-Leadership Influenced Today's Top Management Thinkers* (ed. L.C. Spears). New York: John Wiley & Sons, Inc. pp. 179–193.

57. Bardwick, J.M. (1996) Peacetime management and wartime leadership. In *The Leader of the Future: New Visions, Strategies, and Practices for the Next Era* (eds F. Hesselbeing, M. Goldsmith & R. Beckhard), San Francisco: Jossey-Bass, pp. 131–139.

58. Connor, D.R. (2000) *Leading at the Edge of Chaos: How to Create the Nimble Organization.* New York: John Wiley & Sons, Inc.

59. Bossidy, L. & Charan, R. (2002) *Execution: The Discipline of Getting Things Done.* New York: Crown Business, p. 24.

60. Loos, K. (1994) *Managing Organizational Change: How Leading Organizations are Meeting the Challenge – An Arthur D. Little Management Study Conducted by Opinion Research Corporation.* Cambridge, MA: Arthur D. Little, Inc., p. 13.

61. Isaksen, S.G. (1996) Task appraisal and process planning: managing change methods. *International Creativity Network,* 6: 4–11.

62. Coyne, K.P. & Subramaniam, S. (1996) Bringing discipline to strategy. *McKinsey Quarterly,* 4: 3–12. Dacey, J.S. & Lennon, K.H. (1998) *Understanding Creativity: The Interplay of Biological, Psychological and Social Factors.* San Francisco: Jossey-Bass.

63. Christensen, C.M.A. & Raynor, M.E. (2003) *The Innovator's Solution: Creating and Sustaining Successful Growth.* Boston: Harvard Business School Press. Mintzberg, H. (2000) *The Rise and Fall of Strategic Planning.* Financial Times Prentice Hall.

64. Isaksen, S. G. (1996) Task appraisal and process planning: managing change methods. *International Creativity Network,* 6: 4–11.

65. Isaksen, S.G. & Treffinger, D.J. (1985) *Creative Problem Solving: The Basic Course.* Buffalo, NY: Bearly Ltd.

66. Conner, D.R. (1993) *Managing at the Speed of Change: How Resilient Managers Succeed and Prosper Where Others Fail.* New York: Villard Books.

67. *Ibid.*

68. Katzenbach, J.R. & the RCL team (1995) *Real Change Leaders: How You Can Create Growth and High Performance at Your Company.* New York: Times Books.

69. Rothwell, R. (1977) The characteristics of successful innovators and technically progressive firms. *R and D Management,* 7(3): 191–206. Maidique, M. & Zirger, B. (1985) The new product learning cycle. *Research Policy,* 14(6): 299–309.

70. Cooper, R. (2001) *Winning at New Products (3rd ed).* London: Kogan Page.

71. Mumford, M.D. & Licuanan, B. (2004) Leading for innovation: conclusions, issues and directions. *Leadership Quarterly,* 15(1): 163–171.

72. Charnes, A. & Cooper, W.W. (eds) (1984) *Creative and Innovative Management: Essays in Honor of George Kozmetsky.* Cambridge, MA: Ballinger Publishing. Kuhn, R.L. (ed.) (1988) *Handbook for Creative and Innovative Managers.* New York: McGraw-Hill.

73. Ekvall, G. & Arvonen, J. (1991) Change-centered leadership: an extension of the two-dimensional model. *Scandinavian Journal of Management*, 7: 17–26. Ekvall, G. & Arvonen, J. (1994) Leadership profiles, situation and effectiveness. *Creativity and Innovation Management*, 3: 139–161.

74. Dotlich, D. & Noel, J. (1998) *Action Learning: How the World's Top Companies are Re-creating their Leaders and Themselves*. San Francisco: Jossey-Bass. Garvin, D. (2000) *Learning in Action: A Guide to Putting the Learning Organization to Work*. Boston, MA: Harvard Business School Publishing. Argyris, C. (1993) *Knowledge for Action: A Guide to Overcoming Barriers to Organizational Change*. San Francisco: Jossey-Bass.

75. Gardner, J. (1981) *Self-Renewal: The Individual and the Innovative Society*. New York: W.W. Norton. Gardner, J. (1990) *On Leadership*. Philadelphia, PA: Macmillan.

76. De Geus, A. (1997) *The Living Company: Habits for Survival in a Turbulent Business Environment*. Boston, MA: Harvard Business School Press. Dewey, J. (1938) *Experience and Education*. New York: Macmillan. Hannaford, C. (1995) *Smart Moves: Why Learning is Not All in Your Head*. Arlington, VA: Great Ocean Publishers. Kolb, D.A. (1984) *Experiential Learning: Experience as the Source of Learning and Development*. Englewood Cliffs, NJ: Prentice-Hall. Schön, D.A. (1983) *The Reflective Practitioner: How Professionals Think in Action*. New York: Basic Books. Tichy, N.M. (1997) *The Leadership Engine: How Winning Companies Build Leaders at Every Level*. New York: Harper Collins.

77. Argyris, C. & Schön, D. (1996) *Organizational Learning II*. New York: Addison-Wesley, p. xviii.

78. Senge, P.M. (1990) *The Fifth Discipline: The Art and Practice of the Learning Organization*. New York: Doubleday Currency. Senge, P.M., Kleiner, A., Roberts, C. *et al.* (1994) *The Fifth Discipline Fieldbook: Strategies and Tools for Building a Learning Organization*. New York: Doubleday Currency.

79. Isaksen, S.G. (ed.) (2000) *Facilitative Leadership: Making a Difference with Creative Problem Solving*. Dubuque, IA: Kendall/Hunt Publishing. Kinlaw, D.C. (1993) *Team-Managed Facilitation: Critical Skills for Developing Self-Sufficient Teams*. San Diego, CA: Pfieffer & Company. Rees, F. (1991) *How to Lead Work Teams: Facilitation Skills*. San Diego, CA: Pfieffer & Co.

80. Isaksen, S.G. (1983) Toward a model for the facilitation of creative problem solving. *Journal of Creative Behavior*, 17: 18–31. Isaksen, S.G. (1992) Facilitating creative problem solving groups. In *Readings in Innovation* (eds S.S. Gryskiewicz & D.A. Hills), pp. 99–135. Greensboro, NC: Center for Creative Leadership. Isaksen, S.G. & Dorval, K.B. (1996) *Facilitating Creative Problem Solving*. Sarasota, FL: Center for Creative Learning. Isaksen, S.G. & Dorval, K.B. (2000) Facilitating creative problem solving. In *Facilitative Leadership*, (ed. S.G. Isaksen). Parnes, S.J. (1997) *Optimize the Magic of your Mind*. Buffalo, NY: Bearly Ltd.

81. Greenleaf, R.K. (1973) *The Servant as Leader*. Peterborough, NH: Center for Applied Studies.

82. Puccio, G.J., Murdock, M.C. & Mance, M. (2005) Current developments in creative problem solving for organizations: a focus on thinking skills and styles. *Korean Journal of Thinking and Problem Solving*, 15: 43–76. Reiter-Palmon, R. & Illes, J.J. (2004) Leadership and creativity: understanding leadership from a creative problem solving perspective. *Leadership Quarterly*, 15: 55–77.

83. Kouzes, J.M. & Posner, B.Z. (1993) *Credibility: How Leaders Gain and Lose it, Why People Demand it*. San Francisco: Jossey-Bass.

84. Ekvall, G. & Arvonen, J. (1991) Change-centered leadership: an extension of the two-dimensional model. *Scandinavian Journal of Management*, 7: 17–26.

85. Boyatzis, R. (1982) *The Competent Manager*. New York: John Wiley & Sons, Inc. Shroder, H.M. (1986) *The Development of Management Competencies*. Tampa, FL: Center for Organizational Effectiveness, University of South Florida. Streufert, S. & Swezey, R.W. (1986) *Complexity, Managers and Organizations*. New York: Academic Press.

86. Buckingham, M. & Coffman, C. (1999) *First Break All the Rules: What the World's Greatest Managers Do Differently*. New York: Simon & Schuster.

87. Gleick, J. (1987) *Chaos: Making a New Science*. London: Penguin Books. Masterpasqua, F. & Peran, P.A. (eds) (1997) *The Psychological Meaning of Chaos: Translating Theory into Practice*. Washington, DC: American Psychological Association. Nicolis, G. & Prigogine, I. (1989) *Exploring Complexity: An Introduction*. New York: W.H. Freeman. Wheatley, M.J. (1992) *Leadership and the New Science: Learning About Organization from an Orderly Universe*. San Francisco: Berrett-Koehler. Wheatley, M.J. & Kellner-Rogers, M. (1996) *A Simpler Way*. San Francisco: Berrett-Koehler. Zohar, D. (1997) *Rewiring the Corporate Brain: Using the New Science to Rethink How We Structure and Lead Organizations*. San Francisco: Berrett-Koehler. Zohar, D. & Marshall, I. (1994) *The Quantum Society: Mind, Physics, and a New Social Vision*. New York: William Morrow & Co.

88. Stacey, R.D. (1996) *Complexity and Creativity in Organizations*. San Francisco: Berrett-Koehler Publishers, p. 161.

89. Bennis, W.G. & Biederman, P.W. (1997) *Organizing Genius: The Secrets of Creative Collaboration*. New York: Addison Wesley, p. 8.

90. Block, P. (1996) *Stewardship: Choosing Service over Self-Interest*. San Francisco: Berrett-Koehler Publishers, p. xx.

91. Farson, R. (1997) *Management of the Absurd: Paradoxes in Leadership*. New York: Simon & Schuster, p. 90.

92. Noller, R.B. (1997) *Mentoring: A Voiced Scarf – An Experience in Creative Problem Solving*. Sarasota, FL: Snedley Group. Noller, R.B. & Frey, B.R. (1994) *Mentoring: An Annotated Bibliography (1982–1992)*. Sarasota, FL: Center for Creative Learning.

Chapter 6

OWNING UP
TO CHANGE

leadership in the new reality is very different from leadership in the bureaucratic model of the past. Leadership is much more of a shared process than something that one person does to another. Those in formal leadership roles must be competent in the core task of leadership in the new reality: facilitating transitions – their own and those of their organizations[1]

Introduction

This chapter is written for those who find themselves in senior management positions and must take on the challenges of change. It is also written for those who must work with those managers in implementing change initiatives. This can include facilitators, middle managers and those who must implement the change. Others who consider themselves agents for change may also benefit by examining one of the key aspects that makes for successful implementation of change initiatives. Our intention is to clarify the concept of ownership and illustrate how it relates to the social roles of client and sponsor.

We have had plenty of experience preparing facilitators who have become experts at managing processes, tools and techniques. These facilitators have often been able to provide a process-oriented leadership role within their organizations. Sometimes, these facilitators have been able to make a real difference. In other situations, they have run great sessions, people had some fun filling up flipcharts, but at the end of the day, nothing happened.

In one organization within which we worked, a great deal of time, energy and resources was invested in developing the teams' facilitation skills. The team was seen as a unit that could be deployed throughout the organization to assist with a major quality improvement initiative. In one division, the senior manager asked for her team's support in implementing their own version of the quality program. She invested lots of time and energy working with the facilitator team to plan their approach, specify the need and set appropriate boundaries and expectation. She showed up at all the working sessions to answer questions and provided support for what the facilitators were doing. She was always there to see what the participants had produced. The division was very successful in implementing a great deal of the quality initiative (and has become established as a strong division within the company).

A man who was never really committed to the larger initiative led another division within this company. To be politically correct, he requested the facilitators to come into 'his division to see what they could do to implement the corporate commitment to quality'. The facilitators were often utilized as meeting secretaries and rarely had any time with the division director. The meetings and sessions that the facilitators conducted were technically well run, but did not produce results that made a real difference.

We believe that one of the key differentiators between these two divisions was that one leader really owned up to change. Owning up to change means having a personal image of desired results from change, helping to create a climate to support change, assisting in managing the process, and investing in participation and considering the people involved in the change. She not only demonstrated that she owned up to the change, but also encouraged all within her division to own a share in the larger change initiative.

This experience, along with countless others, has reinforced our model of facilitation. Although this model was designed specifically for one particular change method called creative problem-solving (CPS), we believe that a number of aspects are much more generally applicable to a variety of change methods (see Figure 6.1).

The model includes three distinct social roles.[2] The facilitator's role is to provide process leadership. This means that the facilitator has expertise in the change method(s), in managing group dynamics, and in working with the client to create the desired results. The facilitator often engages the resource group in planning and preparation prior to a working session. The facilitator supports the client's pursuit of the change by steering the use of the group and the method to obtain the desired results. The resource group, when a group of others is needed, provides alternatives, input and options. The client owns the content and results from the application of the method or process. We will have more to say about the role of the client later, but for now think of this model's primary application as providing three distinct social roles during a small-group application of any change method.

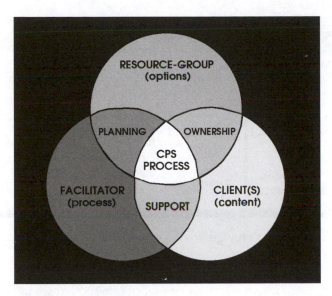

Figure 6.1 A model for CPS facilitation

One of the key benefits of applying this model to the use of change methods is the clear separation of process from content. Many ineffective meetings and problem-solving sessions clearly illustrate the difficulty in trying to manage both process and content at the same time. In most meetings and working sessions we've experienced without a facilitator to manage the process, content quickly becomes the main (and often only) focus. It is far more effective to separate these two responsibilities and assign specific roles to each.

When qualifying clients for the use of creative problem-solving (CPS), we discovered the importance of ownership.[3] Broadly speaking, we felt that the three characteristics of interest, influence and imagination had to be present or we would not pursue the use of any change method. We also learned that it took special roles to make the change process work. We knew that CPS was a powerful change method, but that it was not designed to handle all tasks. The tasks CPS was uniquely designed for had to imply novelty, ambiguity or complexity so that some sort of creative response was necessary. Other change methods are designed to deal with other sorts of challenges and opportunities.

We found that ownership cut across a variety of levels when dealing with change and methods that people use in guiding change. At one level, ownership is a personal attribute. Ownership is something an individual has (or doesn't have) for any

Title/(level)	Defining attributes		
Ownership (individual)	Interest	Influence	Imagination
Clientship (group/team)	Clear task priority	Decision-making responsibility	Open to diverse perspectives
Sponsorship (organization)	Commitment	Power	Setting the context for change

Figure 6.2   Owning up to change

particular task. For us, it serves as a general set of criteria that we use to qualify those with whom we will apply CPS as a change method. If all three of the characteristics of interest, influence and imagination are not present, we will not use CPS and would not generally recommend the use of any other change method.

The challenges of dealing with and guiding change are numerous.[4] It takes a great deal of personal courage to take on change. It also takes some hope and faith in a better future. Many people tell us about the pain and frustration that often precedes a personal transformation. There are a number of basic readiness issues to address before owning up to change. Understanding and dealing with barriers to problem solving and creative thinking are part of being ready. Owning up to change is influenced by many factors including the degree of competence people have to change and their level of comfort with change.[5]

When we plan on deploying any change method, we now check very carefully to understand the degree and kind of ownership surrounding the task (Figure 6.2). The remainder of this chapter will describe ownership, the roles of client and sponsor, as well as some suggestions for instilling ownership for change.

Ownership

On a personal level, a key attribute that drives someone's ability to take on change is ownership. When we started to develop this concept, we were noticing that some of our sessions and interactions were working very well and others went well but little seemed to carry through beyond the actual meeting. In fact, a few sessions seemed to end before their time due to lack of interest or energy. We started to ask ourselves questions to find out what was making this difference.

We inquired about the actual tasks and content on which we were working. Often, the nature of the task was well matched for applying CPS. The method we used seemed to work very well, as far as the desired outcome from the session was concerned. For example, if we wanted to explore numerous problem statements, we were able to meet and exceed the target number of problem statements. The context within which we were working also seemed to be fine. The climate and culture supported the need for novelty and often reinforced the use of the method. The people we worked with were open to the method, but often did not have the necessary level of ownership to make a difference.

For us, those activities conducted in the service of someone who really cared and could make a difference were so much more powerful. We searched our experience and then started examining our current work and found three characteristics that captured the essence of what we meant by ownership. These included: interest, influence and imagination. These are individual, personal attributes and they are particularly important for groups and organizations facing the challenges of change.

Interest

Interest means that someone has energy for the task. We know that someone has interest when there is high motivation to work on the task. That individual makes time and shows others a personal interest in something when it is a high priority for the individual's time and attention. We find a good measure of interest to be how easy, or hard, it is to get on the calendar of someone who wants to make a change. Interest and motivation for change is not something a facilitator can assign or provide. As Amabile has asserted in her model of creativity, the kind of motivation that supports change is more intrinsic than extrinsic. Intrinsic motivation is an internal desire to see the change take place for its own sake. Ownership implies an internal drive and desire to see something change – particularly for the better.

The degree of interest or desire someone has for a task relates to how much attention he or she will pay to it. The increased attention may also raise the level of tension, pain or frustration felt or perceived regarding a gap or desired future. Interest tells you how much motivation and passion the person has for any given task, challenge or opportunity.

Influence

Influence means that the individual(s) are able to make something happen. They have an appropriate degree of legitimate power and authority to implement a change. The influence factor relates to your ability to implement solutions. This can include both specific situational factors like a person's role in the hierarchy and personal factors like level of perceived personal power, belief in self, confidence and competence to make something happen.

Just having a 'fire in the belly' is not enough to effectively use a change method. Ownership means having sufficient influence and power in the situation to make a difference. Influence should not be confused with simply feeling empowered. Having influence means that you have the needed authority within the scope of your role to affect change. You know you are working with someone who has sufficient power when resources are assigned, people are given permission to act and others within the situation listen to the requests for change.

Imagination

The third characteristic of ownership is imagination. It means that the individuals seeking change are clearly concerned with coming up with something new. They do not already have an answer and are open to novelty. Having imagination also implies a willingness to tolerate a degree of uncertainty and ambiguity. In order for someone to claim ownership, there must be a need for engaging the imagination to come up with something new or original. Ownership implies that people are willing and ready to engage in 'possibility' thinking.

When you have a need to engage your imagination for a task or challenge, you are looking for something beyond the obvious or current state. Imagination means literally the ability to create images or mental pictures. Ownership for change includes this ability and desire to be open to novelty and originality. The need to engage the imagination to create the possibility for something new to come into existence is the strongest link between creativity and change.

These three characteristics – interest, influence and imagination – comprise what we call ownership. When we seek to qualify the use of any change method, we are concerned that there is at least someone who will own up to the change that is created. We call that person a *client*. When the scope of our change effort is on an entire organization requiring a more systemic application of a change method, we identify that role as a *sponsor*. We will now turn our attention to these two important social roles and will use CPS as the example change method to illustrate each.

Clientship

Clientship is a social role and becomes important when groups and teams are assembled to help make change happen. As you can see in Figure 6.1, the client has primary responsibility for owning the content and results from applying the change method. The facilitator has responsibility for managing the method and process. When others are needed to provide input we refer to them as resource-group members. Group members need to know that their efforts have some meaning and relevance. They want to see that something will be done with their input and suggestions. This can be achieved only if someone within the group has a sincere interest in implementing the solutions that the group generates. Thus, the facilitator must interact with a client before, during and after a session, initiative or meeting. This is the individual who has decision-making authority, responsibility for implementation or ownership over a particular situation or challenge.

When we work to qualify a client, the main attribute we are searching for is ownership for the task. Ownership within a group is made manifest within the role of client. Clients show interest by holding the task as a priority. They demonstrate that they have influence by taking responsibility for making decisions. By staying open to diverse perspectives, they reinforce their need for engaging imagination and pursuing novelty.

In popular use, the word 'client' means being the purchaser, buyer or customer for goods or services. The role of client in CPS groups goes beyond the passive aspects of consumers. Clients supply content-related expertise. That means that for our purposes the client is the expert on the task. The client provides focus and guides decision-making during the group's session. The client helps to keep the group on track by clarifying the situation, choosing directions and approaches, and actually participating in the group's session.

In the final analysis, it's basically the client who needs to have a problem solved or an opportunity fulfilled. It is the client who has the need for approaching a task in a new way. Therefore, the role of client is an important one in determining the effectiveness and productivity of the group's effort.[6]

Clients need support from the facilitator for permitting, encouraging and participating in the generating activities of the group, as well as guidance for making choices and judging at appropriate times. Clients must demonstrate sincere interest in working with the group and the process to bring about change. For clientship to be present, there must be room for a new approach or fresh idea that the client is willing and able to implement. The client must also have enough clear influence to implement the outcomes of the CPS process. This type of ownership builds commitment to the group process and helps in the development of effective groups.

The role of client helps to provide the group access to a clear definition of the task at hand. During a CPS session or intervention the client shares the most important background data and provides other information that the group needs to know before proceeding. Elements of the client's task must be specified and have clear connection to his or her responsibilities. In short, the client provides much of the domain-relevant expertise necessary for productive problem-solving.

Group clientship

Many times it is possible to identify one clear client. At other times, the ownership is distributed among a group. More broadly, there are some challenges and opportunities that have widely distributed ownership. For example, all of us are currently concerned (to varying degrees) about global warming or the threat of nuclear destruction. Managing group clientship provides the facilitator an even more complicated challenge. Usually, group clientship requires special attention to the focusing or converging aspects of CPS. It may be necessary to modify the process and tools, the time frame within which the group will work, and other factors when working with more than one client. Those factors might include the time and energy necessary for effectively working through task appraisal, planning your approach to process, as well as session time for focusing activities that will expand substantially as the number of clients increase.

Exhibit 6.1

During a change session the client:

- provides background information and clarification;
- takes primary responsibility (or ownership) for the content and results;
- provides content-related expertise but allows exploration;
- provides convergence and focus in decision-making (chooses directions and approaches) and makes contributions when generating options.

The client for a session can also be a sponsor of an organizational change. In the best case, there is a clear connection between the client of the session and the sponsor of the change.[7] A sponsor is someone who has the clear and legitimate authority to initiate an organizational change. Often a sponsor can involve someone else in the change initiative who can take on the role of a sustaining sponsor (we will have more to say about sponsorship later). This is someone who has a direct relationship with the sponsor and who can also take legitimate authority to implement the change. These sustaining sponsors can make excellent clients for applying a change method.

As a facilitator, it will be important for you to know who the sponsor is and to confirm the clientship for the session. This may involve having the sponsor or sustaining sponsor serve in the role of client before, during and after the session. This can also involve the sponsor in initiating a session for which the sponsor has delegated clientship to someone else. You will need to be involved in making the delegation agreement clear to ensure a productive session. This ensures that the results of the session will add value to the overall change initiative. It also confirms that someone will take the results of meetings and interventions forward.

As a client, you need to confirm that the task on which you are working has sponsorship and is aligned with the strategy and aims of the organization. When working on tasks that focus on transformation and change, it is helpful to make your assumptions explicit and deliberately engage those who have the appropriate level of authority.

The degree to which clientship is spread out will have an effect on who needs to be involved in the decision-making or focusing when applying a change method. Having a diversity of clients means taking a great deal more time and effort to manage convergence and process planning. However, it assists in deriving the benefit of involving the people who will have influence to actually implement the results of the problem-solving efforts. Having group clientship has the distinct benefit of including a diversity of perspectives regarding the challenge.

Clear task priority

Group members and participants rely on the client to own the content, results and outcomes from their efforts to problem solve and create change. Clients must demonstrate their interest in the task and in the approach being taken to meet the goal or close the gap.

Clients are experts in the problem area

Productive outcomes can often be influenced by the knowledge level and experience of the client. Effective clients are knowledgable in the problem area to the point that they can communicate the nature of the situation in a simple, clear and understandable manner. In effect, they know their area so well that they could describe it to an eight-year-old child. The client's knowledge and expertise is often necessary for making some sense out of the novel perspectives generated during the use of any change method. There may be special applications of any change method with groups of experts within a particular content domain. Generally, however, if there must be an expert in most CPS sessions, it should be the client. Even when you have a session filled with resource-group members who have high levels of expertise regarding the task, the client functions as first among equals.

Clients are genuinely interested in taking action

Effective clients are interested and motivated to deal with the problem situation. They display a positive attitude and commitment by attending and actively participating in planning meetings and group sessions as well as by taking action on the outcomes of meetings. They actively seek involvement and contribution from others. Their attendance at meetings sends the message that the problem or challenge is important and promotes a climate of challenge and involvement.

Clients are aware of process

Effective clients are willing to learn, understand and display that they are comfortable with the change method to be applied. For example, they have a general level of awareness of the roles of a change management session, how the tools will operate, and can effectively communicate with the facilitator and the resource group using a common language specific to the chosen change method. After applying the process, they often engage in a post-session meeting designed to provide feedback about the general level of productivity. This meeting will also help identify the outcomes that were most useful or intriguing, and if the tools applied during the meeting or session generated the variety of outcomes the client desired. The purpose of the meeting is to be able to identify if and how the application of the change method added value.

Clients are committed to the use of a deliberate change method

Effective clients understand the value of the change method they are applying and are willing to provide the time, energy and planning necessary for productive outcomes. They see value in all three roles (client, facilitator and resource group) and take the responsibilities associated with their role seriously. They actively collaborate with facilitators to plan, deliver and debrief the meetings or sessions. They provide feedback to facilitators and resource-group members when they have implemented change.

Clients often become involved in change management activities with which they may not be familiar. Effective clients trust the process in that they follow the guidelines and principles necessary to provide the desired outcome or result. They remain open to the generation of novel and unusual perspectives and tolerate the ambiguity that usually accompanies the use of certain change method's principles and tools.

Decision-making responsibility

Participants need to have confidence that the energy invested by both the client and resource-group members is going to be worthwhile. The client's role implies that the right person is involved, given the scope of the task, to exert the right amount of influence.

Clients assume authority and responsibility for problem situation

Effective clients have the authority and responsibility to take action on the problem situation. They are able to engage in the change method, see value in its use, and take action on its outcomes. It is possible for a client to be a 'sole proprietor' as well as a 'stake holder'. Ownership may be closely held or widely distributed. In either case, the actual level of responsibility and breadth of accountability for implementation must be clearly identified by the client. Clients are able to effectively answer the question: 'Why is this your challenge?'

Clients make decisions deliberately

Good clients make decisions in ways that allow them (and others) to retrace their steps. This usually means committing to the use of deliberate and explicit procedures and tools for focusing and converging. Having made decisions this way allows others to understand and appreciate the focusing and can encourage them to provide input that may allow a change or improvement in the decision itself. Being able to explain decisions helps to build credibility in the client and to engage the participation of others.

Clients provide feedback about results

Following the use of a change method like CPS, those who have been involved in helping the client often appreciate hearing from the client. Closing the feedback loop for those who have been helpful reminds them of the importance of their contribution and builds up their interest in taking part in future problem-solving activities. It's also just good manners to show appreciation for the extra effort and energy people put into change.

Open to diverse perspectives

Group members need to know that the energy they put into generating and focusing is really needed and potentially useful. The client needs to demonstrate that imagination is required in order to solve the problem. The worst case is that the client engages the services of a resource group when the client already has an answer. In this case, the group will feel manipulated and resent the waste of their time and energy. The client must identify when, where and why novelty is needed so that those who are helping can focus their resources in the right direction.

Clients are willing to change or modify paradigms

You know you have a good client when they show you that they can tolerate ambiguity or question some of their assumptions. The whole notion of putting a great deal of time and energy into appraising the task, process and session planning may be an entirely new way of working for many clients. Effective clients are willing to change or modify existing ways of doing tasks. They consciously seek novel and imaginative outcomes. They promote the involvement of 'outsiders' as resources to assist in providing a diversity of novel perspectives. They promote a safe environment for debate and risk-taking.

Clients are flexible in thinking and perceptions

It is often necessary to 'shift gears' and pursue new avenues or directions. Effective clients remain open to the changes in direction. They listen to and accept different approaches taken during various stages and phases of the change method. They stay open to the fact that they might 'change their mind'. When they are presented with an original option or pathway, they are able to let go of other options in order to genuinely consider novelty. They promote an atmosphere of trust and openness.

Other characteristics of effective clients

In addition to the characteristics defined above, there are other characteristics held by many of the most effective clients with whom we have worked. Two of the more important of these characteristics are described below.

Clients have good people skills

Effective clients have the ability to make others feel at home and supported. They 'read' the facilitator and resource-group members and know when and how to respond. They maintain an appropriate level of eye contact with others and listen carefully to options. Their verbal and nonverbal behavior matches the purpose of the session. They provide an appropriate level of encouragement without smothering or controlling the session. They promote idea support.

Having good people skills implies that clients have some degree of emotional intelligence and can appreciate human capital.[8]

Clients have personal integrity

Our best clients have had a strong set of beliefs in the value of diversity and the importance of unleashing human creativity. They see value in working with people to identify and solve problems and meet challenges. They see people as part of the solution, not the problem. They are honest in dealing with others and themselves. When the possibility of a 'hidden agenda' emerges, they are able to identify it openly and find productive alternative approaches. They deal with conflict and do not allow the tension to remain unproductive.

Sponsorship

When we consider creativity and change within the organizational context, the degree of complexity increases dramatically as we go from the individual or work-group level to a cross-functional or system-wide change. When we think about applying change methods within a group context, the ownership concept refers to the role of client. When we are working with change within an organization, ownership needs to be shown by the sponsor who holds a special role in leading change. This social and organizational role is beyond that of engaging in the social role of client for a small-group working session.

The individual or group who legitimizes or sanctions the change is called the *sponsor*. Conner describes sponsorship as the key differentiator between winners and losers in the tactical management of change.[9] He has devoted his research and practice to helping sponsors to better understand their role in piloting organizational change efforts.

There are different kinds of sponsors. The initiating sponsor is one who takes the first steps to put a change into effect. Sustaining sponsors are those who can also take initiative to support and help to bring about the original change. Sponsors are able to make change happen without asking for permission. Although placement within the organization is the basis for someone taking on the role of sponsor, it takes considerably more than that to take an integrated and systemic approach to guiding change.

Sponsors who demonstrate best practice have three characteristics that are related to demonstrating ownership. These include commitment, power and the ability to establish a climate that supports creativity and change. Each of these is described below in more detail.

Commitment

According to Argyris, 'Commitment is about generating human energy and activating the human mind.'[10] In the best case, sponsors demonstrate interest in change when they:

- show that they are dissatisfied with the way things are;
- can share clear goals for change;
- believe that there is a real need for change;
- publicly and privately convey the commitment for the change (even by making sacrifices to ensure success); and
- are willing to pay the price for change in the appropriate currency (time, energy, popularity, money, etc.).

For change to be successfully implemented, the sponsor must demonstrate strong commitment by:

- being dissatisfied with current reality;
- having an image of what must be changed;
- believing that there is a real need for the change;
- understanding the scope and impact of the change (who will or might be affected);
- understanding and committing the needed resources; and
- showing consistent and sustained support for the change.

The role of sponsor includes the commitment to prepare for strategic and tactical aspects of implementing change.

Sponsors communicate effectively

Sponsors know the importance of both verbal and nonverbal communication. They understand that productive two-way communication is at the heart of most human interaction, but particularly during times of change. As Nadler has indicated:

> I can't overemphasize the importance of hammering away at the same central themes over and over again. Earlier I related my observation that most people, particularly during periods of stress, have to hear a message at least six times before it starts to sink in. The same principle holds true in communicating the themes for corporate change. It requires untold repetition over significant periods of time before the organization as a whole comes to understand and accept the themes.[11]

Sponsors prioritize outcomes and needs

It is easy to imagine that senior managers and others who are likely to find themselves in sponsorship roles juggle many different priorities. Many of these things require immediate attention. Others are less urgent. Sponsors demonstrate their commitment to change by clearly aligning their priorities.

They are persistent in holding these priorities. They show self-control when it comes to making themselves available to the other opportunities. Effective sponsors demonstrate their interest in a change by distinguishing between those things that are important from those that are urgent; and then focusing on those important items – especially those that are consistent with the change initiative. This helps to avoid project proliferation or initiative overload.

Power

Sponsors have the power to legitimize and sanction change. Giving permission and approval to a change initiative impacts the degree to which others are enabled to act. Sponsors demonstrate that they have the needed power and influence for change when they:

- are willing to commit the necessary resources for the change;
- use rewards and other pressures to gain support for change; and
- ensure that procedures to track progress and problems are established.

Sponsors cascade clientship and sponsorship

One of the dangers of qualifying sponsorship when leading change is that all change may be held up until the chief executive officer finds the time to focus attention on sponsoring all changes. Connor promoted the notion of cascading sponsorship to find the lowest possible level within the organization to locate the initiating and sustaining sponsors.[12] Katzenbach and his colleagues agreed with this challenge and called for attention to be focused on those deep within the organization to be real change leaders.[13] The goal is to push ownership and enliven sponsorship throughout the organization, rather than to wait for permission from those at the top.

Connor defined change agents, targets and advocates as other critical roles when an organization is faced with change.[14] The change agent is the individual or group responsible for implementing the change. Beckhard would call them those who make it happen.[15] Targets are those who must actually change. Advocates are those who want or desire to achieve a change but do not have the real power to legitimize it. They can take on Beckhard's idea of being those who help it happen or let it happen. Finally, there are those who will get in the way or who may actively resist the change.

All the change roles outlined by Connor must have a degree of ownership for the change, but the sponsor(s) must have acknowledged and confirmed that the change is appropriate, needed and supported. The challenge is to locate the lowest possible level within the organization for the sponsor to both initiate and sustain the change. Part of cascading clientship is about finding and using the right levers for change within the entire organizational system.

Sponsors provide sufficient resources

Power is also about having the needed strength and force to make change happen. One of the unique abilities of an effective sponsor is to assign the needed finances, attention, personnel and other resources to the change effort. This may mean redirecting current resources and negotiating these assignments within an already lean organization. These decisions and acts of leadership send visible messages about the commitment for the change, the actual resources themselves enabling those involved in the change to take initiative and actions to move in the desired direction.

Legitimize the change

Sponsors decrease the anxiety by reinforcing the priority and the 'rightness' of the change. During periods of fast-paced change, people within organizations need to know that what they are doing is appropriate and that the changes they are being asked to absorb and cope with are authentic. Sponsors have the unique leadership position within the organization to influence, reinforce and symbolize the value of the change making it worthwhile to believe in.

Setting the context for creativity and change

Sponsors and those who lead change efforts are responsible for creating an environment that supports the taking of initiative to support change. They must know their role and their place within the entire system that is changing. The irony is that although sponsors may have the highest degree of formal authority and legitimacy to set priorities, they must also instill ownership for the change throughout the organization (see Chapters 11, 12 and 13 for more information on creating the context for change).

One of the ways that sponsors can demonstrate the need for imagination and creativity is to establish a climate that supports the taking of initiative. There is increasing research to demonstrate that climate makes a difference when examining those organizations that are successful and creatively productive from those that are stagnated.[16] There is some evidence that different organizational environmental conditions are needed for different kinds of creative productivity.[17] Sponsors can establish a climate conducive to creativity and change by working on the following tasks.

Sponsors envision the future

Those who have the courage to lead change also have the responsibility to conceive and communicate the image they have for the desired future. This future focus can come from examining trends and putting forward the logical and linear predictions of what could happen. It can also include a discontinuous image designed to fundamentally transform an organization. Either way, sponsors must demonstrate a personal involvement in using their imaginations by developing and sharing a compelling image of the future. The way they envision the future fosters constructive discontent within the organization regarding the status quo.

Sponsors model creative leadership

Sponsors demonstrate both visible commitment to change and official positions of leadership within organizations. Leaders, managers and supervisors create the climate within which work can productively get done. Sponsors, through their language, interactions and behavior, do little direct work; they are far more likely to have an effect on the climate which, in turn, influences the quality of the outcomes.[18] It is through their modeling of leadership and management behaviors and practices that people in the environment pick up clues as to the general atmosphere and how receptive it is to creativity and change.[19]

Sponsors build up resilience

Those who sponsor change must also engage the imaginations of those who must accept and implement the initiative. Leaders of change must deal with the concept of learned helplessness and self-efficacy.[20] Building up resilience means helping people learn from the full spectrum of experience and strengthening their ability to cope with future change. This includes providing people with, as our colleague Reg Talbot calls it, the means, motive and opportunity for individual, group and organizational learning.

Sponsors are mindful about climate and culture

Sponsors take responsibility to establish the climate that is conducive to creativity and change. Part of encouraging others to use their imaginations is ensuring that the conditions are appropriate within their organizations. Deliberately assessing the climate in order to conduct a strategic stocktaking helps them to find the key levers for improving their organizations. Over time, understanding and developing this climate will help them more firmly establish the culture (deeper values and traditions) that will continuously sustain the use of human imagination.

Instilling ownership

Although we see ownership as a personal (or individual) attribute, we are convinced that interest, influence and imagination must be available to a wide number of people if change is to happen. Leading creative change is not done with the simple writing of a memo or issuing a commandment from the top of the organization. Ownership and change roles must be considered. When it comes to using any particular change method, there must be a client or customer for the outcomes of all sessions, initiatives or interventions. The anticipated results must be legitimized by confirming that the client is either the sponsor, or has the appropriate degree of sponsorship, for authorizing the outcomes of the work.

Although we have identified a number of distinct roles in owning up to change, the major challenge to guiding change efforts has to do with sharing the energy and excitement for the change. The goal is to encourage everyone associated with the change to have some degree of ownership in the initiative.

Evidence is building that the shift toward increasing involvement is not just morally right and not just a response to pressures from masses. Participation shows positive impacts on productivity. Practices in the highest-performing organizations across industries are practices that optimize involvement.[21]

Further support for spreading or sharing ownership comes from Nadler who indicated that:

> As people participate they develop a sense of ownership. Rather than perceiving change as something that someone is doing to them, they see it as something they have a hand in creating. If someone is imposing the change upon them, they derive a sense of power from messing it up; if they feel ownership, they get a sense of accomplishment from making it work.[22]

Conclusions

Those who own up to change take a stand that puts them in an extremely visible position. Today, more than ever, those who take on change need to consider the entire system (see Chapter 1 on taking a systemic approach to change). As Nadler indicated:

Challenging those multiple forces of tradition is what integrated change is all about. It is based on the principle that if you hope to change complex human organizations, you have to consider every aspect of the enterprise, every possible leverage point. It demands a disciplined assessment of every component of the congruence model – strategy, structure, people, processes, and operating environment – and an appreciation that isolated change anywhere in the system will falter and eventually fail if unsupported by a full arsenal of related initiatives.[23]

Making a real difference requires ownership – interest, influence and imagination. Ownership is an important characteristic of best practice for both clients and sponsors of change. Sponsors have the unique social role that demonstrates ownership through having the ability to legitimize the change. Clients have the responsibility to implement the results of sessions, meetings and projects aimed at delivering change. Ownership has to do with making a real difference in the world. This has less to do with playing any particular role, and more to do with the human spirit.

The main characteristics of ownership provide a preliminary checklist of corresponding attributes of clients and sponsors. Those who take on these roles should seek to demonstrate them.

As you consider the defining attributes of the two social roles that have ownership for change (client and sponsor), you may also want to remember that taking on these roles requires the expenditure of a variety of costs in a number of currencies. These can include financial, time, energy, other priorities for change, image, etc. Owning up to change implies a conscious commitment to be mindful of the costs as well as the benefits of taking on such an initiative.

Appendix 6.1

Levels of commitment

'Fist to five' exercise

We often work with groups to obtain a common statement of vision, mission or values. At times, we find that it is important to conduct a quick assessment of the degree of commitment that the individuals within the group have for the outcome under consideration. As a quick method of assessing the levels of commitment, a thumbs down to five-finger scale can be used as described below. Each individual can hold up the appropriate number of fingers for a quick public assessment. We have also asked for a more private polling of commitment by taking a quick written ballot. The scale we use is described below.

Highly committed (5 fingers)

I really want it. I will create whatever 'laws' or structures that are needed to make it happen. I have a great deal of energy for it!

Enrolled (4 fingers)

I want it. I will do whatever can be done within the 'spirit of the law'. Call me a 'joiner' or member of the group who supports the idea. I have a lot of energy for it.

Genuinely compliant (3 fingers)

I see the benefit of the item and will do everything that's expected and more. I will follow the 'letter of the law'. Complies and shows some initiative in carrying out actions to support the idea. 'Good soldiers.' I have some energy for it.

Formally compliant (2 fingers)

I see the benefits of the idea and will do what is expected and no more. 'Pretty good soldier.' I will obediently carry out actions that support the direction.

Grudgingly compliant (1 finger)

I do not see the benefits of the idea, but do not want to lose my connection or position. I will do enough of what's expected because I have to. 'I'm not really on board.' I have very low energy for it.

Apathetic (fist)

Neither for nor against it. I have a lack of interest, emotion or energy for the option. 'Is it five o'clock yet?'

Noncompliant (thumb down)

I do not see the benefit of it and will not do it. 'I won't do it; and you can't make me!' In fact, I have negative energy for it. I will work against it.

References

1. Noer, D.M. (1997) *Breaking Free: A Prescription for Personal and Organizational Change.* San Francisco: Jossey-Bass.
2. Isaksen, S.G. (1983) Toward a model for the facilitation of creative problem solving. *Journal of Creative Behavior*, 17: 18–31.
3. Isaksen, S.G. & Treffinger, D.J. (1985) *Creative Problem Solving: The Basic Course.* Buffalo, NY: Bearly Ltd.
4. Taffinder, P. (1998) *Big Change: A Route-Map for Corporate Transformation.* New York: John Wiley & Sons, Inc.
5. Noer, D.M. (1997) *Breaking Free: A Prescription for Personal and Organizational Change.* San Francisco: Jossey-Bass.
6. Firestien, R.L. & Treffinger, D.J. (1983) Ownership and converging: essential ingredients of creative problem solving. *Journal of Creative Behavior*, 17: 32–38. Jay, A. (1977) Rate yourself as a client. *Harvard Business Review*, 55: 84–92.
7. Conner, D.R. (1993) *Managing at the Speed of Change: How Resilient Managers Succeed and Prosper Where Others Fail.* New York: Villard Books.
8. Thomson, K. (1998) *Emotional Capital: Maximizing the Intangible Assets at the Heart of Brand and Business Success.* Oxford: Capstone Publishing.
9. Conner, D.R. (1993) *Managing at the Speed of Change: How Resilient Managers Succeed and Prosper Where Others Fail.* New York: Villard Books. Conner, D.R. (1998) *Leading at the Edge of Chaos: How to Create the Nimble Organization.* New York: John Wiley & Sons, Inc.
10. Argyris, C. (1998) Empowerment: the emperor's new clothes. *Harvard Business Review*, 76: 98–105.

11. Nadler, D.A. (1998) *Champions of Change: How CEOs and Their Companies are Mastering the Skills of Radical Change.* San Francisco: Jossey-Bass, p. 153.

12. Conner, D.R. (1993) *Managing at the Speed of Change: How Resilient Managers Succeed and Prosper Where Others Fail.* New York: Villard Books.

13. Katzenbach, J.R. & the RCL team (1995) *Real Change Leaders: How You Can Create Growth and High Performance at Your Company.* New York: Times Books.

14. Conner, D.R. (1993) *Managing at the Speed of Change: How Resilient Manager Succeed and Prosper Where Others Fail.* New York: Villard Books.

15. Beckhard, R. (1969) *Organizational Development: Strategies and Models.* Reading, MA: Addison-Wesley Longman.

16. Ekvall, G. (1996) Organizational climate for creativity and innovation. *European Journal of Work and Organizational Psychology,* 5: 105–123. Davis, T. (2000) *Innovation Survey and Growth: A Global Perspective.* London: PricewaterhouseCoopers.

17. Ekvall, G. (1997) Organizational conditions and levels of creativity. *Creativity and Innovation Management,* 6: 195–205.

18. Ekvall, G. & Ryhammar, L. (1998) Leadership style, social climate and organizational outcomes: a study at a Swedish university college. *Creativity and Innovation Management,* 7: 126–130.

19. Kouzes, J.M. & Posner, B.Z. (1995) *The Leadership Challenge: How to Keep Getting Extraordinary Things Done in Organizations.* San Francisco: Jossey-Bass.

20. Seligman, M.E.P. (1975) *Helplessness.* San Francisco: W.H. Freeman. Bandura, A. (1977) *Social Learning Theory.* Englewood Cliffs, NJ: Prentice-Hall.

21. McLagan, P. & Nel, C. (1995) *The Age of Participation: New Governance for the Workplace and the World.* San Francisco: Berrett-Koehler.

22. Nadler, D.A. (1998) *Champions of Change: How CEOs and Their Companies are Mastering the Skills of Radical Change.* San Francisco: Jossey-Bass, p. 102.

23. *Ibid.,* p. 308.

Chapter 7

TEAMWORK FOR TRANSFORMATION: APPLYING VIEW TO HELP MAKE TEAMS PRODUCTIVE

> I will say that teamwork – particularly among executives – is not synonymous with a love fest. It helps enormously if team members admire and care about each other, but teamwork is essentially about working together for the common good, being committed to the same goals, and helping each other to achieve these goals. Failure to create that kind of teamwork can be fatal to the entire change effort[1]

Teamwork is an important concern whenever you expect small groups of people to work together collaboratively toward a common goal or outcome. Effective teams have mutual and shared accountability for their team's goal; their results may impact the evaluation of the individuals and the team as a whole. In order to be effective, teams must also be able to maintain their collaboration, effective communication, and positive interactions over a sustained period of time. When you are facing organizational change and transformation, you will often need to apply teamwork.

When you deploy teams there will be a number of challenges and opportunities. One of the most significant issues is helping team members understand and deal effectively with differences. In this chapter, we will explore the productive potential of using *VIEW: An Assessment of Problem Solving Style*[SM] to help deal with some of the key dynamics of teamwork, particularly teamwork for transformation.

When you are responsible for building or guiding teams, you can apply VIEW in several ways. VIEW can provide a common language or vocabulary for exchanging information about the similarities and differences among team members. This will help the team members to recognize and respect differences, rather than viewing others with differing preferences as 'odd', 'wrong' or 'ineffective'. Team members need to understand that 'differences are not deficits'. Group members can also sustain their team's working relationship when they are able to celebrate each other's strengths and use their differences to complement each other.

Deciding to use a group

Many people who have attempted to use groups for problem solving find out that using groups is not always easy, pleasurable or effective. Using groups has both positive and negative aspects. Table 7.1, describing assets and liabilities of using groups, has been developed by weaving together the work of numerous scholars.[2]

Table 7.1 Potential assets and liabilities of using a group

Assets	Liabilities
1. Greater availability of knowledge and information.	1. Social pressure toward uniform thought limits contributions and increases conformity.
2. More opportunities for cross-fertilization; increasing the likelihood of building and improving upon ideas of others.	2. Group think: groups converge on options, that seem to have greatest agreement, regardless of quality.
3. Wider range of experiences and perspectives upon which to draw.	3. Dominant individuals influence and exhibit an unequal amount of impact upon outcomes.
4. Participation and involvement in problem-solving increases understanding, acceptance, commitment, and ownership of outcomes.	4. Individuals are less accountable in groups allowing groups to make riskier decisions.
5. More opportunities for group development; increasing cohesion, communication and companionship.	5. Conflicting individual biases may cause unproductive levels of competition; leading to 'winners' and 'losers'.

When considering the use of small groups, the leader or facilitator needs to evaluate the liabilities and assets of using groups. The goal is to maximize the positive aspects of group involvement while minimizing the liabilities. For example, as the facilitator or group leader can increase the productive use of diversity, the likelihood of individual dominance should decrease. In general, if there is a need to provide for participation to increase acceptance, if the information is widely held, if there is a need to build on and synthesize the diverse range of experiences and perspectives or if it is important to develop and strengthen the group's ability to learn, you may choose to involve a group.

All teams are groups; but not all groups are teams

Teams are one of the basic building blocks of every organization. After individuals, they may be considered the most important resource in any organization. Teams conduct so much real, day-to-day work within organizations. This explains the interest in high-performance work systems, electronic groupware, small-group facilitation skills, and a host of other strategies for improving the way that groups work. One of the reasons that teams are so essential within organizations is the growing complexity of tasks. Increasingly complex tasks frequently surpass the cognitive capabilities of individuals and necessitate a team approach.

Before we continue, it would be helpful to explore what we mean by a team. Many people use the words 'group' and 'team' interchangeably. In general, the word 'group' refers to an assemblage of people who may just be near to each other. Groups can be a number of people that are regarded as some sort of unity or are classed together on account of any sort of similarity. For us, a team means a combination of individuals who come together or who have been brought together for a common purpose or goal in their organization. A team is a group that must collaborate in their professional work in some enterprise or on some assignment and share accountability or responsibility for obtaining results.

There are a variety of ways to differentiate working groups from teams. One senior executive with whom we have worked described groups as individuals with nothing in common, except a zip/postal code. Teams, however, were characterized by a common vision. Smith described a team as 'a small number of people with complementary skills who are mutually committed to a common purpose, a common set of performance goals, and a commonly agreed upon working approach'.[3]

Characteristics that promote teamwork

Authors, researchers and practitioners have offered many suggestions for productive teamwork.[4] The following dozen characteristics of productive teams have been formulated from reviewing the work of numerous writers and researchers on creative teamwork.[5] The quotes come from a study that we conducted on high-performance teamwork.

A clear, common and elevating goal

Having a clear and elevating goal means having understanding, mutual agreement and identification with respect to the primary task a group faces. Active teamwork toward common goals happens when members of a group share a common vision of the desired future state. Creative teams have clear and common goals. 'The most important factor accounting for my team's creative success was, undoubtedly, each member's drive to attain the end goal, knowing the benefits that would be derived from the results.' The goals were clear and compelling, but also open and challenging. Less creative teams have conflicting agendas, different missions and no agreement on the end result. 'Everyone did their own thing without keeping in mind the overall objective that the group was charged to achieve.' The tasks for the least creative teams were tightly constrained, considered routine and were overly structured.

Results-driven structure

Individuals within high-performing teams feel productive when their efforts take place with a minimum of grief. Open communication, clear coordination of tasks, clear roles and accountabilities, monitoring performance, providing feedback, fact-based judgment, efficiency, and strong impartial management combine to create a results-driven structure.

Competent team members

Competent teams are comprised of capable and conscientious members. Members must possess essential skills and abilities, a strong desire to contribute, be capable of collaborating effectively and have a sense of responsible idealism. They must have knowledge in the domain surrounding the task (or some other domain that may be relevant) as well as with the process of working together. Creative teams recognize the diverse strengths and talents and use them accordingly. 'Each individual brought a cornucopia of experience and insight. All of this, together with the desire to meet the end goal was the key to success.' Less creative teams have inadequate skill sets and are unable to effectively utilize their diversity.

Unified commitment

Having a shared commitment relates to the way that individual members of the group respond. Effective teams have an organizational unity; members display mutual support, dedication and faithfulness to the shared purpose and vision, and a productive degree of self-sacrifice to reach organizational goals. Creative teams 'play hard and work even harder'. Team members enjoy contributing and celebrated their accomplishments. 'All team members were motivated to do the best job possible in reaching the end goal, so everyone was willing to pitch in to get the job done.' There is a high degree of enthusiasm and commitment to get the job done. Less creative teams lack that kind of motivation. There is a lack of initiative, ideas and follow-through on suggestions. Less creative teams had a 'lack of motivation and the inability to recognize the value provided by the end result'.

Collaborative climate

Productive teamwork does not just happen. It requires a climate that supports co-operation and collaboration. This kind of situation is characterized by mutual trust – trust in the goodness of others. Organizations desiring to promote teamwork must provide a climate within the larger context that supports cooperation. Creative teams have an environment that encourages new ideas and allows the development of new ways of working. 'No matter what the disagreements, we all knew that we had to bring our ideas together to get the job done.' Everyone feels comfortable discussing ideas, offering suggestions because

... ideas are received in a professional and attentive manner ... people feel free to brainstorm to improve others' ideas without the authors' feelings getting hurt. In less creative teams new ideas are not attended to or encouraged because 'individuals place their own priorities before the teams'.

They are characterized by not being able to discuss multiple solutions to a problem because team members cannot listen to any opinion other than their own. In these teams, members are 'expected to follow what had always been done and finish as quickly as possible'.

Standards of excellence

Effective teams establish clear standards of excellence. They embrace individual commitment, motivation, self-esteem, individual performance and constant improvement. Members of teams develop a clear and explicit understanding of the norms upon which they will rely.

External support and recognition

Team members need resources, rewards, recognition, popularity and social success. Being liked and admired as individuals and respected for belonging and contributing to a team is often helpful in maintaining the high level of personal energy required for sustained performance. With the increasing use of cross-functional and interdepartmental teams within larger complex organizations, teams must be able to obtain approval and encouragement.

Principled leadership

Leadership is important for teamwork. Whether it is a formally appointed leader or leadership of the emergent kind, the people who exert influence and encourage the accomplishment of important things usually follow some basic principles. Principled leadership includes the management of human differences, protecting less able members, and providing a level playing field to encourage contributions from everyone. This is the kind of leadership that promotes legitimate compliance to competent authority. In creative teams, the leader 'leads by example, encouraging new ideas and sharing best practices'. Leaders provide clear guidance, support and encouragement, and keep everyone working together and moving forward. Leaders also work to obtain support and resources from within and outside the group. In less creative teams, the leader 'creates a situation where everyone is confused and afraid to ask questions'. Leaders 'tear down people's ideas', 'set a tone of distrust' and 'stifle others who have ideas and energy to succeed'. They 'keep all control, but take no action'.

Appropriate use of the team

Teamwork is encouraged when the tasks and situations really call for that kind of activity. Sometimes, the team itself must set clear boundaries on when and why it should be deployed. One of the easiest ways to destroy a productive team is to overuse it or use it when it is not appropriate to do so.

Participation in decision-making

One of the best ways to encourage teamwork is to engage the members of the team in the process of identifying the challenges and opportunities for improvement, generating ideas and transforming ideas into action. Participation in the process of problem-solving and decision-making actually builds teamwork and improves the likelihood of acceptance and implementation.

Team spirit

Effective teams know how to have a good time, release tension and relax their need for control. The focus at times is on developing friendship, engaging in tasks for mutual pleasure and recreation. This internal team climate extends beyond the need for a collaborative climate. Creative teams have the ability to work together without major conflicts in personalities. There is a high degree of respect for the contributions of others. Communication is characterized by 'the willingness of team members to listen to one another and honour the opinions of all team members'. Members of these teams report that they know their roles and responsibilities and that this provides freedom to develop new ideas. Less creative teams are characterized by an 'unwillingness to communicate with one another because people do not make the effort to understand each other'. There are instances of animosity, jealousy and political posturing.

Embracing appropriate change

Teams often face the challenges of organizing and defining tasks. In order for teams to remain productive, they must learn how to make necessary changes to procedures. When there is a fundamental change in how the team must operate, different values and preferences may need to be accommodated. Productive teams learn how to use the full spectrum of their members' creativity.

Challenges to watch for with teams

There are also many challenges to the effective management of teams. We have all seen teams that have 'gone wrong'. As a team develops, there are certain aspects or guidelines that might be helpful to keep them on track. Hackman has identified a number of themes relevant to those who design, lead and facilitate teams. In examining a variety of organizational work groups, he found some seemingly small factors that if overlooked in the management of teams will have large implications that tend to destroy the capability of a team to function.[6] These small and often hidden 'tripwires' to major problems include the following types of challenges.

Group versus team

One of the mistakes that is often made when managing teams is to call the group a team, but to actually treat it as nothing more than a loose collection of individuals. This is similar to making it a team 'because I said so'. It is important to be very clear about the underlying goal structure. Organizations are often surprised that teams do not function too well in their environment. Of course, they often fail to examine the impact of competition in their rating or review process. People are often asked to perform tasks as a team, but then have all evaluation of performance based on an individual level. This situation sends conflicting messages, and may negatively affect team performance. Teams include mutual accountability for agreed goals and working approach, something that may not necessarily be present in all groups.

Ends versus means

Managing the source of authority for groups is a delicate balance. Just how much authority can you assign to the team to work out its own issues and challenges? Those who convene teams often 'overmanage' them by specifying the results as well as how the team should obtain them. The end, direction or outer limit constraints ought to be specified, but the means to get there ought to be within the authority and responsibility of the group. Teamwork is often underutilized because the desired ends are unclear and unspecified. As a result, teams are often given too much guidance on the means (the how) rather than sufficient emphasis on the ends (the what and why). Effective teams are given clear indications of what is the acceptable outcome and end goal and responsibility for working out how to get there.

Structured freedom

It is a major mistake to assemble a group of people and merely tell them in general and unclear terms what needs to be accomplished and then let them work out their own details. At times, the belief is that if teams are to be creative, they ought not be given any structure. It turns out that most groups would find a little structure quite enabling, if it were the right kind. Teams generally need a well-defined task. They need to be composed of an appropriately small number to be manageable but large enough to be diverse. They need clear limits as to the team's authority and responsibility, and they need sufficient freedom to take initiative and make good use of their diversity. It's about striking the right kind of balance between structure, authority and boundaries – and freedom, autonomy and initiative.

Support structures and systems

Often, challenging team objectives are set, but the organization fails to provide adequate support in order to make the objectives a reality. In general, high-performing teams need a reward system that recognizes and reinforces excellent team performance. They also need access to good-quality and adequate information, as well as training in team-relevant tools and skills. Good team performance is also dependent on having an adequate level of material and financial resources to get the job done. Calling a group a team does not mean that they will automatically obtain all the necessary support needed to accomplish the task.

Assumed competence

Many organizations have a great deal of faith in their selection systems. Facilitators, and others who manage or lead groups, cannot assume that the group members have all the competence they need to work effectively as a team, simply because they have been selected to join any particular organization. Technical skills, domain-relevant expertise and experience, and abilities often explain why someone has been included within a group. These are often not the only competencies individuals need for effective team performance.[7] Members will undoubtedly need explicit coaching on the skills they need to work well in a team. Coaching and other supportive interventions are best done during the launch, at a natural break in the task, or at the end of a performance or review period. The start-up phase is probably the most important time frame to provide the necessary coaching or training.

One of the ways to help teams obtain many of the desired characteristics and avoid the trip wires it to consider how teams develop. The next section outlines what team development is, and how VIEW can be used to encourage productive teamwork.

Problem-solving style differences

After more than two decades of research and development, we know that problem-solving style is an important dimension of creative productivity. Information from problem-solving style assessments helps us to address problems that cut across all markets, functions and disciplines – especially the constant challenge of 'doing more with less', and the always present need to anticipate, create, innovate and manage change from both internal and external sources.

Problem-solving styles are consistent individual differences in the ways people prefer to plan and carry out the generating and focusing of ideas, in order to gain clarity, or

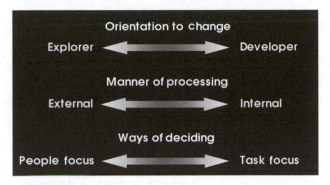

Figure 7.1   Problem-solving style differences

prepare for action when solving problems or managing change. *VIEW: An Assessment of Problem Solving Style*^{SM} is an assessment tool that helps individuals and teams gain a practical understanding of these individual style differences, positioning them to leverage that understanding for competitive advantage.[8]

VIEW addresses three dimensions of style preferences that are crucial in understanding and guiding the efforts of individuals and teams to solve problems and manage change effectively. Each dimension involves two contrasting styles (Figure 7.1). We will describe the three dimensions and six styles below.

Orientation to change

Orientation to change focuses on a person's preferences for managing change and solving problems creatively. How someone perceives opportunities and challenges surrounding change is based on three main issues.

1. How much structure do you need in order to understand and deal effectively with the change?
2. How much will you need to have the guidance and direction from sources of authority?
3. What kind of novelty or originality do you prefer to pay attention to?

The two contrasting styles on this dimension are the *explorer* and the *developer*.

The explorer style

An 'explorer' is someone who prefers to venture into uncharted directions and follows possibilities wherever they might lead. Explorers enjoy initiating many tasks. They thrive on novel, ambiguous situations and challenges. They seek to create many original options that, if developed and refined, might provide the foundation for valuable contributions. Explorers see unusual possibilities, patterns and relationships. These highly novel alternatives may not be very workable or easy to implement. Explorers often 'plunge right in', feeding on risk and uncertainty, and improvising as situations unfold. They often find externally imposed plans, procedures and structures confining. Explorers prefer that sources of authority maintain their distance and limit their influence on their thinking and doing.

The developer style

A 'developer' is an individual who prefers to bring tasks to fulfillment, or who organizes, synthesizes, refines and enhances basic ingredients, shaping them into a more complete and useful result. Developers are concerned with practical applications and the reality of the task. They think creatively by emphasizing workable possibilities and successful implementation. They are usually careful and well-organized, seek to minimize risk and uncertainty, and are comfortable with plans, details and structures. They are able to move tasks or projects forward efficiently and deliberately, and they appreciate close guidance from sources of authority.

Manner of processing

This dimension of VIEW allows people to describe their preference for processing information as well as when and how they prefer to interact with the environment. The main issues included within this dimension include how you prefer to manage information, when you share your thinking, and whether or not interacting with others builds or spends energy. The two styles on this dimension include those who prefer to process *externally* and those who prefer to process *internally* when managing change and solving problems.

The external style

Interacting with others is a source of energy for individuals who prefer the external style. Externals enjoy discussing possibilities and building upon the ideas of others. When learning difficult material, they clarify their ideas and understandings through discussion. When solving problems, they seek a great deal of input from others before reaching closure. They prefer action to reflection, and may seem to rush into things before others are ready to proceed. Externals prefer to share their ideas and thinking early in the process and may be seen as doing so too early by internals. When problem solving, externals will often share their preliminary thinking with others in order to flesh it out. The ideas they share are not very well thought through and are meant to start the problem-solving.

The internal style

People with an internal style preference look first to their inner resources and they draw energy from reflection. Initially, they prefer learning and working alone before sharing their ideas, taking action only after careful consideration and processing information at their own pace. Since their natural preference is to keep their thinking and processing inside, they may seem quiet and might be perceived by externals as pensive or withdrawn. When problem-solving, internals will work with their ideas inside, sharing them when they are more fully developed or near perfection.

Ways of deciding

The deciding dimension involves the initial emphasis a person places on maintaining harmony and interpersonal relationships (i.e. *people*) versus attention to the more logical or rational aspects and obtaining results (i.e. *task*) when making decisions or managing change. The main issues for this dimension relate to your first priorities when you must focus, narrow down choices or make decisions. Your preference for ways of deciding provides insight into how you will prefer to make trade-offs during decision-making.

People-oriented deciders

Individuals who prefer the people style consider first the impact of decisions on people's feelings and on the need for maintaining positive relationships. They prefer emotional involvement when setting priorities, are often seen as warm and caring, and are often quick to become aware of, and to respond to, the needs of others. They seek solutions that others can 'buy into', but may be seen by task-oriented deciders as 'soft' and 'indecisive'. They tend to see task-oriented deciders as being overly concerned about the quality of the outcome, without sufficient consideration being given to the needs of people. People-oriented deciders make decisions and engage in evaluation by considering both the suggestion and the person as a whole, making it more likely that their feedback is more considered and thoughtful of both. People-oriented deciders will make trade-offs in favor of establishing and maintaining good relationships with people over ensuring the highest quality results.

Task-oriented deciders

Individuals who prefer the task style look first at decisions that are logical and objective. They make judgments based on well-reasoned conclusions. They seek in-depth information to reach the 'best solution', or one they can readily justify. They stress staying cool and emotion-free, while seeking clarity and logical order, and may be seen by people-oriented deciders as 'judgmental' and 'uncaring'. They tend to see people-oriented deciders as 'soft', sacrificing outcome quality to the demands of maintaining harmony and relationship. Task-oriented deciders tend to separate the person from their suggestion, enabling them to be more critical of the idea in order to transform it into a more perfect outcome. When they make trade-offs, they will more likely favor obtaining good quality results over maintaining personal relationships.

There are three major levels to consider when it comes to using VIEW to promote teamwork for transformation. The first is to promote insight into an individual's preference and to help them utilize their strengths within the team. The second is when individual team members need to work outside their personal preferences to work together effectively and obtain the desired results. This level of application is called 'coping' and takes energy for those who need to work outside their preferences for extended periods. The third general level of application is when diverse individuals come together and work to complement each other's styles. We call this 'coverage' – having others provide the natural energy that comes from their different preferences to more adequately accomplish the work.

Team development

Once the leader has decided that the resources of a team should be convened, there are a number of dynamics to consider. One of the first of these is the notion that teams go through certain phases of development.[9] Groups and teams are not static. Like individuals, they are unique, dynamic, complex living systems, capable of learning and development. Like any living system, teams go through identifiable stages of development. Some writers refer to this as a natural life cycle for teams. Figure 7.2 depicts our model for team development. According to this model, the stages a team goes through while moving toward some desired goal are relatively identifiable and predictable. In reality, it is quite clear that in practice these stages are not necessary linear and sequential. Some teams seem to skip stages or spend more time in one than other

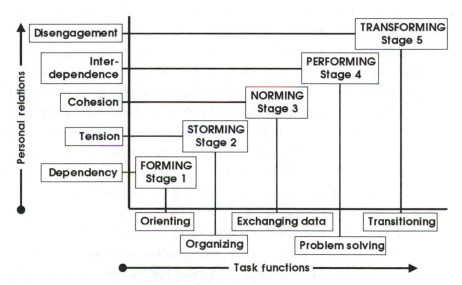

Figure 7.2 A model for team development
Source: Adapted from: Tuckman, B.W. & Jensen, M.A. (1997) Stages of small group development revisited. *Group and Organizational Studies*, 2: 419–427. Reproduced with permission.

stages. Some teams may approach them in reverse order. Still others will reach a level and need to begin all over again because a new member has joined the team.

A model for team development

Understanding where teams are and where you want them to be can be helpful in planning for maximum effectiveness and productivity. Development of a team usually includes two interrelated internal processes. The first deals with internal member-to-member interaction and the nature of the interpersonal relationships. We refer to this as 'personal relations'. The other deals with interaction focused on the task, the work to be done. In other models these dimensions go by other names, but a number of scholars have identified these two dimensions as being central to the process. The classic leadership dilemma is getting the work done while at the same time maintaining positive human relations. Some balance, or appropriate equilibrium, is sought between concern for people and concern for task.[10]

The personal relations dimension refers to the 'human side' of the activity that occurs within the team. Whether it is a task group or a growth group, people progress in development from individuals to group members, to people who feel some attachment to each other, and also to people who are able to link up in creative kinds of ways. People also need to be ready to leave their team and join other teams. Personal relations involve how people feel about each other, how people expect each other to behave, the commitments that people develop to each other, the kinds of assumptions that people make about each other, and the kinds of problems that people have in joining forces with each other in order to get work done. Personal relations characterize the nature and quality of the interaction among team members. The assumption is that the kinds of groups that are referred to here are all organized for the purpose of achieving goals, tasks, production, etc., and that personal relations refers to the human component in the accomplishing of this purpose.

The other dimension is task functions. Characteristic behaviors can also be identified in the different stages of group development with regard to task. A group comes together, learns what the task is, mobilizes to accomplish the task, does the work, and then gets ready to move on. So the two dimensions, personal relations and task functions, form a matrix in which there is an interaction between characteristic human relations and task-oriented behaviors at the various stages of group development. Of course, no two-dimensional model can completely or holistically describe all group interaction without a loss of some precision. The purpose of looking at group development in this relatively simplistic way is to underline the importance, not only of the two dimensions – human and task – but also to provide a common language whereby group members can explore the emerging characteristics and parameters of the team. It is our hope that this will help the teams you work with move through the appropriate stages of development more effectively.

Stage one: forming

In the initial stage, called 'forming', personal relations are characterized by dependency, and the major task functions concern orienting. In the beginning of the team's life, the individual members must resolve a number of dependency problems and characteristic behaviors on the personal relations dimension. They tend to depend on the leader to provide all the structure: the group members 'lean' on the facilitator, chairman or manager to set the ground rules, establish the agenda and to do all the 'leading'. The parallel stage in the task function to be accomplished is the orientation of group members to the work that they are being asked to do. The issues have to be specified. The nature of the work itself has to be explored so that there is a common understanding of what the group has been organized to do. Common behavior at this point is questioning why we are here, what are we supposed to do, how are we going to get it done, and what are our goals.

People who have different styles will have diverse needs in terms of orientation and dependency. Explorers will likely want or prefer minimum guidance and structure, while developers will prefer to have very clear guidance and boundaries. Externals will prefer to get going right away on getting the work done, while internals may prefer to ensure that all the details are worked out before any action is taken. Task-oriented deciders may prefer to emphasize the results that are required, while people-oriented deciders may prefer to clarify their relationship with the leader and other group members.

If you are responsible to lead teams, it will fall to you to encourage everyone to participate and productively engage in clarifying the boundaries of the task and the desired results. Team members will look to you to provide the right level of structure to create a sufficient degree of clarity and help team members understand your role and theirs as well.

Stage two: storming

Stage two is characterized by conflict in the personal relations dimension, and organizing in the task functions dimension. It is referred to as 'storming' because interpersonal conflict inevitably ensues as a part of small-group interaction. It may be that the conflict remains hidden, but it is there. We bring to small-group activity a lot of our own unresolved conflicts with regard to authority, dependency, rules and agenda, and we experience interpersonal conflict as we organize to get work done. Who is going to be responsible for what? What are going to be the rules? What are going to be the limits? What is going to be the reward system? What are going to be the criteria? The variety of organizational concerns that emerge reflect interpersonal conflict over leadership structure, power and authority.

Managing interpersonal tension regarding options or diverse points of view is critical at this stage. Keeping this kind of tension separate from personal tension where individuals might attach the person to the idea is also important. Groups must often be helped through this stage or they will not form into a more cohesive unit capable of high-level performance. This is the stage at which effective application of facilitative leadership is needed. Developers and explorers are likely to have very different concepts of the kind of change required. Internals and externals will have different ways of surfacing the tensions. Task- and people-oriented deciders will have challenges with the way they evaluate alternatives, particularly with differences in the level of personal tension associated with the differences.

You will need to carefully guide the team through this stage, as this is when the individual differences in problem-solving style are most pronounced. You will need to model effective and sensitive listening and encourage others to do the same. Working with the team to establish clear and agreed norms or guidelines for behavior can be very helpful at this stage. Your goal is to help the team traverse this stage and emerge into the next by building a real consensus and challenging each member to contribute toward achieving the desired results.

Stage three: norming

In stage three, the personal relations area is marked by cohesion, and the major task function is exchanging information. It is during this 'norming' stage of development that the people begin to experience a sense of 'groupness', a feeling of clarification at having resolved interpersonal conflict. They begin sharing information, ideas, feelings, giving feedback to each other, soliciting feedback and exploring actions related to the task. This becomes a period during which people feel good about what is going on; they feel good about being a part of a group, and there is an emerging openness with regard to task. Sometimes during stage three there is a brief abandonment of the task and a period of play that is an enjoyment of the cohesion that is being experienced.

When teams reach this stage, it will be important for the facilitator or team leader to provide some recognition and celebration of the success of the group. It would be analogous to the feast following the hunt or the song after successfully managing a boat through the whitewater. A major challenge for the facilitator is to channel this positive energy toward making further progress on the task. Now the group may want to cooperate on every task and get hung up when they can't be 'all for one and one for all'. The challenge is to let the celebration of consensus last long enough to recharge and refocus the group, but not too long so as to invest unnecessary energy in managing the group for the group's own sake.

Developers and explorers will likely have different points of view regarding the scope of the challenges that the team might tackle. For example, the team may have come to agreement that an innovative breakthrough is required. You can be relatively certain that explorers and developers have very different meanings for the same words. Internals and externals may need to celebrate in different ways and may reach this stage at different times. Task- and people-oriented deciders may have different needs in preparing to move forward.

During norming, your challenge is to provide the time and focus to ensure that all team members have actually achieved consensus on the work to be done. You will also need to confirm and reinforce the norms for how the team will work, and the specific action steps to be taken during the next stage.

Stage four: performing

This fourth stage is called 'performing' and is marked by interdependence on the personal relations dimension and problem-solving on the task functions dimension. Interdependence means that members can work singly, in any sub-grouping or as a total unit. They are both highly task-oriented and highly person-oriented. The activities are marked by both collaboration and functional competition. The group's tasks are well-defined, there is high commitment to common activity, and there is support for experimentation and risk-taking.

It is during the performing stage that individual members are both empowered and aligned. They have a shared vision for why they are together and how they are operating. It is at this point where it is appropriate to use the label 'team'. It is important to remember that groups will not stay at this stage forever (nor should they). During the norming process, the group has very probably formed around an implicit set of assumptions. Occasionally, the facilitator will need to test the boundaries or even question their existence.

Developers will enjoy working within the detailed structure and focus on working within the established norms. Explorers may drift from both the agreed structure and ground-rules. Internals may enjoy working alone, but externals will still need some interaction and discussion. Task-oriented deciders will seek quick closure (sometimes premature), while people-oriented deciders may tend to delay closure (sometimes too long).

It is during this stage that the investment in the project plan should pay dividends, allowing you to remind team members about the required actions and deliverables. The same is true for the norms or guidelines you developed. You may also need to periodically remind some team members about these. A key leadership dynamic for you is keeping the team on track while providing them the space to perform. You may need to work with the team to develop clear and balanced criteria upon which to evaluate the results and outcomes.

Stage five: transforming

The fifth stage is called 'transforming' and is characterized by transitioning on the task dimension and disengaging on the personal relations dimension. Transitioning is when the team works to reach closure on the work while getting ready for other and different tasks. Disengagement is when team members detach or separate from the current team members while getting ready to re-engage with other groups and tasks. New members may be entering the existing team to replace some members, necessitating some forming and storming before enabling performing.

During the transforming stage, team members are finishing up the task and getting themselves ready to work with other people, while celebrating the relationships, learning and outcomes from the current team. The major challenge facing the team is dependent on the need for the teamwork to continue beyond one or a few of its members leaving, or the requirement to bring the team to an end as a result of delivering the outcome.

Explorers may perceive that the real work has not yet been accomplished, as they may continue to redefine the task. Developers may have already obtained closure and are ready to move on. Externals may wish to prematurely disengage or, at the other extreme, want to continue with the group interaction beyond the delivery of the results. They may also be much more willing to accept a 'good enough' solution, while the internals may be attempting to pursue perfection. Task-oriented deciders may be more than ready to move on, while people-oriented deciders may not be looking forward to making another transition.

For those responsible for the teamwork, this stage represents the point where the team that has been performing must either redefine itself or bring an end to its work. If the team must disband, your challenge is to ensure that all the desired results are accomplished and that the team has the opportunity to reflect on its success and learn from what has been done. If some members of the team must leave and others remain, your challenge will be creating a transition plan so that the required hand-offs can be accomplished and new members can be acclimated to the project and norms. In either case, you will need to address the need for some sort of recognition and appropriate ways for team members to experience the conclusion of their need to be together.

Conclusion

When applying the model, it is important to remember that this is not a static description of how groups develop. In other words, it is highly unlikely that a particular group would work their way through this process in a systematic manner. Teams will continually develop. Each time a new member joins or a new task is introduced, the development process begins anew. It is also possible that the problem-solving style preferences may play out differently than expected, particularly if you can invite balanced coping and appropriate coverage by playing to the preferences of the different members of team.

Understanding some of the dynamics and patterns that occur within groups is essential if a leader wants to diagnose and describe the current status of any group; predict what might occur in the future; and provide behavior and influence that might help the group move on to a more productive level of development. Taking some time to debrief or reflect on what the team accomplished as well as how it worked together can accelerate team development, particularly if team members can learn the tactics and strategies you deployed. As teams learn to apply these insights they can become more high-performing and will be in a much better position to support organizational transformation.

References

1. Duck, J.D. (2001) *The Change Monster: The Human Forces that Fuel or Foil Corporate Transformation and Change*. New York: Crown Business, p. 95.
2. Maier, N.R. (1970) *Problem Solving and Creativity: In Individuals and Groups*. Belmont, CA: Brooks/Cole. VanGundy, A.B. (1984) *Managing Group Creativity: A Modular Approach to Problem Solving*. New York: American Management Association. Vroom, V.H. (1974) Decision-making and the leadership process. *Journal of Contemporary Business*, 3: 47–67.
3. Smith, D.K. (1996). *Taking Charge of Change: 10 Principles for Managing People and Performance*. Reading, MA: Addison-Wesley.
4. Belbin, M. (1981) *Management Teams: Why They Succeed or Fail*. San Diego, CA: Pfieffer & Co. Belbin, M. (1981) *Team Roles at Work*. San Diego, CA: Pfieffer & Co. Carnevale, A.P., Gainer, L.J. & Meltzer, A.S. (1990). *Workplace Basics: The Essential Skills Employers Want*. San Francisco: Jossey-Bass. Guzzo, R.A. & Salas, E. (eds) (1995) *Team Effectiveness and Decision Making in Organizations*. San Francisco: Jossey-Bass. Katzenbach, J.R. & Smith, D.K. (1993). *The Wisdom of Teams: Creating the High-Performance Organization*. Boston, MA: Harvard Business School Press. Katzenbach, J.R. (1998) *Teams at the Top: Unleashing the Potential of Both Teams and Individual Leaders*. Boston, MA: Harvard Business School Press.
5. Bales, R.F. (1988) *Overview of the SYMLOG System: Measuring and Changing Behavior in Groups*. San Diego, CA: SYMLOG Consulting Group. Isaksen, S.G. & Lauer, K.J. (2002) The climate for creativity and change in teams. *Creativity and Innovation Management*, 11: 74–86. Larson, C.E. & LaFasto, F.M.J. (1989) *Teamwork: What Must Go Right – What Can Go Wrong*. Newbury Park, CA: SAGE Publications. McGregor, D. (1967) *The Professional Manager*. New York: McGraw-Hill.
6. Hackman, J.R. (ed.) (1990) *Groups That Work (and Those That Don't): Creating Conditions for Effective Teamwork*. San Francisco: Jossey-Bass.
7. See: Cook, N.J., Salas, E., Kiekel, P.A. & Stout, R. (2003) Measuring team knowledge: a window to the cognitive underpinnings of team performance. *Group Dynamics: Theory, Research and Practice*, 7: 179–199.
8. Selby, E.C., Treffinger, D.J., Isaksen, S.G. & Lauer, K.J. (2004) Defining and assessing problem-solving style: design and development of new tool. *Journal of Creative Behavior*, 38: 221–243. Selby, E.C., Treffinger, D.J., Isaksen, S.G. & Lauer, K.J. (2004) *VIEW: An*

Assessment of Problem Solving Style – Technical Manual. Sarasota, FL: Center for Creative Learning. Selby, E.C., Treffinger, D.J., Isaksen, S.G. & Lauer, K.J. (2004) *VIEW: Facilitator's Guide.* Sarasota, FL: Center for Creative Learning.

9. Bales, R.F. & Strodtbeck, F.L. (1951) Phases in group problem solving. *Journal of Abnormal and Social Psychology*, 46: 485–495. Jones, J.E. (1983) *An Updated Model for Group Development.* A paper presented at the 29th Annual Creative Problem Solving Institute, Decker Memorial Lecture, Buffalo, NY. Lacoursiere, R.B. (1980) *The Life Cycle of Groups: Group Developmental Stage Theory.* New York: Human Service Press. Tuckman, B.W. (1965) Developmental sequence in small groups. *Psychological Bulletin*, 63: 384–399.

10. Blake, R.R. & Mouton, J.S. (1964) *The Managerial Grid.* Houston: Gulf Publishing Co.

Part 3

TRANSFORMATION METHODS

Chapter 8

MANAGING CHANGE METHODS

do not assume that what's worked for you before will work again. One of the challenges of management is to assess all the techniques and tactics available in the 'managerial kit bag.' You've got to decide which ones are required and why . . . of all the experiences you've had, of all the methodologies you've tried over the years, what is most likely to work here and why?[1]

Introduction

This chapter is about managing change methods. It is written for those of you who must guide change and transformation efforts. You will not need to have a deep background in any particular change method. You probably have a few methods you can (and do) use to guide change. The chapter will define change methods, provide a few reasons why we have so many of them, and offer some ways to deal effectively with them in guiding change systemically.

Before we attempt to deal with the concept of change methods, we will first deal with the word 'managing'. Traditionally, managing means handling or controlling. A synonym for manage is 'conduct'. This word means to guide or escort. Conducting also means leading or directing. Directing implies a constant guiding and regulating to achieve a smooth operation. When we put manage in front of change methods, we mean guide. The emphasis is more on directing the process and keeping a mindful eye on the flow of activity. This idea links very strongly to taking a facilitative approach to leadership as outlined in this book.

We need to rethink the traditional way in which we make change happen. Most change efforts have been unsuccessful and there are numerous reasons for this failure (see Chapter 1 on taking a systemic approach to change). When managers, leaders, consultants and others face situations calling for change, they often pull out their last solution, conduct a quick update or revision and then try to implement it. Often the approach many executives take is to come up with the answer for a big strategic challenge and then announce it to the organization. The expectation is that telling people the answer is sufficient to make the organization change.

This ignores what we know about changing behavior. Daniels has outlined a summary of what the behavioral sciences offer to those who seek to manage change.[2] He outlines the ABCs of behavior. The A stands for 'antecedent'. This is the condition that exists prior to the change. For example, you walk into a room and find that it is too dark. The B stands for 'behavior'. This is the action that is taken to change the current condition. Following the example, you flick the light switch. The C stands for the 'consequences' of the behavior. In the example, the lights come on in the room.

Sending the message that change is needed is more of an antecedent. It sets the conditions for change. When an executive sends a message it must outline the behaviors that need to change. The key is to have a plan for how the consequences will be managed. When people behave in the way that is needed and desired, the consequences must reinforce the appropriate behavior and extinguish or negatively reinforce the behaviors that are out of line. The most powerful kind of reinforcement for encouraging people to take initiative is immediate, positive and concrete. Changing behavior is not an easy affair and is assisted by taking a systemic approach.

At the heart of managing change methods is the idea that there are times when you need to be conscious and deliberate about choosing change methods. In short, we need to change the way we change.

What is a change method?

Change often involves something new, may create some ambiguity and usually contains some level of complexity. To varying degrees, responding to change creates a need for people to use their problem-solving ability and creativity.

A change method gives people a structure or framework to help them understand and achieve a needed transformation. It organizes your approach to change. Methods are ways to obtain various solutions. Change methods are ways that individuals, groups and organizations deal regularly with demands for novelty and improved effectiveness. These can be changes in the marketplace, customer needs, technology, regulations, weather or the structure of knowledge. They are ways in which people cope with modifications and respond to revolutionary shifts or incremental improvements.

Change methods can be reactive or proactive; implicit or explicit; deliberate or unintentional. A well-known (and perhaps overused) reactive organizational change method is to engage in 'cost reduction' when profits dip and costs escalate. This method has created all sorts of solutions like head count reduction or rightsizing. A proactive method, used for the same conditions, is new product or service development. The solutions this method encourages include the introduction of line extensions for revenue generation and the creation of new services.

One of the main reasons for changing the way we change is that we now have many more change methods from which to choose.

Why so many change methods?

The number of change methods has increased because we face more challenges requiring change, increased complexity and a demand for faster change. Each of these reasons is described in more detail below.

More change challenges

The reason for the large number of change methods is, in part, due to the existence of, and need to cope with, many different types of change. Organizations face intense competition on a day-to-day level and at the same time they face other large-scale strategic challenges. Changes within the marketplace are placing heavy demands on organizations. It is no longer possible to deal quietly and calmly with only a few selected changes at a time. A full diversity of change challenges every part of the organization, every day. An implication is that change can no longer be managed by a select few in elite management positions.

More complexity

Organizations are becoming more complex as well. There are increasing efforts to work across functions and cultures. There are all sorts of changes that increase complexity of working within organizations like mergers, acquisitions and new ways of partnering or creating alliances. An implication of this complexity is that parts of the organization are faced with different types of change at different points in time. It would be futile to mandate the use of any single method throughout the organization, particularly for those that must operate on a cross-functional or global level. Another implication is that the tasks are increasingly complex, requiring perspectives and involvement from multiple disciplines. As a result, it becomes necessary to have and use common frameworks and language to encourage collaboration.

Increased speed

The increasing speed with which organizations must deal with change continues to put pressure on the demand for more and better approaches. It is not only the diversity of the changes, but that they must now be dealt with more swiftly than the competition, which creates even more demand for change methods. Given the need for speed, organizations can no longer afford a 'not invented here' mentality or invest precious time and resources in 'reinventing the wheel'. They must now build in a capacity to deal deliberately with change. This means having a deliberate commitment to developing the knowledge and skill of many within the organization.

Changing the way we change

These needs for change have promoted the proliferation of methods. It is a simple reality, of course, that no single method, however powerful, can function effectively the same way for all people, situations or needs. Methods that make the claim of universal application are, upon close examination, likely to have weak conceptual foundations and questionable evidence for validity. There is a need to identify and use change methods across a broader spectrum.

Just as no single method will satisfy all the needs for change, launching an uncoordinated flurry of programs and initiatives is likely to be unsuccessful. If this flurry is accompanied by a random array of methods or approaches, it is unlikely that any productive results will follow. A survey conducted by Bain & Company Planning Forum found that between 1990 and 1994, the average company committed itself to 12 of the 25 popular management tools and techniques from corporate visioning and total quality management (TQM) programs to empowerment and reengineering processes.[3] The study found no relationship between the number of methods that organizations were using and their financial performance.

Most attention is paid to the more public product innovation. Around 70% of innovations are in process, and of these, organizational restructuring is the most common process innovation. Human resource management innovations are the most likely to benefit employees, and more specifically, work design innovations have the highest and most consistent benefits for employee and customer relations. Such innovations require high levels of investment, and have to be pervasive (that is extend to more of the organization) and novel (in comparison to what the organization has done before) in order to translate into improvements in financial performance.[4] However, the majority of organizations adopting 'best practices' have done so piecemeal.[5] For example, the most commonly adopted practices have been those related to support project selection and management, and soliciting customer requirements, but relatively few organizations have paid equal attention to the fuzzy front end of new concept development or facilitation and teamwork necessary for successful implementation.[6]

We have seen three basic barriers to effectively applying a change method. The first is a lack of readiness to apply the method. This can stem from a pure lack of knowledge or awareness of methods in general, or any specific method. It can also stem from not having the right people, situation or task focus. The second and related barrier is a lack of skill and ability to apply the method well. This happens when people have not learned a method well, or do not have the needed experience and the behavioral tools or skills to use the method. The third barrier is that people may not be willing to learn or apply the method. They may be ready (in most ways) to learn the method and understand the need to learn it well, but unwilling to invest the time and energy to do so. These barriers show themselves in various ways including the following responses.

We don't have the time for this!

This usually means that the people involved do not see the value in a method. They are so overwhelmed by the short-term crises they are currently facing that they cannot possibly handle another thing. They may be completely overloaded.

We've tried that before!

This means that not only do we not have the time, but also last time we tried to use a method it didn't work. Rather than learning how to better apply the method, it is perceived as a complete waste of time. This can also be due to a lack of understanding about the nature of change itself (i.e. that there is a natural order to any change initiative).

My *method's better than yours!*

This means that a particular method may already have strong discipleship and that the key to resisting it is that your method could not be as good as mine. This is a restatement of the 'not invented here' idea.

Once the barriers have been broken, those who learn and apply change methods need some way to decide which method to use for what purposes. The methods they choose to use also need to fit both the people involved and the situation in which the method is applied. The implication is that it now requires a bit more discipline to choose and apply change methods.[7] Those who are choosing methods must now look beyond which guru is hot or what is currently being served as the popular flavor of the month. Taking a systemic approach offers a productive alternative.

This stands in sharp contrast to what we often see as the predominant approach to change. Very often, the temptation when facing the need for change is to take out the previous project plan or just to use the favorite approach. We often observe that many who lead organizational change simply look around for what has worked elsewhere and then attempt to copy and apply those solutions – often with disastrous results.

Different kinds of change

One way to sort out the abundance of change methods is to consider the differences in the kinds of change being demanded. Some situations call for an incremental or continuous kind of change. These situations may involve limited resources, clear and agreed upon measures of success, outcomes close to the strategic objective, attention to detail, and focus on short-term benefits and optimization. Such situations demand the effective use of a more developmental kind of creativity (see Chapter 2 on building the Janusian organization). This kind of creativity is more likely to emerge as important within relatively stable environments and involves a high need for structure. This kind of creativity and change is relatively easy and preferred by those who lead and manage organizations due to the ability to introduce more prediction and control.

Other situations call for a more discontinuous kind of change. These situations may involve a grand but unclear vision for a great future opportunity, a radically new design, the occurrence of a disruptive technological breakthrough, or need for paradigmatic shift. They are often stimulated by urgent crises (often with high stakes), a precipitative event, and strategies that call for changing the game because incremental change is not seen as working. These situations demand the effective use of a more exploratory kind of creativity and usually contain a lower need for structure than those requiring more developmental change. Change methods that take a single, predetermined pathway cannot respond well to both exploratory and developmental change. Responding to different kinds of change requires a more flexible or descriptive approach.

Given the broad spectrum of possible changes and the fact that many organizational functions develop and use their own special or favorite approaches, we have seen a proliferation of diverse change methods. Some of these methods may be more appropriate for exploratory change, and others better suited for developmental change. For example, many continuous improvement methods may be better for producing adaptive or developmental change. Reengineering may be a better fit for innovative or exploratory change (see Figure 8.1).

Many different commercially available change methods can be documented (see Chapter 9 on alternative change methods). Also, as a result of working with large and complex change efforts inside some of the world's largest organizations, it is clear that the 'flavor of the month' syndrome is alive and well. If people within organizations are not confused by the speed with which different methods are introduced, then they

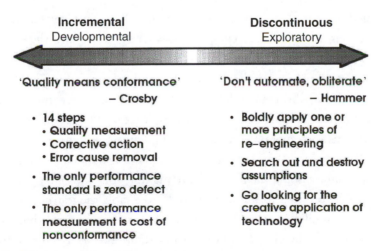

Figure 8.1 Change methodology spectrum

may be challenged by the fact that each method seems to have its own language and appears friendly to one or only a few functions. Using the spectrum of change outlined above may be helpful in choosing the most appropriate method.

One organization, for example, 'rolled out' a continuous improvement initiative only to have it replaced in a little more than a year by business process reengineering. People who had been trained in learning and applying the continuous improvement method and tools were confused, frustrated and uncertain how their investment in this learning was to be used within the new context of reengineering. One of the ways people cope with the vast number and kind of change methods is to use only their favorite one, or cynically dismiss the need to learn and apply any (because they will certainly be replaced by another flavor very soon).

Most organizations seem to manage change methods by discovering the need for change and prescribing the quickest method possible. They may also choose a method that aligns with one favorite or particular guru. This usually results in a single change initiative being launched within the organization. CEOs will often get together and exchange their favorite change methods. It is no accident that GE's Jack Welch's Work Out became IBM's (Lou Gerstner) Accelerating Change Together.[8] Other organizations try to figure out the range of changes that they are currently facing (and might face in the future) and put together a program to manage change. The main question is: How do you manage change methods?

The need for navigation

Managing methods for change requires navigation. You must have a destination in mind (we call this a desired outcome), know where you are and the capabilities of your mode of transportation (context), as well as who is (or how many are) with you (people). Charting your course indicates how you will get to your destination (method). Of course, even with the most efficient and detailed plan, weather conditions or mechanical difficulties, among other things, may force you to modify your plan.

Most change methods contain specific tools, guidelines and language to guide thinking and problem-solving behavior. These resources are usually at the cognitive level – knowing them enables doing them. If you are making your journey by sailboat, there are specific things you need to know how to do to enable the journey.

Navigation is at a different level than cognition. It requires you to think about your thinking (and that of others). We call this meta-cognition. The skipper of the sailboat may know all about the tools and resources on board (and also the capabilities of the deck hands!) but must also maintain focus on where the boat is, current weather conditions and the relative location of the ultimate destination. Certain tasks can be accomplished and completed, but navigation is a constant and ongoing responsibility.

Navigation is key to managing change methods. It involved deliberate planning as well as constant monitoring to allow for adjustments and modifications to the plan. The next section will detail how you can deliberately navigate your use of change methods. We refer to this as 'planning your approach'.

Planning your approach to change

Planning your approach means investing time and energy to clearly determine if you should address a change, and then designing how you might actually accomplish the desired results. If you have only one approach that fits all situations, then you will find planning your approach to be a waste of time. If, on the other hand, you have a method that allows flexibility in application, or a variety of methods from which to choose, you will find these suggestions useful.

Planning your approach includes two major stages. The first is taking the time to reflect on the needs, people and context, as well as the methods themselves. It results in a decision about whether or not to take on the change. This stage is called *Appraising Tasks* and is described in more detail below. The second stage involves the designing of the approach you will take and is called *Designing Process*. This stage is also described in more detail below.

The next section briefly describes the history of this component of managing change methods to help you see where these stages came from.

Key historical CPS developments

Although our focus has been the improvement of a specific change method called creative problem-solving (CPS), the resultant learning can apply to anyone attempting to manage any change method. As we were attempting to improve the Osborn–Parnes model of CPS, we had made several improvements within the system including clarifying the roles of facilitator, client and resource group, and developing specific convergent or focusing guidelines and tools to improve the balance of the process. These improvements were made within the prevailing Osborn–Parnes paradigm of a five-step model that focused primarily on the cognitive activity of generating options as CPS. These historical developments within CPS have helped us discover the importance of being mindful about planning your approach to change.[9]

The first deliberate move toward a meta-cognitive approach to CPS involved adding an explicit stage on the 'front end' of the model that dealt with ownership, outcomes and obstacles, personal orientation and situational outlook.[10] Although the concepts of objective finding and 'fuzzy mess' were within the earlier Osborn–Parnes paradigm, they were not explicitly included in deliberate instructional or application efforts. Instead, they were seen as starting positions for entry into the Osborn–Parnes' five steps.

We originally packaged these concepts within the mess-finding stage of the process, but soon found that by addressing these issues as a part of the process, people were precluded from running through our process the way they did with the Osborn–Parnes five-step model. As a result, we broke the process into components in order to package the stages more closely to the way people actually used them. We also found that there were many variables outside the method that had a profound impact on how CPS was used.[11]

It became apparent that the issues we had packaged into the front end of the CPS process were, in fact, a separate and important aspect of process management. Further, during the early 1990s we purposely moved away from using CPS as a prescribed and preordained sequence of steps to an approach that was designed to meet the needs of any particular situation. Rather than setting out the optimal, prescribed and preferred way through the creative process, we embraced the idea that there were many possible pathways through the creative process. Thinking about and planning for any particular pathway through the process is a component we now call 'planning your approach' and includes the stages of Appraising Tasks and Designing Process.

Since we saw CPS as 'software of the mind', we used the metaphor of computer software to explain this new development. The three main components of CPS were like specific applications. One component dealt with obtaining clarity. Another dealt with generating ideas. A third component dealt with planning for action. If you are familiar with Microsoft Office, these could be seen as PowerPoint, Excel and Word. The navigation component, called 'planning your approach', could be seen as the operating system, allowing you to choose and move around among the specific applications.

Contingencies for Appraising Tasks

In order to effectively plan your approach to change, you will need to have a basic understanding of the task to be accomplished. Appraising Tasks allows you to inquire and reflect on what actually needs to be done. Some preliminary considerations for various tasks were outlined, and a five-year study of the decision-making and problem-solving literature provided support for these and added another.[12] The main issue is considering what you would like to know before you actually design your approach to the change method. The factors shown in Table 8.1 have been identified as key to Appraising Tasks.

Problem-solvers and those who manage change will always have to put these contingencies in context. These are broad issues that provide the purpose for Appraising Tasks. It is quite possible that people involved with the task will have different perspectives on each of the factors. One of the goals of Appraising Tasks is to obtain some degree of consensus surrounding the issues.

These factors provide a base for understanding what the task is. We have provided a task appraisal model to help obtain information and insight on these contingencies. The model reflects the larger system described in Chapter 1 (on taking a systemic approach to change). One main dimension includes the people and the situation. The other dimension includes the content and process. There is interaction within each dimension and between the two dimensions. It is from inquiring and considering these dimensions, and their interactions, that you can make effective decisions and judgments to guide the design of your particular approach.

A task appraisal model

A task is any piece of work or project to be done. Appraising Tasks provides a deliberate structure for thinking about problem-solving for tasks that require change, creativity and innovation. Given the learning from our research and practice, it was no longer possible or desirable for us to force a particular, predetermined and prescribed sequence of steps. We needed an explicit way to better understand the need, people and context before qualifying, modifying or choosing a method.

Appraising Tasks is helpful within our current view of CPS, but is also productive for managing other change methods.[13] Appraising Tasks provides a deliberate opportunity to qualify the use of the method, examine and better understand the people involved in the change, the context surrounding it and the desired outcome or needed result (see Figure 8.2). By considering this system, you are in a better position to make estimates and decisions regarding the factors outlined in Table 8.1.

As the practitioner, consultant, manager or facilitator involved in choosing and then applying a method, you will have the responsibility for Appraising Tasks. As a client

Table 8.1   Factors for Appraising Tasks

Factor	Question
Importance	To what extent is this task a high priority for you and for others?
Kind and degree of ownership	Is this a task about which people care, have enthusiasm and in which they are interested?
	Do they have the authority and opportunity to take action?
	Are they willing to use their imaginations to think up new possibilities?
Ambiguity	To what extent is the task 'messy', ill-defined or lacking in structure?
Complexity	Is the task simple and distinct, or complex and made up of many different elements?
Novelty	To what extent are you seeking new possibilities that will break new ground, or be surprising departures from reality?
	Are you seeking options that are familiar, easy to implement, or considered safe?
Timeline	Does this task require immediate attention and action or can you work on it over a longer period of time?
	Will the task require a single (one-time) effort, or will it require many different efforts?
History	To what extent does the task depend upon understanding the background information?
	What have you already tried to accomplish?
Involvement of others	Should someone work on this task alone, with a few others or with many others?
Vision of desired future	To what extent might people view the task as an obstacle or threat to be overcome, a gap to be closed or an opportunity to be achieved?

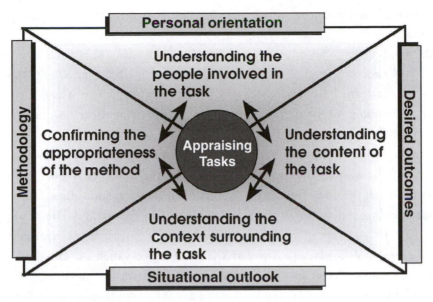

Figure 8.2   The Task Appraisal Model

or sponsor, you will find value in considering each of the elements within the Task Appraisal Model to help you make better decisions about your approach (see Figure 8.2).

You may appraise tasks on challenges that you are facing on your own, or as a facilitator working with a client, or when you are facing a larger change initiative. Others who use or design change methods can use Appraising Tasks to qualify the appropriate application of methods and enhance their understanding of the people, situation and desired outcomes from the method. Those who are responsible for implementing the change will also benefit from Appraising Tasks. The four basic elements of the task appraisal model are described in more detail below.

Personal orientation

Appraising Tasks includes understanding something about the people who might be involved. Working to understand personal orientation includes a focus on ensuring that there is sufficient ownership to effectively use the method (see Chapter 6 on owning up to change). For example, you may be the actual sponsor of the change, the agent responsible for implementing the change, the target who must actually change, or an advocate who wants to achieve a change but lacks the legitimate power to make it happen.

Understanding personal orientation also includes knowing about the level of both content and process expertise of the people involved in the task. When Appraising Tasks, you can learn how much your clients know about their area and their ability to clearly communicate the content. You may also learn something about their awareness level of the method or approach you intend to use.

Becoming aware of the personal preferences and cognitive styles of the people involved may be helpful to more fully comprehend and influence the decisions about how to approach the task. This aspect of Appraising Tasks ensures the necessary focus on understanding the nature of the people involved in the change. For example, we use *VIEW: An Assessment of Problem Solving Style*^{SM} to assist in learning about people's preferences for change, the way that they process their information, and the way that they make decisions (See Chapter 7 on teamwork for transformation).

Some of the key questions you may want to ask when developing an understanding of personal orientation include:

- Who are the leaders or sponsors behind this change, and do they have the influence, clout or leverage to implement any new alternatives?
- Who has a stake in this area and what is it? Who else is involved? Why?
- Do the people involved have all the needed knowledge and information to deal effectively with this task?

After inquiring about personal orientation, there are three possible options. You may find that there is sufficient change leadership to proceed. In other words, you are working with the right people who know enough about the task and can take action without having to ask permission. A second option is that you may want to modify the task so that you can continue to work with the same people. The task might be modified or redefined so that it is within their area of ownership. The third option is that you may keep the task and find the right sponsor or client. In fact, you could probably even use the people with whom you are working to help locate the more appropriate client or sponsor. Of course, for some situations, it would be tough politics to change the people with whom you may be working.

Having sufficient ownership for the task is a go or no-go decision. We find that one of the key reasons any method is unsuccessful is that there is no one responsible for following through on the results. The other aspects of expertise and style inform your use of the method.

Situational outlook

Another aspect of Appraising Tasks includes examining situational outlook. Situational outlook focuses on understanding the context surrounding the task (see Chapter 12 on the climate for innovation and growth). When considering situational outlook, the main issue is that what you learn about the context helps you determine and design your approach. The climate and culture surrounding the task can be examined through the use of formal and informal assessments. Knowing a few of the core values driving the organization you are working with can also be very helpful. For example, learning that safety was a core value helped us understand why certain behaviors were forbidden in one organization with which we worked (e.g. among many other rules, we couldn't run when on the property).

When considering the outlook of the situation, it is helpful to learn about the perceived priority, importance and immediacy of the task. The degree to which the task fits the strategy of the organization can tell you about the perception of the task's importance. Learning about the level of desire for the outcome can also influence how soon you will need to begin to deliver results.

Other issues in understanding the situational outlook include the level of resources, time and budget available for the task. When you learn about the context, you obtain information about the structure and systems as well as many other factors. This information can help you learn about the kinds of resources that are available and the procedures that may be necessary to obtain them.

Some key questions you may want to ask when examining situational outlook include:

- What are the culture and/or climate like?
- How does this task fit the strategic priorities? Will the resources be there?
- How ready are the individuals, teams and organization to take on the needed changes?

When considering situational outlook, you may again end up at three different places. The context may be ready for the task and the method to be used. Second, you may need to intervene to modify either the context itself or the task upon which you will work. Finally, after considering the context you may decide to wait or withdraw.

One of the insights you obtain by exploring the situational outlook is whether or not the climate will support the kind of novelty required by the task. If the task requires exploratory novelty, then certain dimensions within the climate may be necessary (especially trust, risk-taking and idea-time). If the task requires developmental novelty, then it may be more important that the context contains well-structured and ordered procedures as well as deliberate plans for improvement.[14]

Desired outcomes

Comprehending the desired outcome provides you with information about the actual content and the needs within the task. The desired outcome is the end result of the change effort. In considering the desired outcome you will learn about the level of content knowledge on the part of the people involved. Knowing about the needed results helps you to understand how you will measure your success and provides key input into your questions within the other areas of appraising the task.

Understanding the desired outcome also includes knowing the kind and degree of novelty that is necessary, as well as acquiring an image of the preferred future. The degree or level of novelty informs you about how original or unique the outcome needs to be. If it is highly original, it may take a method designed for deliberate effort and stretch. It may also require a certain type of situation and a certain level of involvement from selected individuals. The kind of novelty tells you if the results need to be revolutionary (exploratory) or evolutionary (developmental).

If you are facilitating the application of change methods, you are focused on learning about the client's ability to clearly communicate the image of the preferred future. As you listen to the client(s) describing their perceptions of the desired outcome, you can assess the clarity of the image(s). If you are working with a group, you can learn about the degree of alignment that the clients share. You may even have them draw the desired future state. The focus is on obtaining clarity and agreement regarding what the client is shooting for.

As a client or person responsible for implementing the outcomes from the change method, it is your responsibility to think through the future image. You will need to be clear about the end result while providing some degree of freedom regarding how others with get there.

Some questions you may want to ask to clarify the desired outcomes include:

- Can you provide me a clear picture of what you're looking for?
- What kind of novelty are you looking for? How different is the future state from what exists today?

- What is stopping you from getting what you want? What are the barriers and obstacles to obtaining your desired results?
- How would you know that you have successfully reached your desired outcome?

After acquiring enough information about the desired outcome, you are in a better position to understand the need for novelty and the image of the preferred future. This allows you to proceed to qualify the method you want to use. You may need to modify the task to adjust it so that it includes a clear need for novelty. If not, you may need to modify the expectations that people have for the method. If there is a need for low level of novelty, then those who are using a given change method should not expect that method to produce magic results.

Methodology

Task appraisal also provides for deliberate qualification of the method(s) to be employed. Methodology implies that you are studying the method(s) that you are planning to apply. You may have a specific method in mind or you may have a number of possible methods from which to choose. In either case, this part of Appraising Tasks helps you to consider the appropriateness of the method you have in mind (see Chapter 9 on alternative change methods).

To determine the appropriateness of the method, you need to know the costs and benefits of the various options. There are many different methods available to help you with change, but there is no single and perfect method to fit all situations, people and outcomes. Each one has its own strengths and challenges. Some professional services firms with whom we work have catalogs of hundreds of methods with comprehensive evaluations and case studies to help people make choices. These resources help professionals make deliberate choices regarding the methods that they apply by linking their diagnosis of the desired outcome, situation and people with best-case application.

The level of knowledge and skill that people have in using the methods is another consideration. Some methods are naturally more familiar to people, others may be well known because they have been designated for use in particular places. You may need to use a method that has the support of key people within the organization. On other occasions, you may be able to bring in people from the outside with the needed expertise.

The guiding question for this aspect of task appraisal is: 'Does the method fit the people, situation and desired outcome?' In other words, rather than starting with your method and trying to find the opportunities to apply it, you are better off starting with the desired outcome and a good understanding of the people and the context. Then find a method that has the greatest likelihood of obtaining the outcome, and that fits both the people involved and the context in which it will be applied.

Some questions you may want to ask to confirm the appropriateness of the alternative method include:

- What methods are currently used? What is the level of skill and experience in these methods?
- How might the people involved respond to the alternative method?
- How likely is it that the alternative method will obtain the results?

Once you have enough knowledge of these issues, there are three possible options regarding methodology. It can be applied as designed. What you have learned from the other areas of Appraising Tasks has qualified the method that you had in mind. A second option is that the method can be adjusted, modified, redesigned or combined with another method for appropriate application. Finally, you may decide that the method should not be used at that point in time. Perhaps an alternative method that better fits the people, situation and desired outcome should be applied.

Designing Process

Once the decision is made that a method is appropriate for any particular task, the next challenge is to design the process approach that you will take to apply it. Now you know that the task is appropriate for a change method, you need to figure out *how* to make the change happen. We call this 'Designing Process'. Its purpose is to determine how to proceed with the operation of the specific method(s) and requires an understanding of the method to be employed, the people to be involved, and the situation within which you will be working. It also means designing the series of actions or operations you must take in order to approach the task. Figure 8.3 previews the key aspects of Designing Process.

Designing Process includes more than just project planning and the technical aspects surrounding the design of your approach. Engaging in Designing Process allows you to be mindful and reflective about the spirit of the approach, as well as build motivation and commitment for participating in the process. The following general

Figure 8.3   Designing Process

contingencies will be help your Designing Process efforts across a variety of more specific methods.

Determining scope of application

As a result of appraising the task, you will know about the desired outcome of the change initiative. This information will guide your decision-making regarding the size or scope of the task. The size of the task determines the level of interaction, the kind of method to be applied, and what may happen in the context as you apply the method.

Some tasks may need only a single workshop, meeting or session. An example of this kind of scope was a situation with one of our client organizations where the senior management team would set research and development priorities once a year. The challenge was that this relatively large management team consisted of 13 very strong-willed individuals who very rarely came to consensus on issues. After completing an appraisal of the task with the CEO, we decided that we needed a single meeting (one day) with the main purpose of acquiring clear consensus on investment in research and development. We used a specific tool called 'paired comparison analysis' to allow each individual to rank the importance of nine distinct criteria, and then compiled the results to allow for a focused discussion. The result was a clear set of prioritized criteria that helped the vice president of research and development realign spending and scheduling in his area.

Larger and more complex tasks may require a series of meetings or sessions. We define a project as a coordinated series of meetings or sessions with specific goals and deliverables. A project allows for an individual or group to maintain their focus on the day-to-day work and take on a change effort. For example, one client organization was in the direct mail publishing business. The customer service function was measured by how many calls were handled each hour. The challenge was to change their main focus. That meant changing from processing cancellations as quickly as possible, to working to retain customers. Following an appraisal of the task, we decided to observe a few customer service representatives and then discuss the challenge with them. Following this, we held a series of short problem-solving sessions to get their ideas about how we could meet the challenge. After a one-day planning meeting with the global head of customer service, we held a series of short implementation sessions with each geographical unit. The result was a significant improvement in customer retention, and even some additional revenue through sales of other products.

An initiative includes a series of projects targeting long-term objectives and deliverables. Initiatives can last as long as two or three years or be accomplished within a few months. Figure 8.4 shows an example that will illustrate what we mean. A president of a global business unit within an international publishing company approached us to help with their new product development initiative. After conducting an Appraising Tasks meeting with the president and two of his assistants, we diagnosed the need and created general images for a new product development program for their global business unit. The desired outcome was sufficiently large and complex that we designed a two-year program containing a variety of different forms of interaction including meetings, workshops, global teamwork projects, conferences and coaching sessions.

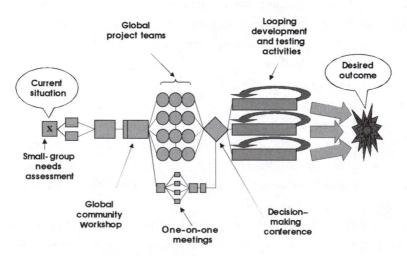

Figure 8.4 An example of Designing Process

Each stage of the process required different kinds of outcomes that lead to later stages (see Figure 8.4 for a visual overview). Therefore, we designed different structures for each activity depending on the outcome needed for that part of the process. For example, in one part, we identified key global market opportunities to pursue, and clarified key customer needs to address. In another part, we generated 12 new concepts that were likely to meet key customer needs. For other parts, we had global project teams talk with customers to confirm their needs, and develop business cases for pursuing concepts. Each part of the process used different approaches based on the required results.

The nature of the task will dictate the character of the method. Coaching, mentoring or some other approach might be best for some tasks. Others may require a single working session or workshops containing multiple sessions. These interactions may be planned as a long-term program or project, rather than a single intervention. Still other tasks may require multiple levels of meetings, sessions, interactions or work groups, and demand systemic project management and integration.

Level of involvement and interaction

People are key to implementing all change efforts. In fact, organizations don't change; people do. In order to successfully approach the task, you may need to gather particular expertise. If you involve others, it may be on the basis of their common and deep knowledge, experience and skill. For other tasks, you may need a diverse array of perspectives. For these, you may gather other people who have different cultural, gender, age or functional backgrounds. Some tasks are more concerned with implementation and acceptance or engagement. For these tasks, it may be less a matter of expertise and more an issue of politics, representation and influence.

Some tasks will require a high level of involvement and participation in the process. These tasks often depend on having a high degree of acceptance of the outcomes or on including a diverse array of perspectives. Other initiatives may be closely held by the individual or group having more exclusive ownership, or they may require more of a top-down approach. This may influence if and how you will work on an individual level, in small groups, large groups or on an organization-wide level.

Certain required results may demand particular kinds of interaction (see the end of this chapter for a list of 100 different ways of interacting). Most of our meetings occur in the same place at the same time. The movement and need to use other forms of interaction is growing. An implication is that your process planning may include organizing your meetings at the same time but at different places (video-conferencing, tele-conferencing, etc.), different places at different times (web sites, bulletin boards, written and print media, etc.), or at the same place but at a different time (message systems, databases, visible displays, learning centers, etc.). These approaches may require specific technology or other material resources.

In our new product development example, we had to manage many different forms of interaction throughout the overall process plan. Some interactions involved one-on-one conversations while others involved small-group work teams. In some cases, we needed to involve a large number of people using global conferences. The level of involvement was determined by what needed to happen at that part of the process. For example, during one part of the process, the focus was on decision-making. Therefore, we pulled together the core decision-makers (a subset of the entire community taking part in the initiative) and involved them in a criteria clarification meeting. It was important that the strategy for decision-making in new product development be clear and consistent with the overall organizational strategies. Therefore, the group responsible for setting strategy in this business unit was involved in creating and defining the criteria.

Then, one-on-one follow-up meetings were held between the core decision-makers and other key influencers to ensure the list of criteria was complete and to get their buy-in to the criteria themselves. A subsequent workshop was then held that involved the core decision-makers and these key influencers (all in one place at the same time) to clarify the priorities associated with the criteria, and then begin making decisions about the new product concepts.

The level of interaction for each part of the process was determined based on the purpose of that stage in the process. At some points, it was necessary to involve a small group, particularly when the issue was decision-making. When a diversity of opinions and expertise was needed, the larger community of people was involved.

From an understanding of the desired outcome, the context and the people involved in the task, you will be in a better position to know if it is necessary or useful to use a group. If the method can be employed effectively with a group, additional planning may be helpful and necessary. For example, when using a group it may also be necessary to prepare the client for interacting with the group members as well as define and clarify roles prior to the session. Decisions made during these planning activities will influence the concrete and specific plans for the actual working session.

Many long-term and strategically important initiatives will have a dedicated project team assigned to them. Often, this team will have a project sponsor, leader and members with specified roles. When planning your approach you may want to work with the entire team to work out the design from the start.

Meeting the need

One key outcome from appraising a task is a clear understanding of the need. Change methods are designed to meet a variety of needs, so part of Designing Process is making decisions about what method, or what parts of methods will help you obtain the desired outcomes.

For example, CPS has three main components including understanding the challenge, generating ideas and preparing for action. Within each of these components, there are numerous stages. Within the understanding the challenge component you can construct opportunities, explore data or frame problems. If you needed to set a new strategic direction for your business unit, you would find constructing opportunities the most appropriate stage. In this stage, you could generate numerous opportunities and obstacles and set about selecting the most important. Then you could integrate these into specific plans for your business. The stage of constructing opportunities helps you use the right kind of language and tools to meet the need.

Constraints from the context

When planning your approach you may learn that the situation in the organization requires a certain degree of visible structure and support. For example, certain organizations (Polaroid, DuPont, Kodak, Exxon, Lucent) have found it useful to have a distinct center for creativity. These central structures offer information, training, facilitation and application services across functions and traditional product categories. Others have relied on a broad skills transfer initiative or a 'swat-team' approach. Often, this had been led through the human resource function due to its focus on building competencies. The constraints from the context may influence the amount and kind of resources that will be available (people, staff, use of external consultants, time, money, technology, etc.). Still other organizations prefer a more informal or low-key approach (i.e. the creeping quiet virus approach).

Certain situations may require that results be shown early in the process. Some organizations may demand quick wins from any change program. Others may take a long-term perspective and allow for investments in other aspects of the process. In either case, you can learn how quickly results must be delivered and shape your approach accordingly. If the sponsor is asking for a fundamental, big and innovative change and the situation is calling for quick, simple and cheap results, you're in for a challenging piece of work!

Another constraint that may affect Designing Process is how many projects have already been launched. You may find that some places suffer from initiative overload. People in these places have too many existing projects and can barely make progress on what's already 'on their platter'.

Our new product development example shows how the constraints of the context have a strong influence on Planning Process. The organization was in the process of creating strategies for new product development. However, at this point in time, a few things were clear. First, they needed to make their core business financially stable in two years. Second, they wanted the approach to new product development to be global. In other words, they wanted to move away from localized new product development, toward products that targeted global markets. And third, they had just clarified their organizational values, one of which focused on customers. Therefore, the process had to focus on the customers' needs. Since the organization had a financial challenge, this was all to be done while minimizing costs associated with the new product development initiative.

These factors in the context helped us target who was involved in the process, how they would be involved, and where the information came from that would stimulate new product develop concepts. It also gave us the general time frames in which steps within the method were to be completed.

Process contingencies

In making decisions about various methods, you will need to consider a number of different features about the method(s) you have at your disposal. Again, the assumption is that you have more than one method from which to choose.

Methods can differ on how broadly they can be applied. Some methods are more amenable to individual application (e.g. some interactive CD technology). Others are more appropriate or have been designed primarily for small-group application (e.g. targeted innovation sessions). Still others are specifically designed for large-group use (e.g. open-space technology). Finally, some methods are best used across an entire organization (e.g. balanced scorecard). Closely related to the breadth of methods is how dependent they may be on the use of specific hard or soft technology.

Methods have been developed to respond to specific purposes. Some are focused on particular kinds of change. Quality methods might be more analytic and promote incremental improvement within organizations. These methods may be more about closing gaps, improving existing products and services and identifying deviations from standards. Creativity methods might be aimed at rethinking the total purpose of the business or enterprise. These methods may be more exploratory and respond better to needs that require a fresh perspective. Still others may be designed for particular organizations or functions. The purpose or need that stimulated the original development of the method can tell you a great deal about the best-case application of that method.

The new product development example involved different processes including creative problem-solving (CPS), consumer research and new product development. Of all the methods available, these were chosen for their unique contribution to the desired outcome and for how each fits the demands of the task. Other methods were not chosen because they did not fit the constraints of the task. For example, we use a method in new product development called 'deep dive discovery'. It helps organizations identify unarticulated and unexplored consumer needs, and helps to turn them into new product concepts. It takes time to engage in this kind of project since it involves understanding needs that customers are unable to consciously explain. At the same time, it also provides a powerful strategic advantage over competitors in that you understand customer's needs that the competition is not likely to know about. However, we could not build 'discover' into the process of this approach because the time frame set on the total initiative was profitability in two years. Acquiring the benefits of discovery may have taken longer than the time frame in which we were working and would have been too exploratory.

Other aspects to consider when selecting methods have already been identified from reflective practitioners. One list of nine criteria was shared with us by Rita Houlihan (from IBM Consulting) and is included, in an adapted format, below.

Will the method:

- Be portable? Will I be able to use the process with a minimum amount of training? Will I be totally dependent on a consultant and that specific consultant's personality or style?
- Be repeatable? Will I be able to count on consistent results from multiple teams using the method?
- Be research-based? Will the method maintain the value of my base educational investment? Will a team of researchers enrich and improve the method and its documentation based on new findings and developments?
- Provide a common language? Will there be easy-to-use prompts that guide a novice or old-timer through the method? Will the language of the method allow independent use? Will the language of the method help bridge the natural gaps between

functions and divisions? Will the common language help to get to the real issues and avoid emotional delays?

- Be comprehensive? Will the method be rigorous and comprehensive enough to address a diversity of situations? Will the method be flexible enough to be compatible with our current tools and processes?

- Have qualified instructors? Will qualified instructors be available to assist the learning of the method? Are the instructors qualified on some explicit skill base? Are they aware of a diversity of research and practical experiences to provide depth to the learning experience?

- Be supported by an internal network of practitioners? Is the method capable of being learned and applied by a variety of internal users? Will the method be friendly to an internal network of facilitators and coaches?

- Be supported by a community of external users? Will I be able to learn and exchange experiences with other corporate users? Will I be able to learn from a diversity of others who use the method?

- Be affordable? Will the method have an acceptable return on investment? Will the method have evidence that it makes a productive difference? Is there a good payback?

These criteria provide an excellent sample of the questions we have heard from many of our students, colleagues and clients over the years. You can apply them to your favorite method, or to a variety of other methods to help you make comparisons.

Many methods, especially those that are more open and flexible, may require an additional level of planning. Some methods are more self-contained and are characterized by the process driving the change. These may require less adjustment and design to allow for use. Others are designed to allow the change to drive the process. These will require some degree of customization or design to tailor the method to best fit the particular application.

If you had qualified the use of CPS for a particular task, then Designing Process would include designing your specific approach to process. This includes determining your entry within the CPS framework, scaling for the needed level of involvement, structuring the necessary kinds of interaction, and preparing the participants, the task summary and agenda as well as the context (location, logistics and events). Of course, you would use the learning and results from Appraising Tasks to help manage your process-planning efforts. For example, the identified needs from the desired outcome will drive decision-making about which CPS components may be most useful, which CPS stages may be employed and which CPS tools may be utilized. Additional planning or scoping may happen for small-group sessions and other levels of application including:

- one-on-one or personal application;
- sessions within larger meetings, conferences, or workshops;
- workshops, sessions, and meetings within projects;
- projects linked within programs.

One of the reasons we used CPS as the core method in the new product development example was that it is very flexible and was able to include other methods. For example, we were able to use the method for individual, small-group and large-group application. We were also able to use only those elements of CPS that were needed for the particular interaction. One workshop during the program involved understanding the core problems to address, and generating ideas to meet the customer needs. One meeting involved generating and clarifying the criteria to be used for deciding on which concepts to pursue. One series of meetings involved developing and strengthening different potential concepts. Each interaction involved tailoring how CPS was applied to meet the individual or group's needs. In addition, some meetings used other methods or parts of other methods.

When combined, Appraising Tasks and Designing Process help determine the need (content) and the readiness (process) to engage in the change method. The method becomes the servant of the people using it. It becomes a means to various but selected ends rather than an end unto itself.

Although Appraising Tasks and Designing Process have been developed within our current approach to CPS, they are useful for those who use a variety of change methods. Those who learn and apply the methods may find Appraising Tasks and Designing Process to be a productive way to qualify their methods and plan their approaches. Those involved in the management of change can use these mechanisms to determine core contingencies for any particular context. These can then function as design parameters for various process interventions.

Making the change happen

Up to now, we have been talking about thinking and planning. Ultimately, the reason for engaging in planning is making a difference. Making the change happen includes the implementation of the plan and minding the store. Implementation is about taking the plan and doing it. It involves driving the change into the organization or work unit. Minding the store is about taking care of the rest of the organization while you focus on implementing the change

Implementing the plan

The key point about implementing the output from Appraising Tasks and Planning Process is that your target is dynamic. While you have been thinking, problem-solving and planning, the place you will affect has also been changing. Your plan must often be ready to change during the actual implementation.

While we were working with a senior management team on an entirely new strategy, we learned about the importance of keeping the plan flexible. The team worked through the issue of moving from a one-product and service R&D facility, to one organized around business units. This represented quite a change. We left our meeting with a comprehensive plan to develop and launch six business units. Each unit had a project plan and these were all outlined in parallel.

When the senior management team returned to work, a few additional challenges faced them. While they were working on these challenges, the start dates on a few of the business unit plans went by. They had to begin to tinker with the entire plan as it included deliverables by date. Fortunately, we had an on-site facilitator who could work with the management team to keep the plan alive. The net result was that four of the units did materialize and save the jobs at the facility.

Implementing the change means keeping your focus on the long-term, cross-functional and strategic design of the initiative. It includes maintaining the blueprint of the change effort, but also keeping the blueprint flexible. It includes starting or initiating the change, following through and sustaining the change, and reaching a destination.

Minding the store

Another key aspect of making the change happen is minding the store. At the same time you focus on implementing the change, some of your time and attention must go to keeping the organization afloat. Even though a great deal of effort has just gone into creating a blueprint for change, you will need to deal with a host of day-to-day operational issues and challenges.

The key point to remember is that the store is always bigger than the change. This means that although you may have some excitement and enthusiasm about the change, it usually must fit within the larger organizational context. The change will almost by necessity create tension between the actual behavior of building and the design on the blueprint. While you are dealing with this dynamic tension, there are still phone calls, employees, clients and customers, and the many other facts of organizational life with which to contend.

This is the reason that good sponsorship is so important to making the change happen. Although the plans may have been great at the end of the senior management retreat (or advance), they must be continually modified, updated and communicated to reflect the balance between the strategic intent and the tactical reality. Appraising Tasks and Planning Process is necessary, but not sufficient to making change happen.

Minding the store also means taking the time (even when it hurts) to learn from and about the change process. As Jacques Nasser has said about his experience with driving change at Ford:

> We realized that the change had to be understood on the individual level. Every manager, every designer, every engineer, every person in the plants had to change his or her way of thinking. And the only way to change at the individual level, I believe, is through teaching. Teaching we've found, is an amazingly effective way to change an organization. With the teaching programs we've used over the past three years, our people have delivered $2 billion to our bottom line, either as increased revenues or decreased costs. And they've delivered them because their mind sets have changed.[15]

Deliberate planning for acceptance

Having a written plan will not always be enough to ensure effective and successful implementation. Research has identified several factors to help increase the power of your implementation plan. For example, Everett Rogers identified five factors to increase the effectiveness of your planning and implementation. He suggested that if your plan shows the relative advantage of your solutions over previous approaches and their compatibility or consistency with existing values, experiences or needs, the likelihood of them being implemented increases. Also, as you make the plan easy to understand and use (less complex), observable, and give people a chance to try parts of it, the greater the chance of successful implementation.[16]

We have used these five categories to develop a checklist to help you examine the effectiveness of your plan and to identify places where it might be strong or need improvement or modification.

Relative advantage

Being better than the previous solution:

- How well does my plan show how much better off people will be when they adopt the plan?
- Why is this plan better than what has been done before?
- What advantages or benefits might there be to accepting the plan?
- Who will gain from the implementation of the plan?
- How will I (or others) be rewarded by adopting the plan?
- How might I emphasize the plan's benefits to all?

Compatibility

Consistent with values, experiences and needs:

- How well does my plan demonstrate that it is compatible with current values, past experiences and needs?
- Is the plan consistent with current practice?
- Does the plan meet the needs of a particular group?
- Does it offer better ways to reach our common goals?
- Who will naturally support and agree with the plan?
- Can it be favorably named, packaged or presented?

Complexity

Being difficult to understand and use:

- How well does my plan provide for easy communication, comprehension and use?
- Is the plan easy for others to understand?
- Can it be explained clearly to many different people?

- Will the plan be easily communicated?
- How might the plan be made more simple or easy to understand?
- Is the plan easy to use or follow?

Trialability

May be experimented with on a limited basis:

- How well does my plan allow for trialability?
- Can the plan be tried out or tested?
- Can uncertainty be reduced?
- Can we begin with a few parts of the plan?
- How might others be encouraged to try out the plan?
- Can the plan be modified by you or others?

Observability

Results are visible to others:

- How well does my plan provide results that are easily observed and visible to others?
- Is the plan easy for others to find or obtain?
- Can the plan be made more visible to others?
- How might I make the plan easier for others to see?
- Will others be able to see the effects of the plan?
- Are there good reasons for not making the entire plan visible?

Other questions

The following are some general questions that will help your planning and implementation efforts.

- What other resources will I need; how might I get them?
- What obstacles exist? How might we prevent or overcome them?
- What new challenges might be created; and dealt with?

- How might I encourage commitment to the plan?
- What feedback about the plan is needed?

Chapter 9 on alternative change methods contains bibliographic information on a variety of alternative methods or approaches. We also make some suggestions for the use of some key vocabulary.

Ways of interacting

1. One-on-one conversation
2. A small group
3. Multiple small groups
4. Across functions
5. Within functions
6. Organization wide
7. Across organizations
8. At workplaces
9. Between workplace and home
10. At homes
11. Conferences
12. Training courses
13. Workshops
14. Conventions
15. Trade shows
16. E-mail
17. Letters through the mail
18. Phone conversations one-on-one
19. Video conferences
20. Telephone conferences
21. Web or Internet
22. Bookmarks
23. Signs
24. Clothing
25. Flipcharts
26. Music
27. Dance
28. Games
29. Role-playing
30. Arena or stadium events
31. Out-of-doors
32. Indoors
33. Smoke signals
34. Sign language
35. Braille
36. Audio tapes
37. Compact disc (CD)
38. Within cultures
39. Across cultures
40. On pens
41. Paging systems
42. Cell phones
43. Answering machines
44. Voice mail
45. Articles
46. Fax
47. Intercom
48. FedEx
49. DHL
50. UPS
51. Networks (people)
52. Bulletin boards

53. Mailboxes
54. Notes
55. AOL Instant message
56. Group ware
57. Body language
58. Newsletters
59. Brochures
60. Place mats
61. Advertisements
62. Magazines
63. Books
64. Billboards
65. TV
66. Radio
67. White boards
68. Posters
69. Flyers
70. Parties
71. PowerPoint presentations
72. Paintings, art and sculpture
73. Drawings and illustrations
74. Graphic images and icons
75. Cafes
76. Over meals
77. On planes
78. On trains
79. On buses
80. On cars
81. On boats
82. Lounges, pubs and bars
83. Sending messages with flowers
84. Singing telegrams
85. Telex
86. LAN
87. Carrier pigeons
88. Focused on self (introspection)
89. Focused on others
90. Talking
91. Listening
92. Whispering
93. Shouting
94. Seeing
95. Tasting
96. Smelling
97. With content
98. With silence
99. With meaning
100. Storytelling

References

1. Schacht, H., cited in Nadler, D.A. (1999) A success story: The case of Lucent Technologies. In *The Leader's Change Handbook: An Essential Guide to Setting Direction and Taking Action* (eds J.A. Conger, G.M. Spreitzer & E.E. Lawler III), pp. 3–25. San Francisco: Jossey-Bass.
2. Daniels, A.C. (2000) *Bringing Out the Best in People*. New York: McGraw-Hill
3. Rigby, D.D. (1994) Managing the management tools. *Planning Review*, Sept.–Oct., 20–24.
4. Totterdell, P., Leach, D., Birdi, K., Clegg, C. & Wall, T. (2002) An investigation of the contents and consequences of major organizational innovations. *International Journal of Innovation Management*, 6(4): 343–368.

5. Tidd, J. & Boldey, K. (2002) The affect of project novelty on the new product development process. *R&D Management*, 32(2): 127–138. Tidd, J. & Hull, F. (2003) *Service Innovation: Organizational Responses to Technological Opportunities and Market Imperatives*. London: Imperial College Press.

6. Dooley, K.J., Subra, A. & Anderson, J. (2002) Adoption rates and patterns of best practices in new product development. *International Journal of Innovation Management*, 6(1): 85–103.

7. Coyne, K.P. & Subramaniam, S. (1996) Bringing discipline to strategy. *McKinsey Quarterly*, 4: 3–12.

8. Tichy, N.M. & Sherman, S. (1993) Walking the talk at GE. *Training and Development*, 47: 26–35.

9. Isaksen, S.G. & Treffinger, D.J. (2004) Celebrating 50 years of reflective practice: versions of creative problem solving. *Journal of Creative Behavior*, 38: 75–101. Treffinger, D.J. (2000) Understanding the history of CPS. In *Facilitative Leadership: Making a Difference with Creative Problem Solving* (ed. S.G. Isaksen), pp. 35–53. Dubuque, IA: Kendall/Hunt. Treffinger, D.J., Isaksen, S.G. & Firestien, R.L. (1982) *Handbook for Creative Learning*. Sarasota, FL: Center for Creative Learning.

10. Isaksen, S.G. & Treffinger, D.J. (1985) *Creative Problem Solving: The Basic Course*. Buffalo, NY: Bearly Limited.

11. Isaksen, S.G. & Treffinger, D.J. (1987) *Creative Problem Solving: Three Components and Six Specific Stages*. Instructional handout. Buffalo, NY: Center for Studies in Creativity. Isaksen, S.G. & Treffinger, D.J. (1991) Creative learning and problem solving. In *Developing Minds: Programs for Teaching Thinking*, Volume 2 (ed. A.L. Costa), pp. 89–93. Alexandria, VA: Association for Supervision and Curriculum Development. Isaksen, S.G. & Dorval, K.B. (1993) Changing views of CPS: over 40 years of continuous improvement. *International Creativity Network*, 3: 1–5. Isaksen, S.G., Dorval, K.B., Noller, R.B. & Firestien, R.L. (1993) The dynamic nature of creative problem solving. In *Discovering Creativity: Proceedings of the 1992 International Creativity and Innovation Networking Conference* (ed. S.S. Gryskiewicz), pp. 155–162. Greensboro, NC: Center for Creative Leadership.

12. An initial outline of task contingencies was published in: Isaksen, S.G., Puccio, G.J. & Treffinger, D.J. (1993) An ecological approach to creativity research: profiling for creative problem solving. *Journal of Creative Behavior*, 27: 149–170. A later study confirmed these and added a few more. This can be found in: Baldwin, S.A. (1998) *In Search of Relevant Task Contingencies for Effective CPS Performance*. Unpublished masters project. Buffalo, NY: Center for Studies in Creativity.

13. Holmes, K. (1994) *Profiling Creativity: An Innovator's Pathway*. Unpublished masters project. Buffalo, NY: Center for Studies in Creativity. Isaksen, S.G. & Mance. M. (1996) *Making Effective Choices about Change Methods*. A presentation at the Annual Creative

Problem Solving Institute. Buffalo, NY: Creative Education Foundation. Mance, M. (1996) *An exploratory examination of methodology core contingencies within task appraisal.* Unpublished masters project. Buffalo, NY: Center for Studies in Creativity.

14. Ekvall, G. (1997) Organizational conditions and levels of creativity. *Creativity and Innovation Management*, 6: 195–205.

15. Wetlaufer, S. (1999) Driving change: an interview with Jacques Nasser. *Harvard Business Review*, 77: 77–88, cited from p. 81.

16. Rogers, E.M. (1995) *Diffusion of Innovations* (4th edn). New York: The Free Press.

Chapter 9

ALTERNATIVE CHANGE METHODS

First, useful change tends to be associated with a multistep process that creates power and motivation sufficient to overwhelm inertia. Second, this process is never employed effectively unless it is driven by high-quality leadership, not just excellent management

John Kotter (1996). *Leading Change.*
Boston: Harvard Business School Press, p. 20.

There is no shortage of change methods. This chapter provides a listing of 20 alternative methods and approaches for stimulating and implementing change. There are many others, but these selected methods were identified through our network of clients and practitioners.

Since the deliberate management of change, creativity and innovation is a relatively young field, and so many different disciplines are involved, it is pretty clear that we lack a common vocabulary for our work. As a result, we will start by offering a suggested vocabulary for understanding and comparing methods.

A vocabulary for understanding methods

There are many different providers of models, methods, theories, and tools and techniques. In the field of change management, some focus on creativity and innovation, others focus on communication and diffusion, and still others focus on organizational development and culture change. Everyone comes to the field with their own perspectives and theories. These differences are often reflected in the language these professionals use when talking or writing about change.

In order to avoid confusion within our own work, we have developed the following definitions and uses of some of the frequently used words within the field.

Method versus model

A method is a specific manner or way of doing something. It is a mode or way in which we approach something. A model is a structural design used to visualize something that cannot be directly observed (like the creative process). Models represent or illustrate something. Methods usually imply certain processes or procedures. Methods usually contain multiple tools in order to make the methods operational.

Process and procedures

Process means a series of actions or operations conducing to an end. There are many models of how change does or should occur. These models often describe a particular method or process for dealing with change. The following section of this chapter contains citations for various methods and models of those methods. This is not meant to be a comprehensive listing, but does point out some of the variety from which you can choose.

Tool versus technique

A tool is an instrument or implement that is used in performing a specific operation. Technique refers to the manner in which the technical details are treated or how a specific tool is used. Many methods contain a variety of specific tools to help perform specific operations. One of the most well-known tools for generating alternatives is brainstorming. There are many variations on the use of this tool, which we would call techniques. For example, brainwriting is a brainstorming technique to help generate options. It is a modification of the brainstorming tool that asks individuals to write and then nonverbally share their options. This technique can help bring out individuals who are more internal or can encourage people to participate if there are various reporting levels involved in the group.

An example of the 'muddle'

One of the challenges facing the reflective professional practitioner of change methods is keeping current with the growing amount of information in the field. In an ongoing effort to address this challenge, we recently embarked on a project exploring the current palette of tools that are available for use with creative problem-solving.

Besides the issue of keeping current, the objectives of this project were the identification of new tools or approaches that have emerged, and further to identify gaps or challenges that may exist in the current palette of tools available for the practitioner of change methods.

Our approach

To accomplish this task we identified a number of potential sources of creativity tools and ultimately selected 25 sources. These selected sources included online compilations, published edited lists and books on creativity tools and techniques by acknowledged experts and practitioners. Every attempt was made to identify the broadest set of source materials in creating the overall list of reported creativity tools.

From these assembled sources we compiled a list of 1270 items that had been presented in the sources as tools. Utilizing the definition of tool previously defined in this chapter, we sorted those items and as a result we discovered that of the 1270 reported tools 783 met the definition and were determined to be tools. The others were found to include a variety of principles, approaches, processes, techniques and methods unto themselves.

Based on the stated purpose and outcome of the tools, or by our analysis if such information was missing in the original source, we classified them as either tools for generating (coming up with many, varied or unusual options) or for focusing (screening, selecting or strengthening alternatives). This classification yielded 669 generating and 114 focusing tools.

Further analysis of the compiled list of tools resulted in some findings that bear reporting. We found that there is lack of agreement or a muddle in the language that is used to define what is, and what is not, a tool. In addition, we found that there is a bias or overemphasis on certain types of tools.

In the compiled list of tools there is considerable repetition where the same fundamental tool is presented with some minor variation as a totally different tool. In some cases, the variation is as simple as changing the name of the tool. In other cases, items were presented as new tools when in fact the variation was in technique (how the tool is used) and not in the basic concept of the tool. The best example of this is the many slight variations and multiple renaming of brainstorming that resulted in the listing of over 20 purportedly 'new' tools – which ended up being a minor variation of the well-established brainstorming tool.

There is a lack of consistent definition of what a tool is, resulting in a language muddle when it comes to the description and presentation of tools. In the beginning of this chapter we have carefully presented our working definitions of tool, technique, method and process. Although the case for such definitional clarity has been previously presented in the literature, it is clear that there is not widespread use of common definitions. If these definitions were consistently used it would begin to reduce some of the confusion that currently exists.

The review we completed supports the continuing existence of a bias in the creativity-oriented change methods. Multiple earlier sources in the literature have identified a tremendous emphasis that has been placed on the creation of and use of generation tools. These tools help individuals and groups come up with many, varied and unusual alternatives and options. This bias has been a consistent and long-standing fact in the field. This work confirms that while some progress has been made, there continues to be significant emphasis on and bias for generating tools (669 generating tools versus 114 tools for focusing).

There is a gap that exists in the availability and use of tools that go beyond the rational, cognitive and semantic-based approach that the majority of the tools in this study represent. While some additional tools have been created that are based upon the irrational, affective and visual, the number of practitioners including these tools in their work and general acceptance of these 'softer' approaches is lacking particularly in the business world.

In this study, while we utilized published sources (both print and online) as sources for the input, it is possible that practitioners are using in their day-to-day practice tools that are not included in this study. We will continue our efforts to identify and understand emerging tools in the field.

The change methods

Coaching

Coaching is the development of an ongoing partnership designed to help individuals produce fulfilling results in their personal and professional lives. Coaching methods help people improve their performance and enhance the quality of their lives.

The International Coach Federation is the professional association of personal and business coaches that seeks to preserve the integrity of coaching around the globe. International Coach Federation web site: **www.coachfederation.org**

Selected references

Anderson, D. & Anderson, M. (2005) *Coaching That Counts: Harnessing the Power of Leadership Coaching to Deliver Strategic Value*. Amsterdam: Elsevier Science and Technology.

Flaherty, J. (2005) *Coaching: Evoking Excellence in Others*. Amsterdam: Elsevier Science and Technology.

Hargrove, R. (1995) *Masterful Coaching*. San Francisco: Pfieffer.

Hendricks, W. & associates (1996) *Coaching, Mentoring, and Managing*. Franklyn Lakes, NJ: Career Press.

Kinlaw, D. (1993) *Coaching for Commitment: Managerial Strategies for Obtaining Superior Performance*. San Francisco: Pfieffer.

McAdam, S. (2005) *Executive Coaching: How to Choose, Use and Maximize Value for Yourself and Your Team*. London: Thorogood.

Parsloe, E. & Parsloe, L. (2005) *Coaching and Mentoring: Practical Conversations to Improve Learning, Performance and Potential*. London: Kogan-Page.

Peterson, D. & Hicks, M.D. (1996) *Leader as Coach*. Minneapolis: Personnel Decisions.

Waldroop, J. & Butler, T. (1996) The executive as coach. *Harvard Business Review*, 74: 12–21.

Conflict resolution

Conflict resolution (along with dispute resolution) usually refers to methods of resolving a dispute or a conflict permanently, by providing for each side's needs, and adequately addressing their interests so that they are satisfied with the outcome. Conflict resolution as a method incorporates mediation and negotiation.

The Association for Conflict Resolution is a professional organization dedicated to enhancing the practice and public understanding of conflict resolution.

The Association for Conflict Resolution website is: **www.acrnet.org**

Selected references

Blake, R. & Mouton, J. (1984) *Solving Costly Organizational Conflicts*. San Francisco: Jossey-Bass.

Dana, D. (2000) *Conflict Resolution*. New York: McGraw-Hill.

Fisher, R. & Ury, W. (1991) *Getting to Yes: Negotiating Agreement without Giving in*. New York: Penguin Books.

Folberg, J. & Taylor, A. (1984) *Mediation: A Comprehensive Guide to Resolving Conflicts without Litigation*. San Francisco: Jossey-Bass.

Kestner, P. & Ray, L. (2002) *The Conflict Resolution Training Program Participant's Workbook*. San Francisco: Jossey-Bass.

Kheel, T.W. (1999) *The Keys to Conflict Resolution: Proven Methods of Resolving Disputes Voluntarily*. New York: Four Walls Eight Windows.

Rahim, A.M. (1992) *Managing Conflict in Organizations* (2nd edn). Westport, CT: Praeger.

Weeks, D. (1994) *The Eight Essential Steps to Conflict Resolution*. Los Angeles: Tarcher.

Creative problem-solving

Creative problem-solving (CPS) is a method that emphasizes the development of novel solutions to situations and challenges. It is unique in that is a systemic approach that takes into consideration all elements of the situation (person, process, product and press).

For further information on Creative Problem Solving:

www.cpsb.com (The Creative Problem Solving Group, Inc.).

www.creativelearning.com (The Center for Creative Learning, Inc.).

Selected references

Cougar, J.D. (1995) *Creative Problem Solving and Opportunity Finding*. Boston: Boyd & Fraser.

Firestien, R.L. (1996) *Leading on the Creative Edge: Gaining Competitive Advantage Through the Power of Creative Problem Solving*. Colorado Springs, CO: Piñon Press.

Isaksen, S.G., Dorval, K.B. & Treffinger, D.J. (2000) *Creative Approaches to Problem Solving* (rev. edn). Dubuque, IA: Kendall Hunt.

Isaksen, S.G., Dorval, K.B., Noller, R.B. & Firestien, R.L. (1993) The dynamic nature of creative problem solving. In *Discovering Creativity* (ed S.S. Gryskiewicz), pp. 155–162. Greensboro, NC: Center for Creative Leadership.

Isaksen, S.G. & Treffinger, D.J. (2004) Celebrating 50 years of reflective practice: versions of creative problem solving. *Journal of Creative Behavior*, 38(2): 75–101.

Osborn, A.F. (1953) *Applied Imagination*. New York: Scribner's.

Parnes, S.J. (1988) *Visionizing: State of the Art Processes for Encouraging Innovative Excellence*. East Aurora, NY: DOK Publishers.

Parnes, S.J. (ed.) (1992) *Sourcebook for Creative Problem Solving: A Fifty-Year Digest of Proven Innovation Processes*. Buffalo, NY: Creative Education Foundation Press.

Parnes, S.J. (1997) *Optimize the Magic of Your Mind*. Buffalo, NY: Bearly Ltd.

Treffinger, D.J., Isaksen, S.G. & Dorval, K.B. (2006) *Creative Problem Solving: An Introduction* (4th edn). Waco, TX: Prufrock.

Goal setting and performance improvement

Goal setting is the term commonly given for the process of setting and working toward specific, defined purposes. Various methods exist for the creation of goals and the execution of them, and include performance improvement methods that seek to influence human behavior and accomplishment.

Selected references

Cairo, J. (1990) *Motivation and Goal Setting: The Keys to Achieving Success*. Shawnee Mission, KS: National Press Publications.

Daniels, A. (1999) *Bringing out the Best in People: How to Apply the Astonishing Power of Positive Reinforcement*. New York: McGraw-Hill.

Gowen, C.R. (1986) Managing work group performance by individual goals and group goals for an interdependent group task. *Journal of Organizational Behavior Management*, 7: 5–27.

Locke, E.A. & Latham, G.P. (1984) *Goal Setting: A Motivational Technique that Works!* Englewood Cliffs, NJ: Prentice Hall.

Smith, D. (1999) Make success measurable: a mindbook-workbook for setting goals and taking action. New York: John Wiley & Sons, Inc.

Zander, A. (1971) *Motives and Goals in Groups*. New York: Academic Press.

Kepner/Tregoe®

This method emphasizes the 'rational' rather than the 'creative'; it is essentially a method for fault diagnosis and repair rather than for disorganized or systemic problem domains. The method helps solve deviations from the standard rather than make sense out of complex and ambiguous problem spaces.

Selected references

Cook, M. (1982) 25 years of change: a dialogue with two pioneers of our profession – Chuck Kepner and Ben Tregoe. *Training and Development Journal*, 36: 132–140.

Kepner, C.H. & Iikubo, H. (1996) *Managing Beyond the Ordinary: Using Collaboration To Solve Problems, Make Decisions, and Achieve Extraordinary Results*. New York: Amacom.

Kepner, C.H. & Tregoe, B. (1997) *The New Rational Manager: An Updated Edition for a New World*. Princeton, NJ: Kepner-Tregoe.

Kepner, C.H. & Tregoe, B.B. (1976) *The Rational Manager*. Princeton, NJ: Kepner-Tregoe.

Kepner-Tregoe Problem Solving and Decision Making (1994) Princeton, NJ: Kepner-Tregoe.

Longman, A. & Mullins, J. (2005) *The Rational Project Manager: A Thinking Team's Guide to Getting Work Done*. New York: John Wiley & Sons, Inc.

Spitzer, Q. & Evans, R. (1997) *Heads You Win: How the Best Companies Think*. New York: Simon & Schuster.

Tregoe, B.B. (1989) *Vision in Action: Putting a Winning Strategy to Work*. New York: Simon & Schuster.

Lateral thinking, six thinking hats

A way of thinking that seeks the solution to intractable problems through unorthodox methods, or elements which would normally be ignored by logical thinking.

Edward de Bono's web site: **www.edwdebono.com**

Selected references

De Bono, E. (1969) *The Mechanism of Mind*. New York: Simon & Schuster.

De Bono, E. (1970) *Lateral Thinking: A Textbook of Creativity*. Harmondsworth, UK: Penguin.

De Bono, E. (1971) *The Use of Lateral Thinking*. Harmondsworth, UK: Penguin.

De Bono, E. (1986) *Six Thinking Hats*. New York: Little, Brown & Co.

De Bono, E. (1992) *Serious Creativity: Using the Power of Lateral Thinking to Create New Ideas*. New York: HarperCollins.

De Bono, E. (1994) *De Bono's Thinking Course* (rev. edn). New York: Facts on File.

Farnham, A. (1994) Teaching creativity tricks to buttoned-down executives. *Fortune*, 129: 98.

Sloane, P. (2003) *The Leader's Guide to Lateral Thinking Skills: Powerful Problem-Solving Techniques to Ignite Your Team's Potential*. London: Kogan-Page.

Neuro-linguistic programming

Neuro-linguistic programming (NLP) studies the structure of how humans think and experience the world, leading to models of how these things work. From these models, techniques for quickly and effectively changing thoughts, behaviors and beliefs that limit individuals have been developed.

The web site address for the Society for NLP is: www.nlp.net

Selected references

Bandler, R. & Grinder, J. (1979) *Frogs into Princes: Neuro-Linguistic Programming.* Moab, UT: Real People Press.

Bandler, R. & Grinder, J. (1980) *Neuro-Linguistic Programming: Volume 1 – The Study of Subjective Experience.* Cupertino, CA: Meta Publications.

Bandler, R. & Grinder, J. (1982) *Reframing: Neuro-Linguistic Programming and the Transformation of Meaning.* Moab, UT: Real People Press.

Dilts, R. (1983) *Applications of Neuro-Linguistic Programming.* Cupertino, CA: Meta Publications.

O'Connor, J. & Seymour, J. (1990) *Introducing Neuro-Linguistic Programming: Psychological Skills for Understanding and Influencing People.* San Francisco: HarperCollins.

Roberts, M. (1999) *Change Management Excellence: Putting NLP to Work in the 21st Century.* Bancyfelin, Carmarthen, Wales: Crown House.

New product development

New product development includes the overall process of strategy, organization, concept generation, product and marketing plan creation and evaluation, and commercialization of a new product.

The Product Development and Management Association (PDMA) is an information source for product development and management professionals. Their mission is to improve the effectiveness of individuals and organizations in product development and management.

The web site address for the PDMA is: www.pdma.org

Selected references

Belliveau, P., Griffin, A. & Somermeyer, S. (2002) *The PDMA Toolbook for New Production Development.* New York: John Wiley & Sons, Inc.

Bower, J.L. & Christensen, C.M. (1995) Disruptive technologies: catching the wave. *Harvard Business Review*, 73: 43–53.

Clark, J. (1995) *Managing Innovation and Change: People Technology and Strategy.* London: SAGE.

Drucker, P.F. (1998) The discipline of innovation. *Harvard Business Review*, 76: 149–157.

Kanter, R.M., Kao, J. & Wiersema, F. (eds) (1997) *Innovation: Breakthrough Thinking at 3M, DuPont, GE, Pfizer and Rubbermaid.* New York: Harper Business.

Kegan, R. & Lahey, L. (2001) *How the Way We Talk Can Change the Way We Work.* San Francisco: Jossey-Bass.

Klein, K.J. & Sorra, J.S. (1996) The challenge of innovation implementation. *Academy of Management Review*, 21: 1055–1080.

Tidd, J., Bessant, J. & Pavitt, K. (2005) *Managing Innovation: Integrating Technological, Market and Organizational Change.* Chichester, UK: John Wiley & Sons, Ltd.

Tushman, M.L. & O'Reilly, C.A. (1997) *Winning Through Innovation: A Practical Guide to Leading Organizational Change and Renewal.* Boston: Harvard Business School Press.

Von Hippel, E. (1988) *The Sources of Innovation.* Oxford: Oxford University Press.

Preferred futuring

Futuring is a very broad term that encompasses a number of methods for anticipating, forecasting and assessing the future. The concept of visioning is an example of this sort of method.

The World Future Society is an association of people interested in how social and technological developments are shaping the future. The Society strives to serve as a neutral clearinghouse for ideas about the future.

The web site for the World Future Society is: www.wfs.org

Selected references

Albrecht, K. (2000) *Corporate Radar: Tracking the Forces that are Shaping Your Future.* New York: AMACOM.

Barker, J.A. (1992) *Future Edge: Discovering the New Paradigms of Success.* New York: William Morrow.

Collins, J.C. & Porras, J.I. (1996) Building your company's vision. *Harvard Business Review,* 74: 65–77.

Fritz, R. (1989) *The Path of Least Resistance.* New York: Fawcett Columbine.

Godet, M. (2001) *Creating Futures: Scenario Planning as a Strategic Management Tool.* London: Economica.

Hoshmand, A.R. (2002) *Business and Economic Forecasting for the Information Age: A Critical Approach.* Westport, CT: Quorum Books.

Parker, M. (1990) *Creating Shared Vision.* Clarendon Hills: Dialog International.

Royal Institute of International Affairs (1996) *Unsettled Times: Three Stony Paths to 2015* (The 1996 Chatham House Forum Report). London: The Royal Institute of International Affairs.

Salmon, R. & Gembicki, M. (1999) *Competitive Intelligence: Scanning the Global Environment.* London: Economica.

Slaughter, R.A. (1995) *Futures Tools and Techniques.* Melbourne: Futures Study Center and DDM Media Group.

Weisbord, M.R. & Janoff, S. (1995) *Future Search: An Action Guide to Finding Common Ground in Organizations and Communities.* San Francisco: Berrett-Koehler.

Project management

Project management is the art and science of managing a project from inception to closure as evidenced by successful product delivery and transfer.

The American Society for the Advancement of Project Management is the project manager competence-based credentialing organization and an advocate of effective project management practice throughout all organizations.

The web site for the American Society for the Advancement of Project Management is: **www.asapm.org**

Selected references

Andersen, E.S., Grude, K. & Haug, T. (1995) *Goal Directed Project Management.* London: Kogan Page.

Berkum, S. (2005) *The Art of Project Management.* Sebastopol, CA.: O'Reilly Media, Inc.

Bowen, K.H., Clark, K., Halloway, C. & Wheelwright, S. (1994) Make projects the school for leaders. *Harvard Business Review,* 72: 131–140.

Graham, R.J. & Englund, R.L. (1997) *Creating an Environment for Successful Projects: The Quest to Manage Project Management.* San Francisco: Jossey-Bass.

Lewis, J. (2002) *Project Leadership*. New York: McGraw-Hill.

Project Management Institute (2005) *A Guide to the Project Management Body of Knowledge* (3rd edn). Newton Square, PA: Project Management Institute.

Wysocki, R. & McGary, R. (2003) *Effective Project Management: Traditional, Adaptive, Extreme* (3rd edn). New York: John Wiley & Sons, Inc.

Quality methods

Quality methods include a range of approaches that seek to maximize customer satisfaction, achieve unprecedented levels of performance and minimize errors. Within the broad set of quality methods, there are a number of related methods including:

- *Continuous improvement* – the ongoing improvement of products, services or processes through incremental and breakthrough improvements.
- *Total quality management* – is a management approach to long-term success through customer satisfaction. TQM is based on the participation of all members of an organization in improving processes, products, services and the culture in which they work.
- *Lean manufacturing* – a method focused on eliminating all waste in manufacturing processes.

The American Society for Quality (ASQ) is a leading authority on quality, advancing learning, quality improvement and knowledge exchange to improve business results, and to create better workplaces and communities worldwide.

The web site address for the ASQ is: www.asq.org

Selected references

Brassand, M. (1989) *The Memory Jogger Plus+: Featuring the Seven Management and Planning Tools*. Methuen, MA: Goal/QPC.

Crosby, P.B. (1985) *Quality without Tears: The Art of Hassle-Free Management*. New York: McGraw-Hill.

Davenport, T.H. (1993) *Process Improvement: Reengineering Work through Information Technology*. Boston, MA: Harvard Business School Press.

Deming, W.E. (1986) *Out of the Crisis*. Cambridge, MA: Massachusetts Institute of Technology.

Hammer, M. & Champy, J. (1993) *Reengineering the Corporation: A Manifesto for Business Revolution*. New York: HarperCollins.

Horovitz, J. & Panak, M.J. (1992) *Total Customer Satisfaction: Lessons from 50 Companies with Top Quality Customer Service*. London: Pitman Publishing.

Imai, M. (1986) *Kaizen: The Key to Japan's Competitive Success*. New York: Random House.

Ishikawa, K. (1982) *Guide to Quality Control*. Tokyo: Asian Productivity Organization.

Juran, J.M. (1988) *Juran on Planning for Quality*. New York: The Free Press.

Juran, J.M. & Gryna, F.M. (eds) (1986) *Juran's Quality Control Handbook* (4th edn). New York: McGraw-Hill.

Melan, E.H. (1992) *Process Management: Methods for Improving Products and Service*. New York: McGraw-Hill.

Ozeki, K. & Asaka, T. (1990) *Handbook of Quality Tools: The Japanese Approach*. Cambridge, MA: Productivity Press.

Tenner, A.R. & DeToro, I.J. (1992) *Total Quality Management: Three Steps to Continuous Improvement*. Reading, MA: Addison-Wesley.

Walton, M. (1986) *The Deming Management Method*. New York: Perigree Books.

Simplex®

Although a derivative of earlier versions of creative problem-solving, the Simplex method has been designed with more specific organizational application in mind. It places emphasis on ideation and evaluation balance as well as emphasizing problem definition and solution implementation.

Min Basadur's web site address is: www.basadur.com

Selected references

Basadur, M.S. (1987) Needed research in creativity for business and industrial applications. In *Frontiers of Creativity Research: Beyond the Basics* (ed. S.G. Isaksen), pp. 390–416. Buffalo, NY: Bearly Ltd.

Basadur, M.S. (1994) Managing the creative process in organizations. In *Problem Finding, Problem Solving and Creativity* (ed. M.J. Runco). New York: Ablex.

Basadur, M.S. (1994) *Simplex®: A Flight to Creativity*. Buffalo, NY: Creative Education Foundation.

Basadur, M.S. (1995) *The Power of Innovation*. London: Pitman.

Basadur, M.S. (1997) Organizational development interventions for enhancing creativity in the workplace. *Journal of Creative Behavior*, 31: 59–72.

Six Sigma

Six Sigma is a method that provides businesses with the tools to improve the capability of business processes through the implementation of a measurement-based strategy that focuses on process improvement and variation reduction.

Selected references

Brue, G. (2002) *Six Sigma for Managers*. New York: McGraw-Hill.

Keller, P. (2005) *Six Sigma Demystified: A Self-Teaching Guide*. New York: McGraw-Hill.

Breyfogle, F.W. (1999) *Implementing Six Sigma*. New York: John Wiley & Sons, Inc.

Breyfogle, F.W., Cupello, J.M. & Meadows, B. (2001) *Managing Six Sigma*. New York: John Wiley & Sons, Inc.

Eckes, G. (2001) *The Six Sigma Revolution*. New York: John Wiley & Sons, Inc.

George, M.L. (2002) *Lean Six Sigma*. New York: McGraw-Hill.

Harry, M. & Schroeder, R. (2000) *Six Sigma*. New York: Doubleday.

Pyzdek, T. (2003) *Six Sigma Handbook* (2nd edn). New York: McGraw-Hill.

Strategic planning

Strategic planning is a disciplined effort to produce fundamental decisions and actions that shape and guide what an organization is, what it does and why it does it, with a focus toward the future.

The Association for Strategic Planning (ASP) is a nonprofit professional society whose mission is to enable people and organizations to succeed through improved strategic thinking, planning and action.

The ASP web site address is: **www.strategyplus.org**

Selected references

Bryson, J.M. (1988) *Strategic Planning for Public and Nonprofit Organizations*. San Francisco: Jossey-Bass.

Burnes, B. (1992) *Managing Change: A Strategic Approach to Organizational Development and Renewal*. London: Pitman Publishing.

Courtney, H. (2001) *20/20 Foresight: Crafting Strategy in an Uncertain World*. Boston, MA: Harvard Business School Press.

Coyne, K.P. & Subramaniam, S. (1996) Bringing discipline to strategy. *McKinsey Quarterly*, 4: 3–12.

Gryskiewicz, S. (1999) *Positive Turbulence: Developing Climates for Creativity, Innovation, and Renewal*. San Francisco: Jossey-Bass.

Hamel, G. (1996) Strategy as revolution. *Harvard Business Review*, 74: 69–82.

Harper, S.C. (2001) *The Forward-Focused Organization*. New York: AMACOM.

Marsh, N., McCallum, M. & Purcell, D. (2002) *Strategic Foresight: The Power of Standing in the Future*. Brisbane: Crown Content.

Mintzberg, H. (1994) The fall and rise of strategic planning. *Harvard Business Review*, 72: 107–114.

Montgomery, C.A. & Porter, M.E. (eds) (1991) *Strategy: Seeking and Securing Competitive Advantage*. Boston: Harvard Business Review.

Nolan, T., Goodstien, L. & Pfeiffer, J.W. (1993) *Plan or Die! Ten Keys to Organizational Success*. San Diego, CA: Pfeiffer.

Porter, M.E. (1980) *Competitive Strategy: Techniques for Analyzing Industries and Competitors*. New York: The Free Press.

Robert, M. (1998) *Strategy II: Pure and Simple – How Winning Companies Dominate Their Competitors*. New York: McGraw-Hill.

Schwartz, P. (2003) *Inevitable Surprises: Thinking Ahead in a Time of Turbulence*. New York: Gotham Books.

Synectics®

Coined from the Greek *syn* (meaning 'to bring together') and *ectics* (for 'diversity'), Synectics is a method that encourages fundamental problem analysis and, on the other hand, the alienation of the original problem through the creation of analogies. The work of George Prince focused on group application and William Gordon on the interpersonal.

Selected references

Gitter, D.L., Gordon, W.J.J. & Prince, G.M. (1964) *Operational Mechanisms of Synectics*. Cambridge, MA: Synectics.

Gordon, W.J.J. (1956) Operational approach to creativity. *Harvard Business Review*, 34(6): 41–51.

Gordon, W.J.J. (1961) *Synectics: The Development of Creative Capacity.* New York: Harper & Row.

Gordon, W.J.J. (1974) Some source material in discovery by analogy. *Journal of Creative Behavior*, 8(4): 239–257.

Gordon, W.J.J. & Poze, T. (1977) *The Metaphorical Way of Learning and Knowing.* Cambridge, MA: Porpoise Books.

Gordon, W.J.J. & Poze, T. (1980) *The New Art of the Possible: The Basic Course in Synectics.* Cambridge, MA: Porpoise Books.

Prince, G.M. (1970) *The Practice of Creativity: A Manual for Dynamic Group Problem Solving.* New York: Macmillan.

Prince, G.M. (1976) Mindspring: suggesting answers to why productivity is low. *Chemtech*, 6: 290–295.

TRIZ

TRIZ is an algorithmic approach for solving technical and technological problems. This method was developed by reviewing thousands of patents. The patents were catalogued by considering the generic problem that needed to be solved, and the solution concept used to generate the resulting patentable innovation.

The web site address for the Technical Innovation Center is: www.triz.org

Selected references

Altshuller, G. (1996) *And Suddenly the Inventor Appeared – TRIZ: The Theory of Inventive Problem Solving.* Worcester, MA: Technical Innovation Center.

Altshuller, G. (1998) *40 Principles Extended Edition: Triz Keys to Technical Innovation.* Worchester, MA: Technical Innovation Center.

Clarke, D.W. (1997) *TRIZ: Through the Eyes of an American TRIZ Specialist – A Study of Ideality, Contradictions, Resources.* Southfield, MI: Ideation International.

Fey, V. & Rivin, E. (2005) *Innovation on Demand.* New York: Cambridge University Press.

Kaplan, S. (1996) *An Introduction to TRIZ: The Russian Theory of Inventive Problem Solving.* Southfield, MI: Ideation International.

Terninko, J., Zusman, A. & Zlotin, B. (1998) *Systematic Innovation: An Introduction to TRIZ (Theory of Inventive Problem Solving).* Boca Raton, FL: St Lucie Press.

Theory of constraints

The theory of constraints (TOC) is a method of improvement based on the fact that, in any complex system at any point in time, there is most often only one aspect of that system that is limiting its ability to achieve more of its goal. For that system to attain any significant improvement, that constraint must be identified and the whole system must be managed with it in mind.

The web site address for Goldratt is: www.goldratt.com

Selected references

Dettmer, H.W. (1997) *Goldratt's Theory of Constraints: A Systems Approach to Continuous Improvement.* Milwaukee, WI: American Society for Quality Control Press.

Goldratt, E.M. (1984) *The Goal: A Process of Ongoing Improvement.* Croton-on-Hudson, NY: North River Press.

Goldratt, E.M. (1990) *Sifting Information out of the Data Ocean: The Haystack Syndrome.* Croton-on-Hudson, NY: North River Press.

Goldratt, E.M. (1990) *The Theory of Constraints Journal – Volume 1 #6: The Paradigm Shift – Looking Beyond the First Stage.* New Haven, CT: Avaham Y Goldratt Institute.

Goldratt, E.M. (1990) *What is This Thing Called Theory of Constraints and How Should it be Implemented?* Great Barrington, MA: North River Press.

Goldratt, E.M. (1994) *It's Not Luck.* Croton-on-Hudson, NY: North River Press.

Goldratt, E.M. & Cox, J. (2004) *The Goal: A Process Of Ongoing Improvement* (3rd rev. edn). Great Barrington, MA: North River Press.

Noreen, E., Smith, D. & Mackey, J.T. (1995) *The Theory of Constraints and its Implications for Management Consulting.* Great Barrington, MA: North River Press.

Scheinkopf, L.J. (1999) *Thinking for a Change: Putting the TOC Thinking Process to Use.* Boca Raton, FL: St Lucie Press.

Schragenheim, E. (1998) *Management Dilemmas: The Theory of Constraints Approach to Problem Identification and Solutions.* Boca Raton: St Lucie Press / APICS Series on Constraints Management.

Value engineering

Value engineering is a systematic method to improve the 'value' of goods and services through function analysis.

SAVE International offers member services such as education and training, publications, tools for promoting the value methodology, certification, networking and recognition.

The web site address for SAVE is: www.value-eng.org

Selected references

Brown, J. (1992) *Value Engineering: A Blueprint.* New York: Industrial Press.

Chowdhury, S. (ed.) (2004) *Next Generation Business Handbook: New Strategies for Tomorrow's Thought.* New York: John Wiley & Sons, Inc.

Cooper, R. (1997) *Target Costing and Value Engineering.* Portland, OR: Productivity Press.

Crum, L.W. (1971) *Value Engineering: The Organised Search for Value.* London: Longman.

Dell' Isola, A.J. (1998) *Value Engineering: Practical Applications.* Kingston, MA: R.S. Means.

Kaufman, J.J. (1989) *Value Engineering for the Practitioner.* Raleigh, NC: North Carolina State University.

Park, R.J. (1999) *Value Engineering: A Plan for Invention.* Boca Raton, FL: St Lucie Press.

Sharp, H.J. (ed.) (1996) *Engineering Materials: Selection and Value Analysis.* New York: American Elsevier.

Younker, D.L. (2003) *Value Engineering: Analysis and Methodology.* New York: Marcel Dekker Inc.

Visualization

Visualization is a method that consists of creating a mental image of a desired outcome, and repeatedly playing that image in the mind.

Selected references

Bry, A. (1978) *Visualization: Directing the Movies of Your Mind.* New York: Harper & Row.

Finke, R. (1990) *Creative Imagery: Discoveries and Inventions in Visualization.* Hillsdale, NJ: Lawrence Erlbaum Associates.

Hansen, Y.M. (1989) *Think Visually: A Handbook of Techniques for Giving Visible Structure to Complexity.* Austin, TX: Gemin-Ideas Press.

Krueger, T.H. (1976) *Visual Imagery in Problem Solving and Scientific Creativity.* Derby, CT: Seal Press.

Leff, H.L. (1984) *Playful Perception: Choosing How to Experience Your World*. Burlington, VT: Waterfront Books.

McKim, R.H. (1980) *Thinking Visually: A Strategy Manual For Problem Solving*. Belmont, CA: Lifetime Learning Publications.

Samuels, M. & Samuels, N. (1975) *Seeing with the Mind's Eye: The History, Techniques And Uses Of Visualization*. New York: Random House.

Holistic systems thinking

Holistic systems thinking is a category of change methods that emphasize integrating creative and rational skills, directing the individual away from narrow specialization to a broader view and the connectedness of the system. These methods move beyond a focus on the product to the thought that precedes it and the broader issues that are involved.

Selected references

Alexander, C. (1984) The state of the art in design methods. In *Developments in Design Methodology* (ed. N. Cross), pp. 309–316. Chichester, UK: John Wiley & Sons, Ltd.

Archer, L.B. (1971) *Technological Innovation: A Methodology*. London: Inforlink.

Cross, N. (1984) *Developments in Design Methodology: Introduction*. Chichester, UK: John Wiley & Sons, Ltd.

Cross, N. (1989) *Engineering Design Methods*. Chichester, UK: John Wiley & Sons, Ltd.

Cross, N. (1992) Research in design thinking. In *Research in Design Thinking* (eds N. Cross, K. Dorst & N. Roozenburg), pp. 3–10. Delft, Netherlands: Delft University Press.

Dorst, K. (1997) *Describing Design: A Comparison of Paradigms*. Delft, Netherlands: Delft University Press.

Dreyfuss, H. (1967) *Designing for People*. New York: Paragraphic Books.

Eekels, J. & Roozenburg, N. (1991) A methodological comparison of structures of scientific research and engineering design: their similarities and differences. *Design Studies*, 12(4): 197–203.

Jackson, M. (2003) *Systems Thinking: Creative Holism for Managers*. Chichester, UK: John Wiley & Sons, Ltd.

Norman, D.A. (1988) *The Psychology of Everyday Things*. New York: Basic Books.

Roozenburg, N.F. & Cross, N. (1991) Models of the design process, integrating across the disciplines. *Design Studies*, 12(4): 215–220.

Valkenburg, R. (2000) *The Reflective Practice in Product Design Teams.* Delft, Netherlands: Delft University Press.

Van der Lugt, R. (2001) *Sketching in Design Idea Generation Meetings.* Delft, Netherlands: Delft University Press.

Chapter 10

APPLYING CREATIVE PROBLEM-SOLVING TO NEW PRODUCT DEVELOPMENT

the greatest invention of the 19th century was the invention of the method of invention[1]

Meeting the innovation challenge

The demand for growth, the need to deal effectively with increasing competition, complexity, and the frenetic pace of change, force those who lead and manage organizations to meet the innovation challenge.

These demands provide the impetus for why 70% of the organizations recently surveyed by the conference board indicate that innovation is a high priority.[2] The same survey indicated that the term 'innovation' is widely used to signal change. But the extent of that change is in the eye of the beholder – some apply the term to shifts that are modest and incremental while others reserve it for changes that are bold and disruptive. In the corporate sphere, innovation may apply primarily to new products and services, but some executives are starting to take a broader view by creating new business models, strategies and processes.

An increasing number of organizations around the world are beginning to broaden their definition of innovation. In response to the demand of competitive pressure to fast-changing consumer needs and trends, innovation is increasingly seen as something that can help organizations work in new ways, enter new categories or channels, as well as produce new products and services.

Sample definitions provided in the Conference Board study include:

Innovation includes new products, improving existing products, break-through production, speed to market, new business segments/models.

(Senior Vice President, consumer products, United States)

We consider innovation to be new products and services, new customer solutions, improved internal operations and services, linked to increased revenues and reduced costs.

(Director, energy services, Europe)

We focus on enterprise-wide efforts to integrate across all lines of business and present a single powerful set of options to each customer.

(Executive Vice President, financial services, United States)

Innovation is introducing new products and redefining business processes – this leads to an improved worldwide network, which provides customers with a superior travel experience throughout our and our partners' network.

(Director, transportation services, Europe)

Innovation contributes to customer loyalty and profitable growth through meeting compelling consumer requirements, creating competitive advantage, and delivering shareholder value.

(Vice President, consumer goods manufacturer, United States)

Many organizations have innovation programs aimed at helping develop new products and services. Some organizations have 'flirted' with creativity, only to find that they generate an overabundance of ideas, and that these ideas have little relevance to their business. This chapter outlines a more systematic and repeatable way to deliberately integrate creative problem-solving into innovation and new product development (NPD) efforts that can be productive for the entire value chain within any organization.

> You can have creativity without innovation, but you can't have innovation without creativity.

Pathways to growth

Organizations have used a variety of strategies to grow their businesses. Some organizations pursue mergers and acquisitions. Still others find ways to create joint ventures or strategic alliances. Some organizations pursue more organic growth strategies like going into new markets or developing new products and services.

Hamel and Getz describe the strategies of mergers and acquisition as agglomeration and call for more emphasis on organic growth through innovation.[3] They say: 'Put simply, innovation is the fuel for growth. When a company runs out of innovation, it runs out of growth.'

Kim and Mauborgne studied more than 30 companies in a variety of industries and they found that high growth is achieved by both small and large organizations, by companies in high-tech and low-tech industries, by new entrants and incumbents, by private and public companies, and by companies from various countries.[4]

What mattered – consistently – was the way that managers in the two groups of companies thought about strategy. The managers of the high-growth companies – irrespective of their industry – all described what is called 'the logic of value innovation'. The managers of the less successful companies all thought along conventional strategic lines.

They went on to study the business launches of 108 companies in order to quantify the impact of value innovation on a company's growth in both revenue and profits. Figure 10.1 illustrates that 86% of the launches were line extensions or incremental

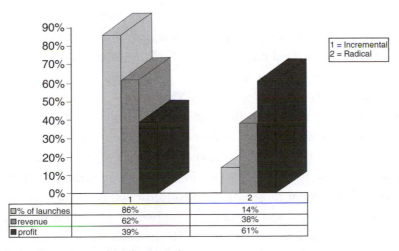

	1	2
% of launches	86%	14%
revenue	62%	38%
profit	39%	61%

1 = Incremental
2 = Radical

Figure 10.1 The roots of high growth

improvements. These accounted for 62% of total revenue and 39% of the profit. The other 14% of the launches were radical value innovations and accounted for 38% of revenue and 61% of profits. Those companies interested in high growth need to pursue a better balance between incremental and radical innovation.

Most companies think about matching or beating their competition. Their strategies tend to converge along the same lines as their rivals'. They share an implicit set of beliefs about how they compete in the market and conventional wisdom about who their customers are, what they value, and the scope of product and services demanded by their market. Value innovation is more about creating new market space.[5] Instead of looking within the accepted boundaries, those companies pursuing value innovation look systematically across them. By taking this approach the value innovators can find unoccupied space that represents real breakthrough.

An example is Michael Dell's success at finding the most efficient way to get his products directly into the hands of consumers. Contrary to the conventional wisdom of the industry, Dell saw that every PC was created with essentially the same components, such as Intel's chips and Microsoft's software, and decided that he could cut out the middleman by assembling his own computers and selling them direct to consumers. Taking his idea even further, he has perfected the art of e-commerce by making the Internet into an effective means for mass customization. By 1999, Dell was the largest seller on the Internet, exceeding sales of Amazon, e-Bay and Yahoo!

Riding two horses

Meeting the innovation challenge requires both incremental and internally focused as well as externally focused and radical change. Each organization must be able to ride two different yet complementary horses.

New product and service development (NPD) provides a natural area within organizations that requires creativity as it demands obtaining new and useful insights from consumers, deliberate development of new ideas and concepts, as well as new and improved marketing concepts and customer service. Keeping the uniqueness and novelty obtained in the front end of NPD alive and relevant throughout the entire life cycle is a core challenge for those who are involved in NPD.

Developing new products and services requires two fundamentally unique, yet complementary kinds of thinking and behaving. The first can be termed 'doing what we do but better' – a 'steady state' in which innovation happens but within a defined envelope around which our 'good practice' routines can operate. This contrasts with 'do different' innovation where the rules of the game have shifted (due to major technological, market or political shifts, for example) and where managing innovation is much more a process of exploration and coevolution under conditions of high uncertainty. A number of writers have explored this issue and conclude that under turbulent conditions firms need to develop capabilities for managing both aspects of innovation.[6]

Once again, the generic model of the innovation process remains the same. Under 'do different' conditions organizations still need to search for trigger signals – the difference is that they need to explore in much less familiar places and deploy peripheral vision to pick up weak signals early enough to move. They still need to make strategic choices about what they will do – but they will often have vague and incomplete information and the decision-making involved will thus be much more risky – arguing for a higher tolerance of failure and fast learning. Implementation will require much higher levels of flexibility around projects – and monitoring and review may need to take place against more flexible criteria than might be applied to 'do better' innovation types.

For established organizations, the challenge is that they need to develop the capability to manage both kinds of innovation. Much of the time they will need robust systems for dealing with 'do better', but from time to time they risk being challenged by new entrants better able to capitalize on the new conditions opened up by discontinuity – unless they can develop a 'do different' capability to run in parallel. New entrants don't have this problem when riding the waves of a discontinuous shift – for example, exploiting opportunities opened up by a completely new technology. But they will, in turn, become established incumbents and face the challenge later if they do not develop the capacity to exploit their initial advantage through 'do better' innovation process, and also build capability for dealing with the next wave of change by creating a 'do different' capability. The challenge is, therefore, to develop an ambidextrous capability for managing both kinds of innovation within the same organization.

Many organizations have figured out how to take a concept and work it through their value chain to get it to the market. The Stage-Gate™ approach is probably the most well-known model for this part of NPD. The kind of thinking and behaving within this approach is very similar to what most people would call 'good' management.[7] This is the likely reason that more than half of the Fortune 500 companies use a Stage-Gate™ approach (Figure 10.2).[8]

The processes and ways of thinking and problem-solving can be detailed, structured and communicated. Decisions can be made rationally, and resources allocated based

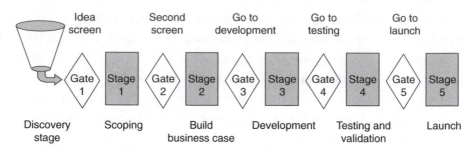

Figure 10.2 Stage-Gate approach to NPD

on relatively clear measures of performance. Timelines and projects can be managed. The activities and nature of the work is very similar to business-as-usual.

The Stage-Gate™ approach has been a source of improved efficiency and effectiveness for many organizations. The best practices are relatively well known and documented.[9] But, even when organizations have mastered their Stage-Gate™ approach, they may not get the kind of results they need to keep up in the marketplace. Models of this kind have been widely applied in different sectors, both in manufacturing and services.[10] We need to recognize the importance here of configuring the practice system to the particular contingencies of the organization – for example, a highly procedural system that works for a global multiproduct software and hardware company, like Siemens or Lucent, will be far too big and complex for many small organizations. And not every project needs the same degree of scrutiny – for some, there will be a need to develop parallel 'fast tracks' where monitoring is kept to a light touch to ensure speed and flow in development.

We also need to recognize that the effectiveness of any stage-gate system will be limited by the extent to which it is accepted as a fair and helpful framework against which to monitor progress and continue to allocate resources. This places emphasis on some form of shared design of the system – otherwise there is a risk of lack of commitment to decisions made and/or the development of resentment at the progress of some 'pet' projects and the holding back of others.

The 'front end' of this process requires a very different kind of thinking and behaving (Figure 10.3). This area is referred to as the 'fuzzy' front end (FFE) because it has been much more difficult to figure out the structure to the process, to make decisions based on trusted data, and to allocate resources to the most potentially productive possibilities.[11] This style is much more difficult and challenging for most organizations that prefer logic, analysis, predictability, structure and control. But, at the end of the day, organizations must be able to master and integrate both styles of problem-solving.

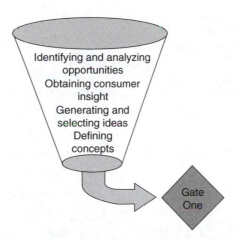

Figure 10.3 Discovery: The front end of innovation

The FFE or discovery stage requires an exploratory kind of thinking and working (or coping) with higher levels of ambiguity and uncertainty. As such, this kind of work appears harder to manage or control. Best practices are not well-known or understood and there are many different meanings for the same term, and many different terms used to describe the same thing. One thing is clear:

> The discovery stage represents the biggest area of opportunity for improvement for those organizations that have already implemented a Stage-Gate™ approach.

To meet the innovation challenge, those who lead and manage organizations must recognize, and then creatively resolve, the inherent tension between these two different kinds of work. Table 10.1 provides a few examples of the differences involved between the more structured Stage-Gate™ part of NPD and the FFE or discovery stage.

The need for more emphasis on the discovery stage is supported by Holman, Kaas and Keeling. They stated that:

> Over the past 15 years, most companies have adopted standard product development processes, with disciplined time lines, strict design reviews, 'gates' to decision-making, and cross-functional development teams. While these changes have made the development of new products much more efficient, further improvements are returning smaller gains. What is needed now is a way of raising product development to a new level.[12]

Table 10.1 The two horses

The front end – one horse	The back end – the other horse
Experimental, often chaotic and filled with 'eureka' moments	Disciplined, goal-oriented, includes well-defined project plans with milestones
Unpredictable 'laboratory' thinking	More certain 'factory' thinking
Venturing, uncertain revenue expectations, speculative	Budgeted and controlled, predictable revenue expectations
Individuals and cross-functional teams with guidance and support of a champion	Cross-functional teams with project leaders
Nonlinear, iterative, nonsequential with little or no consideration of risk	More linear and sequential with deliberate risk mitigation
Favors exploratory problem-solving aimed at delivering new opportunities and insights	Favors developmental problem-solving aimed at delivering better outcomes
Results in strong potential concepts	Results in products ready for commercialization

Radical ideas don't start out as sure-fire bets. A great idea becomes a commercial success through a recursive process of experimentation and learning.[13]

Some common approaches to the discovery and the fuzzy front end

The process of innovation begins with picking up various kinds of trigger signals. These might be about technology, markets, competitor behavior, shifts in the political or regulatory environment, new social trends, etc. – and they could come from inside or far outside the organization. How can an effective searching and scanning process for picking these up in timely fashion be organized and managed? What lessons have organizations learned about effective strategies to improve the range and quality of signals being picked up? And how can we ensure that the sheer volume of all this information coming in does not swamp the important signals with all the 'noise'?

Organizations pick up signals about innovation possibilities through exploring a particular 'selection environment' – essentially a search space made up of knowledge about technologies, markets, competitors and other sources. So we need effective routines to make sure that space is thoroughly explored – and to stretch its boundaries to create new space for large organizations. Significant resources can be devoted to this activity, but for many others it will raise the issue of developing and leveraging networks and connections.[14] There are a number of approaches that can be used to explore and extend this search space.[15]

Defining the boundaries of the marketplace

Essentially this involves asking the deceptively simple question, 'What business are we in?' This kind of question prompts discussion of current and potential markets and assists in looking for new opportunities. Sometimes, innovation can take the form of repositioning – offering the same basic product or service but addressed in a new way to different markets.[16] For example, Amazon.com is seen as an online retailer but is trying to broaden its business by positioning itself also as a software developer and supplier.

Understanding market dynamics

Closely linked to the above is understanding where potential markets may arise as a consequence of various kinds of change. For example, the cellular phone business has moved from a specialist, high-price business tool into the general marketplace as a result of both technological and cultural change. Similarly, low cholesterol and other healthy foods are increasingly becoming relevant to a large segment of the population as a result of changing social attitudes and education. Building up such understanding of the changing marketplace requires various forms of communication and interaction, from monitoring through to customer panels and surveys. Firms like Zara and Benetton have sophisticated IT systems installed in each of their shops such that they can quickly identify which lines are selling well on a daily basis – and tailor production to this.

Trend-spotting

One difficulty in exploring a market space arises when the market does not exist or where it suddenly takes a turn in a new direction. Developing antennae to pick up on the early warnings of trends is important, particularly in consumer-related innovation. For example, much of the development of the mobile phone industry has been on the back of the different uses to which schoolchildren put their phones and delivering innovations that support this. Examples include text messaging, image/video exchange and downloadable personal ring tones where the clues to the emergence of these innovation trajectories were picked up by monitoring what such children were doing or aspiring towards.

Closely related to this is the idea of identifying markets that do not yet exist but which may emerge as a result of identifiable current trends. For example, the figures on rising levels of obesity indicate a likely growth market in products like healthier foods and in services to support healthier lifestyles. The shift in the age profile of many European countries suggests significant growth in age-related services, not just in care but also in 'lifestyle' offerings like holidays and sports/leisure.

Monitoring technological trends

Related to this is the identification of emerging trends in technologies, where existing trajectories may be challenged or redirected as a result of new knowledge. Picking up on these requires active search and scanning at the periphery – for example, through monitoring web sites and chat rooms, visiting conferences, seminars and exhibitions, and building close exploratory links to research labs. As with the case of market trend-spotting, a key skill here is to improve peripheral vision – not only looking in the places where developments might be expected to occur but also exploring at the edges where something unexpected might take off.[17] Research has consistently shown that those organizations that adopt an active as opposed to a parochial approach to seeking out links with possible suppliers of technology or information are more successful innovators. IBM, for example, uses an approach called 'Webfountain' to help it monitor a wide range of potential triggers.[18] Even the CIA makes use of an internal group called In-Q-Tel to act as a 'venture catalyst' to facilitate trend spotting in key technology areas![19]

Procter & Gamble spend about 2 billion dollars each year and employ around 7000 people on research to support the business. But these days, they use the phrase 'connect and develop' instead of 'research and development' and have set themselves the ambitious goal of sourcing much of their idea input from outside the company. The scale of the challenge is huge; they estimate, for example, that in the 150 core technology areas that they make use of there are more than 1.5 million active researchers outside of P&G. Finding the right needle in a global haystack is a critical strategic challenge.

All of this is not to neglect the significant contribution that internal ideas can bring. The company has a wide range of active communities of practice around particular product groups, technologies, market segments, etc., and is able to draw on this knowledge increasingly through the use of intranets. A recent development has been the 'Encore' program in which retired staff of the company – and potentially those of other companies – can be mobilized to act as knowledge and development resources in an extended innovation network.

Forecasting

Various techniques exist for exploring futures, ranging from simple extrapolation of performance parameters and rates of development to complex, nonlinear techniques. Some, like Delphi panels and scenarios, are similar to market forecasting techniques, while others are more closely aligned to technological development models.

Although there are well-proven and useful approaches to forecasting technology and market trends, these often make simplifying assumptions about the wider context in which predicted changes might take place. An alternative approach is to take an integrated view of what different futures might look like and then explore innovation triggers within those spaces. Typical of this approach is the work that Shell and other organizations do with scenarios where a number of people work together to build up pictures of alternative parallel futures.[20]

These are usually richly woven backgrounds that describe technologies, markets, politics, social values and other elements in the form of a 'storyline' – for example, a recent Shell publication looked at possible scenarios for 2020 in terms of two alternatives – 'business class' and 'prism'. The former offers a vision of 'connected freedom' in which cities and regions become increasingly powerful at the expense of central government, and where there is increasing mobility among a 'global elite'. While the latter describes a different world in which people increasingly look to their roots and re-orientate toward values as the focus around which to organize their lives. Neither are necessarily the 'right' answer to what the world will look like by that time, but they do offer a richly described space within which to explore and simulate, and to search for threats and opportunities that might affect the company. In particular, they allow an organization to define particular 'domains' – spaces within the bigger scenario where it can think about deploying its particular competencies to advantage – and to carry out a kind of 'targeted hunting' in its search for innovation triggers.

Working with lead users

Lead users are critical to the development and adoption of complex products. As the title suggests, lead users demand new requirements ahead of the general market of other users, but are also positioned in the market to significantly benefit from the meeting of those requirements. Where potential users have high levels of sophistication – for example, in business-to-business markets such as scientific instruments, capital equipment and IT systems – lead users can help to codevelop innovations, and are therefore often early adopters of such innovations. The initial research by Von Hippel suggests that lead users adopt an average of seven years before typical users, but the precise lead time will depend on a number of factors, including the technology life cycle.[21] A recent empirical study identified a number of characteristics of lead users:[22]

- *Recognize requirements early* – are ahead of the market in identifying and planning for new requirements.
- *Expect high level of benefits* – due to their market position and complementary assets.
- *Develop their own innovations and applications* – have sufficient sophistication to identify and capabilities to contribute to development of the innovation.
- *Perceived to be pioneering and innovative* – by themselves and their peer group.

This has two important implications. First, those seeking to develop innovative complex products and services should identify potential lead users with such characteristics to contribute to the codevelopment and early adoption of the innovation. Second, that lead users, as early adopters, can provide insights to forecasting the diffusion of innovations. For example, a study of 55 development projects in telecommunications computer infrastructure found that the importance of customer inputs increased with technological newness, and moreover, the relationship shifted from customer surveys and focus groups, to codevelopment because 'conventional marketing techniques proved to be of limited utility, were often ignored, and in hindsight were sometimes strikingly inaccurate'.[23] Clayton Christensen and Michael Raynor make a similar point in their book *The Innovator's Solution*, and argue that conventional segmentation of markets by product attributes or user types cannot identify potentially disruptive innovations.

Therefore, a major aspect of the more discovery-oriented FFE is that most organizations need to play with a much larger number of alternatives earlier in their NPD efforts. Most managers already have a great deal on their 'platter' so having to deal with many, varied and original alternatives increases the complexity of their work.

Ultimately, meeting the innovation challenge requires organizations to encompass and include strategic focus on both the discovery and commercialization stages of NPD. Creative problem-solving (CPS) offers one way to help leaders and managers to ride both horses. The rest of this chapter summarizes the current approach to CPS and how this approach can be applied to NPD efforts.

Creative problem-solving: our current framework

CPS is a contemporary framework for solving problems and managing change. CPS enables innovation and change. The CPS framework includes a dynamic balance between creativity and problem-solving. Creativity emphasizes the search for newness and the deliberate generation and development of many and varied alternatives. Problem-solving emphasizes the development of useful and relevant solutions. Over 50 years of research and development on CPS has resulted in the development of a systemic approach that includes a variety of methods, tools and techniques.[24] These developments have strengthened CPS so that it can help integrate the two complementary ways of thinking and problem-solving (Figure 10.4).

CPS includes practical tools to help generate many, varied and original alternatives; and screen, select and strengthen options. Since language and thinking are so closely related, CPS includes clear language that helps differentiate opportunities and problems from ideas, and ideas from concepts or solutions. Having a common vocabulary helps teams be more productive during problem-solving. Guidelines are also included to help you and others effectively generate and focus. Guidelines create norms and agreed sets of behaviors that help you maximize the use of the tools.

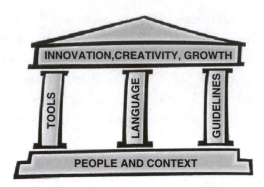

Figure 10.4 The foundation of CPS

CPS is a widely applied method that has been used extensively in business organizations and throughout educational courses and programs. One of the reasons the current version of CPS (CPS Version 6.1™) is so widely used is that it now includes simple mechanisms to help you decide what tools, guidelines and language will be most helpful for the variety of situations and tasks you face. CPS also has a well-defined and learnable skill-base to create effective facilitators of project teams and groups.

The current CPS framework helps you achieve clarity, generate ideas and take action. Since these are three distinct choices and areas into which the tools, guidelines and language of CPS coalesce, you need to be able to navigate your way through its various components and stages. Navigation is obtained by a component called 'Planning your Approach'. Clarity is achieved by Understanding the Challenge. Many, varied and original ideas are obtained by a component called 'Generating Ideas'. The Preparing for Action component includes strengthening potential solutions and developing plans of action. These main components of CPS are described in more detail below.

Planning your Approach

CPS version 6.1™ includes a unique component called 'Planning your Approach', that focuses on producing the desired results as well as consideration of the people involved, the climate within the organization and designing the appropriate process approach.[25] The purpose of this component is to help you navigate your way through the process.

Planning your Approach contains two main stages: Appraising Tasks and Designing Process. These stages deal with the deliberate management of the other

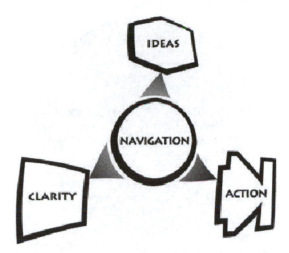

Figure 10.5 The main purpose of CPS

components within CPS. Since we need to be able to personalize and customize CPS for many different applications, these stages help you determine if CPS is an appropriate method and, if it is, to design an effective application of the components, stages and tools (Figure 10.5).

Appraising Tasks

Appraising Tasks involves determining whether or not CPS is appropriate for a given task, and whether modifications of your approach might be necessary. During task appraisal, you consider the key people, the desired outcome, the characteristics of the situation, and the possible methods for handling the task. Task appraisal enables you to assess the extent to which CPS might be appropriate – the method of choice, as it were – for addressing a given task or for managing change in appropriate ways.

When appraising a task we consider the following factors.

People

A key part of the system is to ensure that the proper level of ownership (interest, influence and imagination) and sponsorship are in place. Another important aspect within

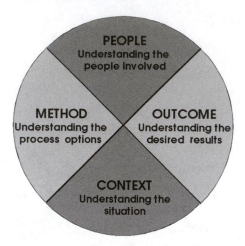

Figure 10.6   Elements of Appraising Tasks

this element is better understanding the different styles of problem-solving of those involved in CPS. Certain styles have been shown to be more successful in some NPD efforts.[26]

Our assessment tool, called *VIEW: An assessment of problem solving style*,™ can be used by individuals and teams to help them obtain an improved understanding and appreciation of style differences (Figure 10.6).[27]

Place

The climate, working atmosphere and culture are important factors in deciding your approach. Considering the context can help you understand if your situation is ready, willing and able to use a particular method. A great deal of research has been done to understand the climate that supports creativity, innovation and change. Our assessment, the *Situational Outlook Questionnaire*,™ can help you know what is working to support your efforts, and what the barriers and challenges are to sustaining innovation.[28]

Outcomes

Having a clear image of the desired results is key to organizational innovation. One source for obtaining this focus can be the business strategy and the product innovation charter. The current approach to CPS requires the development of a task summary that clearly points out the need for originality and the requirements for the outcomes. This statement guides the specific application of the tools and language and helps everyone understand the purpose of the session, project or initiative. Our task summaries act as springboards for effective problem-solving and ensure delivery of desired outcomes.

Methods

There are many methods that can be applied within NPD. Since CPS is an open system, it allows for the integration and use of a number of alternative change methods. The information gained from an improved understanding of the people, context and outcomes guides the choice to use CPS or integrate other methods within your approach.

Designing Process

As a result of Appraising Tasks, you are in the position to design your process approach. This stage includes considering the scope of your work. Will it be a single session, a longer-term project, or an even larger and longer-term initiative? Is the level of your application targeted to an individual, group or team, or at an organizational level? And then, which of the components or stages of CPS will be most helpful? (Figure 10.7).

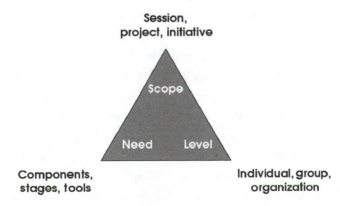

Figure 10.7   Designing Process in a nutshell

Once you have determined the scope and level of application for CPS, you need to decide if the need is for clarity, ideas or action. These are the main purposes of the three remaining components of CPS.

Planning your Approach – applied

A large global consumer products company had developed a very clear screening process for new product concepts. The competition was developing and launching new products much faster in key market segments. We were invited to be the lead and coordinating consultants on project discovery. The goal was to obtain new and different concepts for the laundry, soap and paper sectors. The project was designed using Appraising Tasks and Designing Process allowing the use of five alternative methods to obtain consumer insight. Within 18 months, the company went from having just 25 product concepts (developed over seven years) to 76 new and fundamentally different product concepts that were capable of being tested in the market. The project proved to be so successful that the methods are being taught to everyone who works in product development and research.

Understanding the Challenge

The Understanding the Challenge component includes a systematic effort to define, construct or focus your problem-solving efforts (Figure 10.8). It includes the three stages of constructing opportunities, exploring data and framing problems.

Constructing opportunities involves generating broad, brief and beneficial statements that help set the principal direction for problem-solving efforts. This stage focuses on helping those in the organization identify a business or technology gap that exists between the current situation and a desired future. This allows the organization to capture competitive advantage, pursue value innovation, respond to threats, and focus on acquiring the right kind of data and framing appropriate problems to be solved.

Exploring data includes generating and answering questions that bring out key information, feelings, observations, impressions and questions about the task. These help problem-solvers to develop an understanding of the current situation. This stage is where those managing NPD efforts can search for new consumer insights, identify

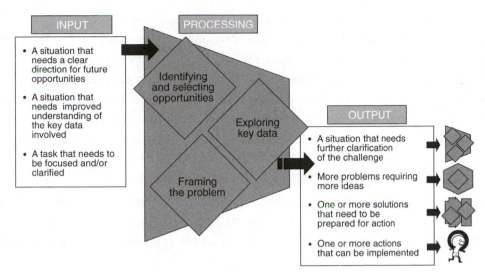

Figure 10.8   Understanding the challenge

trends and use complementary exploratory and confirmatory methods to acquire new data about consumers' needs, wants and desires. For example, when companies need to obtain deep insights into unmet, unknown and unarticulated needs, our Deep Dive Discovery™ method can be applied.

Framing problems involves seeking specific or targeted questions (problem statements) on which to focus subsequent efforts. This stage provides the chance to explore the opportunity or domain in order to identify and detect problems consumers face, whether they consciously know them or not. Potential problem areas within other NPD-related areas can also be identified and addressed (i.e. specific cross-functional NPD issues).

A problem is half-solved if properly stated.

(John Dewey)

Understanding the Challenge – applied

A global university publisher needed to focus their efforts on increasing sales and market share for one of their major divisions. By applying constructing opportunities, the division was able to generate more than 200 opportunity statements and ended up focusing these down to seven key areas for investment and development. By prioritizing these initiatives, they have been able to develop specific action plans much faster, and involve many more stakeholders in the process, than earlier efforts.

A global consumer products company needed to develop some fundamentally new products within one of their major divisions. By applying a Deep Dive Discovery approach to exploring data, they were able to obtain very original insights into consumer needs, and a deeper meaning of what these needs implied, resulting in a significantly improved use of their technology and marketing efforts.

One of our clients produces high-tech medical solutions. By applying framing problems tools to acquire consumer insight, the client was able to redefine their NPD initiative to reengineer their anesthesia equipment. The company ended up with a substantial cost savings and developing a new add-on piece of equipment usable on new and existing machines.

Generating Ideas

The Generating Ideas component and stage includes coming up with many, varied or unusual options for responding to a problem (Figure 10.9). During the generating phase of this stage, problem-solvers produce many options (fluent thinking), a variety of possible options (flexible thinking), novel or unusual options (original thinking), or

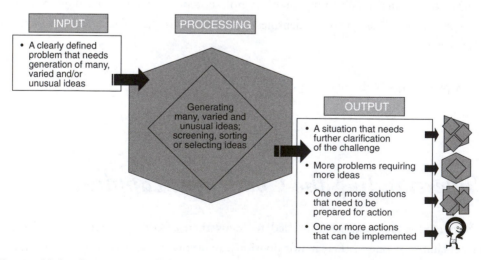

Figure 10.9   Generating Ideas

a number of detailed or refined options (elaborative thinking). The focusing phase of Generating Ideas provides an opportunity to examine, review, cluster and select promising ideas. Although this stage includes a focusing phase, its primary emphasis rests in generating or the commitment of extended effort to seek creative possibilities.

This stage of CPS provides for the development of embryonic forms of new products and services. Ideas are high-level views of the potential alternative solutions envisioned for the identified problem or opportunity

Value innovators look for blockbuster ideas and quantum leaps in value.[29]

Generating Ideas – applied

A global direct marketing/publishing company has applied CPS Generating Ideas tools to 'turbo charge' their use of focus groups resulting in substantially better insights from consumers. In addition, they have used these tools to help a major global division generate fundamentally different product ideas, to help them generate hundreds of new media and marketing channel ideas, and to generate ideas for consideration in their three-year planning process. All were aimed at helping them grow their core business.

Preparing for Action

Problem-solvers use the Preparing for Action component to make decisions about, develop, or strengthen promising alternatives, and to plan for their successful implementation. The two stages included in the component are called 'developing solutions' and 'building acceptance' (Figure 10.10).

During developing solutions, promising options may be analyzed, refined or developed. If there are many options, the emphasis may be on compressing or condensing them so that they are more manageable. If there are only a few promising options, the challenge may be to refine, strengthen or develop each one to make it as strong as possible. This stage can involve ranking or prioritizing a number of possible options, generating and selecting specific criteria for evaluating promising options or selecting the most promising options from a larger pool. The emphasis in this stage is primarily on focusing options and developing promising ideas into plausible solutions.

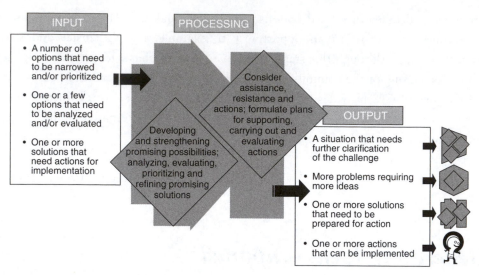

Figure 10.10 Preparing for Action

This stage of CPS transforms the potential product or service ideas into more workable concepts. As a result, the concepts take on a well-defined form that can be described by words, visuals or prototypes. Developing solutions results in a clear definition of the features and benefits, as well as areas that need to be improved to strengthen the concept.

> Execution is not just something that does or doesn't get done. Execution is a specific set of behaviors and techniques that companies need to master in order to have competitive advantage.[30]

The building acceptance stage involves searching for potential sources of assistance and resistance and identifying possible factors that may influence successful implementation of solutions. The aim is to help prepare solutions for improved acceptance and greater value. This stage helps the problem-solver identify ways to make the best possible use of assisters and avoid or overcome possible sources of resistance. By considering these factors, problem-solvers can develop and evaluate a plan of action. Preparing for implementation also provides opportunities to consider alternative possibilities, contingency plans or feedback loops.

This stage of CPS takes the developed concept to another level of preparation for acceptance. When building acceptance on an NPD concept, efforts are focused on getting the concept ready for the more traditional screens within the NPD process and results in a project plan to sustain the uniqueness in the concept. This stage includes examining the levers and barriers that the new concept is likely to face, and modifying and improving the concept as well as making changes to the process, procedures and structures to allow for successful launch.

Preparing for Action – applied

A major manufacturing company needed to obtain more value from their R&D investment decisions. The senior management team worked with CPS developing solutions tools in order to generate and then prioritize the criteria for NPD investment projects. This diverse management team reached a clear consensus on their top 10 criteria for investment and made swift changes to the projects currently under consideration.

A global professional services consulting firm needed to speed up the development and launch of new services. The firm was able to decrease their time to market from 18 to 3 months by applying CPS building acceptance tools to a new suite of service offerings. This resulted in creating and maintaining increased market share.

Key lessons learned

The challenge to create sustainable growth means that organizations must learn how to effectively balance their attention and allocation of resources between incremental and radical innovation. Our current approach to CPS can be a powerful approach to help meet this challenge.

In an effort to understand what differentiated successful innovative organizations from lower performing ones, Davis comprehensively studied nearly 600 companies from seven countries.[31] They identified 10 characteristics that clearly separated the more- from the less-successful organizations. The characteristics they identified included:

1. There is a more active flow of ideas.
2. There are well-defined processes for realizing commercial successes at any level.
3. There is a higher degree of management trust.
4. There are explicit idea management processes that people adhere to.

5. People take responsibility for implementing their own ideas more often.
6. There is a balanced view of risk-taking.
7. Managers have adequate time to explore and test new ideas.
8. Managers involve others in developing ideas into actions.
9. They routinely envision the future based on intimate market knowledge.
10. They do not rely on the board alone for significant new ideas.

In addition, their study identified three general organizational capabilities that provided a clear picture of those companies generating a much higher percentage of revenue (and profit) from new products and services. The high performers not only had deliberate Stage-Gate™ processes. They also had explicit procedures and systems to support the front end of innovation (idea management). Second, leaders in the high-performing organizations reached out to a much larger number of people, involving them collaboratively in turning ideas into action. Finally, these successful companies encouraged the creation of a working atmosphere and climate that supported innovation and initiative.

On the basis of this research, as well as inquiry into the successful development of blockbuster products and our practical experience of more than 20 years, we have identified the following major lessons to guide your future NPD efforts.

1. The more successful efforts focus on an intimate understanding of consumer needs

This is about establishing a clear commitment to look externally to the organization toward those who choose to purchase products and use services. This is also where the front end of innovation is most important. The key is to continuously search for a deeper understanding and appreciation of needs, interests, desires and frustrations of consumers (known and unarticulated; rational and emotional).

CPS has been applied to help obtain deeper consumer insight by 'turbo charging' focus groups, designing and analyzing consumer surveys, and by integrating CPS tools into deep exploratory consumer research. Very often these efforts provide original insights that challenge existing assumptions and ways of working. Those who have been trained in CPS do a much better job of developing workable concepts and retaining the essence of newness from these insights.[32]

2. *Faster, better and more cost-effective NPD requires cross-functional involvement*

This is about having multiple functions and disciplines involved during the front end and throughout the entire NPD process. It's not necessarily about having large chaotic teams, but cross-functional involvement does imply that there is involvement and participation of people from across the entire value chain.

CPS can help teams become more effective when working across functions. CPS provides a common and clear language and approach that facilitates cross-functional collaboration by providing concrete tools to facilitate teamwork.

3. *Most successful launches have had good sponsorship*

Senior managers must guide the process by demonstrating that they are good sponsors of NPD. They do this by showing interest in and commitment to NPD. They allocate appropriate resources, make prompt decisions based on clearly communication priorities, and legitimize and encourage both exploratory and developmental initiatives.

CPS includes deliberate tools to assess, establish and maintain clear sponsorship and clientship, and they have been used extensively and successfully with a variety of senior management teams. Applying CPS at an organizational level helps to instill clear ownership for specific tasks.

4. *A clear and compelling strategy must guide NPD efforts*

There must be a challenging, coherent and authentic strategy to guide NPD efforts. Many successful organizations create a written document outlining the link between the overall organizational vision, mission and purpose with NPD efforts. This 'Product Innovation Charter' is linked to the brand values, overall strategy for the organization and is communicated widely.[33]

It is also usually developed through collaborative and cross-functional involvement. The irony is that in order to obtain creative initiative and risk-taking, an organization must promote clarity of direction and focus on few priorities.

CPS has been applied effectively to develop, communicate and implement Product Innovation Charters. CPS also uses this charter to connect the variety of tasks on which those involved in NPD efforts work. The charter also creates a foundation for a variety of supplementary tasks that require cross-functional involvement and engagement.

5. Meeting the innovation challenge demands deliberate management of creativity

Since so many people must inevitably be involved in NPD, and the desired condition is an idea-rich climate, organizations with multiple brands and global presence must have a formal process to seize opportunities. It takes a climate rich in ideas to ensure successful new product development. The message is very clear: it takes many ideas to create successful new products. It is for this reason that organizations successful with new product development have deliberate processes that work, people sharing ideas from all parts of the organization and a climate that stimulates new thinking.

CPS encourages the generation of many, varied and unique ideas, and also includes deliberate tools and guidelines to help transform ideas into workable concepts. It is based on many years of research and development into how creative people solve problems (the creative process), the characteristics of creative people, and the atmosphere and climate in which creativity can flourish.

6. Sustainable NPD success requires an investment in people

Building the capability for innovation takes a special and more inclusive kind of leadership, deliberate efforts to establish a climate for creativity, and structured methods for idea management. Those organizations that are more innovative do all of these things simultaneously. Innovation requires creativity. Since the only source of creativity is people, sustainable innovation requires a long-term view of training and development of creativity relevant skills.

CPS is a highly portable method, allowing cost-effective training and transfer of skills. More than any other problem-solving method, CPS has a long tradition of research and documented impact. Our approach to CPS has an explicit skill base that can be easily learned and applied to the full spectrum on NPD challenges.

Meeting the innovation challenge is an imperative for any organization that wishes to survive and grow. Best practices of those who are doing so illustrate the benefits of taking a systemic approach (rather than following a single 'silver bullet' approach). Taking a systemic approach implies at least two things. First, the efforts must be conscious, deliberate and disciplined. Second, these efforts must consider all key elements of the system (including people, processes, product and place). CPS version 6.1™ is one helpful method that encourages the integration of two complementary ways of problem-solving and application of a systemic approach to innovation.

References

1. Whitehead, A.N. (1926) *Science and the Modern World*. Cambridge, UK: Cambridge University Press, p. 120.
2. Troy, K. (2004) *Making Innovation Work: From Strategy to Practice*. A research report: The Conference Board (R-1348-04-RR). New York: The Conference Board, Inc.
3. Hamel, G. & Getz, G. (2004) Funding growth in an age of austerity. *Harvard Business Review*, 82: 76–84.
4. Kim, W.C. & Mauborgne, R. (1997) Value innovation: the strategic logic of high growth. *Harvard Business Review*, 75: 104–112.
5. Kim, W.C. & Mauborgne, R. (1999) Creating new market space: a systematic approach to value innovation can help companies break free from the competitive pack. *Harvard Business Review*, 77: 83–93. Kim, W.C. & Mauborgne, R. (2004) Blue ocean strategy. *Harvard Business Review*, 82: 76–84.
6. Christensen, C. & Raynor, M. (2003) *The Innovator's Solution: Creating and Sustaining Successful Growth*. Boston, MA: Harvard Business School Press. Foster, R. & Kaplan, S. (2002) *Creative Destruction*. Boston, MA: Harvard University Press.
7. Tidd, J., Bessant, J. & Pavitt, K. (2005) *Managing Innovation: Integrating Technological, Market and Organizational Change*. New York: John Wiley & Sons, Inc.
8. Cooper, R.G. (2001) *Winning at New Products* (3rd edn). Reading, MA: Perseus.
9. Cooper, R.G. & Kleinschmidt, E.J. (1987) New products: what separates the winners from the losers? *Journal of Product Innovation Management*, 4: 169–184.
10. Bruce, M. & Cooper, R. (2000) *Creative Product Design*. Chichester, UK: John Wiley & Sons, Ltd.

11. Katz, G.M. (2004) The voice of the customer. In *The PDMA Tool Book 2 for New Product Development* (eds P. Belliveau, A. Griffin & S.M. Somermeyer), pp. 167–199. New York: John Wiley & Sons, Inc. Koen, P.A., Ajamian, G.M., Boyce, S. *et al.* (2002) Fuzzy front end: effective methods, tools, and techniques. In *PDMA Toolbook* (eds Belliveau, Griffin & Somermeyer), pp. 5–35.

12. Holman, R., Kaas, H. & Keeling, D. (2003) The future of product development. *McKinsey Quarterly*, 3: 29–39. Cited from page 29.

13. Hamel, G. & Getz, G. (2004) Funding growth in an age of austerity. *Harvard Business Review*, 82: 76–84.

14. Kurtz, C. & Snowden, D. (2003) The new dynamics of strategy: sense-making in a complex and complicated world. *IBM Systems Journal*, 42(3): 462–482.

15. Tidd, J., Bessant, J. & Pavitt, K. (2005) *Managing Innovation: Integrating Technological, Market and Organizational Change*. New York: John Wiley & Sons, Inc.

16. Huston, L. (2004) Mining the periphery for new products. *Long Range Planning*, 37: 191–196.

17. Day, G. & Schoemaker, P. (2000) *Wharton on Managing Emerging Technologies*. New York: John Wiley & Sons, Inc. Seely Brown, J. (2004) Minding and mining the periphery. *Long Range Planning*, 37: 143–151.

18. Seely Brown, J. (2004) Minding and mining the periphery. *Long Range Planning*, 37: 143–151.

19. Day, G. & Schoemaker, P. (2000) *Wharton on Managing Emerging Technologies*. New York: John Wiley & Sons, Inc. Seely Brown, J. (2004) Minding and mining the periphery. *Long Range Planning*, 37: 143–151.

20. Shell (2003) *People and Connections: Global scenarios to 2020*. London: Shell International Ltd.

21. Von Hippel, E. (1986) Lead users: a source of novel product concepts. *Management Science*, 32(7): 791–805. Von Hippel, E. (1988) *The Sources of Innovation*. Oxford: Oxford University Press. Von Hippel, E. (2005) *Democratizing Innovation*. Cambridge, MA: MIT Press.

22. Morrison, P.D., Roberts, J.H. & Midgley, D.F. (2004) The nature of lead users and measurement of leading edge status, *Research Policy*, 33: 351–362.

23. Callahan, J. & Lasry, E. (2004) The importance of customer input in the development of very new products, *R&D Management*, 34(2): 107–117.

24. Isaksen, S.G. & Treffinger, D.J. (2004) Celebrating 50 years of reflective practice: Versions of creative problem solving. *Journal of Creative Behavior*, 38: 75–101.

25. Isaksen, S.G., Dorval, K.B. & Treffinger, D.J. (2000) *Creative Approaches to Problem Solving: A Change Method*. Dubuque, IA: Kendall/Hunt. Treffinger, D.J., Isaksen, S.G. & Stead-Dorval, K.B. (2006) *Creative Problem Solving: An Introduction* (4th edn). Waco, TX: Prufrock Press.

26. Stevens, G., Burley, J. & Divine, R. (1999) Creativity + business discipline = higher profits faster from new product development. *Journal of Product Innovation Management*, 16: 455–468.

27. Selby, E.C., Treffinger, D.J., Isaksen, S.G. & Lauer, K.J. (2004) Defining and assessing problem-solving style: design and development of new tool. *Journal of Creative Behavior*, 38.

28. Isaksen, S.G. & Lauer, K.J. (2002) The climate for creativity and change in teams. *Creativity and Innovation Management Journal*, 11: 74–86. Isaksen, S.G., Lauer, K.J., Ekvall, G. & Britz, A. (2001) Perceptions of the best and worst climates for creativity: preliminary validation evidence for the Situational Outlook Questionnaire. *Creativity Research Journal*, 13(2): 171–184.

29. Kim, W.C. & Mauborgne, R. (1997) Value innovation: the strategic logic of high growth. *Harvard Business Review*, 75: 104–112.

30. Bossidy, L. & Charan, R. (2002) *Execution: The Discipline of Getting Things Done*. New York: Crown Business.

31. Davis, T. (2000) *Innovation and Growth: A Global Perspective*. London: PricewaterhouseCoopers.

32. Dorval, K.B. & Lauer, K.J. (2004) The birth of novelty: ensuring new ideas get a fighting chance. In *The PDMA Tool Book 2* (eds Belliveau, Griffin & Somermeyer), pp. 269–293.

33. Crawford, C.M. & DiBenedetto, C.A. (2000) *New Products Management* (6th edn). Boston: IrwinMcGraw-Hill. Gill, B., Nelson, B. & Spring, S. (1996) Seven steps to strategic new product development. In *The PDMA Handbook of New Product Development* (eds M.D. Rosenau, A. Griffin, G.A. Castellion & N.F. Anschuetz), pp. 19–34. New York: John Wiley & Sons, Inc.

Part 4

THE CONTEXT FOR TRANSFORMATION

Chapter 11

TRANSFORMING THE CULTURE AND CLIMATE

when one brings culture to the level of the organization and even down to groups within the organization, one can see more clearly how it is created, embedded, developed, and ultimately manipulated, managed, and changed. These dynamic processes of culture creation and management are the essence of leadership and make one realize that leadership and culture are two sides of the same coin[1]

It is common to hear leaders and managers proclaim, 'What we need around here is a culture change!' Like many things, this is much easier said than done.

If we take transformation seriously, then we must have a good understanding of what culture is and what it would take to change it. We conjure up images of cultural anthropologists studying far away tribes and civilizations when we think about culture. Those who lead change often find that the actual change they are trying to implement is influenced by many other factors that make a difference. As we discussed in Chapter 1, taking a systemic approach to guiding change includes considering the people involved in the change, the method or approach you are taking and the situation surrounding the effort. Each of these areas provides an entire domain for inquiry and consideration. How much effort you choose to put into each one (or any) depends on how important the change is and how much time and energy you have. Any successful change will require some knowledge and use of each of these areas.

One of the broadest factors to consider is the context for creativity and innovation for transformation. The word 'context' can be taken to mean something as broad as society or national culture as well as something very limited, like the working climate within a team.

This chapter overviews some of the important factors to consider when guiding change within organizations. Then we will focus on the ideas of climate and context for change and creativity. Finally, we will include some strategies leaders can follow to create the context for creativity and change.

What is culture?

Many writers have offered a variety of definition of culture. Thankfully, there are consistent themes among this diversity. Culture consists of deep and enduring patterns of how individuals and groups make decisions and demonstrate priorities about value differences. These value differences can be organized into dichotomies, such as people are good versus people are evil. Cultures can be more or less synergistic depending on the extent to which those who hold contrasting value orientations can and do work with each other. Cultures that hold strictly to one value polarity to the point that the opposing value is consistently put down and not tolerated can become stagnated.

In general, culture is something that:

• Is shared by all or most of the members of some social group.
• Older members usually try to pass on to younger members.
• Shapes behavior and structures perceptions of the world.

As such, culture can be described as collective programming of the mind or, as Geert Hofstede has called it, 'software of the mind'.[2] This collective software of the mind distinguishes the members of one social group from another.

Many writers see culture as something that is stable, deep and reinforced by a history of decisions, use of power and learned strategies for answering fundamental questions. The earliest meaning associated with the word 'culture' was the way in which people in a particular area took care of the soil – as in cultivate, plant, etc. How people worked with soil in the region was influenced by a number of key factors and was aimed at producing the best yield possible given those conditions. Just as this early use reflected the development of a specific way of dealing with certain environmental conditions, our current use of the word 'culture' has been formed based on how different societies have chosen to deal with certain similar issues. In a way, what defines a culture is how those within it have chosen to answer certain basic questions, particularly when they must confront similar problems (dealing with the external environmental forces) as a society.

1. What is the nature of humans? Are people good or evil? Can people change or are they resistant to change?
2. What is the nature of our relationships to each other? Is the focus on me, as an individual or me as a member of a group? What are the implications of being born a male or female? How do we deal with the unequal distribution of power?
3. How do we consider time? Do we make choices about our efforts based on the past, present or future?
4. How do we deal with space? Do we think about our personal and private use of space or do we think in terms of the public domain?
5. What is the nature of human activity? How do we deal with authority or control? Are we more about doing or being?
6. What is the nature of reality and truth? How do we face an uncertain or ambiguous future?
7. What is our relationship to nature? Do we think we should control or dominate it or live in harmony with it?

Cultures differ in their responses to these questions, but the questions are the same for each. The choices certain cultures have made regarding these questions reflect the shared values and deeply held assumptions they hold. Research has identified a number of different dimensions upon which cultures differ. Table 11.1 summarizes the dimensions upon which cultures have found to differ from the point of view of two prominent cultural researchers.

What is organizational culture?

Organizational culture is a different concept from culture. Most people have exercised a choice to join a place of work whereas people are born into particular societies. People who work in organizations usually have limits on how much time they spend there (or at work) and have other discretionary time available. People are generally free to leave an organization and may do so more easily than leaving a society. In any case, we have seen an increased interest in the idea of organizational culture.

Organizational cultures should describe the shared mental programming of those within the same organization, particularly if they share the same nationality. Research has shown that organizational cultures can and do differ in six important areas.

Table 11.1 Dimensions of culture

Fons Trompenaars: Culture is the pattern by which a group habitually mediates between value differences, such as rules and exceptions, technology and people, conflict and consensus, etc. [2]	*Geert Hofstede:* Culture is the collective programming of the mind which distinguishes the members of one group or category of people from another. [2]
Universalism versus particularism – Deals with rules in open spaces and the dilemma when no code or rule seems to cover an exceptional case. Should you shade the evidence for the sake of friendship? *Individualism versus communitarianism –* Is the emphasis on personal freedom, human rights, competitiveness, or social responsibility, harmonious relations, cooperation? *Specificity versus diffusion –* Are we more effective when we analyze things by reducing them to specifics (facts, items, tasks, numbers, units) or when we integrate and configure these into diffuse patterns, relationships, understandings and contexts?	*Uncertainty avoidance –* The extent to which the members of a culture feel threatened by uncertain or unknown situations (expressed through nervous stress, need for predictability, need for written and unwritten rules). *Individualism versus collectivism –* Individualism pertains to societies in which the ties between individuals are loose: everyone is expected to look after himself and his immediate family. Collectivism pertains to societies in which people from birth onwards are integrated into strong, cohesive groups, which throughout people's lifetimes continue to protect them in exchange for unquestioning loyalty.

Table 11.1 *Continued*

Fons Trompenaars: *Culture is the pattern by which a group habitually mediates between value differences, such as rules and exceptions, technology and people, conflict and consensus, etc. [2]*	**Geert Hofstede:** *Culture is the collective programming of the mind which distinguishes the members of one group or category of people from another. [2]*
Achieved versus ascribed status – Is what you've done or track record more important than who you are or your potential connections?	*Power distance* – The extent to which the less powerful members of institutions and organizations within a country expect and accept that power is distributed unequally.
Inner versus outer direction – Should we be guided by our inner convictions, moral compass or conscience, or by signals from the wider social and physical environment?	
Sequential versus synchronous time – Is it more important to do things fast, in the shortest sequence of passing time, or to synchronize efforts so that activities are coordinated?	*Long-term versus short-term* – The relative emphasis on quick results, saving face, respect for social and status obligations regardless of cost and respect for tradition, versus perseverance toward slow results, willingness to subordinate self for a purpose, respect for social and status within limits, and adaptation of tradition to fit a modern context.
Neutral versus affective – Should we communicate the full extent of personal feelings or should we behave 'professionally' with an air of detachment and dispassion so to focus more on the tasks to be accomplished?	*Masculinity versus femininity* – The relative importance of earnings, recognition, advancement and challenge (material success and progress are dominant values) versus working relationships, cooperation, employment security and living in a good location caring for others and preservation are dominant values).

- *Process versus results orientation* – focus on the means or the way things are done, such as quality management or process improvement, versus a bias for action and results, such as 'management by objectives'.
- *Employee versus job* – the classic tension between concern for people, versus concern for the task, for example, the so-called 'European social model' versus the 'Anglo-Saxon' liberal market approach.
- *Parochial versus professional* – identity derived from the internal organization, versus identity with a specific type of job.
- *Open versus closed systems* – broad definition of organizational boundaries with a high degree of interaction with the environment, versus a narrow organizational focus, for example, the 'not invented here' syndrome.
- *Loose versus tight control* – a high degree of autonomy regarding ends and means, versus a more prescriptive and directive approach.
- *Normative versus pragmatic* – a focus on following the bureaucratic rules and procedures, versus meeting the needs of the task or customer.

What does culture include?

Values, beliefs and deeply held assumptions

Values are general beliefs that function to define what is right or wrong, or specify general preferences. They influence behavior because they are broad tendencies to prefer certain states of affairs over others. They are similar to deeply held assumptions . . .

In an organizational context values can sometimes be specific and explicit. When we first started consulting with DuPont's Innovation Initiative in the early 1990s, we were impressed with the many successes with new product development. There were, however, some challenges in implementing some of the strategies included within the innovation initiative. We also ran into a number of rules when we visited numerous factories and locations. We could not run on DuPont property, for example. When we looked deeper into the culture, it became very clear to us that DuPont held a strong value for safety. Later, we were able to visit the site of the founding of the E.I. DuPont de Nemours gunpowder manufactury in Wilmington, Delaware. It was a pretty location on the Brandywine River, which served as the power source in the early 1800s. We noticed that in the buildings in which the gunpowder was produced, three walls were made of very thick stone, but the side facing the river was made of thin wood.

Not a single nail was used in the construction of these buildings for fear that a small piece of metal could fall and make a spark.

The family home was not very far from the buildings that made the gunpowder. So, from the very founding of the company, there was always a great concern for safe operations and limiting the risk of harm to people. This is how many deeply held values are embedded in organizations.

Symbols

Symbols are words, gestures, pictures or other objects that carry and convey meaning to a particular group that share a common culture. In an organizational context they can include flags, status symbols, manner of dress, etc.

Heroes

Heroes are people who can be either dead or living, real or imaginary, who possess highly valued characteristics. As such, they serve as role models for preferred or desired ways of behaving.

Rituals

Rituals and customs are activities that seem nonessential to the actual functioning of the group, but they are considered socially necessary. These behaviors are reinforced over time – forming traditions that are filled with implicit meaning. In an organizational context this could include the way greetings and initial social exchanges occur during meetings.

Rituals, heroes and symbols are visible to the observer; their meaning is invisible and may require interpretation.

Can leadership change culture?

According to Edgar Schein, one of the most cited writers in the field, there are three main sources that form any organizational culture.[3] First, there are the beliefs, values and assumptions of the founder. Next, the learning experiences of members as the organization evolves and grows can also influence culture. Third, organizational cultures can change as a result of new beliefs, values and assumptions brought into the organization from new members and leaders. The most profound of these tend to be the founding leaders. They have strong theories about how things should be done and these get tested early in the organization's life. If the organization makes it through the many early tests of the founders' theory, the beliefs and assumptions of those founders exert a profound influence on the culture of the organization. If circumstances change, and those assumptions are not longer viable, then the organization must change its culture or die.

During the founding stage, the culture is formed primarily by what the founding leaders do and pay attention to. As the organization grows, and the founders may no longer be in the picture, it creates smaller units based on the needs for functional specialization and geographic decentralization, and by creating divisions to deal with unique product, market or technology areas. These smaller units begin the process of culture formation with their own leaders making it even more complex to manage culture change.

Since culture is such a deep, stable, complex set of shared assumptions that are built over relatively long periods of time, it is not an easy task for new leaders to change it. Further, many definitions of culture specifically exclude behavior. When we see what leaders have done to actually influence culture change, they have actually focused their efforts more on the working climate. For example, Schein identified six primary mechanisms the leaders use to embed a culture. These include things like what leaders pay attention to, measure and control, as well as a number of other observed behaviors like the criteria leaders use to allocate scarce resources and rewards.

For example, most large organizations in the private and public sectors now use explicit measures of or targets for performance to try to manage and improve. It has become a cliché, but 'what gets measured gets managed', and the converse, 'what doesn't get measured doesn't get done' is largely true in most organizations. This observation has a number of important practical implications, namely:

1. Performance measures do influence behavior, although clearly they are not the only influence.
2. Measures can effect behavior in positive and negative ways, and therefore, the choice of measures used is critical.
3. It forces managers to review their activities and to decide which are most important. Without measurement it is impossible to determine current performance or to prioritize resources for improvement.

4. It provides a guide to the direction and rate of improvement. Measures provide useful feedback on the relative success of initiatives, and are the basis of continuous improvement and organizational learning.

5. Linking measures of performance with incentives and rewards can help to direct and sustain employee motivation and effort. These include *extrinsic* rewards, such as appraisal, income and promotion, and *intrinsic* rewards such as personal pride, acknowledgment and competitive instincts.

However, inappropriate measures can be worse than having no measures at all. A common failing in many organizations is that what gets measured is not that which is most important, but that which is most easily measured. Managers, and more recently civil servants and politicians, tend to focus on those issues for which data already exist or are easily created, however important or relevant such measures might be. For example, many organizations rely on inappropriate measures derived from management accounting because in most cases the data already exist. However, as we shall argue, such measures are at best incomplete, and at worst misleading, because of arbitrary decisions regarding allocation of overheads. In contrast, we will advocate only the measurement of what is considered important to an organization, however difficult or imperfect such measures might be. Common problems include:

1. *Measuring the wrong things*. There is a bias toward financial measures and other easily collected data, rather than developing measures that relate to the underlying processes and performance of the organization. For example, in the UK the government publishes league tables of schools based on examination results. Such data are relatively easy to collect, but do not reflect the quality of the schools in the sense of the value they add. To do this would require some measure of the quality of students upon enrolment.

2. *Failure to define or understand the processes*. Too often measures are imposed by managers (or civil servants or politicians) too remote from the process to understand the detailed requirements. As a result, measures and targets may be unrealistic. For example, targets for growth are often set at an arbitrary level based on the past year's performance, rather than on the basis of the scope for improvement, which might be greater or smaller than the target set. Process analysis makes it easier to understand the underlying operations, and therefore identify appropriate measures and targets for improvement.

3. *Failure to distinguish between measures for control and improvement*. Managers tend to view measurement as a means of control, and therefore often fail to develop measures that can be used by staff for improvement. For example, most measures

adopted by management accounting have been developed to control, rather than to improve. Targets for recovery of overheads do nothing to help reduce overheads, and variance against budget does nothing to encourage cost reductions if budgets are achieved.

4. *Fear of increased management control and lost autonomy.* The flip side of the previous problem is that staff are likely to resist measurement if they believe that this reduces their autonomy and increases management control. For example, in customer call centers used for services such as telephone banking and insurance, staff are continuously monitored. A typical measure used is the time taken to deal with a customer, and targets of a few minutes are common. This can create stress and discourage staff from providing an adequate service to customers.

5. *Fear of exposing poor performance.* Any new measurement regime is likely to identify areas of poor performance, and therefore the managers and staff responsible are likely to resist. In such cases, it is essential to create a secure and positive environment, stressing the potential for improvement and growth, rather than rationalization. For example, for many manufacturing companies the demand for their products is stable or declining. Therefore, any improvements in productivity are likely to result in job losses, which does not encourage cooperation. Under conditions of growth it is much easier to implement productivity and quality improvements.

6. *Additional bureaucracy and administrative burden.* The need to measure can be seen as a distraction from the 'real' job – as an additional overhead. In this case, the potential for improvement needs to be communicated clearly, and the time and training provided to develop, pilot and conduct measurement. For example, in many services there has been a proliferation of service-level agreements and customer feedback and assessment measures.

Figure 11.1 shows the results of a survey of 203 organizations. This confirms suggest that financial and operational measures are the most common, but that measures of quality, innovation and environment are less common.

This survey identifies a number of issues.

- Financial measures of performance are almost universal, and in most cases are included in staff reviews and linked to compensation.
- Measures of operational performance are commonplace, but are much less likely to be included in staff reviews or compensation.
- Less than half of firms have measures of customer satisfaction, but around three-quarters of these include the measures in staff reviews, and just over a third also

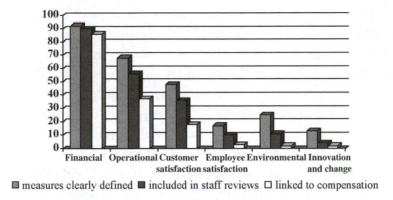

Figure 11.1 Use of performance measures (*n* = 203)
Source: Adapted from Lingle, J.H. and Schiemann, W.A. (1996) From balance score-card to strategic gauges. *Management Review*, March: 56–61.

link these measures to staff compensation. However, in absolute terms less than 20% of firms link customer satisfaction to staff compensation.

- Only a small proportion of firms have measures of employee satisfaction, environmental impact or innovation, and even those that do rarely include these in staff reviews or link to compensation.

We are not suggesting that everything of value can or should be measured, or conversely that only those activities that can be measured are valuable. Every organization is unique in the sense that it has its own history and culture, and operates in an environment of customer demands, competitor threats and regulatory requirements. Together, these internal and external contextual factors will shape and constrain measures of performance. Therefore, the objectives of and approaches to performance measurement will vary, ranging from more traditional goals such as cost reduction or quality improvement, to less common goals such as stimulating innovation or environmental sensitivity. When we examined such mechanisms, we found that they are not actually culture, but more about the perceived behaviors of those who live and work in the organization.

What is climate?

Climate is defined as the recurring patterns of behavior, attitudes and feelings that characterize life in the organization. At the individual level of analysis, the concept is called 'psychological climate'.[4] At this level, the concept of climate refers to the intrapersonal perception of the patterns of behavior, attitudes and feelings as experienced by the individual. When aggregated, the concept is called 'work unit' or 'organizational climate'.[5] These are the objectively shared perceptions that characterize life within a defined work unit or in the larger organization. Climate is distinct from culture in that it is more observable at a surface level within the organization and more amenable to change and improvement efforts.[6] Culture refers to the deeper and more enduring values, norms and beliefs within the organization.[7]

The domain for our inquiry into the climate for creativity and change is the organization. Climate is a scalable concept, in that it can be examined at the level of the work unit or group, the division or function, or at the entire organizational level. As such, it is influenced by the culture and other factors on the model for organizational change (MOC). Together, these factors create the larger context, within which climate is one key intervening variable.

The climate for creativity and change is that which promotes the generation, consideration and use of new products, services and ways of working. This kind of climate supports the development, assimilation and utilization of new and different approaches, practices and concepts.

Culture versus climate

The two terms, culture and climate, have been used interchangeably by many writers, researchers and practitioners. We have found that the following distinctions may help those who are concerned with effecting change and transformation in organizations.

Different levels of analysis

Culture is a rather broad and inclusive concept. Climate can be seen as falling under the more general concept of culture. If your aim is to understand culture, then you need to look at the entire organization as a unit of analysis. If your focus is on climate, then you can use individuals and their shared perceptions of groups, divisions or other levels of analysis. Climate is recursive or scalable.

Different disciplines involved

Culture is within the domain of anthropology and climate falls within the domain of social psychology. The fact that the concepts come from different disciplines means that different methods and tools are used to study them.

Normative versus descriptive

Cultural dimensions have remained relatively descriptive, meaning that one set of values or hidden assumptions were neither better nor worse than another. This is because there is no universally held notion or definition of the best society. Climate is often more normative in that we are more often looking for environments that are not just different, but better for certain things. For example, we can examine different kinds of climates and compare the results against other measures or outcomes like innovation, motivation, growth, etc.

More easily observable and influenced

Climate is distinct from culture in that it is more observable at a surface level within the organization and more amenable to change and improvement efforts.

What is needed is a common sense set of levers for change that leaders can exert direct and deliberate influence over. That is the purpose of the next section of this chapter.

A model for organizational change

A variety of models have been put forward to explore the relationship and role of context in organizational research and theory.[8] Considering these models and our own fieldwork and research with organizations engaged in change initiatives, we have developed a revision and reintegration of some of these works as shown in Figure 11.2.[9]

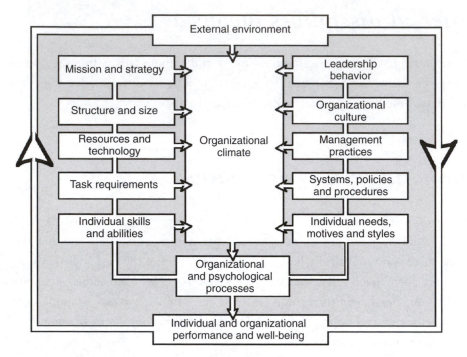

Figure 11.2 A model for organizational change

We see organizational climate as an intervening variable that affects individual and organizational performance due to its modifying effect on organizational and psychological processes. The climate is influenced by many factors within the organization and, in turn, affects organizational and psychological processes. Organizational processes include group problem-solving, decision-making, communication and coordination. Psychological processes include learning, individual problem-solving, creating, motivating and committing. These components exert a direct influence on the performance and outcomes in individuals, working groups and the organization. The model outlines a few of the more important organizational factors that affect climate, which in turn impact the results and outcomes of the organization.

The model for organizational change (MOC) emphasizes those factors that we believe are important to consider when introducing, managing or understanding change within an organizational context. The 14 elements in the MOC describe the key levers for change within organizations. Information and interaction are the content that flows through this larger system. By information we mean the data and knowledge being exchanged. It includes formal and informal news and represents the collective wisdom within the organization. Interactions are the relationships and inter-play between and among people. Interactions can be observed through behavior and patterns of communication and focus on how the information is exchanged and transmitted.

The external environment

The organization exists in a context and is affected by its external environment and affects the external environment by producing both individual and organizational output or performance. This is consistent with the thinking of the general systems theory,[10] and the more recent findings of Burke and Litwin and their colleagues.[11]

The external environment is any condition or situation that is outside the organi-zation itself but can exert an influence on the organization's performance (the market, other organizations, global financial conditions, government, the larger political and social system, technological and scientific developments). Individual and organiza-tional performance and well-being include the actual outcomes or results. These results reenter the external environment as do some of the interactions within the system. They function as indicators of the achievements and efforts of the organization and the people within it. The MOC displays the organization as a system within this larger context. Both the external environment and the organization's operations and perfor-mance have an impact on the climate within the organization.

Therefore, there is unlikely to be 'one best way' to manage and organize change as organization-specific characteristics are likely to undermine the notion of a universal formula for success.[12] For example, research on organizational innovation confirms that the type of organization and scope for innovation are critical differentiating factors,[13] and the broader organization context and industry dynamics are also influ-encial.[14] Managers' assessments of the organizational environment affect the crite-ria used to assess and select projects, and the methods used to manage and resource them.[15]

The effects of context on organization and performance is sometimes called the 'con-tingency theory'. Central to contingency theory is the concept that no single organi-zational form is effective in all circumstances, and that instead there is an optimal organization type that best fits a given contingency, such as size, strategy, task uncer-tainty or technology.[16] Therefore, the better the fit between organization and con-tingency, the higher the organizational performance.[17] This relationship between contingency, organization and performance has been supported by a substantial body of research conducted in the 1960s and 1970s, including qualitative comparative case studies[18] and quantitative analysis of large samples.[19]

Contingency theory has been criticized for being too prescriptive and deterministic, leaving little scope for other influences such as managerial choice or institutional pressures. However, Child offers some accommodation of the competing theories by allowing some 'strategic choice' within boundaries set by contingencies.[20] We adopt a similar position here, and will argue that contingencies do influence the organization and management of change, but that they constrain rather than fully determine 'best practice'.

The transformational factors

The four factors at the 'top' of the model are leadership behavior, organizational culture, mission and strategy, and structure and size. These have been referred to as the transformational variables for organizational change because any alteration within them is likely to be caused by an interaction with the external environment and will require new behaviors within the organization.[21]

Leadership behavior

Leadership behavior includes any actions initiated by leaders aimed at the transformative aspects of the organization. Acts of leadership occur whenever problems are solved, decisions are made, or information exchanges result in actions. Leadership behavior is very visible to individuals in the organization, especially during times of change. Leaders may be senior managers, supervisors and others who hold formal positions of influence, or those who demonstrate an informal influence on others. Leadership behavior has a major influence on the perceptions people have about the climate for creativity and change.[22]

Research over the past 40 years has confirmed that contrary to the common caricature of the lone maverick innovator, 'top management commitment' is one of the most common prescriptions associated with successful innovation.[23] The challenge is to translate the concept into reality by finding mechanisms that demonstrate and reinforce the sense of management involvement, commitment, enthusiasm and support.

In particular, there needs to be long-term commitment to major projects, as opposed to seeking short-term returns.

Leadership can influence cognitive perceptions of the work environment, that is the need for and susceptibility to change, and innovative behaviors, including the generation, testing and implementation of ideas. The critical condition for translation of the situational assessment into innovative behaviors is that a leader judge a need for change, and that the environment is susceptible to change.[24] Clearly, a feedback loop exists from the second to the first appraisal. With greater perceived situational control (authority to act, resources, time, etc.) managers will increase their sensitivity and aspiration for innovation, and conversely if they perceive their control to be lower, their sensitivity in the primary appraisal will be reduced.

There is a recent and growing body of research, experience and practice that indicates that specific leadership styles and practices can have a significant positive effect on creativity and innovation. For example, a useful typology of creative leadership consists of three broad leadership styles: those that accept existing ways of doing things; those that challenge existing ways of doing things; and those that synthesize different ways of doing things.[25] This suggests that leadership styles can be positioned on some scale of leader proactiveness, ranging from avoidance or laissez-faire at the bottom of the range, through transactional somewhere in the middle, to transformational at the top. Others identify a focus on personal values and standards, so-called 'ideological' leadership, and a focus on social needs and requirements for change or 'charismatic' leadership.[26]

One of the most important roles that leaders play within organizational settings is to create the climate for innovation. In the next chapter, we identify the critical dimensions of the climate for innovation, and suggest how leaders might nurture these. By using a Situational Outlook Questionnaire (SOQ) as a diagnostic, we identify nine dimensions to help decide what kind of interventions might be helpful in establishing the appropriate context for innovation.

Organizational culture

Organizational culture includes the values, beliefs, history and traditions that reflect the deeper foundations of the organization. Culture is the cement that holds an organization together. Over time, organizations develop a culture based on deeply entrenched norms and assumptions. These embedded principles and ethics influence patterns of interaction as well as choices and decisions that people make. The culture determines the worldview or mind set for those who belong.[27] It influences the way people behave, particularly how they respond to surprise, ambiguity, creativity and change.

As we have seen, culture is complex, but it basically equates to the pattern of shared values, beliefs and agreed norms that shape behavior – in other words, it is 'the way we do things round here' in any organization. Schein suggests that culture can be understood in terms of three linked levels, with the deepest and most inaccessible being what each individual believes about the world – the 'taken for granted' assumptions.[28] These shape individual actions and the collective and socially negotiated version of these behaviors defines the dominant set of norms and values for the group. Finally, behavior in line with these norms creates a set of artefacts – structures, processes, symbols, etc. – which reinforce the pattern. Given this model, it is clear that management cannot directly change culture – but it can intervene at the level of artifacts – by changing structures or processes – and by providing models and reinforcing preferred styles of behavior. Such 'culture change' actions are now widely tried in the context of change programs toward total quality management and other models of organization that require more participative culture.

However, the idea of a strong shared culture may be too simplistic, and instead we can identify five dimensions or orientations: autonomy, external, interdepartmental coordination, human resources and improvement.[29] Autonomy refers to the degree of discretion employees have at the job or task level. External orientation is derived from an open systems approach, and refers to the relationship with the context. Interdepartmental coordination is included as horizontal differentiation and specialization can create barriers to inter group communication. Human resource issues are an inherent component of organizational culture. The fifth dimension, improvement, reflects the organization's level of ambition, degree of proactiveness and emphasis on results.

Mission and strategy

Mission and strategy define what the business is going to do and subsequently how it will achieve its aim. Mission and strategy include the vision, purpose and the main strategic initiatives that the organization will take to ensure its purpose and reach its vision. The strategy defines for them how this purpose will be achieved. Mission and strategy also influence patterns of behavior, attitudes and feelings of those who develop the direction as well as those who take initiative and implement it.[30]

While we must be careful of vacuous expressions of 'mission' and 'vision', it is also clear that in cases like these there has been a clear sense of, and commitment to, shared organizational purpose arising from such leadership. Changing mind set and refocusing organizational energies requires the articulation of a new vision, and there are many cases where this kind of leadership is credited with starting or turning round organizations. Examples include Jack Welch of GE, Steve Jobs (Pixar/Apple), Andy Groves (Intel) and Richard Branson (Virgin).

Leadership should formulate, define and restate overall values, vision and mission, strategic directions and organizational forms; it can empower and mobilize commitment to new directions, and can energize people in action. Bass considered charisma (later renamed 'influence'), intellectual stimulation, inspired motivation and individual consideration to be significant components of the construct of transformational leadership.[31] Charismatic leadership includes a sense of mission, articulating a future-oriented, inspirational vision based on powerful imagery, values and beliefs, and is highly predictive of organizational performance.[32] Innovation champions provide enthusiastic support for new ideas and relate the innovation to a variety of positive organizational outcomes by using their informal networks to promote the innovation throughout the organization.[33]

Structure and size

Structure refers to the way that people and functions are arranged. It deals with levels of responsibility, decision-making authority and formal reporting relationships with others in the organization. It is often displayed as an organizational chart showing its functions and divisions. Structures are usually designed to ensure that the mission and strategy of the organization are effectively implemented. The structure and the size of the organization, and its working units, influence the use of power in making decisions and the scope of participation. They create the pathways for the flow of information and guide the assumptions that people make regarding relationships and interactions.

Ekvall has shown that the type of structure within departments of an organization (i.e. hierarchical and bureaucratic versus flat and empowered) has an impact on employees' perceptions of the climate in those departments.[34] Much of the early research examined the relationship between formalization, specialization and firm size, the Aston Group being the most influential work on this subject.[35] Galbraith argued that as task uncertainty increases, more information must be processed, which in turn influences the control and communication structures.[36] Similarly, Lawrence and

Lorsch proposed that the rate of environmental change affected the need differentiation and integration within an organization, and found support for this in their comparative study of organizational structures in three different sectors.[37] More recently, management researchers such as Mintzberg[38] and Galbraith[39] have developed these ideas into more prescriptive management frameworks, which attempt to match organizational structural templates to specific task environments.

The transactional factors

The remaining elements of the MOC are generally referred to as transactional variables in that they are aimed at preserving and implementing that which has been decided at the transformative level of the organization. Some might call these more tactical elements in that they focus more on the day-to-day interactions and behaviors within the organization.

Resources and technology

Resources and technology are the basic tools an organization has at its disposal to complete business. These include the people, capital, machines, equipment, materials, patents and copyrights that the organization has acquired for use in its operations. The level of knowledge available to the organization is also a key resource. Resources and technology can impact the feelings and attitudes of people in the organization by either facilitating or inhibiting appropriate behaviors. A lack of key resources can often frustrate and provide barriers to creative thinking and limit initiative.

The type of technology used has long been recognized as having a fundamental effect on organization and performance.[40] However, assessing technology is relatively difficult, the most simple being the scale and flexibility of production processes. Having and effectively using resources and technology can be a stimulant for the climate for creativity and change.[41]

Task requirements

Task requirements are the mixture of skills, knowledge and capabilities needed by the organization to perform assignments effectively. The kinds of tasks to be accomplished, and their corresponding demands, influence the selection of who needs to work on what jobs. Certain tasks may require cross-functional work, others may require co-operation across divisions. The demands made by these tasks influence the behaviors required by the organization to accomplish its purpose, and in turn, affects the climate.[42]

An examination of the research suggests that many contingencies exert a significant influence on organizational and management of innovation, the most significant being the uncertainty and complexity of the tasks undertaken.[43] A review of 21 innovation research projects concludes that

> environmental uncertainty influences both the magnitude and the nature of innovation . . . (which) suggests that future research should adopt environmentally sensitive theories of organizational innovation by explicitly controlling for the degree and the nature of environmental uncertainty.[44]

In particular, perceptions of environmental uncertainty appear to affect the organization and management of innovation.[45] Perrow developed a finer grain typology of task analyzability and variability.[46]

Task complexity is a function of the number of technological components and interactions. Uncertainty is a function of the rate of change of technologies and product markets, whereas complexity is a function of technological and organizational interdependencies. Uncertainty and complexity need to be differentiated, as they appear to have different requirements. Recent research suggests that innovation in complex systems is fundamentally different to that in other fields.[47] For example, a firm exposed to an environment of rapid technological change might require high levels of internal research and development and linkages with the science base, whereas a firm attempting to manage complexity is likely to be embedded in a network of collaborating organizations.[48] Complexity does not necessarily imply uncertainty, or vice versa.[49]

Individual skills and abilities

Individuals' skills and abilities are the capabilities and knowledge held by individuals within the organization. The skills and abilities describe the level and kind of competence available to the organization. They determine how much talent is available within the organization to meet the requirements of the tasks. If a workplace is filled with highly qualified people, with more than sufficient talent to contribute to accomplishing the purpose of the organization, the climate will be positively affected.[50]

A core ability in any learning organization will be the continual discovery and sharing of new knowledge – in other words, a continuing and shared learning process. Mobilizing and managing knowledge becomes a primary task and many of the recipes offered for achieving this depend upon mobilizing a much higher level of participation in innovative problem-solving and on building such routines into the fabric of organizational life.

But organizations do not learn, it is the people within them who do; routines are thus directed at creating the stage on which they act and the scripts they work to. To achieve this employees must understand how to learn; an increasing number of organizations have recognized that this is not an automatic process and have begun implementing training programs designed less to equip employees with skills than to engender the habit of learning. Training – not only in the narrow sense of 'know-how' but also a component of education around the strategic rationale for the change (the 'know-why') – can provide a powerful lubricant for oiling the wheels of such innovation programs.

We are interested in the routines that the organization develops to enable the learning process, and in particular in the ways in which individual and shared learning can be mobilized. For example, the following mechanisms are all important:[51]

- training and development of staff;
- development of a formal learning process based on a problem-solving cycle;
- monitoring and measurement;
- documentation;
- experiment;
- display;
- challenging existing practices;
- use of different perspectives;
- reflection – learning from the past.

Crucially, what is learned and developed is not only new knowledge directly relevant to the organization, but also knowledge about how to manage the process itself. To take an analogy, human beings not only acquire new content of knowledge as they grow, but they also learn to learn; some develop more effective learning strategies than others, while for others it is a case of 'some people never learn'. Over time, successful innovators review and build upon particular courses of action and internalize particular routines for managing the innovation challenge – for example, ways of getting close to users, ways of managing projects, ways of harnessing and sharing information, ways of exciting and supporting creative problem-solving.

Management practices

Management practices refer to the behaviors managers use to run the day-to-day business. Management practices are aimed at maintaining the stability and order of the organization by coordinating, communicating, controlling and planning the use of human, financial and material resources. Typical management practices include conducting performance and business reviews, encouraging and monitoring individual and team goal setting, planning projects and budgeting. How managers behave influences how others in the organization will behave and, therefore, influences the climate for creativity and change.[52]

A key role of effective managers is to provide feedback and evaluation. This evaluative role is critical, but is typically seen as not being conducive to creativity and innovation, where the conventional (but wrong) advice is to suspend judgment to foster idea generation. Senior management inputs are most valued at the early stages of a new project, when problems are being defined and ideas formulated, and at the later stages when feedback and implications need to be identified.

Therefore, managers must invest a great deal of time and effort in evaluation and feedback as their core creative contribution, and should manage the timing and nature of this feedback to minimize the impact on motivation. This can lead to an ongoing cycle of innovation, as leaders and followers engage in a creative exchange.

The quality and nature of the leader–member exchange (LMX) has been found to influence the creativity of subordinates.[53] For example, a study of 238 knowledge workers from 26 project teams in high-technology firms identified a number of positive aspects of LMX, including monitoring, clarifying and consulting, but also found that the frequency of negative LMX were as high as the positive, around a third of respondents reporting these.[54] Therefore, LMX can either enhance or undermine subordinates' sense of competence and self-determination. However, analysis of exchanges perceived to be negative and positive, revealed that it was typically *how* something was done rather than *what* was done.

Systems, policies and procedures

Systems, policies and procedures are the mechanisms that facilitate work and provide structure for the organization. They include pay practices, rewards and recognition policies, management information systems (MIS), performance appraisal, budget and financial controls, and human-resource allocation procedures. Systems, policies and procedures provide the checks and balances that keep things on track and prevent costly errors. They act as early warning systems and help establish repeatable processes, create stability and prevent anarchy. How they are implemented and what people think about them has an influence on the climate.[55] They can also prescribe certain kinds of behavior.

Despite the claims of purveyors of highly standardized IT-based systems such BPR (business process reengineering) and ERP (enterprise resource planning), different contexts will demand different systems, policies and procedures. For example, our research has identified at least five distinct system configurations necessary to support different goals, ranging from traditional service or manufacturing factories, through to project-based organizations and professional bureaucracies.[56] However, any system configuration needs to provide several common elements, including:

- organizational mode of bringing people together;
- control mechanisms, either impersonal (standards, documentation, common software) or interpersonal (collocated teams);
- shared knowledge and/or technical information base;
- external linkages, e.g. customers and/or partners/suppliers.

Individual needs, motives and styles

Individual needs, motives and styles provide the basic drive and source of energy for the organization. They are psychological factors that provide a sense of worth or desire for peoples' actions and thoughts. Needs for affection, belonging and recognition influence what people do. Their motives determine what kinds of tasks they have energy and commitment. Their preferred style tells us about the way that they might like to work, think, solve problems and manage change. Needs, motives and styles tell us how much energy people have for various kinds of work and will impact their behaviors, attitudes and feelings.[57]

Individuals may have different vocabularies, different motives and represent organizations of widely differing cultures. Three approaches to improving communication are commonly used: mechanistic, psychological and interpretive.

- *Mechanistic* – which assumes that the process is essentially linear and rational, and that the sender and receiver of information share common perceptions, and therefore, the receiver will attribute the same meaning to the message as intended by the sender. This is the basis of the common cascade approaches to top-down communication.
- *Psychological* – which considers how individual characteristics such as attitudes, cognitions and perceptions influence communication. Individual motivations, perceptions, likes and dislikes determine *what* information is reacted to and *how* it is processed. However, this approach has been criticized for ignoring or underplaying the influence that the context has on communication.
- *Interpretive* – which looks at how social context and meaning systems influence individual behavior. Social structures and meaning systems are locally constructed and communication is highly context-specific. Actors are guided by experience and past behavior, and form cognitive maps that filter information and guide behavior. For example, sociological factors, such as the relative power of different members of a social group, their existing intellectual and technical commitments and control of valued information, can have a significant effect. Thus, local 'rigidly held perceptions' and 'pervasive sets of beliefs' will influence the way in which information is interpreted and acted upon.

The MOC provides the conceptual framework to help us define climate and to see it as an intervening variable in influencing organizational change. The MOC outlines those organizational attributes that influence climate as well as those that climate influences.

Conclusions

In this chapter, we have argued that a focus on organizational climate is more effective than a focus only on culture. This is because culture is difficult to measure or manage, whereas climate can be broken down into a number of components that can more easily be identified, assessed and influenced. We introduced a model of organizational change that takes into account the contingencies and context of an organization, and incorporates both transactional and transformational factors. In the next chapter, we develop the Situational Outlook Questionnaire (SOQ) to help to assess the organizational climate in more detail, and to provide the basis of a climate for innovation and growth.

References

1. Schein, E.H. (1992) *Organizational Culture and Leadership* (2nd edn). San Francisco: Jossey-Bass, p. 1.
2. Hofstede, G. (1997) *Cultures and Organizations – Software of the Mind: Intercultural Cooperation and its Importance for Survival.* New York: McGraw-Hill. Hofstede, G. (2001) *Culture's Consequences: Comparing Values, Behaviors, Institutions, and Organizations across Nations*, p. 5. Thousand Oaks, CA: SAGE. Trompenaars, F. & Hampden-Turner, C. (2004) *Managing People Across Cultures*, p. 22. West Sussex, UK: Capstone.
3. Schein, E.H. (1992) *Organizational Culture and Leadership* (2nd edn). San Francisco: Jossey-Bass.
4. Isaksen, S.G. & Kaufmann, G. (1990) Adaptors and innovators: different perceptions of the psychological climate for creativity. In *Creativity and Innovation: Learning from Practice* (eds T. Rickards, P. Colemont, P. Grøholt, M. Parker & H. Smeekes), pp. 47–54. Delft, Netherlands: Innovation Consulting Group TNO. Isaksen, S.G. & Lauer, K.J. (in press) The relationship between cognitive style and individual psychological climate: Reflections on a previous study. *Studia Psychologica*.
5. Turnipseed, D. (1994) The relationship between the social environment of organizations and the climate for innovation and creativity. *Creativity and Innovation Management*, 3: 184–195.
6. McNabb, D.E. & Sepic, F.T. (1995) Culture, climate and total quality management: measuring readiness for change. *Public Productivity and Management Review*, 18: 369–385.
7. Ekvall, G. (1996) Organizational climate for creativity and innovation. *European Journal of Work and Organizational Psychology*, 5(1): 105–123. Schneider, B., Brief, A.P. & Guzzo, R.A. (1996) Creating a climate and culture for sustainable organizational change. *Organizational Dynamics*, 24(4): 7–19.
8. Amabile, T.M. (1988) A model of creativity and innovation in organizations. *Research in Organizational Behavior*, 10: 123–167. Litwin, G.H. & Springer, R.A. (1968) *Motivation and Organizational Climate*. Boston, MA: Harvard Business School Press. Nadler, D.A. & Tushman, M.L. (1977) A diagnostic model for organizational behavior. In *Perspectives on Behavior in Organizations* (eds J.R. Hackman, E.E. Lawler & L.W. Porter), pp. 85–100. New York: McGraw-Hill. Payne, R. & Pugh, D.S. (1976) Organizational structure and

climate. In *Handbook of Industrial and Organizational Psychology* (ed. M.D. Dunnette), pp. 1125–1173. Chicago, IL: Rand McNally College Publishing. Tagiuri, R. & Litwin, G.H. (eds) (1968) *Organizational Climate: Explorations of a Concept*. Boston, MA: Harvard University Press. Weisbord, M.R. (1976) Organizational diagnosis: six places to look for trouble with or without a theory. *Group and Organizational Studies*, 1: 430–447. Woodman, R.W., Sawyer, J.E. & Griffin, R.W. (1993) Toward a theory of organizational creativity. *Academy of Management Review*, 18: 293–321.

9. Isaksen, S.G., Lauer, K.J. & Ekvall, G. (1998) *Perceptions of the Best and Worst Climates for Creativity: Preliminary Validation Evidence for the Situational Outlook Questionnaire.* Creativity Research Unit – Monograph Series #305. Buffalo, NY: The Creative Problem Solving Group. Isaksen, S.G., Lauer, K.J. & Ekvall, G. (in press) Situational Outlook Questionnaire: a measure of the climate for creativity and change. *Psychological Reports.* Isaksen, S.G., Lauer, K.J., Murdock, M.C. *et al.* (1995) *Situational Outlook Questionnaire: Understanding the Climate for Creativity and Change (SOQ™) – A Technical Manual.* Buffalo, NY: Creative Problem Solving Group.

10. Katz, D. & Kahn, R.L. (1978) *The Social Psychology of Organizations* (2nd edn). New York: John Wiley & Sons, Inc.

11. Burke, W.W., Coruzzi, C.A. & Church, A.H. (1996) The organizational survey as an intervention for change. In *Organizational Surveys: Tools for Assessment and Change* (ed. A.I. Kraut), pp. 41–66. San Francisco: Jossey-Bass. Burke, W.W. & Litwin, G.H. (1992) A causal model of organizational performance and change. *Journal of Management*, 18(3): 523–545.

12. Tidd, J. (1997) Complexity, networks and learning: integrative themes for research on innovation management, *International Journal of Innovation Management*, 1(1): 1–22. Tidd, J. (2002) Innovation management in context: environment, organizational and performance. *International Journal of Management Reviews*, 3(3): 169–184.

13. Damanpour, F. (1991) Organizational innovation: a meta-analysis of the effects of determinant and moderators. *Academy of Management Journal*, 34: 555–590.

14. Drazin, R. & Schoonhoven, C.B. (1996) Community, population, and organization effects on innovation: a multilevel perspective. *Academy of Management Journal*, 39(5): 1065–1083.

15. Tidd, J. & Bodley, K. (2002) The affect of project novelty on the new product development process, *R&D Management*, 32(2): 127–138; Tidd, J. (2002) Innovation management in context: environment, organizational and performance. *International Journal of Management Reviews*, 3(3): 169–184.

16. Donaldson, L. (1996) *For Positivist Organization Theory*. London: SAGE.

17. Donaldson, L. (1999) *Performance Driven Organizational Change*. London: SAGE, Drazin, R. & Van de Ven, A.H. (1985) Alternative forms of fit in contingency theory. *Administrative Science Quarterly*, 30: 514–539.

18. Burns, T. & Stalker, G.M. (1961) *The Management of Innovation*. London: Tavistock. Chandler, A.D. (1966) *Strategy and Structure*. Cambridge, MA: MIT Press.

19. Child, J. (1972) Organizational structure, environment and performance: the role of strategic choice. *Sociology*, 6: 1–22; Lawrence, P.R. & Lorsch, J.W. (1967) *Organization and Environment: Managing Differentiation and Integration*. Boston: Harvard Business School Press.

20. Child, J. (1972) Organizational structure, environment and performance: the role of strategic choice. *Sociology*, 6: 1–22.

21. Bass, B.M. (1985) *Leadership and Performance Beyond Expectations*. New York: The Free Press. Burns, J.M. (1978) *Leadership*. New York: Harper & Row. Kouzes, J.M. & Posner, B.Z. (1987) *The Leadership Challenge: How To Get Extraordinary Things Done In Organizations*. San Francisco: Jossey-Bass.

22. Ekvall, G. (1997) Organizational conditions and levels of creativity. *Creativity and Innovation Management*, 6(4): 195–205; Ekvall, G. & Arvonen, J. (1984) *Leadership Styles and Organizational Climate for Creativity: Some Findings in One Company*. (Report 1). Stockholm, Sweden: FArådet – The Swedish Council for Management and Work Life Issues. Ekvall, G., Arvonen, J. & Waldenstrom-Lindblad, I. (1983) *Creative Organizational Climate: Construction and Validation of a Measuring Instrument*. (Report 2). Stockholm, Sweden: FArådet – The Swedish Council for Management and Work Life Issues. Ekvall, G. & Ryhammar, L. (1998) Leadership style, social climate and organizational outcomes: a study of a Swedish university college. *Creativity and Innovation Management*, 7: 126–130.

23. Tidd, J., Bessant, J. & Pavitt, K. (2005) *Managing Innovation: Integrating Technological, Market and Organizational Change* (3rd edn). Chichester, UK: John Wiley & Sons, Ltd.

24. Krause, D.E. (2004) Influence-based leadership as a determinant of the inclination to innovate and of innovation-related behavior, *Leadership Quarterly*, 15(1): 79–102.

25. Sternberg, R.J., Kaufman, J.C. & Perez, J.E. (2003) A propulsion model of creative leadership. *Leadership Quarterly*, 14(4–5): 455–473.

26. Strange, J.M. & Mumford, M.D. (2002) The origins of vision: charismatic versus ideological leadership. *Leadership Quarterly*, 13: 301–323.

27. Hofstede, G., Neuijen, B., Ohayv, D.D. & Sanders, G. (1990) Measuring organizational cultures: a qualitative and quantitative study across twenty cases. *Administrative Science Quarterly*, 35: 286–316.

28. Schein, E.H. (1992) *Organizational Culture and Leadership* (2nd edn). San Francisco: Jossey-Bass.

29. Van den Berg, P. & Wilderom, C.P.M. (2004) Defining, measuring, and comparing organisational cultures. *Applied Psychology: An International Review*, 53(4): 570–582.

30. Collins, J.C. & Porras, J.I. (1997) *Built to Last: Successful Habits of Visionary Companies* (paperback edn). New York: Harper Business.

31. Bass, B.M. (1998) *Transformational Leadership: Industrial, Military and Educational Impact*. New Jersey: Lawrence Erlbaum Associates.

32. Walderman, D.A., Javidan, M. & Varella, P. (2004) Charismatic leadership at the strategic level: a new application of upper echelons theory. *Leadership Quarterly*, 15(3): 355–380.

33. Howell, J.M. & Boies, K. (2004) Champions of technological innovation: the influence of contextual knowledge, role orientation, idea generation, and idea promotion on champion emergence. *Leadership Quarterly*, 15(1): 123–143.

34. Ekvall, G. (1997) Organizational conditions and levels of creativity. *Creativity and Innovation Management*, 6(4): 195–205.

35. Pugh, D.S. & Hickson, D.J. (1976) Organizational structure in its context: the Aston Programme I. Hants: Saxon House. Pugh, D.S., Hickson, D.J., Hinings, C.R. & Turner, C. (1969) The context of organization structure. *Administrative Science Quarterly*, 14(1): 91–114.

36. Galbraith, J.R. (1994) *Competing with Flexible Lateral Organizations*. Reading: Addison-Wesley. Galbraith, J.R. & Lawler, E.E. (1993) *Organizing for the Future*. San Francisco: Jossey-Bass.

37. Lawrence, P.R. & Lorsch, J.W. (1967) *Organization and Environment: Managing Differentiation and Integration*. Boston, MA: Harvard Business School Press.

38. Mintzberg, H. (1983) *Structures in Fives: Designing Effective Organizations*. Englewood Cliffs: Prentice-Hall.

39. Galbraith, J.R. & Lawler, E.E. (1993) *Organizing for the Future*. San Francisco: Jossey-Bass.

40. Woodward, J. (1965) *Industrial Organizational: Theory and Practice*. Oxford: Oxford University Press.

41. Nonaka, I. (1991) The knowledge-creating company. *Harvard Business Review*, 69: 96–104.

42. Amabile, T.M. (1996) *Creativity in Context: Update to the Social Psychology of Creativity*. Boulder, CO: Westview Press.

43. Damanpour, F. (1996) Organizational complexity and innovation. *Management Science*, 42(5): 693–716.

44. Hauptman, O. & Hirji, K.K. (1999) Managing integration and co-ordination in cross-functional teams. *R&D Management*, 29(2): 179–191.

45. Souder, W.E., Sherman, J.D. & Davies-Cooper, R. (1998) Environmental uncertainty, organizational integration, and new product development effectiveness: a test of contingency theory. *Journal of Product Innovation Management*, 15: 520–533.

46. Perrow, C. (1970) *Organizational Analysis: A Sociological View*. London: Tavistock.

47. Dvir, D., Lipovetsky, S., Shenhar, A. & Tishler, A. (1998) In search of project classification: a non-universal approach to project success factors. *Research Policy*, 915–935. Hobday, M., Rush, H. & Tidd, J. (2000) Innovation in complex product systems. *Research Policy*, 29: 793–804.

48. Tidd, J. & Trewhella, M. (1997) Organisational and technological antecedents for knowledge acquisition and learning. *R&D Management*, 27(4): 359–375. Tidd, J. (1995) The

development of novel products through intra- & inter-organizational networks. *Journal of Product Innovation Management*, 12(4): 307–322.

49. Tidd, J. (1997) Complexity, networks and learning: integrative themes for research on innovation management. *International Journal of Innovation Management*, 1(1): 1–22.

50. Torrance, E.P. (1987) Teaching for creativity. In *Frontiers of Creativity Research: Beyond the Basics* (ed. S.G. Isaksen), pp. 189–215. Buffalo, NY: Bearly Ltd.

51. Garvin, D. (1993) Building a learning organization. *Harvard Business Review*, July/August, pp. 78–91.

52. Berryman-Fink, C. & Fink, C.B. (1996) *The Manager's Desk Reference* (2nd edn). New York: American Management Association. Schroder, H.M. (1994) In *Adaptors and Innovators: Styles of Creativity and Problem Solving* (ed. M.J. Kirton), pp. 91–113. London: Routledge.

53. Scott, S.G. & Bruce R.A. (1994) Determinants of innovative behavior: a path model of individual innovation in the workplace. *Academy of Management Journal*, 37(3): 580–607.

54. Amabile, T.M., Schatzel, E.A., Moneta, G.B. & Kramer, S.J. (2004) Leader behaviors and the work environment for creativity: perceived leader support. *Leadership Quarterly* 15(1): 5–32.

55. Pasmore, W.A. (1988) *Designing Effective Organizations: The Sociotechnical Systems Perspective*. New York: John Wiley & Sons, Inc.

56. Tidd, J. & Hull, F. (2003) *Service Innovation: Organizational Responses to Technological Opportunities and Market Imperatives*. London: Imperial College Press.

57. Kirton, M.J. (1994) *Adaptors and Innovators: Styles of Creativity and Problem Solving*. London: Routledge.

Chapter 12

THE CLIMATE
FOR INNOVATION
AND GROWTH

we need to create conditions, even inside larger organizations, that make it possible for individuals to get the power to experiment, to create, to develop, to test – to innovate. Whereas short-term productivity can be affected by purely mechanical systems, innovation requires intellectual effort. And that, in turn, means people. All people. On all fronts. In the finance department, the purchasing department, and the secretarial pool as well as the R&D group. People at all levels, including ordinary people at the grass roots and middle managers at the heads of departments, can contribute to solving organizational problems, to inventing new methods or pieces of strategies.[1]

Leaders and their behavior are a major force in creating the context for change and creativity. The purpose of this chapter is to outline a number of other factors that can make a difference as well as share some specific strategies that can be employed to improve the situation. Rather than focus on only one strategy, it may be helpful to have a number at your disposal.

The key is to examine the situation. This examination can be done from a cultural perspective and from the point of view of values, such as those surrounding the use of power, dealing with uncertainty, the tension between individuals and community, and masculine–feminine issues.[2] From this examination of the culture and climate, a better decision regarding the use of any particular strategy can be made.[3]

The value in using a deliberate assessment approach is that you can increase the likelihood that you will consider more factors while guiding significant change. Knowing more about your situation will help you decide how quickly you need to take action, the needed level of preplanning and the degree of involvement from others.

We have already outlined many of the factors that influence working climate in our model for organizational change (see Chapter 11). Viewed this way, climate is an attribute of the organization. People who belong to the organization, or those who are at least good observers of it, can describe and rate the climate.[4]

Climate can be understood as a 'sandwich' sort of concept. There are factors that can affect it, such as the physical environment, size, the material and machinery, and the quality of interpersonal interaction, among others. In turn, climate also exerts an influence on a variety of organizational processes including problem-solving, decision-making, communication; and psychological processes such as learning, creating, motivating and committing.

The climate of an organization intervenes or mediates these inputs and influences the quality of products or services produced,[5] the well-being of employees,[6] and the overall success of the organization or work unit (division, etc.).[7] As such, climate represents a critical lever for those who lead and manage within any kind of organization.

The Situational Outlook Questionnaire

Since we can define and differentiate climate, it should be possible to measure it. We have developed the Situational Outlook Questionnaire (SOQ) over the past 15 years in order to assess and then improve the climate for creativity and change. It has been translated and modified from the original research conducted by Ekvall and his colleagues.[8] The current version of the measure contains 53 items on nine dimensions. It also uses three open-ended questions that provide narratives to understand what is helping or hindering people in any specific situation. The third question provides concrete suggestions to improve the climate.

The reason we selected Ekvall's measure was its excellent validity. He was able to collect data over the years to clearly illustrate that the climate in innovative organizations was very different from those that were stagnated. Innovative organizations were those able to develop more new products and services, get them to the market faster and obtain more commercial success. As Table 12.1 illustrates, innovative organizations have a better average score than the stagnated, on all dimensions except conflict. Conflict is a negative dimension, so a lower score is better.

Every organization, work unit or division is different. The results from the SOQ are best left to those who are qualified to interpret and intervene. Even so, as someone interested in establishing a context supportive of creativity and change, you are

Table 12.1 International organizations			
Climate variables	Innovative (*N = 10)	Average (*N = 15)	Stagnated (*N = 5)
Challenge and involvement	238	190	163
Freedom	210	174	153
Trust and openness	178	160	128
Idea time	148	111	97
Playfulness/humor	230	169	140
Conflict	78	88	140
Idea support	183	164	108
Debate	158	128	105
Risk-taking	195	112	53

* N = number of companies.
Source: Ekvall, G. CCQ International Norms. Swedish Council for Management and Work Life Issues. Reproduced by permission.

probably able to informally assess your situation and determine if it might have too much, too little or the right amount of any of the nine kinds of behaviors described in the dimensions of the SOQ. This should be done with the utmost of care in that every case will have specific situational constraints and differences.

As you can observe from Table 12.1, even those organizations identified as innovative on the SOQ do not have 'perfect' scores of 300. Those that are stagnated do not have zero scores on the dimensions. This is consistent with our own research with best- and worst-case organizational climates and our experiences working within a variety of organizations.[9]

Climate dimensions and sample strategies

Certain dimensions of climate have been shown to support creativity and change. The following nine dimensions of a climate for creativity and change are those that are assessed by the SOQ. Each dimension will be defined and then followed by an example of how those who guide change might help to create an improved context for change.

Challenge and involvement

Challenge and involvement is the degree to which people are involved in daily operations, long-term goals and visions. High levels of challenge and involvement mean that people are intrinsically motivated and committed to making contributions to the success of the organization. The climate has a dynamic, electric and inspiring quality. People find joy and meaningfulness in their work and, therefore, they invest much energy. In the opposite situation, people are not engaged and feelings of alienation and indifference are present. The common sentiment and attitude is apathy and lack of interest in work and interaction is both dull and listless.

If the score for the challenge and involvement dimension is too low, you may see that people are apathetic about their work, are not generally interested in professional development, or are frustrated about the future of the organization. One of the probable causes for this might be that people are not emotionally charged about the vision, mission, purpose and goals of the organization. One of the ways to improve the situation might be to get people involved in interpreting the vision, mission, purpose and goals of the organization for themselves, and their work teams.

If the score for the challenge and involvement dimension is too high you may observe that people are showing signs of 'burn out', they are unable to meet project goals and objectives, or they spend 'too many' long hours at work. One of the reasons for this is that the work goals are too much of a stretch. A way to improve the situation is to examine and clarify strategic priorities.

Building and maintaining a creative climate involves systematic development of organizational structures, communication policies and procedures, reward and recognition systems, training policy, accounting and measurement systems and deployment of strategy. Leaders who focus on work challenge and expertise rather than formal authority result in climates that are more likely to be assessed by members as being innovative and high-performance.[10] Studies suggest that output controls such as specific goals, recognition and rewards have a positive association with innovation.[11] A balance must be maintained, between creating a climate in which subordinates feel supported and empowered, with the need to provide goals and influence the direction and agenda.[12] Leaders who provide feedback that is high on developmental potential – for example, provide useful information for subordinates to improve, learn and develop – result in higher levels of creativity.[13]

Intellectual stimulation is the most underdeveloped components of transformational leadership, and includes behaviors that increase others' awareness of and interest in problems, and develops their propensity and ability to tackle problems in new ways.

Intellectual stimulation by leaders can have a profound effect on organizational performance under conditions of perceived uncertainty, and is also associated with commitment to an organization.[14]

However, innovation is too often seen as the province of specialists in R&D, marketing, design or IT, but the underlying creative skills and problem-solving abilities are possessed by everyone. If mechanisms can be found to focus such abilities on a regular basis across the entire company, the resulting innovative potential is enormous. Although each individual may only be able to develop limited, incremental innovations, the sum of these efforts can have far-reaching impacts.

Since much of such employee involvement in innovation focuses on incremental change, it is tempting to see its effects as marginal. Studies show, however, that when taken over an extended period it is a significant factor in the strategic development of the organization. For example, a study of firms in the UK that have acquired the Investors in People award (an externally assessed review of employee involvement practices) showed a correlation between this and higher business performance. On average, these businesses increased their sales and profits per employee by three-quarters.[15] Another study involved over 1000 organizations in a total of seven countries, and found that those that had formal employee involvement programs, for example, featuring support and training in idea generation and problem-finding and solving, reported performance gains of 15–20%.[16] But there is also an important secondary effect of high involvement: the more people are involved in change, the more receptive they become to it. Since the turbulent nature of most organizational environments is such that increasing levels of change are becoming the norm, greater formal involvement of employees may provide a powerful aid to effective management of change.[17]

Idea time

Idea time is the amount of time people can (and do) use for elaborating new ideas. In the high idea-time situation, the possibilities exist to discuss and test impulses and fresh suggestions that are not planned or included in the task assignment and people who tend to use these possibilities. When idea time is low, every minute is booked and specified. The time pressure makes thinking outside the instructions and planned routines impossible. Research confirms that individuals under time pressure are significantly less likely to be creative.[18]

If the score for the idea-time dimension is too low, you may observe that people are only concerned with their current projects and tasks. They may exhibit an unhealthy level of stress. People see professional development and training as hindrances to their ability to complete daily tasks and projects. You may also see that management avoids new ideas because they will take time away from the completion of day-to-day projects and schedules. One of the possible reasons for this could be that project schedules are so intense that they do not allow time to refine the process to take advantage of new ideas. Individuals are generally not physically or mentally capable of performing at 100%. A corrective action could be to develop project schedules that allow time for modification and development.

If the score for the idea-time dimension is too high, you may observe that people are showing signs of boredom, that decisions are made through a slow, almost bureaucratic, process because there are too many ideas to evaluate, or that the management of new ideas becomes such a task that short-term tasks and projects are not adequately completed. Individuals, teams and managers may lack the skills to handle large numbers of ideas and then converge on the most practical idea(s) for implementation. You may be able to provide training in creativity and facilitation, especially those tools and skills of convergence or focusing.

The concept of *organizational slack* was developed to identify the difference between resources currently needed and the total resources available to an organization.[19] When there is little environmental uncertainty or need for change, and the focus is simply on productivity, too much organizational slack represents a static inefficiency. However, when innovation and change is needed, slack can act as a dynamic shock absorber, and allows scope for experimentation. This process tends to be self-reinforcing due to positive feedback between the environment and organization.

When successful, an organization generates more slack, which provides greater resource (people, time, money) for longer-term, significant innovation; however, when an organization is less successful or suffers a fall in performance, it tends to search for immediate and specific problems and their solution, which tends to reduce the slack necessary for longer-term innovation and growth.

The research confirms that an appropriate level of organizational slack is associated with superior performance over the longer term.[20] For high-performance organizations the relationship between organizational slack and performance is an inverted 'U' shape, or curvilinear: too little slack, for example being too lean or focused, does not allow sufficient time or resource for innovation, but too much provides little incentive or direction to innovation. However, for low-performance organizations any slack is simply absorbed, and therefore, simply represents an inefficiency rather than an opportunity for innovation and growth. Managers too often view time as a constraint or measure of outcomes, rather than as a variable to influence that can both trigger and facilitate innovation and change. Providing slack but finite time and resources, individuals and groups can minimize the rigidity that comes from work overload, and the laxness that stems from too much slack.[21]

Freedom

Freedom is described as the independence in behavior exerted by the people in the organization. In a climate with much freedom, people are given autonomy to define much of their own work. They are able to exercise discretion in their day-to-day activities. They take the initiative to acquire and share information, and to make plans and decisions about their work. In a climate with little freedom, people work within strict guidelines and roles. They carry out their work in prescribed ways with little room to redefine their tasks.

If there is not enough freedom, people demonstrate very little initiative for suggesting new and better ways of doing things. They may spend a great deal of time and energy obtaining permission and gaining support (internally and externally) or perform all their work 'by the book' and focus too much on the exact requirements of what they are told to do. One of the many reasons could be that the leadership practices are very authoritarian or overly bureaucratic. It might be helpful to initiate a leadership improvement initiative including training, 360-degree feedback with coaching, skills of managing up, etc.

If there is too much freedom, you may observe people going off in their own independent directions. They have an unbalanced concern weighted toward themselves rather than the work group or organization. People may do things that demonstrate little or no concern for important policies/procedures, performing tasks differently and independently, redefining how they are done each time. In this case, people may not know the procedures, they could be too difficult to follow or the need to conform may be too low. You may start to reward improvement of manuals, process improvements, and ways to communicate and share best practices to help correct the situation.

For example, corporate entrepreneurs appear to have some common personal characteristics. The two critical requirements appear to be an internal locus of control and a high need for achievement. The former characteristic is common in scientists and engineers, but the need for high levels of achievement is less common. Entrepreneurs are typically motivated by a high need for achievement (so-called 'n-Ach'), rather than a general desire to succeed. This behaviour is associated with moderate risk-taking, but not gambling or irrational risk-taking. A person with a high n-Ach:

- Likes situations where it is possible to take personal responsibility for finding solutions to problems.
- Has a tendency to set challenging but realistic personal goals and to take calculated risks.
- Needs concrete feedback on personal performance.

Entrepreneurs also tend to have an internal locus of control. In other words, they believe that they have personal control over outcomes, whereas someone with an external locus of control believes that outcomes are the result of powerful institutions, others or chance. Numerous surveys indicate that around three-quarters of entrepreneurs claim to have been frustrated in their previous job. This frustration appears to result from the interaction of the psychological predisposition of the potential entrepreneur and poor selection, training and development by the parent organization. Specific events may also trigger the desire or need to leave, such as a major reorganization or downsizing of the parent organization.

In many cases, innovation happens in spite of the senior management within an organization, and success emerges as a result of guerrilla tactics rather than a frontal assault on the problem. Much has been made of the dramatic turnaround in IBM's fortunes under the leadership of Lou Gerstner, who took the ailing giant firm from a crisis position, to one of leadership in the IT services field and an acknowledged pioneer of e-business. But closer analysis reveals that the entry into e-business was the result of a bottom-up team initiative led by a programmer called Dave Grossman. It was his frustration with the lack of response from his line managers that eventually led to the establishment of a broad coalition of people within the company, who were able to bring the idea into practice and establish IBM as a major e-business leader. The message for senior management is as much about leading through creating space and support within the organization, as it is about direct involvement.

Idea support

Idea support involves the ways that new ideas are treated. In the supportive climate, ideas and suggestions are received in an attentive and kind way by bosses and workmates. People listen to each other and encourage initiatives. Possibilities for trying out new ideas are created. The atmosphere is constructive and positive. When idea support is low, the reflexive 'no' prevails. Every suggestion is immediately refuted by a counterargument. Fault-finding and obstacle-raising are the usual styles of responding to ideas.

Where there is little idea support, people shoot each others' ideas down, keep ideas to themselves, and idea-suggestion systems are not well utilized. It could be that, based on past experience, people don't think anything will be done. You may need to carefully plan a relaunch of your suggestion system with a series of case studies of what has been acted upon and why.

Some situations may have too much idea support. In these cases you may observe that people are only deferring judgment. Nothing is getting done and there are too many options because appropriate judgment is not being applied. Too many people may be working in different directions. One of the reasons for this condition may be that people are avoiding conflict and staying 'too open'. You may need to help people apply affirmative judgment so that a more balanced approach to evaluation prevails.

A supportive climate is vital for gaining information, material resources, organizational slack and political support. This can reduce the energy wasted by individuals through nonlegitimate acquisition and support strategies, such as boot-legging (within the organization) or moon-lighting (outside the organization).[22] Without appropriate support for new ideas, potential innovators grow frustrated: 'If they speak out too loudly, resentment builds toward them; if they play by the rules and remain silent, resentment builds inside them.'[23] It is not sufficient to simply have a policy or process of support; it is necessary for managers to provide the time and resources to generate and test new ideas.

Creative work is not the same as a creative job. Creative work in most organizations is essentially down to an individual choice between the routine and novel. Self-efficacy is the belief that one has the ability to produce productive creative outcomes. It includes the confidence to adopt nonconformist perspectives, to take risks and acting without dependence of social approval, and can encourage broader information search and sustain effort. The creativity of all workers responds positively to support for creativity from supervisors and coworkers, especially those with lower self-efficacy.[24]

Individuals may lack, or believe themselves to lack, the ability to be creative in their work, independent of their performance in their job or job-efficacy. In general, supervisor support, job-efficacy and job complexity are positively associated with creative self-efficacy, but job tenure has a negative effect; that is, the longer the tenure the less creative self-efficacy. However, tenure interacts with job complexity: creative efficacy is positively associated with job tenure for high job complexity, but negatively with job tenure for low job complexity.[25] Therefore, in general, creative self-efficacy requires a sense of general mastery of a complex job as a foundation, and explicit support from supervisors and colleagues beyond that.

Role breadth self-efficacy (RBSE) refers to creating an environment in which people believe in their capabilities to organize and execute their responsibilities to produce given attainments, beyond their prescribed technical requirements. It is associated with employee motivation and effort, coping and persistence, and results in problem-solving, process improvement and innovation.[26]

Exhibit 12.1   Idea support at Nortel Networks[27]

Nortel Networks is a leader in a high-growth, high-technology sector, and around a quarter of all its staff are in R&D, but it recognizes that it is extremely difficult to initiate new businesses outside the existing divisions. It created the Business Ventures Programme (BVP) to help to overcome some of the structural shortcomings of the existing organization, and identify and nurture new business ventures outside the established lines of business:

> The basic deal we're offering employees is an extremely exciting one. What we're saying is, 'Come up with a good business proposal and we'll fund and support it. If we believe your business proposal is viable, we'll provide you with the wherewithal to realize your dreams.'

The BVP provides:

- guidance in developing a business proposal;
- assistance in obtaining approval from the board;
- an incubation environment for start-ups;
- transition support for longer-term development.

The BVP selects the most promising venture proposals, which are then presented jointly by the BVP and employee(s) to the Advisory Board. The Advisory Board applies business and financial criteria in its decision whether to accept, reject or seek further development, and if accepted, the most appropriate executive sponsor, structure and level of funding. The BVP then helps to incubate the new venture, including staff and resources, objectives and critical milestones. If successful, the BVP then assists the venture to migrate into an existing business division, if appropriate, or creates a new line or business or spin-off company:

> The programme is designed to be flexible . . . the key motivators are to grow equity by maximizing return on investment, to pursue business opportunities that would otherwise be missed, and to increase employee satisfaction.

The main problems experienced have been the reaction of managers in established lines of business to proposals outside their own line of:

> At the executive council level, which represents all lines of business, there is a lot of support . . . where it breaks down in terms of support is more in the political infrastructure, the middle to low management executive level where they feel threatened by it . . . the first stage of our marketing plan is just titled 'overcoming internal barriers'. That is the single biggest thing we've had to break through.

Initially, there was also a problem capturing the experience of ventures that failed to be commercialized:

> Failures were typically swept under the rock, nobody really talked about them . . . that is changing now and the focus is on celebrating our failures as well as our successes, knowing that we have learned a lot more from failure than we do from success. Start-up venture experience is in high demand. Generally, it's the projects that fail, not the people.

Conflict

Conflict in the organization refers to the presence of personal, interpersonal or emotional tensions in contrast to idea tensions in the debate dimension. When the level of conflict is high, groups and single individuals dislike or hate each other and the climate can be characterized by 'warfare'. Plots and traps are common in the life of the organization. There is gossip and back-biting going on. When the level of conflict is low, people behave in a more mature manner. They have psychological insight and exercise more control over their impulses and emotions.

Although conflict is a negative dimension, all organizations have some level of personal tension. If conflict is too low you may see that individuals lack any outward signs of motivation or are not interested in their tasks. Meetings are more about 'tell' and not consensus. Deadlines may not be met. It could be that too many ineffective people are entrenched in an overly hierarchical structure. It may be necessary to restructure and identify leaders who possess the kinds of skills that are desired by the organization.

If the score on the conflict dimension is too high you may observe gossiping at water coolers (including character assassination), information hoarding, open aggression, or people lying or exaggerating about their real needs. These conditions could be caused by power struggles of both a personal and professional nature. In these cases, you may need to take initiative to engender cooperation among key individuals or departments.

So the goal is not necessarily to minimize conflict and maximize consensus, but to maintain a level of constructive conflict consistent with the need for diversity and a range of different preferences and styles of creative problem-solving. For example, people will have different preferences and styles: generators, conceptualizers and optimizers.[28] Group members with similar creative preferences and problem-solving styles are likely to be more harmonious but much less effective than those with mixed preferences and styles.

Conflicts can occur over tasks, process or relationships. Task conflicts focus on disagreements about the goals and content of work, the 'what?' needs to be done and 'why?' Process conflicts are around 'how?' to achieve a task, means and methods. Relationship or affective conflicts are more emotional, and characterized by hostility and anger. In general, some task and process conflict is constructive, helping to avoid groupthink, and to consider more diverse opinions and alternative strategies. However, task and process conflict only have a positive effect on performance in a climate of openness and collaborative communication; otherwise, it can degenerate into a relationship of affective conflict or avoidance. Relationship conflict is generally energy-sapping and destructive, as emotional disagreements create anxiety and hostility. However, in some cases this can be beneficial.

Perhaps counter-intuitively, research suggests that friendship within groups can lead to greater emotional conflict, and that this conflict can be harnessed to improve task and process.[29] This is because the bonds of friendship are built on trust, and expressing affective conflict is perceived to be safer and more acceptable. Even with severe conflicts, healthy and open resolution will promote trust and risk-taking.

Risk-taking

Tolerance of uncertainty and ambiguity exposed in the workplace constitutes risk-taking. In the high risk-taking climate, bold new initiatives can be taken even when the outcomes are unknown. People feel that they can 'take a gamble' on some of their ideas. People will often 'go out on a limb' and be first to put an idea forward. In a risk-avoiding climate there is a cautious, hesitant mentality. People try to be on the 'safe side'. They decide 'to sleep on the matter'. They set up committees and they cover themselves in many ways before making a decision.

When the score for the risk-taking dimension is too low, employees offer few new ideas or few ideas that are well outside of what is considered safe or ordinary. In risk-avoiding organizations people complain about boring, low-energy jobs and are frustrated by a long, tedious process used to get ideas to action. These conditions can be caused by the organization not valuing new ideas or having an evaluation system that is bureaucratic, or people being punished for 'drawing outside the lines'. It can be remedied by developing a company plan that would speed 'ideas to action'.

When the score for the risk-taking dimension is too high you will see that people are confused. There are many ideas floating around, but few are sanctioned. People are frustrated because nothing is getting done. There are many loners doing their own thing in the organization and no evidence of teamwork. These conditions can be caused by individuals not feeling they need a consensus or buy-in from others on their team in their department or organization. A remedy might include some team building and improving the reward system to encourage cooperation rather than individualism or competition.

A recent study of organizational innovation and performance confirms the need for this delicate balance between risk and stability. Risk-taking is associated with a higher relative novelty of innovation (how different it was to what the organization had done before), and absolute novelty (how different it was to what any organization had done before), and that both types of novelty are correlated with financial and customer benefits.[30] However, the same study concludes that:

> incremental, safe, widespread innovations may be better for internal considerations, but novel, disruptive innovations may be better for market considerations . . . absolute novelty benefits customers and quality of life, relative innovation benefits employee relations (but) risk is detrimental to employee relations.

The inherent uncertainty in some projects limits the ability of managers to predict the outcomes and benefits of projects. In such cases, changes to project plans and goals are commonplace, being driven by external factors, such as technological breakthroughs or changes in markets, as well as internal factors, such as changes in organizational goals. Together the impact of changes to project plans and goals can overwhelm the benefits of formal project planning and management (Table 12.2).[31]

Table 12.2   Management of conventional and risky projects

Conventional project management	Management of risky projects
Modest uncertainty	Major technical and market uncertainties
Emphasis on detailed planning	Emphasis on opportunistic risk-taking
Negotiation and compromise	Autonomous behavior
Corporate interests and rules	Individualistic and ad hoc
Homogeneous culture and experience	Heterogeneous backgrounds

This is consistent with the real options approach to investing in risky projects, because investments are sequential and managers have some influence on the timing, resourcing and continuation or abandonment of projects at different stages. By investing relatively small amounts in a wide range of projects, a greater range of opportunities can be explored. Once uncertainty has been reduced, only the most promising projects should be allowed to continue.

For a given level of investment, this real option approach should increase the value of the project portfolio. However, because decisions and the options they create interact, a decision regarding one project can affect the option value of another project.[32] Nonetheless, the real options perspective remains a useful way of conceptualizing risk, particularly at the portfolio level. The goal is not to calculate or optimize, but rather to help to identify risks and payoffs, key uncertainties, decision points and future opportunities that might be created.[33] Combined with other methods, such as decision trees, a real options approach can be particularly effective where high volatility demands flexibility, placing a premium on the certainty of information and timing of decisions.

Research on new product and service development has identified a broad range of strategies for dealing with risk. Both individual characteristics and organizational climate influence perceptions of risk and propensities to avoid, accept or seek risks. Formal techniques such as failure mode and effects analysis (FMEA), potential problem analysis (PPA) and fault tree analysis (FTA) have a role, but the broader signals and support from the organizational climate is more important than the specific tools or methods used. For example, internal risks in the organization and management of projects are commonly perceived as being just as important as less controllable external risks in technology, product and commercialization.[34]

Trust and openness

The trust and openness dimension refers to the emotional safety in relationships. These relationships are considered safe when people are seen as both competent and sharing a common set of values. When there is a strong level of trust, everyone in the organization dares to put forward ideas and opinions. Initiatives can be taken without fear of reprisals and ridicule in case of failure. The communication is open and straightforward. Where trust is missing, count on high expenses for mistakes that may result. People also are afraid of being exploited and robbed of their good ideas.

Trust can make decision-making more efficient as it allows positive assumptions and expectations to be made about competence, motives and intentions, and thereby economizes on cognitive resources and information-processing. Trust can also influence the effectiveness of an organization through structuring and mobilizing.[35] Trust helps to structure and shape the patterns of interaction and coordination within and between organizations. Trust can also motivate employees to contribute, commit and co-operate, by facilitating knowledge- and resource-sharing and joint problem-solving.

When the score on the trust and openness dimension is too low you may see people hoarding resources (i.e. information, software, materials, etc.). There may also be a lack of feedback on new ideas for fear of having concepts stolen. Management may not distribute the resources fairly among individuals or departments. One cause for this condition can be that management does not trust the capabilities and/or integrity of employees. It may help to establish norms and values that management can follow regarding the disbursement of resources, and a means to assure that resources are wisely used.

When the score on the trust and openness dimension is too high, relationships may be so strong that time and resources at work are often spent on personal issues. However, trust can bind and blind. It may also lead to a lack of questioning each other that, in turn, may lead to mistakes or less productive outcomes. Cliques may form where there are isolated 'pockets' of high trust. One cause of this condition may be that people have gone through a traumatic organizational experience together and survived (i.e. down sizing, a significant product launch, etc.). In this case, it may help to develop forums for interdepartmental and inter group exchange of information and ideas.

Trust may exist at the personal and organizational levels, and researchers have attempted to distinguish different levels, qualities and sources of trust.[36] For example, the following bases of organizational trust have been identified:

- Contractual – honoring the accepted or legal rules of exchange, but can also indicate the absence of other forms of trust.
- Goodwill – mutual expectations of commitment beyond contractual requirements.
- Institutional – trust based on formal structures.
- Network – because of personal, family or ethnic/religious ties.
- Competence – trust based on reputation for skills and know-how.
- Commitment – mutual self-interest, committed to the same goals.

These types of trust are not necessarily mutually exclusive, although over reliance on contractual and institutional forms may indicate the absence of the other bases of trust. Goodwill is normally a second-order effect based on network, competence or commitment. In the case of innovation, problems may occur where trust is based primarily on the network, rather than competence or commitment. Clearly, high levels of interpersonal trust are necessary to facilitate communication and learning in collaboration, but intra-organizational trust is a more subtle issue.

Trust is partly the result of individuals' own personality and experience, but can also be influenced by the organizational climate. For example, we know that the nature of rewards can affect some components of trust. For example, individual competitive rewards tend to reduce information-sharing and raise suspicions of others' motives, whereas group or cooperative rewards are more likely to promote information-sharing and reduce suspicions of motives.[37] Similarly, the frequency of communication within an organization influences trust, and in general, the higher the frequency of communication, the higher the levels of trust. In a climate of low communication, the level of trust is much more dependent on the general attitudes of individuals toward their peers.[38]

Trust is also associated with employees having some degree of role autonomy. Role autonomy is the amount of discretion that employees have in interpreting and executing their jobs. Defining roles too narrowly constrains the decision-making latitude. Role autonomy is influenced by three key factors: other functions, socialization and tenure.[39] Role autonomy can be affected by the level of influence that other internal functions have on discretion in decision-making, for example, limiting the scope for flexibility or adaptation. Role autonomy can also be influenced by the degree to which organizational socialization encourages employees to internalize collective goals and values; for example, clan cultures focus on developing shared values, beliefs and goals among members of an organization so that appropriate behaviors are reinforced and rewarded, but do not specify task-related behaviors or outcomes. This approach is most appropriate when tasks are difficult to anticipate or codify, and it is difficult to assess performance. However, individual characteristics will also influence role autonomy, including the level of experience, competence and power accumulated over time working for the organization.

So changes to the climate of an organization, such as the nature of rewards, frequency of communication and degree of role autonomy, can help to overcome individual propensities and biases, and improve the levels of trust. This can lead to more general positive organizational citizenship behaviors (OCBs). These are individual discretionary behaviors that in aggregate promote the effective functioning of the organization, and are not directly or explicitly recognized by the reward system. Supportive leadership is associated with these OCBs, in particular helping behaviors such as altruism and courtesy.[40] These OCBs help to maintain organizational trust, and such routines, norms and values are able to survive changes in individual personnel. In this way, organizational learning can take place, including new ways of doing things (operational or lower-level learning), and doing new things through diversification (strategic or higher-level learning).

Debate

Debate involves encounters, exchanges or clashes among viewpoints, ideas and differing experiences and knowledge. In the debating organization many voices are heard and people are keen on putting forward their ideas. Where debates are missing, people follow authoritarian patterns without questioning. Debate focuses on issues and ideas (as opposed to conflict that focuses on people and their relationships). Debate involves the productive use and respect for diversity of perspectives and points of view.

When the score on the debate dimension is too low, you may see constant moaning and complaining about the way things are, rather than how the individual can improve the situation. Rather than open debate, you may see more infrequent and quiet one-on-one conversation in hallways. In these conditions, there will be a lack of willingness by individuals to engage others in conversation regarding new ideas, thoughts or concepts. One of the reasons for this situation is that people may have had bad experiences when they have interacted in the past. It may help to clarify the rationale of debate in the organization and begin to model the behavior.

When the score debate dimension is too high, you are likely to see more talk than implementation. Individuals will speak with little or no regard for the impact of their statements. The focus on conversation and debate becomes more on individualistic goals than on cooperative and consensus-based action. One reason for this may be too much diversity or people holding very different value systems. In these situations, it may be helpful to hold structured or facilitated discussions and affirm commonly held values.

This has important implications for managers. The first concerns the practice of corporate strategy, which should be seen as a form of corporate learning, from analysis and experience, and how to cope more effectively with complexity and change. The implications for the processes of strategy formation include:[41]

- Given uncertainty, explore the implications of a *range* of possible future trends.
- Ensure broad participation and informal channels of communication.
- Encourage the use of multiple sources of information, debate and scepticism.
- Expect to change strategies in the light of new (and often unexpected) evidence.

The mandate for legitimating challenge to the dominant vision may come from the top – such as Jack Welch's challenge to 'destroy your business' memo. Perhaps building on their earlier experiences, Intel now has a process called 'constructive confrontation', which essentially encourages a degree of dissent. The company has learned to value the critical insights that come from those closest to the action rather than assume that senior managers have the 'right' answers every time.

Playfulness and humor

The playfulness and humor dimension represents the spontaneity and ease that is displayed in the workplace. A relaxed atmosphere, including good-natured jokes and laughter, characterizes the organization that is high in this dimension. The opposite climate is characterized by gravity and seriousness. The atmosphere is stiff, gloomy and cumbrous. Jokes and laughter are regarded as improper.

When there is too little playfulness in an organization, personal areas often lack artifacts that provide personal pleasure. People are listless and don't smile or interact beyond required discussion. In these cases, the company may not promote extracurricular activities. A common reason for this condition is that management does not see the business need for playfulness and humor on the job. In these cases, it can be helpful to encourage management to reflect on their own best-case work environment and provide support from literature for the need for playfulness and humor. The point is that work can be fun even when it is not for fun.

When there is too much playfulness in a workplace, personal areas are cluttered with artifacts that may impede work. Good-natured joking turns ugly (i.e. racial/gender jokes, destructive practical jokes). Playful activities become so numerous that individuals lack desire to do them and it may actually be viewed as an obligation or mandate. One reason for this is that it has become an informal policy and part of the organization's culture. In this case, it may be helpful to establish clearer norms regarding the specific conditions under which playfulness is appropriate.

Innovation requires creating new ideas and thinking about new options, playing with them to see if they are practical, economical and marketable, and then doing: making the innovation real. This suggests a new schema for the innovation process: think, play, do.[42] Part of the new potential for greater 'play' results from the application of new technologies to the innovation process itself, including simulation and modeling, visualization and rapid prototyping technologies. When used effectively, innovation technology makes the innovation process more economical and ameliorates some of its uncertainties. These technological changes are accompanied by changing organization structures and skills requirements. The technologies can be used to support fast-moving, creative environments and are most suited to project-based organization. They also require the development of new 'craft' skills to realize the possibilities they create.

Conclusions

Only a few years before the fall of Rome, Sidonius (a key historian of the Roman Empire who wrote *circa* 467 AD) wrote how normal everything was. Within a decade, the Roman Empire was swept into the pages of history. Sidonius was too close to the center of power to observe the forces bearing down upon Rome. These forces were anything but normal, but an individual's perspective can be so inwardly focused or limited in scope that the reality of the situation is overlooked. The same thing happens in some of the largest and best-run organizations in the world today.

If you, as a leader of change, really want to pay attention to the many forces that are already at work within your organization, then one of the best things you can do is to formally assess the climate around you. Rather than trying to measure or understand all relevant factors within the MOC, a single, broad measure can pick up those factors that are most relevant to your particular situation.

The most common mistake managers make is to use only one approach or a limited set of them regardless of the situation. A surprisingly large number of managers have this problem. This would include the hard-boiled boss who often coerces people, the people-oriented manager who constantly tries to involve and support his people, the cynical boss who always manipulates and co-opts others, the intellectual manager who relies heavily on education and communication, and the lawyer-like manager who usually tries to negotiate.[43]

The SOQ has shown that it measures nine key dimensions of a climate that supports creativity and change. In addition, the narrative section picks up factors that are included within the MOC[44] and points out unique ingredients within the situation that can really make a difference. As a result, the SOQ offers an excellent starting point to help you understand the situational outlook surrounding the change effort you wish to implement.

Our experience has shown that it is necessary to work with an experienced user of the SOQ. One very large organization with which we work conducted an SOQ assessment within one of its divisions. When the results were shared, the key leaders wanted to focus on only those dimensions on which they scored below the more productive norm. What they missed was the most significant (and meaningful) difference: that they were scoring well above an appropriate score for debate. The heart of their need for improvement turned out to be the productive avoidance created by too many diverse opinions and no clear strategic direction. This was confounded by the fact that most people in the division really enjoyed a good debate. It certainly was more fun than doing any productive work!

References

1. Kanter, R.M. (1983) *The Change Masters*. New York: Simon & Schuster, p. 23.
2. Offerman, L.R. & Hellmann, P.S. (1997) Culture's consequences for leadership behavior: national values in action. *Journal of Cross-Cultural Psychology*, 28: 342–351.
3. Coyne, K.P. & Subramaniam, S. (1996) Bringing discipline to strategy. *McKinsey Quarterly*, 4: 3–12.
4. Ekvall, G. (1996) Organizational climate for creativity and innovation. *European Journal of Work and Organizational Psychology*, 5, 105–123.

5. Ekvall, G. (1997) Organizational conditions and levels of creativity. *Creativity and Innovation Management*, 6, 195–205.

6. Talbot, R., Cooper, C. & Barrow, S. (1992) Creativity and stress. *Creativity and Innovation Management*, 1, 183–193.

7. Kotter, J.P. & Heskett, J.L. (1992) *Corporate Culture and Performance*. New York: The Free Press.

8. Cabra, J.F. (1996) *Examining the Reliability and Factor Structure of the Climate for Innovation Questionnaire*. Unpublished master's thesis, State University College at Buffalo, New York. Isaksen, S.G., Lauer, K.J., Murdock, M.C., Dorval, K.B. & Puccio, G.J. (1995) *Situational Outlook Questionnaire: Understanding the Climate for Creativity and Change (SOQ™) – A Technical Manual*. Buffalo, NY: Creative Problem Solving Group. Lauer, K.J. (1994) *The Assessment of Creative Climate: An Investigation of Ekvall's Creative Climate Questionnaire*. Unpublished master's thesis, State University College at Buffalo, New York. Speranzini, G.D. (1997) *Understanding the Impact of a Climate Intervention: Debriefing the Situational Outlook Questionnaire (SOQ)*. Unpublished master's thesis, State University College at Buffalo, New York. Sobieck, M.A. (1996) *Examination of Cross-Site Narrative Responses on the CIQ and SOQ*. Unpublished master's thesis, State University College at Buffalo, New York.

9. Britz, A. (1995) *The Assessment of Climate for Innovation in Organizations*. Unpublished master's thesis, Technische Hochshule Darmstadt. Isaksen, S.G., Lauer, K.J. & Ekvall, G. (1999) Situational Outlook Questionnaire: a measure of the climate for creativity and change. *Psychological Reports*, 85: 665–674. Isaksen, S.G., Lauer, K.J. & Ekvall, G. (1998) *Perceptions of the Best and Worst Climates for Creativity: Preliminary Validation Evidence for the Situational Outlook Questionnaire*. Creativity Research Unit – Monograph Series #305. Buffalo, NY: The Creative Problem Solving Group.

10. Judge, W.Q., Gryxell, G.E. & Dooley, R.S. (1997) The new task of R&D management: creating goal-directed communities for innovation. *California Management Review*, 39: 72–85.

11. Cardinal, L.B. (2001) Technological innovation in the pharmaceutical industry: the use of organizational control in managing research and development. *Organizational Science*, 12: 19–36.

12. Jung, D.I., Chow, C. & Wu, A. (2003) The role of tansformational leadership in enhancing organizational innovation. *Leadership Quarterly*, 14(4–5): 525–544.

13. Zhou, J. (2003) When the presence of creative coworkers is related to creativity: role of supervisor close monitoring, developmental feedback, and creative personality. *Journal of Applied Psychology*, 88: 413–422.

14. Rafferty, A.E. & Griffin, M.A. (2004) Dimensions of transformational leadership: conceptual and empirical extensions. *Leadership Quarterly,* 15(3): 329–354.

15. Hambledon Group (2001) cited on DTI website www.dti.gov.uk.

16. Boer, H., Berger, A., Chapman, R. & Gertsen, F. (1999) *CI Changes: From Suggestion Box to the Learning Organisation*. Aldershot: Ashgate.

17. Bessant, J. (2003) *High Involvement Innovation: Building and Sustaining Competitive Advantage Through Continuous Change*. Chichester, UK: John Wiley & Sons, Ltd.

18. Amabile, T.M., Schatzel, E.A., Moneta, G.B. & Kramer, S.J. (2004) Leader behaviors and the work environment for creativity: perceived leader support. *Leadership Quarterly*, 15(1): 5–32.

19. Cyert, R. & March, J. (1964; 1992) *The Behavioral Theory of the Firm*. Blackwell.

20. Tan, J. & Peng, M.W. (2003) Organizational slack and firm performance during economic transitions: two studies from an emerging economy. *Strategic Management Journal*, 24: 1249–1263.

21. Staudenmayer, N., Tyre, M. & Perlow, L. (2002) Time to change: temporal shifts as enablers of organizational change. *Organization Science*, 13(5): 583–597.

22. Jenssen, J.I. & Jorgensen, G. (2004) How do corporate champions promote innovations? *International Journal of Innovation Management*, 8(1): 63–86.

23. Meyerson, D.E. (2001) Radical change, the quiet way. *Harvard Business Review*, 79: 92–101.

24. Madjar, N., Oldham, G.R. & Pratt, M.G. (2002) There's no place like home? The contributions of work and non-work creativity support to employees' creative performance. *Academy of Management Review*, 45(4): 757–767.

25. Tierney, P. & Farmer, S.M. (2002) Creative self-efficacy: its potential antecedents and relationship to creative performance. *Academy of Management Journal*, 4596: 1137–1148.

26. Podsakoff, P.M., Mackenzie, S.B., Paine, J.B. & Bachrach, D.G. (2000) Organizational citizenship behaviors: a critical review of the theoretical and empirical literature and suggestions for future research. *Journal of Management*, 2693: 513–563.

27. Tidd, J., Bessant, J. & Pavitt, K. (2005) *Managing Innovation: Integrating Technological, Market and Organizational Change* (3rd edn). Chichester, UK: John Wiley & Sons, Ltd.

28. Basadur, M. (2003) Leading others to think innovatively together: creative leadership. *Leadership Quarterly*, 12(1): 103–121.

29. Hinds, P.J. & Bailey, D.E. (2003) Out of sight, out of sync: understanding conflict in distributed teams. *Organization Science*, 14(6): 615–632.

30. Totterdell, P., Leach, D., Birdi, K, Clegg, C. & Wall, T. (2002) An investigation of the contents and consequences of major organizational innovations. *International Journal of Innovation Management*, 6(4): 343–368.

31. Dvir, D. & Lechler, T. (2004) Plans are nothing, changing plans is everything: the impact of changes on project success. *Research Policy*, 33: 1–15.

32. McGrath, R.G. & Nerkar, A. (2004) Real options reasoning and a new look at the R&D investment strategies of pharmaceutical firms. *Strategic Management Journal*, 25: 1–21. Paxon, D.A. (2001) Introduction to real R&D options. *R&D Management*, 31(2): 109–113.

33. Loch, C.H. & Bode-Greual, K. (2001) Evaluating growth options as sources of value for pharmaceutical research projects. *R&D Management*, 31(2): 231–245.

34. Keizer, J.A., Vos, J.P. & Halman, J.I.M. (2005) Risks in new product development: devising a reference tool. *R&D Management*, 35(3): 297–306.

35. McEvily, B., Perrone, V. & Zaheer, A. (2003) Trust as an organizing principle. *Organization Science*, 14(1): 91–102.

36. Hoecht, A. & Trott, P. (1999) Trust, risk and control in the management of collaborative technology development. *International Journal of Innovation Management*, 3(3): 257–270.

37. Ferrin, D.L. & Dirks, K.T. (2003) The use of rewards to increase and decrease trust: mediating processes and differential effects. *Organization Science*, 14(1): 18–31.

38. Becerra, M. & Gupta, A.K. (2003) Perceived trustworthiness within the organization: the moderating impact of communication frequency on trustor and trustee effects. *Organization Science*, 14(1): 32–44.

39. Perrone, V., Zaheer, A. & McEvily, B. (2003) Free to be trusted? Organizational constraints on trust in boundary spanners. *Organization Science*, 14(4): 422–439.

40. Podsakoff, P.M., Mackenzie, S.B., Paine, J.B. & Bachrach, D.G. (2000) Organizational citizenship behaviors: a critical review of the theoretical and empirical literature and suggestions for future research. *Journal of Management*, 2963: 513–563.

41. Tidd, J., Bessant, J. & Pavitt, K. (2005) *Managing Innovation: Integrating Technological, Market and Organizational Change* (3rd edn). Chichester, UK: John Wiley & Sons, Ltd.

42. Dodgson, M., Gann, D. & Salter, A. (2005) *Think, Play, Do: Innovation, Technology, and Organization*. Oxford: Oxford University Press.

43. Kotter, J.P. (1999) *John P. Kotter on What Leaders Really Do*. Boston: Harvard Business School Press, p. 43.

44. Sobieck, M.A. (1996) *Examination of Cross-Site Narrative Responses on the CIQ and SOQ*. Unpublished master's thesis, State University College at Buffalo, New York.

Chapter 13

CREATING THE CLIMATE FOR TRANSFORMATION

> changing the culture of an organization by tackling it head on as a single facet of organizational life is really, really tough. To go deep into cultural change you have to be talking about beliefs and values, and these go to the very soul of the organization and its people. It is much easier to change the climate and language of the business[1]

Deliberate climate creation is the main responsibility of leadership within any organization. Some argue that it is the only major thing leaders do. But how can busy leaders who must manage the day-to-day business of the organization deliberately and consciously create the climate for creativity, innovation and transformation?

First, the reality is that all leaders within all organizations are already creating a climate, whether they do it deliberately or not.[2] Unless leaders are totally invisible to others, what they say and do is observed by others and is the greatest influence on the perceived patterns of behavior that characterize life and the atmosphere within the organization. Of all the factors that influence climate outlined in the earlier chapters, leadership behavior is generally the most potent.

Ekvall and his colleagues have found that leadership behavior accounts for a great deal of the variance on climate assessments.[3] In one study, they found a direct relationship among leadership, climate and productivity (Figure 13.1). When they removed (partialed out) the variance from climate, they found a very weak direct relationship between leadership and productivity. Although this was a very preliminary study, it does raise an interesting and provocative issue. Perhaps the most important thing a leader of any organization does to obtain productive results is create the climate and working atmosphere.

Working to deliberately create a climate that is conducive to innovation and change is emerging as a critical factor for organizational survival and growth.[4] There may

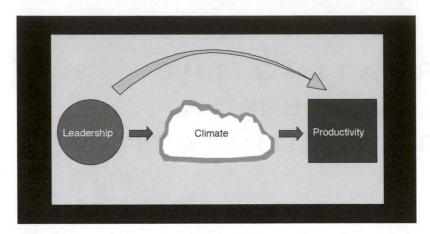

Figure 13.1 Leadership – climate and productivity

be differences in both the degree and style of creativity demanded from employees who face diverse tasks and desired outcomes, but there is an emerging consensus that there is room – in nearly every job – for more creativity. Creating a working atmosphere that allows for creative behavior is one of the biggest opportunities for those who choose to meet the innovation challenge.

One example supporting the need for deliberate climate creation comes from the PwC innovation and growth survey described in Chapter 1. As you may remember, those organizations earning the highest percentage of revenue from new products and services demonstrated that they were more effective on three capabilities. They demonstrated a more inclusive and creative kind of leadership, took deliberate steps to manage their creative and idea management processes, and did not leave their climate or working atmosphere to chance.

The researchers also studied the idea management processes in a representative set of organizations in the sample. They found that those organizations earning more from new products and services were nurturing 115 ideas per day. The average organizations captured and managed 18 ideas per day. The lowest performing organizations only nurtured about one idea per day.

Support for an idea-rich environment is also provided by research into the success curves for industrial innovation. One study found that it took 3000 raw ideas to produce one substantially new and commercially successful new product.[5] Although their research applied to most industries, they indicated for others, including drug companies, the number of raw ideas may actually be higher (6000–8000).

What do we know about leadership behavior?

We have already reviewed the historical and current literature on leadership in Chapter 5. We have also maintained that founding leaders and managers of organizations have a profound affect on the culture, and therefore, the climate of their organizations. Finally, research and practice indicate that new and emerging leaders can also influence the climate within their teams, divisions or entire organizations. Kouzes and Posner provide one example of how this happens.

Kouzes and Posner began their inquiry into leadership because of their disbelief in the popular myth that only a lucky few can decipher the mystery of leadership. Their 15 years of inquiry and research has produced information that suggests leadership is not a mystery. Their Leadership Practices Inventory is based on a huge amount of data – from more than 3000 cases and 100 000 surveys – showing that leadership is an observable, learnable set of practices.[6]

After assessing all of this information, the conclusion they came to was that:

> Leadership is everyone's business. Everyone must function as a leader at some time and in some arena – whether in an organization, an agency, a task force, a committee, a community group, or even a family setting – and everyone can learn to lead effectively.

The 30 items of the LPI are divided into the five practices that were found to occur most commonly in the research Kouzes and Posner conducted. These five practices are described again below with a few implications for climate creation.

Challenging the process

Leaders search for opportunities to change the status quo. They look for innovative ways to improve the organization. In doing so, they experiment and take risks. And because leaders know that risk-taking involves mistakes and failures, they accept the inevitable disappointments as learning opportunities. If leaders can demonstrate the effective deployment of this practice, the effect on the climate could be to encourage people to ask questions about the ways things are being done, take initiative to try new ways of working, and occasionally make some bold changes.

Inspiring a shared vision

Leaders passionately believe that they can make a difference. They envision the future, creating an ideal and unique image of what the organization can become. Through their magnetism and quiet persuasion, leaders enlist others in their dreams. They breathe life into their visions and get people to see exciting possibilities for the future.

When leaders inspire a shared vision they can raise the level of energy and commitment in their organizations. If leaders can couple their communicating about the vision and big picture with effective management tactics surrounding good project management, providing the appropriate level of resources and guiding direction for key projects (without micromanaging), people within their organizations can take initiative to turn the visions into reality.

Enabling others to act

Leaders foster collaboration and build spirited teams. They actively involve others. Leaders understand that mutual respect is what sustains extraordinary efforts; they strive to create an atmosphere of trust and human dignity. They strengthen others, making each person feel capable and powerful.

When leaders enable others to act they bridge the traditional view of leadership with effective management. As we outlined in our model for creative leadership explained in Chapter 5 on leading and managing for transformation, leaders model the behaviors that illustrate appropriate levels of involvement and engagement in change efforts. But this kind of behavior need not stay at the highest levels of the organization. Including those involved in the change effort is one of the best ways to overcome many of the barriers to implementing the desired outcome of the change. Going a step further and working to provide people with the tools, training and resources they need to do a good job is a natural implication of this leadership practice and management competency.

Modeling the way

Leaders establish principles concerning the way that people (constituents, colleagues and customers alike) should be treated and the way that goals should be pursued. They create standards of excellence and then set an example for others to follow. Because the prospect of complex change can overwhelm people and stifle action, they set interim goals so that people can achieve small wins as they work toward larger objectives. They unravel bureaucracy when it impedes action; they put up signposts when people are unsure of where to go or how to get there; and they create opportunities for victory.

When leaders and managers model the way, their words and behavior are seen as consistent. This breeds a higher level of trust and emotional safety in relationships because the rules of the game are clear and consistent. Furthermore, by breaking down larger and more complex projects and initiatives, leaders and managers can reinforce the direction for new initiatives, individual and team problem-solving efforts.

Encouraging the heart

Accomplishing extraordinary things in organizations is hard work. To keep hope and determination alive, leaders recognize contributions that individuals make. In every winning team, the members need to share in the rewards of their efforts, so leaders celebrate accomplishments. They make people feel like heroes.

When leaders and managers encourage the heart by providing a range of reward and recognition for the efforts people take, clear messages are sent about the kind of behavior or initiative that is invited and welcomed within the organization. If the learning that comes from both successful and unsuccessful risk-taking is rewarded, people will engage in the kind of risk-taking that can bring value to the organization. Further, by encouraging the heart, people within the organization can become more committed and challenged by continuing their efforts to produce meaningful work.

Leaders create the working climate by using all the levers within the model for organizational change, as outlined in Chapter 11 on transforming the culture and climate. For example, when leaders create and communicate mission and strategy they can influence the climate. Restructuring is one lever we have witnessed that is utilized very often to create change in the way that people interact (perhaps an overused lever). Leaders and managers can also focus on the transactional elements of the model to create climate. By providing clear task requirements for projects and tasks they can set the tone for the kind of change required.

When leaders want to focus clearly and deliberately on creating the climate that supports change, creativity and innovation, they can also apply the Situational Outlook Questionnaire (SOQ). The dimensions and design of the SOQ is described in more detail in Chapter 12 on the climate for innovation and growth. The following sections of this chapter will focus on some case studies in which a variety of organizations have applied the SOQ in a deliberate change effort. These case studies are not offered as absolute proof of the effectiveness of the SOQ, but are shared to help you better understand what it will likely take to make meaningful and significant changes in your climate.

Case 1: A symphony orchestra

A major world-class orchestra in the North East of the USA had been invited to prestigious festivals all over the world. It was housed in an impressive building in the downtown area of a major metropolitan area and had over 100 musicians and 75 staff, and an operating budget of nearly $30 million. The orchestra had been in existence for over 100 years and had an excellent reputation and programs for classical music, Broadway, jazz and pops.

We started working with the organization to help them develop a strategic architecture in 1997. In the process of this strategic planning effort, the leadership team identified a number of opportunities and threats facing the organization. One of the major threats was their overreliance on endowment to fund their operation. The leadership team identified 11 strategic growth opportunities and initiated a number of assessment efforts to determine their position in the market and their relevance to the community. Over the next year, the leadership team decided to involve their board and address a number of key strategic growth projects.

As a part of their effort to engage the entire organization in their change efforts, the SOQ was administered in January of 1999. The following month, the results of the SOQ were shared with the entire staff and they participated in a workshop to identify improvements that would help the orchestra in the short, medium and long term. Follow-up workshops were held with the senior management team, and each department. We assembled cross-functional teams to address the dimensions of freedom, idea time, conflict, debate and risk-taking. Each team identified actions that needed to be taken to improve the results on one dimension and presented to the senior management team.

A number of the actions were implemented over the next year. A leadership development workshop was held and included the senior management as well as department heads. Workshops on delegation and empowering people were held. The dress code was changed to allow for less formal attire during nonperformance days. Staff meetings were restructured to allow for more participation and to encourage follow-up on many of the actions and projects. Emphasis was placed on more deliberate communication of the strategy and progress on the strategic goals. One team addressed the issue of staff shortages and more effective use of volunteers to ease the pressure of a very heavy workload. Another cross-functional team was charged with the task of 'unclogging the information arteries' by exchanging information across departments. The senior management team also chose to address the need to become less reliant on endowment. They created a research and development function to explore numerous alternatives. They took a bold suggestion to the board to allow the symphony orchestra to extend beyond its education and nonprofit mission and create some for-profit centers. For example, a retail store was created adjacent to the performance hall. Another project was created to review human resource practices and make improvements in staffing, pensions and personal and vacation time.

All of these efforts were linked with the overall strategy of the orchestra and addressed during special and regular meetings of the senior leadership and departments. The follow up assessment of the SOQ, 21 months later, showed some improvement on most of the targeted dimensions (Table 13.1).

During the presentation of the data on the second administration of the SOQ with the senior management team they noticed a major decrease in conflict. They also noticed some improvement in trust and risk-taking. People were putting more thoughts and suggestions forward and the working relationships between managers and

Table 13.1 Numeric comparison

Climate variables	Innovative company averages	2000 averages	1999 averages
Challenge and involvement	238	221	217
Freedom	210	152	149
Trust and openness	178	165	154
Idea time	148	108	109
Playfulness/humor	230	180	172
Conflicts	78	90	134
Idea support	183	151	149
Debates	158	177	166
Risk-taking	195	112	104
Number of Comps or Inds	10 Companies	75 Individuals	63 Individuals

employees were improving. The quantitative scores were supplemented, once again, with narrative feedback from 75 people who took the assessment.

As a result of examining the quantitative and qualitative findings, they reported that people within the organization seemed much more receptive to the changes and the new strategic direction. The management team changed their perception of the employees to reflect much greater respect for their talents and motivations. Communication was improving within and across departments. They were also able to see an improvement on the overreliance on their endowment.

The senior management team also identified needed additional steps to be taken to continue to improve the organization's readiness, willingness and ability to implement the changes. They recognized that idea time had not improved. The feedback from the SOQ detailed the reasons for the lack of improvement being an ever-increasing workload and demands from the projects and community. As of this writing, progress continues. But between the two administrations of the SOQ, they had increased the revenue and decreased dependency on the endowment to a large degree and other new services and sources of revenue streams were under consideration.

Case 2: A medical technology company

A Finnish-based global healthcare organization had 55 000 employees and $50 billion in revenue. The division we worked with was located in the mid-west and employed 700 people. Its mission was to develop, manufacture and market products for anesthesia and critical care.

During January of 1999, the senior management team of the mid-west division conducted an SOQ assessment. They had been doing well on quality and operational excellence initiatives in manufacturing and had improved their sales and marketing results, but were still concerned that there were many other areas on which they could improve. They approached the SOQ assessment as a means to find out what was working well and what needed to be improved.

We held a workshop with the senior team to present the results and engage them to determine what they needed to do to improve their business. We met with the CEO prior to the workshop to highlight the overall results and share the department comparisons. She was not surprised by the results but was very interested to see that some of the departments had different results.

During the workshop, the team targeted challenge and involvement, freedom, idea time and idea support as critical dimensions to improve to enable them to meet their strategic objectives. The organization was facing increasing competition in their markets and significant advances in technology. Although major progress had been made in the manufacturing area, they needed to improve their product development and marketing efforts by broadening involvement internally, cross-functionally and externally by obtaining deep consumer insight. The main strategy they settled upon was to 'jump start' their innovation in new product development for life support.

Key personnel in new product development and marketing were provided training in creative problem-solving, and follow-up projects were launched to apply the learning to existing and new projects. One project was a major investment in re-engineering their main product line. Clinicians were challenged with the current design of the equipment. The initial decision was to redesign the placement of critical control valves used during surgery. The project leader decided to apply CPS on the challenge and used a number of the tools to go out and clarify the problem with the end users. The sessions were videotaped and small-group sessions were held involving project team members from research and development as well as marketing. The result was a redefinition of the challenge and the decision to save the millions of dollars involved in the reengineering effort, and instead, develop a new tactile tool to help the clinicians' problem of having their hands full.

During this process, the employees were involved in the working sessions and were able to observe progress due to a deliberate effort to display and communicate the results. Since the professionals in the research and development lab were also directly involved in obtaining and interpreting the consumer insight data, they understood the needs of the end users and displayed an unusually high degree of energy and commitment to the project.

There were other spin-offs as well. Other employees were trained in the tools and techniques and creative problem-solving. Many of the employees started taking other initiatives to transform their use of space into community sharing events and resources. On one visit to the facility, we observed a resource exchange for employees with children in which they could purchase new learning games or exchange their used ones with each other. We also observed a much greater amount of cross-functional and informal working across departments. Some human resource personnel were replaced and new forms of reward and recognition were developed. Not only was there more consumer insight research going on, but there were more and closer partnerships created with clinicians and end users of the products.

Another SOQ assessment was administered about 18 months later and the results are shown in Table 13.2. During this period of time the CEO tracked revenue growth and profitability of the division and reported double-digit growth.

Table 13.2 A medical technology company's climate averages

Climate variables	Innovative company averages	2001 averages	1999 averages
Challenge and involvement	238	180	166
Freedom	210	147	138
Trust and openness	178	138	133
Idea time	148	126	109
Playfulness/humor	230	166	155
Conflict	78	137	147
Idea support	183	141	121
Debate	158	170	162
Risk-taking	195	119	108
Communication	N/A	120	102
Personal ownership	N/A	144	135
Customer satisfaction	N/A	187	178
Number of Comps or Inds	10 Companies	491	525

Based on the observations with the symphony orchestra, we decided to see if the changes in the climate results were significant and if the SOQ assessment scores were reliable. These data are reported in Tables 13.3 and 13.4.

This case, coupled with earlier cases and applications of the SOQ assessment approach, provided an increasing degree of confidence that the measure could be very useful for informing and guiding change efforts.

Case 3: An electrical engineering division

This organization was a division of a large, global electrical power and product supply company headquartered in France. The division was located in the south-east of the USA and had 92 employees. Its focus was to help clients automate their processes particularly within the automotive, pharmaceutical, microelectronics and food and beverage industries. For example, this division would make the robots that put cars together in the automotive industry or provide public filtration systems.

Table 13.3 Comparing 1999 and 2001

Was the change in scores statistically significant?

Dimension (N = 491)	Univariate F	Statistical significance
Challenge	15.58	$p < 0.001$
Freedom	6.21	$p < 0.05$
Trust	1.89	Not significant
Idea time	21.05	$p < 0.001$
Playfulness/humor	7.45	$p < 0.01$
Conflict	4.08	$p < 0.05$
Idea support	25.78	$p < 0.001$
Debate	5.32	$p < 0.05$
Risk-taking	10.63	$p < 0.001$
Communication	16.54	$p < 0.001$
Personal ownership	5.44	$p < 0.05$
Customer satisfaction	3.44	Not significant

Table 13.4 Sample reliability

Dimension	Items	Reliability coefficient*
Challenge	7	0.88
Freedom	6	0.84
Trust	5	0.74
Idea time	6	0.87
Playfulness/humor	6	0.89
Conflict	6	0.90
Idea support	5	0.90
Debate	6	0.85
Risk-taking	5	0.78

*Cronbach Alpha

When this division was merged with the parent company in 2002, it was losing about $8 million a year. A new general manager was bought in to turn the division around and make it profitable quickly. The general manager attended a senior management development program and learned about the SOQ. He decided that this measure and approach might be helpful to him and his team when doing a short-term turnaround.

In August of 2002, the first general climate assessment was conducted with all the employees of the division. The management team worked to integrate the results on the SOQ with their current understanding of what was needed to make the turnaround work. The team reviewed the results and identified that they were strongest on the debate dimension but were very close to the stagnated norms when it came to challenge and involvement, playfulness and humor, and conflict. They indicated that the quantitative and qualitative assessment results were consistent with their own impressions that the division could be characterized as conflict-driven, uncommitted to producing results, and that people were generally despondent. Their quantitative results are presented in Table 13.5.

Table 13.5 Sample climate 2002

Climate variables	Innovative company averages	Total group averages	Stagnated company averages
Challenge and involvement	238	171	163
Freedom	210	156	153
Trust and openness	178	138	128
Idea time	148	112	97
Playfulness/humor	230	132	140
Conflicts	78	137	140
Idea support	183	135	108
Debates	158	165	105
Risk-taking	195	125	53
Number of Comps or Inds	10 Companies	75 Individuals	5 Companies

The leadership decided, after some debate, that they should target challenge and involvement, trust and openness, playfulness and humor, and conflicts in order to help them implement the needed turnaround. They set a very specific target of obtaining a score of 195–205 on challenge and involvement. This dimension also fit the strategic emphasis on a global initiative on employee commitment. We were a little uncertain about their ability to deliberately affect the trust and openness dimension due to the lack of a significant improvement with the previous cases.

It was clear to them that they needed to soften the climate and drive a warmer, more embracing, communicative and exuberant climate. They developed and then implemented a plan for short-term climate change.

They committed to increase communication by holding monthly all-employee meetings, sharing quarterly reviews on performance and using cross-functional strategy review sessions. They implemented mandatory 'skip level' meetings to allow more direct interaction between senior managers and all levels of employees. The general manager held 15-minute meetings with all employees at least once a year. All employee suggestions and recommendations were invited, and feedback and recognition was required to be immediate. A new monthly recognition and rewards program, based on peer nomination, was launched across the division for both managers and employees.

At a time when making the division profitable was the highest priority, the management team reestablished training and development and encouraged employees to engage in both personal and business-related skills development. They also provided mandatory safety training for all employees.

Another category of initiatives included providing a clear and compelling mission, strategy and values for the division. The management team formed employee review teams to challenge and craft the statements in the hopes of encouraging more ownership and involvement in the overall strategic direction of the business.

In general, they focused on relaxing the climate. They used the suggestions provided by the narrative parts of the survey to identify actions that needed to be taken. They modified rules regarding the dress code, adapted more flexible working hours, and allowed plants and flowers in the workplace. They scheduled parties and social events, and fostered open debate and feedback without repercussions. Managers who could not follow the new behavioral norms were coached, and some were removed from their positions. It was critical to encourage everyone to understand how their specific role and responsibilities fit into the overall flow of the business, so they did extensive work on detailing the definition of roles and process ownership. Their stated aim was to create an unstoppable 'bubble of excellence' in North America and to challenge the 'tyranny of the average'.

Table 13.6   Sample climate change over one year

Climate variables	Total group 11/2002 averages		Total group 10/2003 averages	DELTA	Significant
Challenge and involvement	171	Target	204	33	☺
Freedom	156		160	4	
Trust and openness	138	Target	163	25	☺
Idea time	112		124	12	
Playfulness/humor	132	Target	154	22	☺
Conflicts	137		94	−43	☺
Idea support	135	Target	158	23	☺
Debates	165		184	19	☺
Risk-taking	125		134	9	
Number of Inds	75		77		

In September of 2003, the leadership team wanted feedback on how they were doing in their efforts to change the climate, so they requested a second administration of the SOQ. The results of this second assessment, along with the comparison to their first is included in Table 13.6.

The four dimensions they targeted improved significantly. In addition, two additional dimensions showed significant improvement, even though they were not specifically targeted. The conflict dimension showed the largest change in the more positive direction. We also noticed a significant improvement on the trust and openness dimension. This could have been the result of the level of intensity with which the management drove the climate change.

The division showed a $7 million turnaround in 18 months and has now begun to deliver profit much closer to projections. In 2003, the division won a worldwide innovation award. They are building specific innovation metrics into their balanced scorecard and continue to identify areas of improvement, despite a promotion of the general manager to a national position.

General themes across cases

Each of the organizations identified above were very different. Despite the different purposes, industries and sizes, there were some common themes that may help you take deliberate efforts to improve your own climate.

Leaders and managers accepted their key role

In each case, those charged with the strategic responsibility and day-to-day work owned up to their role in climate creation. They faced both the good and bad news that came with the assessment and then focused on what needed to be done to make improvements.

Those who owned up to change, and took their sponsorship and clientship responsibilities seriously, were able to accomplish their desired outcomes, involve people and make progress on their deliberate methods. Having access to climate data helped them celebrate what was working and remove the barriers within the context to create an atmosphere conducive to the release of creativity. They did not try to discount the data or measure (or the people presenting them). Instead, they faced the reality of the climate data with a positive attitude.

Focused on interpretation and integration

The leaders and managers sought to understand both the numbers and narrative results and then carefully considered which dimensions and actions could help them move the organization forward.

Climate creation was not a goal or objective all on its own. The results from the SOQ assessment served to provide leadership teams with important insights to help them look at the current organizational context in light of the direction they needed to go, the quality of the working relationships among people, and how well their current methods or approaches were working. Based on these insights, the leadership teams were able to engage others (usually on a cross-functional level) to make the needed changes and improvements.

Targeted key dimensions

In each case, the leadership and management teams selected dimensions of climate that were critical to their own unique purposes and markets.

The SOQ provides quantitative data on nine dimensions and narrative comments and themes in response to what is helping or hindering creativity and what specific actions need to be taken to improve the situation. This amount of information could overwhelm an already overburdened management team. The teams in these cases certainly paid attention to all the data, but they were able to take advantage of the understanding of the business needs and integrate these with the critical insights about the climate. As a result, they focused their efforts on a selected number of high-priority dimensions and actions that helped them achieve results and improve the climate.

Demonstrated follow-through

Each of these cases demonstrated the value of taking actions over time. Rather than using the SOQ as a report card or a short executive intellectual exercise, the management teams understood that it was all about changing behavior. This often required the leaders to transform their own behavior first, but nearly always cascaded through the organization. Rather than thinking that climate creation was a single event, they knew that this kind of work was a process or journey – and they stayed the course.

Used external resources

Although the ultimate value of any climate assessment must be internally relevant to the organization, each of these organizations saw value in using an external assessment that was normative and having the results presented and interpreted by an objective outsider.

Each of the senior leaders and members of the management teams realized the benefit of using a well-developed assessment tool and qualified individuals who knew how to use the measure to help obtain results. Having access to clear benchmarks and, often, results from other organizations in similar industries, helped the management teams and employees understand the importance and value of the climate creation efforts.

Our experience has shown that it is necessary to work with a qualified user of the SOQ. One very large organization with which we work conducted an SOQ assessment within one of its divisions. When the results were shared, the key leaders wanted to focus on only those dimensions on which they scored below the more productive norm. What they missed was the most significant (and meaningful) difference: that they were scoring well above an appropriate score for debate. The heart of their need for improvement turned out to be the productive avoidance created by too many diverse opinions and no clear strategic direction. This was confounded by the fact that most people in the division really enjoyed a good debate. It certainly was more fun than doing any productive work!

Climate creation enables a systemic approach to change

We have asserted the value of taking a systemic approach to change. Change efforts that only focus on a single element of the organizational system are far more likely to fail. When leadership teams take deliberate steps to examine their climate, they open themselves up to the entire system.

Since climate is an intervening set of variables, when you target specific climate dimensions, you are very likely to be able to create and implement actions that will not only improve those selected dimensions, but others as well. This is the nature of climate. It is the patterns of behavior that characterize life within the organization. Many factors affect the climate, and the climate influences the organizational and psychological processes throughout the organization.

One of our colleagues conducted a study that demonstrates how systemic change can happen. He studied the effects of almost a full semester of training in CPS on the communication behavior of small groups.[7] Hotels in the western New York area have a real problem with occupancy rates during the winter months, so a number of area hotel managers served as clients for a real problem-solving session. Each session was recorded and each group received the same instructions for the outcome and the way that they were to work together (Table 13.7).

After analyzing the communication behavior of the groups, Firestien found that there were significant differences between the trained and untrained groups. The trained groups generated more responses to the task, had fewer verbal criticisms and more verbal support and laughter. The members of the trained group smiled more frequently and generated more ideas. These findings clearly illustrate a link between training in deliberate process tools and approaches and the effects on working climate.

Table 13.7 Effects of CPS training 1

On communication behavior in groups

	Untrained	Trained
Total responses	26.00	39.00
Verbal criticisms	2.20	0.09
Verbal support	1.40	3.70
Laughter	2.10	6.00
Smiles	2.60	39.00
Ideas generated	13.00	27.00

Source: Firestien, 1990.

Table 13.8 Effects of CPS training 2

On communication behavior in groups: idea quality results combined rating of three criteria used

Rating	Untrained	Trained
5	281	618
4	500	1342
3	352	917
2	253	648
1	29	140

Source: Firestien, 1990.

This illustrates a key link among two of the elements of the system described in this book. Deliberately developing the CPS skills of people not only raises their level of creativity; it also affects the working climate within the teams. Table 13.8 shows the results from the evaluation by the client team of the ideas generated during the small-group session.

Although the CPS trained groups enjoyed working together and generated more ideas than the untrained groups, the differences did not end there. As you can see from the Table 13.8, there were significant differences in the quality of the ideas they generated.

The management of the hotels rated the ideas on a five-point scale. One was the lowest value, and five was the highest. The trained group generated many more lower-quality ideas than the untrained group, providing support for the key guidelines of brainstorming, allowing for silly ideas and deferring judgment.[8] The trained groups also significantly outperformed the untrained groups when it came to the higher-quality ideas. If you consider those receiving a ranking of four or five higher-quality ideas, the trained groups produced more than 250% more high-quality suggestions.

Deliberate training of CPS tools and skills not only had an impact on the climate within the groups. There were meaningful and significant differences in the quantity and quality of the outcomes.

Conclusions and implications

Leaders and their behavior are a major force in creating the context for change and creativity. The purpose of this chapter has been to outline a number of other factors that can make a difference, as well as to share some specific strategies that can be employed to improve the situation. Rather than focus on only one strategy, it may be helpful to have a number at your disposal.

The key is to examine the situation. This examination can be done from a cultural perspective and from the point of view of values such as those surrounding the use of power, dealing with uncertainty, the tension between individuals and community, and masculine-feminine issues.[9] From this examination of the culture and climate, a better decision regarding the use of any particular strategy can be made.[10]

The value in using a deliberate assessment approach is that you can increase the likelihood that you will consider more factors while guiding significant change. Knowing more about your situation will help you decide how quickly you need to take action, the needed level of preplanning and the degree of involvement from others.

If you, as a leader of change, really want to pay attention to the many forces that are already at work within your organization, then one of the best things you can do is to formally assess the climate around you. Rather than trying to measure or understand all relevant factors within the MOC, a single, broad measure can pick up those factors that are most relevant to your particular situation.

The experiences outlined above indicate that the SOQ helps leaders and managers understand the readiness, willingness and ability to transform their organizations. The SOQ has shown that it measures nine key dimensions of a climate that supports creativity and change. In addition, the narrative section picks up factors that are included within the MOC and points out unique ingredients within the situation that can really make a difference.[11] As a result, the SOQ offers an excellent starting point to help you understand the situational outlook surrounding the change effort you wish to implement.

The three cases in this chapter all use the SOQ for organization-wide change and transformation. We have been able to apply the SOQ to a variety of profit and non-profit organizations including churches, educational institutions and community or social service agencies. The SOQ has shown itself to be useful with a variety of organizational types and at a number of different levels.

The SOQ has been used to help teams function more effectively. You would expect that improvements in the overall organizational climate would also have a general positive effect on teamwork. The SOQ has been able to distinguish between best and worst case creative teams, and has been used by teams who were charged with helping to make organizational transformation happen.

The SOQ has also been applied to help develop leaders. A number of organizations have incorporated the SOQ as an assessment in their leadership development programs. The participants in these programs take the SOQ as a self-assessment and then invite those who are good observers of their leadership behavior to take the assessment as well, prior to the program. During the program, the participants are provided their quantitative and qualitative results so that they can compare them with those of their observers. They can also compare their results with the norms from innovative versus stagnated organizations and best and worst case teams. The exercise usually provides those who are developing their leadership talents with powerful insights and implications for further skill development and behavior change.

References

1. Thomson, K. (2000) *Emotional Capital: Maximising the Intangible Assets at the Heart of Brand and Business Success.* Oxford, UK: Capstone Publishing Ltd, p. 240.
2. Shalley, C.E. & Gilson, L.L. (2004) What leaders need to know: a review of social and contextual factors that can foster or hinder creativity. *Leadership Quarterly*, 15: 33–53.

3. Ekvall, G. & Ryhammar, L. (1998) Leadership style, social climate and organizational outcomes: a study of a Swedish university college. *Creativity and Innovation Management*, 7: 126–130. Ekvall, G. (1997) Organizational conditions and levels of creativity. *Creativity and Innovation Management*, 6(4): 195–205. Ekvall, G., Arvonen, J. & Waldenstrom-Lindblad, I. (1983) *Creative Organizational Climate: Construction and Validation of a Measuring Instrument* (Report 2). Stockholm, Sweden: FArådet – The Swedish Council for Management and Work Life Issues.

4. Shalley, C.E. & Gilson, L.L. (20004) What leaders need to know: a review of social and contextual factors that can foster or hinder creativity. *Leadership Quarterly*, 15: 33–53.

5. Stevens, G.A. & Burley, J. (1997) 3,000 raw ideas = 1 commercial success. *Research Technology Management*, 40: 16–27.

6. Kouzes, J.M. & Posner, B.Z. (1987) *The Leadership Challenge: How to Get Extraordinary Things Done in Organizations*. San Francisco: Jossey-Bass.

7. Firestien, R.L. (1990) Effects of creative problem solving training on communication behaviors in small groups. *Small Group Research*, 21: 507–521. Firestien, R.L. & McCowan, R.J. (1988) Creative problem solving and communication behaviors in small groups. *Creativity Research Journal*, 1: 106–114.

8. Isaksen, S.G. & Gaulin, J.P. (2005) A reexamination of brainstorming research: implications for research and practice. *Gifted Child Quarterly*, 49: 315–329.

9. Offerman, L.R. & Hellmann, P.S. (1997) Culture's consequences for leadership behavior: national values in action. *Journal of Cross-Cultural Psychology*, 28: 342–351.

10. Coyne, K.P. & Subramaniam, S. (1996) Bringing discipline to strategy. *McKinsey Quarterly*, 4: 3–12.

11. Sobieck, M.A. (1996) *Examination of Cross-Site Narrative Responses on the CIQ and SOQ*. Unpublished master's thesis, State University College at Buffalo, New York.

INDEX